STREET ARCHIVES AND CITY LIFE

Radical Perspectives

A *RADICAL HISTORY REVIEW* BOOK SERIES

A series edited by Daniel Walkowitz and Barbara Weinstein

EMILY CALLACI

Street Archives and City Life

Popular Intellectuals in Postcolonial Tanzania

Duke University Press   Durham and London   2017

© 2017 Duke University Press
All rights reserved
Printed in the United States of America on acid-free paper ∞
Typeset in Chaparral Pro by Westchester Publishing Services

Library of Congress Cataloging-in-Publication Data
Names: Callaci, Emily, [date—] author.
Title: Street archives and city life : popular intellectuals in
    postcolonial Tanzania / Emily Callaci.
Description: Durham : Duke University Press, 2017. | Series:
    Radical perspectives
Identifiers: LCCN 2017027317 (print) | LCCN 2017042414 (ebook)
ISBN 9780822372325 (ebook)
ISBN 9780822369844 (hardcover : alk. paper)
ISBN 9780822369912 (pbk. : alk. paper)
Subjects: LCSH: City and town life—Social aspects—Tanzania—
    Dar es Salaam—20th century. | City and town life—Tanzania—
    Dar es Salaam—History—20th century. | Intellectuals—
    Tanzania—Dar es Salaam—History—20th century. |
    Urbanization—Tanzania—Dar es Salaam—
    History—20th century.
Classification: LCC HT148.T34 (ebook) | LCC HT148.T34 C355 2017
    (print)
DDC 307.7609678/232—dc23
LC record available at https://lccn.loc.gov/2017027317

Cover art: Illustration by Julienne Alexander

Support for this research was provided by the University of
Wisconsin–Madison Office of the Vice Chancellor for Research
and Graduate Education with funding from the Wisconsin Alumni
Research Foundation.

Contents

vii Acknowledgments

1 Introduction

18 CHAPTER 1
TANU, African Socialism, and the City Idea

59 CHAPTER 2
"All Alone in the Big City": Elite Women, "Working Girls,"
and Struggles over Domesticity, Reproduction, and Urban Space

102 CHAPTER 3
Dar after Dark: Dance, Desire, and Conspicuous Consumption
in Dar es Salaam's Nightlife

141 CHAPTER 4
Lovers and Fighters: Pulp-Fiction Publishing and the
Transformation of Urban Masculinity

180 CHAPTER 5
From Socialist to Street-Smart: A Changing Urban Lexicon

207 Conclusion

215 Notes
253 Bibliography
277 Index

Acknowledgments

This book is the product of many journeys, conversations, and collaborations I have had in Tanzania over nearly a decade. Among those who taught me, assisted with my research, or helped shaped my thinking, I am especially indebted to Walter Bgoya, Muhiddin Mwalim Muhammad Gurumo, Stephen Hiza, Hamza Kalala, Jackson Kalindimya, Patrick Kamaley, Maele Kushuma, Freddy Macha, Mohamed Majura, Fatuma Mdoe, Clemence Merinyo, Issa Michuzi, Jumaa Mkabarah, Kikubi Mwanza Mpango, Grace Mtawali, Amne Mbaraka Mwinshehe, Telson Peter Mughogho, Kajubi Mukajanga, Christina Nsekela, Mpeli Nsekela, Farid Hammie Rajab, Mohamed Said, Zigi Saidi, and Mzee Ally Sykes. F.E.M.K. Senkoro, Deogratias Ngonyani, Yusta Mganga, and Nahya Karama taught me *Kiswahili*. Professors Yusuf Lawi and M. M. Mulukozi generously made time to meet with me at the University of Dar es Salaam, and our conversations about history and literature have greatly enriched my thinking. *Asanteni sana.*

On a more personal note, I thank Khadija Suleiman, Chandrika Pattni, Sunnah Sylvester, and Fadhili and Binti Msemo, who welcomed me into their homes. Some of my best memories of the years I have spent in Tanzania are of long, hot Sundays spent in the home of Fadhili and Binti, sitting under the papaya tree in the yard, playing trucks and chasing chickens with their sons Kassim and Mohamed. I first met Amne and Taji Mwinshehe because of their famous relative, the great songwriter Mbaraka Mwinshehe, yet our friendship quickly eclipsed my research. I miss being part of the community of neighbors, extended family, musicians, and Quranic students who gathered in their mosaic-tiled courtyard in Mwananyamala to share laughter, conversation, prayer, food, and music.

The preoccupations that gave shape to this research were in the making years before I ever thought about writing a book or becoming an academic historian. When I was an undergraduate student at Kenyon College, Clifton

Crais's classes on African history captured my imagination, challenged my thinking, and ultimately shaped the direction of my life. Athman Lali Omar was my professor and mentor during a semester abroad in Mombasa Kenya, and it was under his tutelage that I developed a love of ethnography, oral history, and the Swahili language. Steve Ashcroft was my dearest friend during my college years. He inadvertently helped to send me on a path into academia by sharing his infectious enthusiasm for the writings of Ben Okri, Ranajit Guha, and Steve Biko and by nudging me to take my first class in African history. I dearly wish that he were still here with us to see his name in these acknowledgments.

I had an extraordinary community of mentors and friends during my years as a graduate student at Northwestern University. My gratitude, admiration, and fondness for Jonathon Glassman continues to grow with time. As an advisor, he is relentlessly devoted, rigorous, and supportive. I am grateful for the ways in which his scholarship has inspired and influenced me, and I am even more grateful for the ways in which he encouraged me to invest in, nurture, and articulate ideas of my own. David Schoenbrun's gift for asking brilliant and unexpected questions often gave me a sense of intellectual freedom, space, and joy even as I sweated and fretted my way through graduate school. Butch Ware filled our seminar rooms with energy and intensity and always pushed us to keep the academic study of African history connected to bigger questions of social justice. James Brennan's generosity to colleagues and dedication to the field of Tanzanian history makes all of us who study it better at what we do. My fellow graduate students Pamela Khanakwa, Andreana Prichard, Rhiannon Stephens, Kate DeLuna, Zachary Wright, and Aurelien Mauxion formed my community in graduate school, while the friendship of Teri Chettiar and Amy Tyson sustained me personally. Throughout the entire process of researching and writing my dissertation, in Chicago, Dar es Salaam, and New York, John West gave steadfast support and kindness. My debt to him can never be repaid.

Many colleagues have given their time and critical eye to drafts of this project. I am grateful to Derek Peterson, Lynn Thomas, Karin Barber, Michael Schatzberg, Aili Tripp, Preeti Chopra, Jo Ellen Fair, and Louise Young, who read and advised me on a first draft of this book as part of the First Book Program at the University of Wisconsin–Madison Center for Humanities, under the leadership of Sarah Guyer and with support from the A. W. Mellon Foundation. Additionally, James Brennan, Alex Perullo, Kate DeLuna, and Andreana Prichard all read individual chapters of this manuscript, and Tom Spear read a full draft. My thinking was also enhanced by several opportunities to present portions of this book, especially at the Emory University Institute for African Studies, the University of Wisconsin–Madison Institute for Research in Humanities, and the Columbia University Seminar on Contemporary Africa. To all who have taken the time to listen or read along the way, I offer my heartfelt thanks.

The University of Wisconsin–Madison has been a supportive and engaging environment in which to work and think. I am grateful for Florencia Mallon's mentorship and for the collegiality, energy, and dedication of my colleagues Neil Kodesh, James Sweet, and Florence Bernault. As I wrote the manuscript, I benefited from the feedback, camaraderie, and encouragement of Lucas Graves, Molly Steenson, Judd Kinzley, Stephen Young, Kathryn Ciancia, and Elizabeth Hennessy. I thank Aili Tripp and Marja-Liisa Swantz for sharing with me the research notes from the social surveys that the latter conducted with students at the University of Dar es Salaam in the 1970s. During the years that I've spent working on this, Priya Lal, Lucas Graves, and Molly Steenson were my friends, fellow first-book writers, and traveling companions.

I have also been fortunate to receive generous financial support for my work. During my graduate school years, I completed my research and writing with the support of a Jacob Javits Fellowship and a Fulbright-Hays DDRA Fellowship. In the years since, my writing and research have been enabled by grants from the American Council of Learned Societies, the University of Wisconsin Institute for Research in Humanities, and the Office of the Vice Chancellor for Research and Graduate Education at the University of Wisconsin–Madison (with funding from the Wisconsin Alumni Research Foundation). I finished writing this book while a scholar in residence, first at the Institute for Research in Humanities at UW–Madison, under the direction of Susan Friedman, and then at the Institute for Comparative Literature and Society at Columbia University, under the direction of Stathis Gourgouris and Lydia Liu. I hope that communities and resources such as these continue to be available and to enrich future generations of humanities scholars.

When I scan my bookshelves, a substantial number of the scholars that have most inspired my thinking have had their work published by Duke University Press, and having worked with Duke on this manuscript, I can see why. I am grateful to the entire team, and especially to Gisela Fosado, as well as to two anonymous readers whose generous and detailed feedback greatly improved and clarified this book.

I thank my parents, Debbie and Jack Callaci, for their love and encouragement, in this and in all of my life endeavors. My mother Debbie's unwavering support for my various interests, obsessions, and joys over the course of my lifetime has helped me find the confidence and freedom to follow my heart in my career and in life. Through his example, both as a parent and as an activist, my father, Jack, instilled in me a sense of why ideas and history matter. My friends and family members in places including Rhode Island, Western Massachusetts, New York, Jersey City, Boston, Seattle, Stockholm, Chicago, and Austin have boosted my spirits year after year. The final days I spent working on this book were happy ones, filled with love and music and punctuated by Sunday roasts, kitchen discos, and joyful meanderings around New York City, Cape Cod, and Madison with Stephen Young. His support, engagement and insight have made me a better historian, and this a better book. He has my gratitude, my admiration and my heart.

My grandmother, Dorothy Callaci, is the most brilliant, tough, righteous, and generous person I know. Throughout my life, she has fed my soul by taking me to museums, concerts, and political demonstrations, filled my bookshelves with great literature, and modeled for me, in the streets and at the dinner table, what it looks like to stand up for what you believe in. For me, she is the example of a life well lived. I am lucky to be her granddaughter, and it is to her that I dedicate this book.

Introduction

The migration of millions of young African men and women from rural villages and towns to cities during the second half of the twentieth century has been one of the most dramatic demographic shifts in human history. Yet in the midst of this urban revolution, many African-nationalist intellectuals, political leaders, and artists argued that Africans were an inherently rural people.

Nowhere was this contradiction more stark than in the postcolonial nation of Tanzania, where from 1967 through 1985 President Julius Nyerere launched a campaign to relocate citizens—at first on a voluntary basis, and later by force—into collectivized rural villages as the central policy of his program of African socialism. Nyerere envisioned the Tanzanian nation as a network of self-sufficient, egalitarian villages. Yet when by 1973 most Tanzanian peasants had not voluntarily organized themselves into village units, he launched a campaign to create African socialist villages by force. Simultaneously, in the cities, the ruling party TANU (Tanzania African National Union) carried out periodic campaigns to arrest unemployed youth and relocate them to the countryside. In the city, TANU periodically deployed its militant youth branch, the TANU Youth League, to dismantle new squatter settlements, while the Ministry of Information launched a vigorous propaganda campaign to educate youth—both urban-dwellers and villagers who might potentially choose to make the journey to the city—about the miseries of urban life and the rewards of rural development. Yet despite official policy, unprecedented numbers of young people from throughout East and Central Africa left their rural homes and made their lives in Tanzania's largest city of Dar es Salaam during the socialist era.[1]

Then as now, young Tanzanians would explain that they went to the city *kutafuta maisha*: to "search for life."[2] Like their counterparts across the global south, Tanzania's urban sojourners sought material security, emotional satisfaction, and social recognition in circumstances radically different from those of their parents' and grandparents' generations. Earlier, in the late 1950s and early 1960s, many Tanzanians had believed that decolonization would mean that the benefits that had been attainable to only a small elite living under colonial regimes would now become available to the African masses. Yet upon arrival in Dar es Salaam, Tanzanians encountered a dramatically different material reality. By the mid-1970s, Dar es Salaam was, like many cities in Africa in the era of the global recession and state decline, a city in dire economic straits. The urban population and the boundaries of the city expanded rapidly every year not as part of a collective and planned vision of African prosperity, but informally, and often illicitly, as the growth of a city of squatters. The gap between the expectations of urban citizens and the material realities of the city grew greater each year over the course of the 1970s as the economy slowly collapsed, the central government systematically starved the city of resources, and rural socialism failed in the countryside, sending greater numbers of migrants to the city in search of life.

What did it mean to plan one's life in an unplanned city? How did these urban sojourners reconcile the promises of national liberation and collective economic uplift with the realities of inequality, scarcity, and infrastructural collapse that they encountered in the postcolonial African metropolis? In what ways did the expectations, aspirations, and imaginations of urban migrants shape the city itself? To answer these questions, this book explores the city as encountered by those socialist-era urban-dwellers who articulated visions of how life in the postcolonial African city should be. These popular urban intellectuals include investigative journalists and newspaper gossip columnists, songwriters, Christian women's advice writers, nurses and social workers, university sociologists, and underground pulp-fiction writers and publishers. Nearly all of these urban intellectuals were recently arrived migrants and part of a new generation of cultural producers in the city.

This book is both a literary history of Dar es Salaam and a retelling of Africa's twentieth-century urban revolution. Taken together, these case studies of urban cultural production reveal a paradox: despite the Tanzanian government's antiurban political philosophy and its systematic neglect and disinvestment from the city, the 1970s fostered the creation of a new kind of popular public intellectual who would innovate new modes and visions of urban community. While most African nationalist intellectuals developed a moral terminology premised on a global order of things that presumed the nation-state as the primary actor, this book explores how migrants in the city theorized the postcolonial predicament based on their urban experiences. This book is about those intellectuals who addressed their visions to their fellow urban-dwellers, creating urban publics and mentalities that were connected to concrete conditions and practices of urban life. These popular urbanists developed a moral vocabulary for the postcolonial city that was distinct from the moral vocabulary of African-nationalist liberation and nation building.

City, Country, and African Socialism

Tanzania's program of African socialism drew on a philosophy encapsulated in the term *Ujamaa*: a concept that, in Swahili, means "familyhood." Priya Lal has shown that, in articulating its distinctive political vision, Ujamaa's creators drew on multiple intellectual sources: variants of socialist thought from throughout the continent and Third World, *long durée* East African regional political idioms, colonial-era policies, and the Cold War–era nonaligned movement.[3] The intellectual genealogy of Ujamaa philosophy also contained deeply antiurban strands, including colonial-era social science theories about the dangers of "detribalization," Gandhian rural romanticism, and Third World agrarianism.[4] Like other newly sovereign African nations, postcolonial Tanzania faced a severe lack of industrial infrastructure and skilled manpower and a seemingly impenetrable "development barrier" that appeared to separate their economic path from that of the rest of the world.[5] While urban industrial development remained a goal for some postcolonial African nations—notably Ghana under Kwame Nkrumah[6]—other African leaders envisioned models of socialism that could be attained in the absence of an industrial revolution and the creation of a robust urban proletariat. One way these Third World intellectuals, politicians, and activists claimed socialism as their own was through programs of rural reorganization. The argument that a productive countryside would be the engine of national economic and political liberation circulated widely in anti-colonial and socialist intellectual circles, inspired by a range of political thinkers from Frantz Fanon to Mao Zedong.

Lacking the infrastructure and skilled manpower of the industrialized global north, African countries aspired to rely on their own natural resources and the physical labor of their bodies. "We must run while others walk," Nyerere often said, echoing the words of India's first prime minister,

Jawaharlal Nehru. What he meant was that the nation's uplift must be based on physical labor, for that was the resource that Africans possessed and that would be used without incurring debts to foreign entities. African physical labor in rural areas would make up for the inequalities wrought by the legacy of what the political theorist Walter Rodney called *under-development*.[7] In that sense, rural development brought about by physical labor was linked with self-reliance—in Swahili, *kujitegemea*.[8] Cities, by contrast, were understood to be unproductive sites where urban-dwellers shirked their duties to the nation and profited unfairly from the efforts of the peasantry.

Nyerere enshrined antiurbanism in the Arusha Declaration, the document that officially inaugurated and defined the socialist program and the concept of Ujamaa in 1967. In theory, for rural communities, socialism would entail the spatial reorganization and modernization of rural life, as peasants would be relocated from dispersed settlements into the spatially condensed unit of "village," or *kijiji*. More than the urban proletariat, in African socialism it was the rural peasant who would be the nation's common man and ideal citizen: the one on whose behalf state actions would be carried out. Agricultural development, it was argued, would make the nation of Tanzania self-sufficient and independent from the outside world, whereas the building of modern cities would require equipment, materials, and loans that would keep Tanzanians perpetually indebted to the outside world.[9] As a counterpart to rural villagization policies, the Tanzanian government carried out urban campaigns to remove women and unemployed youth from the city through forcible repatriations, while members of TANU's militant youth branch the TANU Youth League (TYL) patrolled city streets and carried out squatter demolitions in attempts to stem the tide of urban growth.[10]

Yet meanwhile, like other cities in the global south, Dar es Salaam was undergoing a dramatic transformation, both in size and in character. While earlier historical periods of urban growth throughout the world coincided with industrialization and economic growth, cities in Africa and much of the global south expanded rapidly in the face of economic decline, decreasing real wages, and collapsing state capacities and infrastructures.[11] AbdouMaliq Simone describes this trend as "the reorganization of the city from being the center for a modernist elaboration of formal public and private employment to an arena for highly improvised small-scale entrepreneurial enterprise."[12] In 1973, in the midst of this global urban shift, anthropologist Keith Hart first coined the phrase *informal sector* to describe the extralegal income-generating activities he observed in the city of Accra, Ghana, and the term quickly caught on among academics and policy makers.[13] At the same time, many Western observers and policy makers cultivated panic about crowded cities in the global south as sites of potential catastrophe by invoking the specter of an impending "population bomb."[14] From 1975 through 1977, Indian prime minister Indira Gandhi declared a state of emergency and oversaw the coercive sterilization of millions of poor people in the name of population control and national development in Delhi.[15] Signaling the recognition of these new urban patterns as a global trend and collective concern of the international community, in 1976 the United Nations General Assembly convened "Habitat 1": its first conference on the problem of rapid unplanned urbanization in the "developing world." In Africa, struggles to control urban growth, formalize the economy of the city and to bring urban activities within the actionable sphere of national governments were not new to the 1970s. Yet in the context of postcolonial nation-building efforts, mass urban migration took on new political significance since rapid unplanned urban growth ran counter to the narrative of state-controlled development, modernization, and sovereignty.

Dar es Salaam, like many of the burgeoning cities of Africa and the global south in the 1960s and 1970s, was a city of migrants. By 1971, 82 percent of people living in Dar es Salaam had been born elsewhere.[16] According to World Bank estimates, during the 1970s, Tanzania was the country with the third-fastest urbanization rate in the world, after Mozambique and the United Arab Emirates.[17] In 1967, the year that rural socialism was inaugurated, Dar es Salaam was a city of 272,515 people, and yet when Nyerere left office eighteen years later, it had quintupled in size. Today, according to some estimates, Dar es Salaam remains Africa's fastest-growing city.[18] In the 1970s, Tanzania was simultaneously one of the most rapidly urbanizing places in the world and the African nation with the most overtly antiurban policies and rhetoric.

This book is a history of the socialist period written from the perspective of those who left their rural villages and made their lives in Dar es Salaam. Writing a history of Tanzania from the standpoint of urban migrants and the problem of migration constitutes a departure from an academic historiography of Tanzania that is strikingly bifurcated between studies of rural socialism and studies of Dar es Salaam. The last decade has seen the burgeoning of a rich and sophisticated historiography of Dar es Salaam, making it one of the most well researched cities on the continent.[19]

Additionally, in recent years, scholars have begun to revisit and rethink the history of Ujamaa villagization.[20] Yet one of the shortcomings of this scholarship about twentieth-century Tanzania is that, writ large, it inadvertently reproduces, rather than investigates, the presumed distinction between city and country that Nyerere found so morally potent and politically expedient.

As Raymond Williams has argued, representations of city and country perform critical political work.[21] In postcolonial cities in the global south, from Jakarta to Calcutta to the Zambian Copperbelt, intellectuals have used contrasting images of city and country to contest political legitimacy and sovereignty, to define patriotism and deviance, and to name insiders and outsiders.[22] This book shows how, by contrasting images of an idyllic, authentically African countryside with images of a decadent, miserable, un-African metropolis, Nyerere displaced accountability for urban inequality and suffering from international and state actors onto urban-dwellers themselves.[23] Tanzanians who had, over the decades since World War II, begun to envision prosperous futures that would arise out of wage labor and urban living now were to be convinced through TANU ideology to imagine a rural future. It was not peasants and farmers who were the primary audience for a nationalist iconography consisting of bucolic images of rural life, but rather urban youth and restless rural youth considered to be at risk of migrating. The discursive dichotomy of urban and rural was a political tactic aimed at the control of mobility and an attempt to shrink or contain the city. Rural romanticism, in other words, was about the countryside in only a superficial sense. In this way, the national vision of socialist villagization and the challenge of managing the urban crisis were part of the same process.

By bringing the history of Dar es Salaam and the history of Tanzania's vision of rural socialism into the same analytic lens, a new history of the city—and of Ujamaa—becomes possible. The history of Dar es Salaam as it exists today is largely a history of those who left rural villages in the 1960s and 1970s. The people who filled the streets and squatter settlements came from rural peasant families, and their presence in the city threatened the moral political legitimacy of socialism and its central mythologies. Observers of urban life witnessed not only the urbanization of Tanzania, but also a simultaneous ruralization of Dar es Salaam.[24]

Dar es Salaam's newcomers were problematic to socialist boosters and ideologues not only because of the material claims they made on the city, but also because of what they potentially revealed about the rural areas from whence they came and about the ideology of Ujamaa more generally. Through their very occupation of the city's peripheral spaces, they contradicted the central premises of African agrarian socialism: that it could reverse the inequalities of colonialism, that the countryside was prosperous, that to live as rural villagers was to be authentically African, and that the Tanzanian people would choose it willingly. When urban migrant intellectuals rethought these premises and proposed new ways of living in the city, they—intentionally or not—forced a collective confrontation of the assumptions of Nyerere's central ideologies.

To explore Tanzania's socialist era from the standpoint of the city of migrants is to reframe the history of postcolonial Africa as a history of mobility, both in the physical and metaphorical sense. Sojourners "searched for life" in the cities to pursue what they did not find in their rural homes. The aspirations to social mobility implied by those who fled villages for the city threw into dramatic relief the incongruity between the desires of citizens and the state's ability to make those desires attainable. This mobility was not simply a technical problem, but rather the revelation of a more devastating truth: imperialism impoverished Africa, and yet national sovereignty and socialism alone did not deliver a just resolution.

Popular Urbanists

In recent years, a sophisticated body of scholarship has explored the tensions of national cultures in postcolonial Africa.[25] By shifting the frame from national cultures to popular urban intellectuals, this book illuminates new themes, both building on and departing from this rich field of academic inquiry. The urgent questions of urban expressive cultures that I examine in this book sometimes touched on matters of national culture, but more often probed personal questions about what it meant to leave a rural homeland behind, how to form viable personal relationships in an unfamiliar environment, and whether to resist or give into the temptations of new forms of wealth and pleasure in the city. From an itinerant songwriter composing songs and performing them in neighborhood bars to the mission-educated elite writing advice for young Christian girls in the city, how urban popular intellectuals portrayed the city and the countryside revealed an array of hopes for, and diagnoses of, a rapidly changing urban condition.

This book offers to the study of postcolonial Africa the category of *popular urbanists*. In a sense, it takes up and elaborates on Karin Barber's

1987 classic essay "Popular Arts in Africa," in which she identifies a "new kind of art created by a new emergent class, the fluid heterogeneous urban mass. Located at the perceived source of social change, popular art was both produced by a new situation and addressed to it."[26] Neither urban planners nor policy makers, nor simply "urban-dwellers" or the subaltern landless urban masses, "popular urbanists" are intermediate figures who are able to conjure urban publics.[27] My focus on popular urbanists, rather than more generally on urban-dwellers, highlights an approach that seeks out organic intellectuals who not only lived and survived in the city, but also theorized the urban predicament for a broader audience. Like Steven Feierman's category *peasant intellectuals*, these popular urbanists are defined as such neither by an objective measure of their intelligence nor by their academic or professional credentials, but rather by their ability to shape discourse and to call together an urban public.[28]

The work of these popular urbanists in socialist Tanzania was shaped by three historical circumstances. First, in Tanzania and beyond, across Africa and the global south, the growth of cities outpaced investments in infrastructure, economic growth, and planning. As time went on, as many African states faced financial strain and collapse in the late 1970s, the city and its trajectory gradually became unmoored from the prerogatives of nation building. State propaganda had encouraged people to organize their lives in rural nuclear-family households, to see themselves as economically self-sufficient, and to earn their living through agricultural production or, for a small minority, regularized wage labor. Yet these lifestyles never became the norm and countless other arrangements in the city continued to exist alongside these prescribed models. As state investments shrunk and the city grew, alternative forms of city-based community became increasingly important to the life of the city.[29]

Second, the larger political ethos of the time inspired people to think about the city in moral political terms, linking their personal and collective struggles to larger historical questions about Africa's place in an unequal world order. Participants in public debates drew from a wide range of sources in crafting their visions. They invoked utopian promises of African prosperity, critiques of neocolonialism and underdevelopment, Marxism, and discourses of Third World solidarity, and they combined these ideas with older regional moral idioms of sexual discipline, masculinity, and adulthood. They also drew on official Ujamaa rhetoric, and even moral narratives and characters from global popular cinema in genres including kung fu, Bollywood, blaxploitation, and spaghetti westerns. Urban popular intellectuals assembled and combined images of racial and economic justice from various sources, held them up against the urban realities they witnessed, and used the contrast as a starting point from which to voice critique and produce new visions of what a just and meaningful urban life might be.

Third, the expansion of networks of communication and media and the concurrent dramatic rise of literacy rates made it possible for people to communicate their urban visions to a wide audience. The Tanzanian socialist state was remarkably successful at raising rates of education and literacy through a rigorous and comprehensive grassroots literacy campaign that spanned the territory in the early 1970s.[30] Additionally, state investments in music and dance festivals, theatre workshops, and poetry competitions encouraged more Tanzanian youth to see themselves as producers of culture. Paradoxically, the infrastructural, cultural, and educational investments of colonial and postcolonial regimes made possible expressive cultures and visions that were unintended by, and sometimes at odds with, the developmentalist states that built them. Moreover, state protectionism and censorship against foreign cultural imports during those years produced a ready-made market for locally produced cultural goods.

As a literary history of migrant Dar es Salaam, this book follows the itineraries of a generation of urban cultural and intellectual producers who were grappling with the quotidian realities of decolonization, economic recession, and everyday life in an unplanned city. Ujamaa socialism and the mythologies of Tanzanian nationhood structured, but did not contain, the conditions of their production and thinking. By decentering the nation as the narrative through line, we can ask a different kind of question that does not center on the success or failure of the nation-state or of Nyerere's experiment with socialism. Instead, we can ask: at what moments do urban-dwellers understand the stakes of their experiences in national or socialist terms, and at what moments do they rely on, or innovate, other shared moral logics?

Cities, Textualities, and "Street Archives"

All cities are interwoven with stories. The stories people tell about their cities shape the urban environment in concrete, if not always straightforward, ways. For example, narratives about risk and sexual danger shape the terms on which differently gendered people occupy and move through urban space. Judith Walkowitz's now classic *City of Dreadful Delight* shows how Victorian-era Londoners produced, consumed, and deployed sensational narratives of sexual danger—such as stories about Jack the Ripper—as vehicles for shaping politics, policies, and unequal subjectivities in the city.[31] Historians and social scientists have also documented the mutually reinforcing relationship between crime narratives and concrete practices of racial segregation and securitization in cities ranging from São Paulo to Johannesburg and beyond.[32] Urban inhabitants design and construct domestic spaces that reflect their perceptions of crime and criminality and, in so doing, collectively transform the built environment in ways that entrench inequalities and perceptions of danger. At the same time, stories about cities also travel internationally in ways that impact global circuits of capital. Narratives that bolster a city's reputation for being modern or "world class" can attract capital foreign investment, while narratives of pathology or corruption can perpetuate conditions of marginality, whether or not these narratives are true.[33] Along these lines, Louise Young identifies Japan's "Tokyo-centrism" as a phenomenon that is simultaneously literary and material.[34] City stories change in tandem with changing global-historical circumstances: a process that Gyan Prakash illuminates in his 2010 book *Mumbai Fables* by tracking how the city of Bombay/Mumbai was transformed from a city of cosmopolitan colonial modernism to a "city of slums" in the collective national and global imagination over the course of the twentieth century. Prakash distills one of the questions at the heart of urban studies: what makes possible the telling of some city stories, but not others, at different moments in time?[35]

This is not an abstract question, for stories don't simply flow unmediated between author and audience. At least in Tanzania, the production of city stories not only has material effects, but is also itself a process shaped by material possibility and constraint. By the end of the 1970s in Dar es Salaam, basic commodities such as ink and paper were often unavailable in government cooperative stores, and basic services such as electricity and public transportation were frequently unavailable. Moreover, histories of urban narratives cannot take for granted a public that can access and interpret those narratives in a predictable, uniform way. Mass literacy was a new and growing phenomenon in postcolonial Tanzania, and as Rappaport and Cummins have argued, literacy is not a universal skill or technology that spreads evenly across a homogenous modernizing world, but is rather "a social process" that builds on various preexisting cultures of orality and expressive idioms. All of these factors shape how authors can convene audiences for their city stories.[36]

In other words, narratives—urban or otherwise—do not float freely apart from the physical forms, genres, and social contexts in which they are expressed. As Brad Weiss argues, "Imaginative acts are in fact materially grounded in social activities . . . too often the act of imagining is unmoored from the specific forms, times, and places through which persons project their possible lives."[37] Stories about the city and its possibilities become durable, shared, and embodied through specific forms of communication or expression. While in theory, anyone can create a narrative about a city, not everyone is equally empowered to shape urban practices and successfully assemble others into a shared moral community, nor are popular intellectuals completely free to choose the terms and forms in which they do so. By analyzing city stories in such a way as to include the genres and media in which they are expressed and the spaces in which they circulate and proliferate, this book aims to make visible the material inequalities and possibilities of cities that make some versions of urban life sayable, actionable, durable, and others not.

This book investigates texts, instead of narratives, to reveal the interplay of material, discursive, and social forms that give shape and substance to city stories. Karin Barber defines "text" broadly as a "tissue of words." She writes, "Though many people think of 'text' as referring exclusively to written words, this is not what confers textuality. Rather, what does is the quality of being joined together and given a recognizable existence as a form."[38] A collection of "urban texts" might include novels, newspapers, magazines, or religious books, as well as advertisements, graffiti, or the slogans printed on the sides of buses. It might also include oral texts, such as song lyrics, proverbs, and praise poems. It might include the Friday sermons amplified out from the speakers of mosques or the sales pitches of street hawkers shouted out of a megaphone: formulaic in some ways, yet also improvised and reshaped based on the dress and comportment of different potential customers encountered on the street.

Though often improvised, texts are not spontaneous or random; they are organic to the social worlds in which they resonate. Texts are both durable and mutable, revealing change and continuity over time. They are durable, for to perform work, they rely on social convention, genre, defined relationships between author and audience, and the expectations each has of the other. At the same time, they are mutable in that they change and can be deployed for different ends by their authors. Authors can create new texts by dis- and reaggregating old ones, through extracting and recasting fragments, through quoting or misquoting, and through combining multiple texts to constitute new communities and audiences in changing circumstances. In this way, texts reflect the constraints and possibilities of the worlds in which authors produce them.

This book examines text-making as a mode of city-making.[39] In this sense, I am not proposing to interpret texts produced in Dar es Salaam as evidence of urbanism; more than that, I argue that they are *constitutive* of urbanism. The Dar es Salaam texts collected and explored in this book instantiate the active efforts of urban-dwellers in the past to call together new publics, to innovate new spatial practices, and to construct urban moral communities that were at times separate from, and at times overlapping with, those of the ruling party and its documentary and bureaucratic conventions. Rather than reading texts as sources that deliver up to the historian an urban reality beyond themselves, I seek here to read texts as active components of the social worlds in which they were produced. How did the people who produced them seek to "matter," and in what way, and to whom? How, in a time of material scarcity, did urban intellectuals assemble the resources to produce and circulate texts for urban audiences? What were the contours of the social relationship that was being called into being through the author and her audience?

Such an approach to urban textualities is especially germane to the urban history of postcolonial Africa and other locations characterized by urban growth that occurs outside of the purview of state-based urban planning. Dar es Salaam during the socialist years was a city undergoing a massive transition. If the rhetoric of national citizenship in the late colonial and early postcolonial "developmentalist" years led to a vision of urban life that consisted of full employment, the upgrading of housing, and better services and working conditions as the components of citizenship, by the end of the 1970s and early 1980s, urban-dwellers from Abidjan to Harare to Lagos to Dar es Salaam began talking instead about being prepared to hustle; to "improvise" or "bluff," to "use the brains" to respond to unpredictable changes, or to forgo straight and predictable paths and "zigzag" through the city.[40] While historians have defined the post–World War II era as a time of policies of stabilization in African cities,[41] economic anthropologist Jane Guyer, writing about Nigerian cities in the wake of the oil boom and currency devaluation, identifies *destabilization* as a defining characteristic of urban life in recent African history.[42] In this context, ethnographers have taken a broad and creative approach to analyzing forms of contemporary urban life. In the absence of conventional forms of state and private urban infrastructure, AbdouMaliq Simone tells us, urban-dwellers invest in social networks above all else, mobilizing "people as infrastructure."[43]

This shift in the language and tactics of urban citizenship was accompanied by changes in the official documentation of city life. If, as Frederick Cooper has observed, the era of so-called stabilization went along with new forms of official documentation of the lives of Africans by the colonial state,[44] the retreat of the state from these forms of urban citizenship makes for a different kind of documentary record. As Jean Allman has argued: "At least in Ghana's case, the state has not adopted the same role as the colonial state in naming, preserving, categorizing, classifying, withholding, or destroying its records. As importantly, it appears to be either unable to do so or uninterested, especially compared to its predecessor, in the archives' panoptic potential."[45] Contrary to theories that emphasize surveillance and social engineering of top-down repressive states,[46] Bähre and Lecocq have argued that one of the defining features of the postcolonial state is its *inability* to see its citizens.[47] While Bähre and Lecocq see this as a sign of the weakness or incapacity of the state, Ananya Roy defined a lack of government documentation of the city of Calcutta not so much as an inability to see the city as an active strategy of neglect and flexibility, which she calls *unmapping*.[48] How will historians investigate these vital forms of urban life that, by their very definition, elude conventional forms of state documentation and archiving?

One of the central arguments of this book is that the popular and vernacular texts that were produced and circulated in socialist Dar es Salaam formed infrastructures of urban sociality. These texts can be read as unintended archives of an unmapped city: each collection of texts an unofficial "street archive." Reading these texts critically, as active components of city-making, reveals the everyday acts of creativity and imagination, as well as ad hoc logics of community and governance, that people deployed in their attempts to make durable forms of urban life. They reveal that, while Nyerere and his international allies saw the exploding squatter city as a diagnosis of crisis to be resolved by curbing the flow of migrants from the countryside, many urban sojourners saw it as an opportunity: to create and sell commodities, to assemble Christian converts, to redefine adulthood on new terms, to map new solidarities, to establish a reputation, or to engage in a salvationist project of uplift. Reading collections of popular texts from the past as archives of the city can reveal these soft infrastructures that sustained urban lives and imaginaries.

My point is not to romanticize urban textualities and the moral universes they improvised as a kind of democratic, liberating, or entrepreneurial alternative to the promises of state-directed urban modernity. In contrast with the more conventional narratives of modern African political history that seek to diagnose regimes in terms of success or failure or as stories of democracy or corruption, the popular urban intellectuals that appear in these pages elude these reductionist narratives. They did not see the Tanzanian socialist experiment as something to support or resist, but rather as a set of circumstances that they had no choice but to inhabit.[49] Approached as an alternative archive of city life, Dar es Salaam's popular texts reveal urban communities called together in circumstances not of their choosing and that many of the new urban arrivals identified as unacceptable and unjust. These street archives reveal urban-dwellers grasping toward new languages of political critique of the very circumstances in which they expressed their visions. Moreover, while street archives might reveal the ad hoc labor of producing networks, moral communities, and solidarities, like more conventional archives, they simultaneously reveal the work of power, hierarchy, and exclusion.

In the pages that follow, I mine texts produced in the city, along with interviews with the authors, producers, and sellers of these texts, to investigate the history of the migrant city. In this way, this book deploys the study of texts and textuality as a mode of urban historical investigation.

Method and Structure

My research method was to collect popular urban texts and analyze both their content and the ways in which they moved through the city and summoned urban communities. These texts were preserved in various, dispersed urban sites, and seeking out these texts and understanding how they were produced and circulated took me to many unexpected corners of the city. Over the course of my research, I spent time in church bookshops and the libraries of mission schools and Christian girls' hostels, sifting through the storage trunks of itinerant used booksellers, in conversation with pirated cassette tape sellers, and at the rehearsal spaces where songwriters composed songs and practiced with their bands. I spent much of my time interviewing those who authored, published, disseminated, or sold texts. I asked men and women about their knowledge and experience as text producers, focusing on the mechanics of producing various kinds of texts in Dar es Salaam in the socialist era. These interviews also took the form of more general and open-ended conversations about the experience of migration to Dar es Salaam in the 1960s and 1970s. The chapters that follow draw on this combination of textual analysis, ethnography, and oral-history interviewing.

Chapter 1 weaves together an intellectual history of representations of rural and urban locations in twentieth-century African nationalist thought and an accounting more specifically of how Dar es Salaam came to occupy a central symbolic place in constructions of race, nation, and authenticity in African socialism. Drawing on the pedagogical texts and propaganda produced by state ministries, it examines the relationship between the ruling party and the city of Dar es Salaam, the historical conditions that made Dar es Salaam a site of cultural production during an era defined by rural romanticism and antiurban sentiment, and the attempt of the ruling party to cultivate a citizenry that defined itself as rural. It goes on to examine the city and its publics as imagined by "roving reporters" and investigative journalists who wrote for the newspapers produced in Dar es Salaam over the course of African socialism. It tracks the takeover of the press by the ruling party and the rise of a new authorial mode in which reporters constructed a dichotomy of rural racial authenticity and urban foreignness as a way of defining criminality and sexual deviance in the city. This shift in perspective reveals a larger historical process by which the ruling party, TANU, distanced itself from its urban origins and its claims to represent urban constituencies and began to portray the city as the nation's foil.

Chapter 2 examines the intellectual and cultural work of middle-class Christian African women reformers who sought to model a modern urban African womanhood by composing advice literature for unmarried "girls" in the city. Through advice and prayer books, didactic novellas, newspaper advice columns, and public health pamphlets, these middle-class educated women advised female urban newcomers on how to live respectable Christian lives as workers in a city that had, until recently, been predominantly Muslim. The creation of distinctly female reading publics was linked with the attempts of reformers to make spaces of respectability and safety for women in the city, including the promotion of hostels for unmarried women and of improvements in transportation and workplaces to promote women's physical safety. In their advice to women about how to comport themselves in the city and in their broader attempt to politicize urban womanhood, reformers shared in common a privileging of monogamy, Christianity, and the nuclear family as the desired life outcome for young urban women. Yet regional norms of sexuality and extended-family-household composition and the economic precariousness of city life meant that this vision had limited appeal to most women for whom flexible sexual and domestic alliances were often a source of security, community, and material well-being in the city.

Chapter 3 uses songs and social rituals as an entrée into the nightlife of socialist-era Dar es Salaam. It explores networks of musicians, waitresses, bouncers, stage dancers, taxi drivers, and consumers who created a subculture in dancehalls and nightclubs of Dar es Salaam. Contrary to ruling-party ideals of austerity and physical discipline cultivated through national youth cultural curriculum, these influential urban denizens and social commentators elaborated an urban ethos from the stage and the dance floor in which access to leisure spaces, economic networks, and gendered modes of belonging were linked to cosmopolitan cultural knowledge displayed through dress, dance, and conspicuous consumption. The songs they wrote, the social rituals they choreographed, and the slang lexicon they developed to describe urban social types reveals a precarious sexual economy in which reputations and belonging were crafted through the exchange of money, scarce luxury items, and sex. Economic scarcity put strain on this highly gendered sexual economy, and young participants increasingly expressed frustrated desire and ambitions as gendered animosity.

Chapter 4 uncovers the existence of a thriving literary movement started by a group of young urban migrant men, known as "briefcase publishers," whose self-published crime thrillers and romance novellas modeled a new urban masculinity while generating powerful critiques of ruling political elites. These writers drew on international genres of romance and crime thrillers, set their stories in recognizable locations in Dar es Salaam, featured local urban characters as villains and protagonists, and composed their works in a colloquial Swahili idiom. Underground Swahili pulp-fiction novellas valorized the struggles of young migrant men to find livelihoods and social recognition in the city of Dar es Salaam. I show that the plotlines of the novellas mirrored the production process of the books themselves. In creating a publishing industry out of pilfered paper and ink and distributing their texts through informal trade networks, writers not only described urban communities and reputations, but also created them.

If the question asked by party leaders was whether or how Ujamaa was possible in the city, by the end of the period, urban-dwellers had innovated another term to capture the ethos of the era: *bongo*. In a way, the terms *Ujamaa* and *bongo* form chronological bookends to this study. Chapter 5 tracks the collapse of African socialism in the 1980s and the rise of the popular concept of bongo: an urban ethos valorizing an ability to survive in a precarious economic urban environment through creativity and street-savvy. The term *bongo* literally means "brains," and it refers to the kind of creativity and street-savvy one needs to survive in the city. This chapter steps back from the case-study structure of the earlier chapters and tracks a changing urbanist lexicon across Dar es Salaam's multiple "street archives," including popular terminology for black-market trade, prestige, beauty, masculinity, and sexual prowess. I argue that for Dar es Salaam's urban intellectuals, the ethos of bongo emerged as a shift toward a cynical realism about the place of Africa's growing numbers of urban strivers in an uneven world economy.

Taken together, the various texts created by urban-dwellers about urban life do not congeal around a single urban vision, yet they do share a set of concerns and moral idioms centering on the question of entanglement with the city and its networks. Whether to engage in informal-sector trade; whether to accept a gift from a lover; whether to wear the uniform of the TANU Youth League, or to accept a ride in a car from a wealthy man and move easily through town, rather than waiting in vain for the inefficient and maddeningly slow public transport; whether to cohabit with a romantic partner or bring a pregnancy to term in the city before securing the recognition of rural relatives; these were all weighty decisions. To be sure, the challenges faced by these generations of postcolonial African urban sojourners were, on one level, economic decisions about survival and household composition. Yet they were also far more than that. The kinds of obligations that shape social networks are not simply about survival, but are the very substance of how personhood, respectability, and community are constructed.

CHAPTER 1

TANU, African Socialism, and the City Idea

In 1965, the story on the front page of the Tanzanian newspaper *Ngurumo* carried the headline, "Give Your Vote to Julius Nyerere." Below the headline were two contrasting images. The first was a house constructed of mud brick walls and a thatched roof. The caption read, "the shoddy homes of the ruled." The second photo was of a "modern" house, constructed of whitewashed cement walls with windows and a *bati*, a corrugated metal sheet roof. Underneath the second photo was the caption, "the new houses of the free." These two images were followed by an injunction to "remember to make your black mark [on the ballot] for Nyerere. He builds Tanzania."[1] The message was clear: modern housing was a kind of political liberation.

To build the nation—*kujenga nchi*—would become one of the rallying calls of the Tanganyika African National Union, TANU, and its members. The phrase *TANU yajenga nchi!* [TANU builds the nation] was the official party anthem sung or chanted at government events and celebrations, and over the next decade, politicians would use the phrase *build the nation* over and over again as a generic phrase to label a wide range of patriotic acts. Yet in the early days following independence, in Dar es Salaam, TANU's promise "to build" meant something quite literal. Frequently, the front pages of the newspapers and TANU's news magazine featured photographs of Tanzania's new urban works of construction, including community centers, government buildings, roads, and especially *nyumba za kisasa*, or up-to-date houses, built under the directives of TANU. In these promotional campaigns, the physical improvement of the city was deemed synonymous with the progress of sovereign nations.

Within a few years after taking office, Nyerere sought to rein in this equation of liberation with urban modernization as Dar es Salaam swelled with migrants from the countryside and grew at a rate that far outpaced state capacity for urban planning, housing, and infrastructure. In the early and mid-1970s, in the context of economic crisis, unmanageable rates of urban migration, and a shift in policy to forcible rural villagization, many of the social benefits an earlier generation had associated with collective African uplift, such as houses roofed with bati, would be reframed by members of the ruling party as the signs of a "colonized mentality." According to politicians, the aspirations of Tanzanians for the trappings of urban modernity strained the capacities of a resource-poor state.[2] In 1977, Nyerere wrote an essay reflecting on the first decade of African socialism and the realities of persistent poverty and inequality in his country, offering a reinterpretation of the role of urban development. After having run for office promising cement houses with metal roofs as a symbol of freedom and decolonization, he returned again with a new take on the matter of housing: "The present widespread addiction to cement and tin roofs is a kind of mental paralysis. A *bati* roof is nothing compared with one of clay tiles. But those afflicted with this mental attitude will not agree. Cement is basically 'earth' but it is 'European soil.' Therefore people refuse to build a house of burnt bricks and tiles; they insist on waiting for a tin roof and 'European soil.' If we want to progress more rapidly in the future we must overcome at least some of these mental blocks!"[3]

Nyerere's two statements about houses, uttered twelve years apart, reflect a broad shift in TANU's relationship to the economic expectations of Dar es Salaam's urban residents over the course of the socialist era, from its inception in 1967 through its demise in 1985. The promise that liberation would mean the pursuit of a universal economic modernity was replaced with an ethos of cultural authenticity. For Tanzanians to desire the material trappings of urban modernity no longer signaled African economic self-sufficiency in the global economy, but rather the opposite: a cultural dependence on the West.

Between Tanzanian independence in 1961 and the mid-1970s, leaders within TANU transformed the organization from a political party that mobilized urban aspirations as synonymous with political liberation into a party that mobilized antiurban sentiment as a patriotic discourse. This chapter tracks the shifting relationship between TANU and Dar es Salaam, exploring how the metropolis went from being portrayed as the modernizing metaphor of the nation to being portrayed as its foil. It also raises the question: what are the consequences of defining civic virtue as rural at a time when African youth were increasingly leaving rural villages and seeking to make a life in the city? In other words, what political work did antiurban sentiment perform?

The history of print media and literacy in Dar es Salaam both illuminates TANU's antiurban transformation and served as a factor in shaping it. In the texts produced by TANU, representations of city and country legitimized new configurations of state power. Through a romanticization of rural village life and the vilification of cities, TANU attempted to prevent urban migration. By controlling mobility, the party aimed to control the aspirations and material demands of its citizens. To an extent, this shift is part of what Issa Shivji recognized as TANU remaking its politics as it transformed itself from an anti-colonial movement to the ruling party of a newly sovereign nation, responsible for building and directing the economy of a socialist society.[4] Yet while it is no surprise that TANU's vision changed once it was in power, the embrace of virulent antiurban sentiment as part of TANU's ideology was a political choice rather than a foregone conclusion. As Raymond Williams argued in his classic *The Country and the City*, representations of rural and urban scenes create and reinforce a geographical constellation of city, country, and towns in relation to the power of nation-states and their economic elites, naturalizing certain economic modes as legitimate while coding others as deviant.[5] Though his main emphasis was on the history of capitalism in Great Britain, scholars of postcolonial cities have opened up new lines of questioning by extending Williams's analysis to the decolonization of the global south. Writing about the political trajectories of cosmopolitan radical thinkers in twentieth-century Johannesburg—namely, Nelson Mandela and Mohandas Gandhi—Jonathan Hyslop attributes the transformation of urban nationalist freedom fighters into champions of rural romanticism to the attempt of politicians to neutralize the radicalism of urban politics once they themselves are in power.[6] In Zambia, James Ferguson shows how 1970s images of the virtuous and nurturing African countryside, as compared with images of Copperbelt cities imbued with the historical evils of capitalism and colonialism, became a way of legitimizing policies such as low wages for urban workers and of providing an idealized example meant to inspire or discipline urban-dwellers.[7] In India in the 1990s, Ananya Roy showed how the Communist Party of Calcutta contrasted positive images of the Bengali peasant with dystopian images of urban capitalism as a tactic of "setting boundaries and securing consent for its exclusions," especially their exclusion of the urban poor.[8] The contrast between rural authenticity and urban foreignness in postcolonial contexts has often been grafted onto narratives of decolonization in which the city comes to represent the unjust world of the colonizers and the countryside signifies the world of the oppressed.

The first half of this chapter charts the history of TANU in relation to the history of Dar es Salaam. The party's membership drew from the different corners of the territory with both rural and urban components, yet by the 1970s, the voices that represented urban constituencies had largely faded from the mainstream party platform. The second part of the chapter focuses specifically on texts produced by TANU after coming to power as they consolidated their authority as the ruling party of a sovereign nation. Their changing representations of city and country reflect the negotiation of multiple tensions, including struggles over gender and generation and over the geopolitics of decolonization. In Tanzania, the literary network of newspapers, workers' cooperative magazines, and later, didactic texts produced by TANU for the nation's educational system show a change in the relationship between TANU and the city between the late 1960s and the late 1970s. The shift in TANU literature took shape both in the content and in the literary form. In the content of TANU literature, writers shifted from portraying the city as a site of uplift, modernity, and citizenship from the late 1950s to late 1960s to portraying the city as a site of outsiders and shirkers of national duties by the early 1970s onward. TANU ideologues simultaneously changed the authorial stance and intended effect on audience, from portraying the city from the perspective of the young migrant male insider to portraying it from the view of a militant national outsider. This transformation of TANU's relationship with Dar es Salaam and the recoding of the city as "foreign" would have both discursive and concrete consequences.

Cosmopolitan Dar es Salaam

As a city to think with, Dar es Salaam exemplifies the synergies and tensions between nativism and cosmopolitanism that are at the heart of nationalism. Dar es Salaam stretches west from a concave half-moon–shaped harbor on the Indian Ocean. Initially envisioned as a city in the 1860s by Sultan Majid of Zanzibar, over the twentieth century, Dar es Salaam became one of East Africa's largest cities and a center of culture, print media, government, and commerce. The earliest inhabitants of the coastal region of Dar es Salaam are the Zaramo and Shomvi, groups who were able to capitalize on their deep roots in the region to become among the most

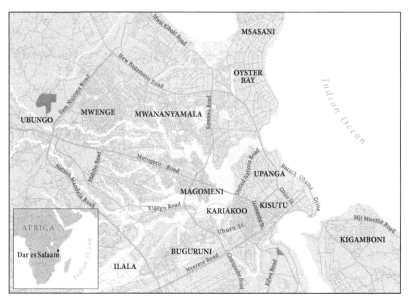

Map 1.1 Dar es Salaam and its neighborhoods. Map by University of Wisconsin Cartography Laboratory.

prominent landlords and neighborhood leaders in Dar es Salaam as the city grew in the eras of German and then British colonialism. Dar es Salaam grew from a tiny outpost of the Zanzibar sultanate to a colonial metropolis over the course of the early twentieth century. In his social survey of Dar es Salaam, based on research conducted in the mid-1950s, J. A. K. Leslie counted at least 100 ethnic identities present, hailing from locations in the present-day nations of Tanzania, Kenya, the Democratic Republic of Congo, Malawi, and Zambia.[9] Over the course of Dar es Salaam's history, as opportunities for work expanded in the growing colonial port economy, increasing numbers of people migrated from inland to settle—sometimes temporarily, and sometimes permanently—in Dar es Salaam.

Dar es Salaam's inhabitants trace their lineages from throughout central and southern Africa, as well as across the Indian Ocean from locations in present-day Yemen, Oman, and the Indian subcontinent. Throughout its history, Dar es Salaam has been home to substantial Arab and South Asian minorities. In the twentieth century, the Asian population of Dar es Salaam was made up largely of Muslims, but has also included Goan Catholics, Hindus, and Sikhs. The Muslim Indian population includes a minority of Sunnis, as well as three Shi'a communities: Ismaili Khojas, Ithansheri

Khojas, and Bohoras.[10] This cosmopolitanism is reflected aesthetically in the city's eclectic colonial and Indian Ocean architecture, Arabic- and Congolese-inflected music, and in the Swahili language: a Bantu language with borrowings from multiple languages including Arabic, Gujarati, and English.[11] By the 1960s, Dar es Salaam would stage new layers of cosmopolitanism in the form of pan-African and socialist solidarities when the city became a pilgrimage site and home away from home for pan-Africanist and socialist intellectuals from around the world. Many black activists, including freedom fighters from Southern Africa and members of the American Black Panther Party, found safe haven and intellectual companionship in the cafes of Dar es Salaam, while the University of Dar es Salaam became home to an inspired community of expatriate anti-colonial and Marxist intellectuals.[12]

It might seem paradoxical that while Dar es Salaam staged these multiple Indian Ocean and pan-Africanist global circuits, Tanzania's postcolonial political philosophy valorized and politicized indigeneity and nativism. Nyerere's articulation of Ujamaa philosophy placed precolonial tradition and conceptions of African authenticity at the center of a national vision, while public intellectuals labeled racial and cultural "others" as scapegoats for societal ills. The same milieu that fostered a distinctive and celebrated cosmopolitanism, ethnic fluidity, and an ability to incorporate different kinds of people into its diverse social fabric also fostered the opposite impulse: exclusionary nativist nationalism.[13]

Swahili cities have historically been built on trade rather than military might and are deserving of their reputation for cultural sophistication, diversity, and worldliness. It would be misleading, however, to read the cultural openness and racial diversity of Dar es Salaam as evidence of a peaceful tolerance of diversity. A new arrival in Dar es Salaam in the 1950s would have encountered a city shaped by historic cosmopolitanism, but they also would have encountered deep tensions and inequalities, exacerbated by the effects of European colonial segregation schemes. When British colonizers reconfigured the German East African colony as the British Protectorate of Tanganyika following World War I, they further entrenched earlier German policies in Dar es Salaam through the creation of three economic zones, which resulted in the de facto racial segregation of the city. Zone One was predominantly populated by Europeans, Zone Two by Asians, and Zone Three by Africans. In Zone One up along the coast, European expatriates built large, breezy suburban homes interspersed with older fishing villages inhabited by local residents. Zone

Two, which would become the de facto Asian residential and commercial district, consisted of numerous multistory stone tenement buildings. The densely populated Zone Two was the economic heart of the city.[14] The African residential Zone Three, mostly located in the neighborhood of Kariakoo, was separated from Zones One and Two by a "neutral zone": a *cordon sanitaire* that would later become known as "Mnazi Moja Park," where crowds would gather for religious festivals, competitions between neighborhood dance groups, and TANU rallies.[15] Zone Three housing in Kariakoo was largely restricted to mud and thatch houses inhabited by Africans and was home to many of the city's most important cultural institutions for black Tanzanians, including the headquarters for soccer teams, music clubs, dance associations, religious institutions, the Kariakoo market, the headquarters of the African Association, and, later, the offices and main headquarters of TANU.

James Brennan has shown how race-based policies governing access to property and credit entrenched racial divisions in Dar es Salaam. The result was that Asian residents could invest in real estate and owned multiple-story stone buildings, or *ghorofa*, while African residents held temporary year-to-year leases on single-story houses built from mud bricks and thatch: a distinction that adds significance to the later politicization of housing in Nyerere's speeches. At the same time, the immigration of Yemeni workers to Dar es Salaam in the 1950s led to the displacement of many Africans from housing, retail spaces, and commercial niches, exacerbating the sense that the city's inequalities could be understood in racial terms. Despite historic connections and centuries of intermarriage between people from Africa and the Arabian peninsula, Arab shopkeepers in Dar es Salaam were targets of racial violence several times throughout the 1950s.[16] In later years, with the policy of housing nationalization in 1971, it was primarily Indian families who lost all of their property.[17]

With both its colonial-era racial politics and its location as a node in global intellectual circuits, Dar es Salaam fostered multiple strands of nationalist thought, including some that would later shape the political platform of TANU. Dar es Salaam's coffee shops, bookstores, and printing presses brought together a wide range of political ideas and philosophies, including both regional political idioms and international intellectual currents ranging from Garveyism to Gandhiism. This intellectual ferment is evident in Dar es Salaam's rich colonial-era independent press. For example, in the 1930s and 1940s, Erica Fiah, a Ugandan-born journalist, established himself as an important Dar es Salaam public intellectual through the publication of his newspaper *Kwetu*—meaning, literally, "Our Home," or perhaps more accurately given the political context, "Our Homeland." Fiah was an avid reader of pan-Africanist literature, and through his newspaper he helped bring the ideas of pan-African intellectuals such as Marcus Garvey and Booker T. Washington into public political discourse and to apply those ideas as a lens for interpreting political matters in colonial Dar es Salaam.[18] Additionally, several Indian-owned newspapers, especially the *Tanganyika Herald* and the *Tanganyika Opinion*, fostered connections with Hindu intellectuals on the Indian subcontinent. They publicized images of mass anti-colonial protest abroad and reframed local grievances in terms of anti-colonial resistance.

The cosmopolitanism of Dar es Salaam fostered intellectuals who would reframe and invert ideologies from nearby and elsewhere, shaping them such that they would resonate in the city of Dar es Salaam, calling moral publics into being in the city.[19] The racial nationalism that would become so prominent as a TANU political discourse was formed both in conversations with, and in contrast to, Dar es Salaam's multiracial communities.

City of Migrants

In addition to its various Indian Ocean sojourners, Dar es Salaam's polyglot communities included migrants from East, Central, and Southern Africa. Another strand of East African nationalism emerged out of regional gender politics of the far-flung communities in which migrants remained embedded. These gender struggles emerged out of a post–World War II context in which the mobility of youth posed new problems to elders and patriarchal political systems that had been shored up, codified, and emboldened by colonial policies of indirect rule.[20] The urban revolution in Africa in the years following World War II was, in many communities, also a sexual revolution as increasingly mobile youth with access to cash and commodities forged new social bonds through the reconfiguration of sex, money, and community in cities rather than through elder rural gatekeepers who guarded access to land and marriage rites. For many of these urban sojourners, especially women, the city offered potential liberation from oppressive family dynamics, physical abuse, or economic marginalization that they experienced in their rural homes. Yet for those who stayed in rural areas, urbanization and particularly the movement of women to cities signified a potentially disastrous loss of communal control over youth labor, wealth, and reproductive capacity.

Urban migrants who left their rural homes behind to seek income or life experience in the city were products of a new economic predicament as Africa was incorporated in new and uneven ways into the global economy; yet they were also acting in a way that was consistent with a longer tradition in which mobility was linked with the pursuit of adulthood. For centuries prior to colonial rule, adolescent men throughout East Africa had traveled away from their homes as porters, traders, or soldiers to seek wealth and a reputation outside their natal communities. This separation from their families, if successful, would be part of their transition to respectable adulthood.[21] In the nineteenth century, with the extension and intensification of long-distance trade routes into East and Central Africa from the coast, young men traveled to Indian Ocean port cities with the caravan trade, working for cash wages as porters or seasonal laborers. These opportunities for travel and work would potentially allow men to bypass generational hierarchies and attain the trappings of male wealth and status—consisting of the rights to land, marriage, and economic dependents—through the control and distribution of newly available commodities such as imported cloth and firearms.[22] In later years, over the course of the colonial era, a growing number of young men gained access to the cash economy, allowing more of them to challenge the authority of elders and chiefs by finding alternative ways to achieve the components of adulthood.[23]

By the 1960s, as young urban newcomers continued to forge new social arrangements outside the context of rural households, many newly independent African countries responded on behalf of patriarchal "ethnic patriots" by restricting the mobility and dress of youth, especially women.[24] Across multiple African contexts, politicians responded to the sense of societal upheaval by deploying patriarchal metaphors of the rural family as symbols of political virtue.[25] These gender politics manifested most visibly in campaigns of urban reform and gender discipline across postcolonial Africa. One of the most notable manifestations of this broader perceived gender crisis was the banning of the wearing of miniskirts in several African countries. At the same time, cities saw increased incidences of physical attacks on "westernized" African women by young men in public spaces and increasingly strict measures to prosecute suspected prostitutes.[26]

This gender and generational upheaval that rocked colonial African metropolises in the late colonial era fed into racial politics and, in Tanzania, into a politically powerful strand of antiurban discourse. Post–WWII migration to Dar es Salaam augmented and altered preexisting urban dynamics of the coastal city. Between 1948 and 1971, Dar es Salaam's population quadrupled, and the vast majority of that growth happened in the form of migration from outside the city. Roughly half of those migrants were from coastal regions just outside Dar es Salaam and to the south, as far south as Mtwara and the northern coast of Mozambique. Many migrants maintained their access to land and their connections with agricultural communities, and they shared elements of coastal Islamic culture in common with each other and with longer-established urban notables. The rest of the migrant population came from farther afield in the interior of the territory, and greater numbers of them were Christian. They tended on average to have more exposure to Western education than migrants from the coastal region, and they occupied some of the most coveted jobs as clerical workers and bureaucrats in the postcolonial city. Because they traveled longer distances to seek out life in the city, they potentially had more to lose and fewer social networks to fall back on if things didn't work out.[27]

Anxieties over youth migration to cities became one of the catalysts that informed how East African political thinkers articulated a collective racial predicament as colonized Africans. Many, for example, saw the migration of youth to cities as a threat to African economic prosperity. In the interwar years, Dar es Salaam's African intellectuals expressed ambivalence about the city, which, in a colonial order of things, seemed to fuel the systemic subordination of Africans through menial labor, loss of land, and discrimination in urban institutions. Anxious public intellectuals filled the pages of newspapers with commentaries about the dangers of urbanization. They expressed fear about what Africans were losing by seeking lives in cities that were economically dominated by Asians and Europeans. In one editorial for his newspaper *Kwetu*, Erica Fiah wrote: "Reduced to a wage slave, he leaves the stricken family behind him cursing those responsible for home breakers, for destroyers of health, and for murderers of unborn babies! *Race murder*, to be brief. Wages, wages, always wages; temporary wealth but eternal moral as well as economic ruin. Once the lad is away from home 'on service,' in the townships, his doom is firmly sealed."[28]

In this way, Fiah links the loss of wealth of individual African migrants with the greater collective fate of Africans as victims of colonial urbanization. This fear that the growth of cities would impoverish black Africans as a community would continue to find resonance over the next several decades, in various political contexts.

The equation of African uplift with life in the rural village overlapped with the thinking of interwar European colonial anthropologists and administrators who articulated a set of fears and assumptions encapsulated in the term *detribalization*: a term that referred to Africans who moved to the city, away from their rural "tribe." The assumption was that Africans are a tribal, rural people and that when they are in the city, far away from the salutatory and chastening effect of tribal norms, they become a social threat.[29] Through low wages, barriers to African access to credit and financial products, and restrictions on mobility, the architects of colonial states defined Africans as rural. They defined urban Africans—particularly African men—as temporary migrant workers.[30] On this point, thinkers ranging from colonial officials to proto-nationalist intellectuals agreed, though for different reasons.

The behavior of youth in cities was a constant preoccupation of the various African public intellectuals who wrote for colonial-era newspapers. These anxieties over gender and generation found expression in a language of racial and ethnic exclusivity. Across East and Central Africa in the late colonial years control of urban women became a raison d'etre of ethnic associations. Community leaders called for ethnic endogamy in an attempt to control the free movement of youth and to end prostitution, drinking, and promiscuous dancing so that people would invest their wealth and labor at home and perpetuate rural communal institutions. Dar es Salaam's ethnic associations, including the Haya Union, Usambara Union, and the Nyamwezi Association, committed themselves not only to the well-being of voluntary members, but also to keeping tabs on itinerant youth by cultivating the loyalty and social discipline of young urban migrants in towns.[31] For example, the Nyamwezi Association in Dar es Salaam sponsored a dance association in which participants performed "traditional" dances of their western Tanzanian homeland.[32] Participants in the dance association organized themselves into a rigidly structured hierarchy, with titles, ranks, and different roles assigned to each member. The leader—often a woman—would be formally installed on a throne with a lion's skin in a public ceremony in Dar es Salaam. The association and its leader were rendered legitimate through the presentation of a letter of permission from the leader of the association's homeland branch in Tabora.[33] One of the central goals articulated by the organization's spokespeople was to promote the good behavior and sexual discipline of young migrants from their ethnic group in the city.[34]

There was a punitive flip side to this cultivation of ethnic identities and boundaries in the city. Kenda Mutongi describes how the Kenyan Kavirondo Welfare Association would send elders into the city of Kisumu to forcibly repatriate girls who were there against the will of elders. Mutongi describes public spectacles in which girls who resisted repatriation were body-punched, stripped, put into a burlap sack, and paraded around the village to be publicly shamed.[35] As Derek Peterson argues, Haya ethnic patriots, many of them vocal young men, sought to assert authority in their community by controlling the movements and sexuality of their female Haya age mates in the city. "In their activism," Peterson argues, "they valorized rural life as the ground of virtue and assigned to local government the task of supervising women's conduct." Ethnic identities solidified around attempts to manage female sexuality through efforts to control female migration and the behavior of wayward daughters in town. In a precursor to Ujamaa rhetorical strategies, the performance of authentic ethnic identity and rural heritage became a way of disciplining youth in the city.

Throughout much of sub-Saharan Africa, a romantic iconography of rural African life and negative portrayals of reckless female sexuality in cities became the available language with which to respond to the dislocations of migrant labor and a crisis in the family and sexuality.[36] Controlling female sexuality within the imagined community—whether that imagined community was a regional ethnicity or the race as a whole—was a building block of nationalist thought, spatially configured over the rural-urban divide. Echoing the earlier sentiments expressed by thinkers as seemingly divergent as Erica Fiah and colonial anthropologists, many imagined the rural African village as a solution to the ills of colonial expropriation, youth rebellion, and the loss of older forms of political authority. Shaped ideologically by the rise of racial nationalisms across the continent and fueled by the urgency of the social dislocations caused by new regimes of migration and the feminization of rural poverty, images of the city and country became resonant in a new way in the 1950s. Alongside concerns about the sexual endogamy of women, interracial sexual relationships and mixed-race children, known in Swahili as *chotara*, were singled out as especially controversial in the public sphere.[37] Rural romanticism became a moral language that conflated both the enforcement of female virtue and the policing of racial boundaries.

In light of these controversies, Dar es Salaam occupied a precarious place in TANU's mobilization, for the city simultaneously represented

Tanzania's modernization ambitions and a threat to zealously guarded gendered and generational social orders. In the 1950s and onward, the city increasingly staged the pursuit of new kinds of economic and sexual autonomy, and many young people moved to Dar es Salaam *kutafuta maisha*: to look for life. Young people, like generations before them, saw opportunities for advancement and new forms of adulthood and prestige.[38] But this potential for opportunity and upward mobility also made Dar es Salaam appear as a threat to a social order rooted in rural patriarchy and elder control of youth. Migration to the cities and the threats and social dislocations posed by this new mobility were an impetus for nationalist thought, placing antiurban thought as a central and defining component of racial nationalism in the city of Dar es Salaam.

TANU and the City of Dar es Salaam

When the colonial government sociologist J. A. K. Leslie conducted his survey of Dar es Salaam in 1956 and 1957, he observed near-universal support for TANU among the city's black population, leading him to label Dar es Salaam "a TANU town."[39] The new political party mobilized, honed its message, and gained momentum within Dar es Salaam's polyglot urban milieu. In the final years of colonialism and in the early days of independence, for many in the city, the trajectory of Africans in Dar es Salaam and of TANU was one and the same.

At the time that TANU was founded in 1954 in Dar es Salaam, the city's politics were shaped both by tensions of race and cosmopolitanism and by the broader territorial politics of youth migration to the city. Dar es Salaam's TANU branch was one of three powerful constituencies within the party's territory-wide coalition. The other powerful blocs included members from the wealthy and agriculturally fertile northeastern coffee-growing region and the Great Lakes Region of the northwest.[40] In Dar es Salaam, TANU organizers worked to link the grievances of urban-dwellers with a nationalist vision. The demands of urban supporters included workers' rights, better infrastructure, the ability to own and occupy urban real estate and to obtain trading licenses, and access to urban spaces that had barred entry to black Africans.[41] Channeling these demands into a vision of national sovereignty, TANU's urban branches envisioned decolonizing the city by opening its resources and opportunities up to its African inhabitants.

TANU's earliest core members in the city included not only educated elite men conversant in international anti-colonial politics, but also soon included other groups, including unemployed and marginally employed young urban male migrants and Muslim women traders. The TANU organizers who traveled through the city to recruit new members worked to recast the grievances and aspirations of the city of migrants through a national lens; TANU sought to channel the energy of urban male migrants by recruiting unemployed urban young men into the TANU Youth League. These energized TANU youth functioned as a kind of security force parallel to the colonial police, drilling with imitation rifles, physically intimidating TANU's rivals, and registering new party members. The organization established its popular legitimacy by promising to bring development and social control and claiming the ability to prevent youthful disorder in the city.[42] Brennan argues that it was in this context that TANU transformed urban grievances into a political movement defined along racial lines, framing claims to urban space in terms of the rights of black Tanzanians in a process that he calls "racial recruitment."[43] African urban residents who were restricted from access to property and credit, denied the best jobs, and subjected to de facto segregation began to see national sovereignty and citizenship as the solution to their grievances.[44]

Urban Muslim women were also active in Dar es Salaam's TANU mobilization. Following the example of the formidable Bibi Titi Mohamed, a divorced businesswoman and an urban property owner, women organized support through female urban social and economic networks, including *ngoma* (dance) associations and communities of brewers and traders who plied their wares together in the *pombe* (alcohol) markets.[45] Muslim women in Dar es Salaam were especially effective as political organizers, in part due to a culture of economic autonomy for women and the flexible shape of household composition, which allowed women relative control over their time and freedom to participate in political activities.

Dar es Salaam's independent press, which was built on the foundations laid by entrepreneurs like Erica Fiah, helped link urban grievances and aspirations with TANU's vision of Tanzanian national sovereignty. Two independently owned newspapers were part of TANU's organizing effort: *Mwafrika* (*The African*) and *Ngurumo* (*The Roar*). Robert Makange, one of the founding editors of *Mwafrika*, moved to Dar es Salaam as a young man in his twenties in the mid-1950s, during the years when TANU was first gaining momentum as a political and social force in the city. As part of an increasingly influential minority of Western-educated migrant men in Dar es Salaam, he found work as a colonial civil servant before joining TANU and becoming a member of the party's central planning committee at the headquarters in Kariakoo. There, he met fellow TANU member Kheri Rashidi Bagdelleh, and together they founded the newspaper *Mwafrika*.[46] By its fourth weekly issue, publication had grown from a print run of 4,000 to 20,000.

The second newspaper, *Ngurumo*, was founded and published by Randhir Thakers, a TANU supporter of South Asian descent who, despite widespread anti-Asian sentiment in the party, enjoyed close relationships with leading TANU figures.[47] By the 1960s, at 10 cents per copy, the paper sold for less than half the price of other mainstream national newspapers.[48] During those years, it was the most widely circulating newspaper in Dar es Salaam, reaching a regular print run of 40,000.

The editors of *Mwafrika* and *Ngurumo* supported TANU, but the newspapers were not officially linked with the party. Sometimes, their rhetoric acted as a catalyst to TANU members, cultivating support for the party agenda. At times, the editors were more radical than TANU politicians could afford to be. In 1958, Makange and Bagdelleh were arrested and charged with sedition for their virulent criticism of British colonial policies in the pages of *Mwafrika*.[49] Upon their release, Makange and Bagdelleh were welcomed by crowds of cheering members of the TANU Youth League in the street. These media outlets articulated, circulated, and amplified a vision that linked African racial solidarity and anti-colonialism to a vision of Tanzanian national sovereignty. At the same time, their formal institutional separation from TANU meant that the party would not be punished by the colonial state for the views of their supporters.

As a historical source, the pages of *Mwafrika* and *Ngurumo* reveal how members of TANU's potential constituency sought to portray the city in the construction of an urban political community. In the years following Tanzania's political independence, *Mwafrika* and *Ngurumo* popularized an optimistic vision of an upwardly mobile modern trajectory for Tanzania's urban-dwellers. *Mwafrika*'s writers parsed debates happening in Parliament, showcased new African-owned businesses that were opening throughout the city (including the entrepreneurial endeavors of Makange himself), and celebrated pan-African political and cultural figures that came through Dar es Salaam. The stories, imagery, and advertisements of *Mwafrika* reproduced 1950s developmentalist images of pan-African racial respectability and uplift,[50] framing liberation as the embrace of a global urban modernity in which Dar es Salaam's residents could be active participants.

At the same time, *Mwafrika*'s urban reporters highlighted their insider knowledge of the city's neighborhoods and public spaces. One of the regular features of *Mwafrika* in its final few years of publication was the *Mitaani* series. *Mitaani*, which means, "On the Street," featured "reporting" from Dar es Salaam and sometimes Tanga and Mwanza—Tanzania's other two major cities—as well as occasional dispatches from Kampala, Uganda, and Nairobi, Kenya.[51] The stories worked familiar scenes, specific locations, and characters into sensationalized and cinematic descriptions of urban life. In this series, the regular reporters included Kenyan reporter Bob Muthusi and the Tanzanian reporters Omar Bawazir and Maurice Sichalwe, better known by his pen name of "Kashkash." The columns were written in colloquial Swahili, peppered with slang from Swahili and English, and populated with young male characters with catchy nicknames like "Pennywaiz" and "Masta Plan." From week to week, the writers in the "On the Street" series crafted personas based on a mobility made possible by their vast network of social connections. They promised to "uncover and reveal the real city." The narratives in the "On the Street" series took place in public urban places, away from the domestic worlds of families, wives, and children. Monetary exchange propelled their movement through the story, allowing access to commercial leisure spaces, while also facilitating the making and breaking of relationships of reciprocity and indebtedness with barmaids, friends, and relatives. The vantage point for explorers like Kaka Sukari, Kashkash, Muthusi, and Bawazir was that of an active participant in urban life, multiply entangled, but morally impartial.

After independence in 1961, *Mwafrika* struggled to remain financially viable, and the Nairobi-based East African Publishers, looking to make inroads into the Dar es Salaam market, bought the majority of the publication's shares and continued to publish the newspaper for Dar es Salaam's audience. Makange continued to run the newspaper until shutting it down in 1964. He explained that he did so because, once TANU was victorious, he felt the paper had served its purpose.

The "roving reporters" who wrote for *Ngurumo* made the same boast of realism as the "on the street" observers of the city in *Mwafrika. Ngurumo*'s roving reporters fanned out across the city into the bars, nightclubs, ports, markets, and courts probing into disputes between husbands and wives, the cases being heard in local neighborhood courts, and the sexual escapades of town notables.[52] In both instances, the vantage point is that of the mobile male observer, who has ease of movement through his knowledge of, and emotional detachment from, the city. He is young and has no dependents in the story, allowing him special mobility. Especially distinctive in *Ngurumo*'s investigative reporting is a gendered dynamic in which the male explorer takes on the role of an anonymous "everyman," while the women who are the focal points of the stories are identified in precise detail. A reporter who suspected a woman of prostitution, abortion, adultery, or other forms of delinquency might print her name, the names of her relatives, her address in the city, and the name and location of her ancestral village in the newspaper.

In this sense, the press accounts were a continuation of the post–World War II tradition of men observing and disciplining female migrants in the city on behalf of an ethnic group, race, or nation. As a ruling party and source of authority, TANU legitimacy drew on an older moral idiom of policing female sexuality in the city.

TANU's Urban Moment

As we saw in the newspaper story that opened this chapter, print media also became a vehicle for promoting images of urban modernity as symbols of TANU legitimacy. In the years immediately following independence in 1961, commentary in the Dar es Salaam press celebrated independence as a call for modernization and renewal in the city. Within a few years, a construction boom was underway in the city's central locations. Prominent new government buildings, including a drive-in movie theatre, a new National Library, and massive works of public housing in the working-class neighborhood of Magomeni, were erected and announced with great fanfare as harbingers of a coming postcolonial prosperity.[53] Modern office buildings in brutalist style were constructed to house new government ministries, while several new hotels promoted Tanzania as a global tourist destination.[54] Government agencies showcased these buildings in regular newspaper advertisements, in *Jenga*, or *Build*, the magazine published by the National Development Corporation, and in the pages of *Nchi Yetu*, the publication of the Ministry of Information.[55] Boosters of these urban construction projects emphasized that these new buildings were built after independence, under the leadership of an African regime. These new structures proclaimed African self-reliance and a home-grown modernity before a global audience. Modernization, the narrative went, did not require foreign intervention, but would be delivered by the benevolence and competence of TANU.

Images promoting urban modernization also depicted the cultivation of modern urban workers and lifestyles. The publication of dozens of worker magazines in the 1960s for employees of public and private firms are historical artifacts of this vision. Nurses, teachers, postal workers, doctors, police officers, diamond mine employees, electrical workers, and engineers all had their own magazines produced by and for employees.[56] These publications contained discussions about the profession as well as portrayals of the social lives of the workers and their families. Some magazines also gave tips on urban life, instructing their readers on how to open a bank account and how to plan healthy, nutritional meals after work in the evenings. A 1965 issue of *Civil Servants Magazine*, which was published for the nation's expanding cadre of civil servants, featured an article that advised workers on how to obtain bank loans and how to invest in urban real estate. In the context of shortages of government and employer-provided housing, the article instructed the reader on the process for purchasing land, at what prices, and on which neighborhoods were up and coming.[57] These publications all envisioned an urban middle-class readership that would invest in the future of the modern city of Dar es Salaam.

The flip side of these images of urban modernization was the efforts of the Ministry of Culture to showcase the preservation of rural African traditions. TANU's directors of national culture oversaw the gathering and display of artifacts of "village culture" in community centers and museums and choreographed dance and music performances to be staged on holidays and in state-sponsored competitions.[58] In youth programs at community centers and in public schools, teachers instructed children on how to perform the traditional dances of various ethnic groups, while professors sent their college students to their home villages during school holidays to record the oral traditions of their elders.[59] Part of urban modern citizenship was an awareness of one's rural heritage. As one of the centerpieces of this articulation of a national tradition, in July 1966, the National Museums of Tanzania opened the *Kijiji cha Makumbusho*, or Village Museum, on what were then the outskirts of Dar es Salaam, on the road to the university from downtown.[60]

Between its founding in 1954 and the early years of independence, the histories of TANU and of Dar es Salaam became intertwined, though they were never synonymous. TANU's urban constituencies were one powerful strand in the party's platform, and in its early years, their interests were vocalized through images of urban modernization and inclusion.

Projected for a national audience, Dar es Salaam's modernization was a synecdoche of the nation and its progress, while the image of the idyllic village represented the past and the collective soul of the country.

The City, the Village, and African Socialism

TANU made official the beginning of its public retreat from earlier promises of urban modernization in 1967, when Julius Nyerere produced the Arusha Declaration, which inaugurated what would become Tanzania's eighteen-year experiment with socialism. The central policy platform of the socialist program was the organization of the population of the nation into collective rural villages. In theory, for rural communities, this would mean a reorientation and modernization of rural life as people were relocated from dispersed regions into reconstituted village units, allowing more efficient distribution of government services such as transportation, water sources, schools, and clinics. Urban citizenship would be reserved for a small number of citizens who would work in parastatal factories or in salaried government positions, though these urban professionals would remain a minority in the broader scheme of a socialism that was predominantly rural in nature. It was the rural peasant, and not the urban proletariat, who would be embraced as the nation's common man: the one on whose behalf state actions would be carried out.[61]

The rural romanticism and antiurbanism that would shape Ujamaa discourse in the socialist era drew on several political registers. One was a global register of anti-colonial nationalism, crafted in conversation with socialist thinkers throughout the African continent, particularly in socialist-leaning Ghana, Guinea, Mali, and Zambia.[62] The argument that a productive countryside would serve national liberation circulated widely in anti-colonial intellectual circles. Frantz Fanon, in his classic text *The Wretched of the Earth*, argued that urban elites lacked revolutionary zeal because of their structural position as beneficiaries of the colonial economy. "In an underdeveloped country," he wrote, "the leading members of the party ought to abandon the capital city as if it had the plague. They ought, with few exceptions, to live in the country districts."[63] For Fanon and others, liberation from colonial economies and racial hierarchies required the rejection of colonial cities as the spatial manifestation of a colonial economic world order. According to Fanon, nationalists should instead live alongside the peasantry, whose radical perspectives followed naturally from their structural position. Economically and culturally in-

dependent of colonial cities and outposts, peasants had no stake in preserving colonial and capitalist systems and so could be relied upon to
be authentic revolutionary nationalists.[64] *The Wretched of the Earth* was
widely read by Tanzanian intellectuals, cited often in the popular press,
and eventually appeared in two Swahili translations in 1977 and 1978.[65]

The projection of the rural African village as the site of political liberation also resonated with a global political project of Third World solidarity that emphasized agricultural production as a source of liberation
and economic autonomy from the industrialized global north in the era
of the Cold War.[66] The vision of the African village as a site of cultural and
economic production was consistent with a geopolitical vision embraced
by many Tanzanian leaders and their socialist allies in other parts of the
global south, captured in the words of the Chinese military leader Lin
Biao, who, in 1965, said, "Taking the entire globe, if North America and
Western Europe can be called 'the cities of the world,' then Asia, Africa
and Latin America constitute 'the rural areas of the world.'"[67] Lacking
the infrastructure and skilled manpower of the industrial north, African
countries had to rely on their natural resources and the physical labor of
their bodies. In a context in which colonial underdevelopment had left
the country with scant infrastructure and little skilled manpower, Nyerere was especially inspired by the example of China under Mao Zedong.
The many Tanzanian and Zanzibari political leaders, intellectuals, and
students who traveled to China and met Chinese delegations in Tanzania during the 1960s saw China's agricultural modernization scheme as a
path toward the future that bypassed colonial modernization trajectories
designed to serve the economic interests of the former colonizers.[68]

The Arusha Declaration's embrace of the village and rejection of the city
was both ideological and pragmatic. Nyerere urged Tanzanians to recog-
nize that Tanzania's material impoverishment placed political constraints
on their modernization trajectory. Development that required cash, Nyerere argued, would require foreign aid and make Tanzania dependent on,
and therefore vulnerable to, the outside world. "Gifts and loans," the declaration argued, "will endanger our independence." Within a national geography, this view of the world was mapped onto the older dichotomy of
city and country, for industrial development in cities, it was argued, could
only be accomplished through foreign loans. Because urban investments
required currency, Nyerere and his allies linked cities and urban-dwellers
with Tanzania's continued subordination to the outside world of former
colonizers. Echoing Fanon, the Arusha Declaration cautioned, "If we are

not careful we might get to the position where the real exploitation in Tanzania is that of the town dwellers exploiting the peasants." By contrast, agricultural development, fueled by natural resources and African labor, would make the nation of Tanzania self-sufficient, which would in turn deliver not only prosperity, but political sovereignty and self-determination.

Yet unlike Mao Zedong or Frantz Fanon, who had little use for "tradition," Nyerere linked his modernizing vision of villagization to a recoverable African past. Literally "familyhood," Ujamaa invoked the image of a rural extended family. Nyerere defined African socialism as natural and inherent to Africa's history and culture. He argued—contrary to linguistic and historical evidence—"I doubt there is such thing as class in African languages"; the concept of "class" or "caste" was nonexistent in African society.[69] He described a precolonial African village-based society where people acted in each other's best interests and yet relied only on themselves for survival. The African socialist relied on no one for wealth and yet gave freely to others. Tanzania's African socialists argued that African tradition was the wellspring of socialism, yet as Lal argues, "Nothing could be less traditional than this map of the ideal rural village."[70] Like all traditions, Ujamaa included elements that were invented and shaped by the needs of the political moment rather than the direct transmission of an unchanging past.[71]

TANU intellectuals selectively deployed historical narratives to naturalize villagization as an act of cultural recovery and to vilify urban migration as an act of racial betrayal. When referencing a national public history, many TANU ideologies portrayed Tanzania's coastal cities as historic sites of racial violence committed by non-Africans against Africans, drawing on some of the nationalist rhetoric that circulated around the time of the Zanzibar Revolution in which the Omani monarchy was overthrown in 1964.[72] Though Dar es Salaam had never been a significant slave-trading port, commenters often lumped it together with coastal sites in the slave trade such as Bagamoyo and Zanzibar as part of a larger and more generalized narrative of the enslavement of Africans by Arabs. The narrative of enslavement and emancipation resonated with African nationalists from many parts of Africa in the years following independence, both those from regions that had been subjected to the predations of the slave trade and those from regions that had not. These narratives cast the history of slavery and the Swahili coast through a drama of racial antagonism between two discrete racial groups—Africans and non-Africans—belying the forms of cosmopolitan citizenship and mixed racial heritage that had shaped the coastal history of Swahili cities, including Dar es Salaam. As Tanzanian policy makers took an antiurban turn in the early 1970s, this historical narrative was also mapped onto a dichotomy between rural and urban. Urban migrants, many argued, were suffering from a slave mentality or had a colonized consciousness, seeking out material goods and lifestyles that they had been indoctrinated into by members of other exploiting races.[73] When Nyerere announced a bold plan to officially shift the national capital from Dar es Salaam to Dodoma beginning in 1972, many portrayed the move as the replacement of a foreign capital city with an authentically African one.[74]

While Nyerere initially believed that Tanzanians would take on villagization voluntarily, with mounting evidence to the contrary, in 1973, Nyerere announced Operation Vijiji, or Operation Villages, in which he deemed villagization mandatory. Yet far from a top-down high-modernist scheme, as James Scott has described it, the implementation of this decree was highly uneven across different regions.[75] In some locations, such as Dodoma and Mtwara, villagization directives were taken on voluntarily at the grassroots, while in others, they were carried out by physical force against a resistant population. In some cases, officials who did not carry out the centrally mandated order would lose their posts and be replaced with more compliant managers.[76] At the national level, though, Operation Vijiji marked a dramatic shift in socialist policies from a voluntary collective project of uplift to a set of coercive measures.

Meanwhile, as villagization was carried out in the countryside, Dar es Salaam was increasingly becoming a city of squatters who were born outside the city and who were coming from increasingly farther afield. By 1971, 83 percent of Dar es Salaam's residents were migrants from elsewhere. The squatter population grew dramatically each year, at an estimated 24 percent per year between 1969 and 1972.[77] By the end of the decade, it made up 65 percent of the population.[78] The majority of these squatters did not work in salaried formal labor occupations. While state propaganda portrayed urban migrants as irresponsible youth who were abandoning their rural communities as though on a lark, the reality was far more complex. Like generations of young men and women before them, many migrants sought out economic opportunities in the coastal economy as an alternative to the pathways to wealth accumulation and adulthood available to them in rural areas. Others, many of them women, came to the city to escape violence or precarious domestic arrangements.[79] Yet most of these migrants, far from abandoning their rural homes and connections, remained deeply invested in them. In a survey, Richard Stren found that five out of every six squatters still intended to move back to their rural community and inherit land later in life.

The reorientation of the economy according to the principles of the Arusha Declaration coincided with several changes in urban land policy. In 1972, after the National Housing Commission (NHC) had ended its first five-year plan in 1969 and abandoned the program to build public housing in the city, they adopted a new plan that instead moved toward a policy of providing land that urban-dwellers could lease and improve themselves. The state would level sparsely populated plots of land and equip them with basic infrastructure. They would then invite applicants to build houses on the upgraded plots according to strict modern standards, relying on the capacity of individuals to build and invest in their own housing. This change in the provision of housing reflected a broader sea change in the rhetoric of citizenship whereby the expectation of Tanzania as a modernizing welfare state was replaced with the rhetoric of individual self-sufficiency. At first, the plan required citizens to construct their houses using expensive durable materials, like the cement and bati houses that had been celebrated as symbols of liberation in Nyerere's 1965 election campaign. Yet the expense of such materials and of hiring people to actually construct the housing made this vision out of reach for most Tanzanians. In the face of collapsing real wages, the National Housing Commission (NHC) lowered its construction standards.[80]

Socialist-era thinking about the city also again took up some of the discursive strands of the gender politics of the 1940s and 1950s. Female mobility, long associated with threats to ethnic and racial prerogatives in the 1940s, took on an additional set of meanings in the postcolonial context. As the Arusha Declaration stated, "The energies of the millions of men in the villages and thousands of women in the towns which are at present wasted in gossip, dancing and drinking, are a great treasure which could contribute more towards the development of our country than anything we could get from rich nations." Media commentators portrayed women in cities as rejecting their parents and their farms and threatening their social role as rural modernizers and as "mothers of tomorrow."[81] In this new postcolonial discourse, wayward women were not only betraying their elders or the members of their ethnic group; now, they were also betraying the nation and the race and perpetuating the reliance of the African continent on the outside world. Reanimated through the rhetoric of Third World agrarian solidarity, negative images of female mobility would make African urban women into scapegoats for global racial injustice: a shift that served to sanction violence against urban "modern" women across the continent in the 1960s and 1970s, including in Malawi, Zambia, and Uganda.[82] In Tanzania, TANU Youth League members took this up through Operation Vijana, or Operation Youth: a campaign ostensibly aimed at preserving the dignity of African culture in cities through the imposition of a "respectable" dress code and the public enforcement of that dress code, especially among women.[83]

Meanwhile, images of Dar es Salaam's expanding squatter settlements remained a thorn in the side of state policy makers, undermining the narrative of national sovereignty that TANU strove so hard to project, both at home and abroad. The image of burgeoning unplanned urban settlements revealed the failure of earlier promises of liberation through the building of modern houses for all. More importantly, by the early 1970s, these squatter areas belied the images of rural modernization and prosperity that were increasingly central to TANU's self-image: if the African peasantry were prosperous, and if villagization was indeed a successful model, and if the countryside was self-sufficient, and if national sovereignty could be achieved through the sweat of agricultural work, why were so many people fleeing those idyllic circumstances and choosing instead a life of urban poverty?

State officials took a punitive approach to the problem of urban expansion. In the cities, this took shape in a number of campaigns, including the 1972 policy Operation Kupe, or Operation Bloodsucker: a renewed campaign to arrest the urban unemployed and relocate them forcibly to rural areas. Another version of this policy was enacted in 1976 with "Operation Kila Mtu Afanye Kazi," or "Operation Every Person Must Work," in which eleven thousand unemployed Dar es Salaam residents were arrested and repatriated to Ujamaa villages outside the city.[84] These measures established that the right to the city was based on salaried employment, which would remain a possibility for only a select few.

Meanwhile, as more and more rural migrants made their way into the city's squatter settlements, the socialist state systemically neglected the city of Dar es Salaam. In 1974–78, as part of the broader policy of decentralization, the government dissolved the municipal structure of Dar es Salaam and divided the city into three regions. Political representatives in these districts would be appointed by the central government, rather than elected locally. In this way, the city of Dar es Salaam was no longer an officially recognized political entity. Public health funding was redirected away from urban hospitals, dispensaries, and preventive care and instead was channeled toward the building of rural clinics. This led to improved health outcomes in rural areas, but also to severely overburdened urban health clinics where patients often waited for hours in long lines before being seen by a doctor or nurse. Low immunization rates and poor public health measures in Dar es Salaam led to rising rates of malaria and tuberculosis in the city.[85] In perhaps the most dramatic gesture to separate the trajectory of the nation from that of Dar es Salaam, in 1972, Nyerere announced that Dar es Salaam would no longer be the nation's capital and that a new national capital would be built from scratch in the central, sparsely populated region of Dodoma.[86]

By the end of the first decade of socialist policies, the Tanzanian state had retreated from earlier promises of urban modernization and instead projected the collectivized rural village as the site of the nation's future. TANU enacted this rural reorientation through coercive policies including the repatriation and arrest of migrants in the cities and coercive villagization in many rural areas. Alongside these heavy-handed programs was a subtler ideological project of naturalizing the village as virtuous homeland and the city as a foreign and dangerous space. One of the ways they achieved this was through the production of literature and the cultivation of a nation of readers. They did this through two vehicles: first, the educational system and its network of literacy programs, and second, the state-owned press.

Cultivating Rural Socialists: The Literacy Campaign

Paradoxically, at the same time as the shifting politics of TANU resulted in the abandoning of the city as a metaphor of the nation, the city remained the nation's center of written knowledge production. This reinforced its prominent place in the national imaginary and as the site from which Nyerere's modernizing vision was disseminated. All major national newspapers were headquartered in Dar es Salaam, and most of their reporters were based in the city. They traveled up-country as stringers for short trips and then came back to Dar es Salaam, where they lived, worked, and raised families, to file reports on life in the villages at the newspaper central offices. As of 1972, newspapers were all owned either by the Tanzanian government or by TANU. The TANU newspapers were distributed throughout the country through ruling party networks, available at local TANU headquarters, office branches, and the homes of TANU ten-cell leaders:

local-level liaisons to the party who were selected from every group of ten houses.[87] Additionally, the University of Dar es Salaam was the preeminent university in the country and a prestigious institution where national elites from Tanzania and other African countries studied before going on to hold influential positions in government and industry. The University of Dar es Salaam was the institution that published the nation's social-science research on the effects of Tanzania's socialist programs, and its literature departments and university press produced Swahili plays, poetry, and novellas that would be performed throughout the country, many of them on patriotic themes of socialism and rural life. Advancement through the ranks of TANU required party members to spend time in Dar es Salaam. Rising TANU party cadres and civil servants throughout the country traveled to Dar es Salaam to be educated at Kivukoni College, which was TANU's ideological institute, before then being sent to work in Ujamaa villages in the rural regions.[88] In these different sources of knowledge—media, academic research, and propaganda—even negative portrayals of Dar es Salaam kept the city at the center of national narratives.

In this context, invocations of rural village virtue held different meanings and promises for different urban-dwellers. For example, some writers, many of them women, imagined Ujamaa villages as sites of feminist uplift. If coming to the city made women and girls vulnerable to the predations of corrupt "big men," adulterous husbands, and foreigners, women who were fed up with abuse, economic reliance on men, and sexual harassment in the street could, in these literary depictions, return to rural villages and find respectable work, social status, and community.[89] For example, Martha Mvungi's 1975 detective novel *Hana Hatia*, or *He/She Is Not to Blame*, includes a subplot about a man named Petro who leaves his virtuous and devoted wife, Maria, for a city mistress after he and Maria have trouble conceiving a child. Maria, cut loose from her natal familial home and marriage, needs to make a living for herself, and when she finds herself unable to find support in the city, she returns home to an Ujamaa village, where she finds a satisfying career as a village schoolteacher.[90] In the end, we learn that Maria was wronged: Petro, it turns out, is the one who was infertile, and moreover, his mistress turned out to have been a spy of his political rival. Meanwhile, in village life, Maria finds material and emotional security that she was unable to find in her marriage in the city. These romantic depictions of female uplift in the village were common in academic literary circles and were often written by educated elite women, most of whom resided in Dar es Salaam, including Martha Mvungi, who was a professor at the University of Dar es Salaam. While these critiques of the dehumanization of women in the city were powerful, their utopian portrayals of village life often glossed over the poverty, gender inequities, and violence that led many rural women to leave their village and migrate to the city in the first place.

At the same time as increasing migration belied the idea that communal village life was based on the natural cultural inclination of Africans, TA-NU's regional branches stepped up a propaganda campaign aimed at cultivating African socialist behaviors in its citizens. Nyerere and his allies made the case that rural socialism would liberate Tanzania from colonial economic legacies. Yet to realize this vision, they had to stem the tide of urban migrants, and if they couldn't do that, they had to at least neutralize them politically. The mass literacy campaign became a vehicle for producing rural African socialists and inculcating antiurban sentiment, while TANU publishing outlets produced texts that recast the city as un-African and unpatriotic.

In 1970, the state launched its famously successful adult-education program. The spirit of the campaign was inspired, in part, by the works of Marxist Brazilian educator Paolo Freire, whose 1968 book *Pedagogy of the Oppressed* advocated breaking down class hierarchies through a participatory approach to mass literacy and education. Freire visited Dar es Salaam in 1972 to speak with those who worked in the adult-literacy program, and as a token of solidarity, he gave the Tanzanian state the rights to Swahili translations of his book. Promoters of the mass education campaign saw literacy as central to the creation of socialist consciousness. In learning to read, Tanzanians would gain a "national attitude and awareness of social and economic obligations in all the national efforts on development." There were also material aspects to this vision as the circulation of texts could help build awareness of better material conditions and foster modern material aspirations in rural people. As an official guide to the program stated: "The desire of the farmer for a better life will be translated into effort to acquire the money income to satisfy material needs out of his farming activities and will lead to improved productivity. The Government has, therefore, decided to attach special priority to community development action, the essential purpose of which will be, by adult education, exhortation and example, to enlighten both men and women on possibilities of attaining a different, higher and more satisfying standard of living."[91]

Figure 1.1 An adult literacy class is held in Ihangiro, Bukoba District, 1969. Reprinted courtesy of the Tanzania Ministry of Information.

The kind of literacy promoted by the state would create not only readers, but also the right kinds of communal attitudes, national consciousness, and material aspirations that would modernize the countryside. This would also help expand consumer markets for goods produced in Tanzania, while it might also inspire citizens to become more economically productive.[92] The cultivation of a desire for modernization was a delicate balance, however. One of the core positions of Tanzanian officials and ideologues was that it was the unrealistic material desires of rural villagers that were to blame for urban migration and the related ills of delinquency, crime, and poverty. Education would have to inspire in students a desire for only the specific kinds of prosperity associated with village life.

The first cohort of officers of the adult-education program were trained in Dar es Salaam at Kivukoni College—TANU's ideological institute—and were then sent out to the district and village levels to organize and run the programs. In rural areas, classes were held at party headquarters, schools, churches, and sometimes out in the open air. In cities, classes were held in community centers and often in the workplace. Workers in the parastatal factories at Dar es Salaam were often required by their supervisors to either stay late or arrive early for work to attend a literacy class where they would learn to read and be taught how their work fit into a larger economic and political structure in Tanzania's socialist program.[93] The literacy program was intended to cultivate citizens who would not only possess a modern skill set, but who would also be open and receptive to Ujamaa propaganda. So, for example, TANU literacy primers would teach readers about the villagization program and its political ideals. They would also teach developmental topics, such as better farming techniques, family planning, hygiene, child-rearing, and household budgeting.

In 1972, the same year that Paolo Freire visited Dar es Salaam, the Tanzania Publishing House was opened as a state entity. Under the leadership of Walter Bgoya, the Tanzania Publishing House published the English-language scholarly works of internationally acclaimed socialist thinkers from the University of Dar es Salaam, including Issa Shivji and Walter Rodney, as well as Swahili translations of works by Frantz Fanon and Kwame Nkrumah. Additionally, as part of the literacy campaign, the Tanzanian state, in conjunction with intellectuals from the University of Dar es Salaam, promoted the writing, publication, and dissemination of novels in Kiswahili. Cultural policy makers and university intellectuals saw literacy as an indispensable skill for a modern citizenry, and more importantly, they believed that the content of an emerging national literature would work to cultivate the habits and sensibilities of national citizenship in its Tanzanian readership. Reflecting state campaigns to discourage urban growth, the majority of these Ujamaa-era novellas told stories about urban migration, unfolding as young men or women moved to the city in search of love or money and describing either the inevitable descent of the urban migrant into poverty, criminality, or prostitution or their redemption when they returned to rural areas to join an Ujamaa village.

The main curriculum of the adult-education program would take the form of primers, produced by a team consisting of an agricultural officer, a Swahili-language expert, and an adult-education officer.[94] The manuscripts were sent for review to ministries of national education and agriculture before being published by the Tanzania Publishing House or other state presses.[95] Often, the primers would feature a short story and then contain a series of discussion questions for students in the adult-literacy class to engage in with their instructor. For example, in 1973, the Tanzania Publishing House launched a series of primers called *Mazungumzo*, or *Discussions*, to be assigned as curriculum in the state literacy campaign. The texts were written in simple Swahili, with a small core vocabulary suitable for new readers. They were designed to incite conversation about socialist values and behaviors.

The third primer in the *Mazungumzo* series took up the theme of urban migration. The author, S. K. Msuya, composed the parable in the form of a conversation between a man and his grandson in an unnamed rural village in a mountainous region of Tanzania. After the boy shares his dreams of moving to the city, his grandfather tells his own story of wayward youth. He describes his naïve childhood hopes of finding a life of prosperity and material comfort in the city and his hopes that the wages earned in the city would allow him to properly provide for his fiancée. Yet once in the city, he was unable to find work and found himself isolated and destitute, scorned by his neighbors and living on the street. In describing this scene to his grandson, he lamented how the traditional cultures of the village were destroyed in the city as youth like him mistook foreignness for "development." He angrily criticized the urban girls, whom he saw bringing shame on their parents by walking around the city in miniskirts. Eventually, filthy, naked, and destitute, he climbed onto the back of a vegetable truck heading in the direction of his home village, where he was welcomed with open arms by sympathetic rural villagers. As a young man, the grandfather had gone from being a hooligan and vagrant in the city to becoming a leader in the development and modernization of his village, "the land of milk and honey." Through hard work and community development projects, he went on to have a successful career, making his village a far more desirable place to live than the city.[96]

In contrast with young men and women who went to the city kutafuta maisha, to look for life, it was in the process of making a victorious return to rural life that the grandfather narrator attained adulthood and respectability. In this way, idioms of generation were used to code differences between city and country. If, as Raymond Williams suggests, a conventional capitalist narrative portrays the country as the site of childhood innocence and cities as sites of adulthood and complexity, with nations that are urbanized seen as having "come of age,"[97] here an alternative narrative is being offered. While rural areas are sites of childhood innocence, cities don't represent adulthood so much as stalled adolescence and the inability to attain proper adulthood. It is only when returning to villages that such growth and maturity can be reached.

The back cover of the *Mazungumzo* books revealed the pedagogical approach of TANU's mass education program. The description reads: "This looks at the behavior of city-dwellers and compares differences between life in the city and in the country. It also shows how the entry of foreign power led to life in the city with wealth that comes from the country. This book is written with short sentences in literary Swahili. It will suit adult readers who are learning to read and write."[98]

The books were marketed not toward consumers, but rather toward party cadres at the district levels who would decide which books would be assigned in the adult-literacy program in their regions. This description makes explicit the connections between historical narratives, attempts to curb urban growth, and the model of party-led "education" of citizens, revealing how party intellectuals attempted to weave this spatial logic into the ethos of citizenship through mass education and literacy. They were written in the style that Lila Abu-Lughod calls "development realism."[99]

At the same time as books and government educators were circulating out into the countryside on behalf of the literacy campaign, within the city, slum demolitions and the mass arrest and repatriation of unemployed urban-dwellers continued. The fictional stories of heroic rural return would serve to recast the punitive nature of forcible repatriations and slum demolitions as a narrative of racial and social restoration. Whether the story was of voluntary or forced return to the rural areas to perform nation-building work, official party propaganda instructed readers to understand these rural returns as part of a broader racial and historical narrative in which the contrast between village virtue and urban delinquency was a bigger story about foreign incursion and racial betrayal. These pedagogical texts show how TANU sought to cultivate a socialist citizenship and national consciousness in which the urban was foreign and therefore illegitimate. They demonstrated how the ruling party wanted citizens to understand policies such as Operation Kupe, Operation Vijiji, and the broader push to move to rural villages.

The texts of the literacy campaign articulated a new geography of city and country in socialist policy and rhetoric in which movement to the city was associated with decline and exploitation, while movement into Ujamaa villages was associated with collective uplift. More than content, the literary mode of TANU texts promoted a relationship between author and audience in which the authoritative former would improve the latter. The literature reflected the attempt of bureaucrats to cultivate the desire of citizens for rural prosperity while discouraging urban aspirations. They did so by portraying cities as inauthentic, impoverished, and depraved, while portraying rural areas as sites for the attainment of prosperity and adulthood. It was with that same logic that Nyerere would, in 1977, in the context of economic crisis and infrastructural collapse, recast the desire to live in cement houses with metal roofs from an argument about economic entitlements and liberation to an argument about race and authenticity. The literature of Ujamaa wove together historical narratives of racial violence and collective redemption with individual stories of struggles for adulthood, respectability, and emotional satisfaction. Within this narrative logic, village life promised respectable adulthood for the individual and racial uplift for the nation.

TANU's Man on the Street

By the 1970s, TANU's relationship with the Dar es Salaam press also changed, reflecting an attempt to shape and control, rather than harness and direct, urban political grievances. While we've seen that earlier independent newspapers such as *Mwafrika* and *Ngurumo* were a way of mobilizing and channeling urban moral community toward a shared racial nationalism, by the early 1970s, newspapers sought more to cultivate particular modes of citizenship. The authorial stance of the urban insider, in which young male reporters would observe the city as knowledgeable insiders, would all but disappear from the media with the government seizure of newspapers by 1972 as the state gradually consolidated control over media.

The government takeover of the press began in 1968 with the passage of the Newspaper Ordinance, which gave the president the authority to close down any publication that was deemed antithetical to national interests. Soon afterward, the state took over the English-language paper the *Tanganyika Standard* based on the accusation that it represented foreign interests.[100] In 1970, then, newspapers that circulated in Dar es Salaam included the central government–owned *Daily News* and its Sunday version, *Sunday News*, the TANU-owned *Uhuru* and its Sunday version, *Mzalendo*, and *Nchi Yetu*, a monthly news publication of the Ministry of Information. Meanwhile, *Mwafrika* had shut down in 1964 as *Ngurumo* declined gradually, finally closing its doors in 1974. The *Tanganyika Standard* was then folded into the *Nationalist*, the English-language party daily newspaper, to form the *Daily News*. By the mid-1970s, all major newspapers in circulation were owned by either the state or the ruling party.

The state takeover of the press was part of a broader process of centralization of control over information, bolstered by a developmentalist premise: the role of the media was to "educate" people into the values of socialist citizenship. In a 1972 editorial in the *Daily News*, the journalist

Guido Magome captured the predominant industry belief about the role of media. He wrote:

> The greatest challenge in new nations is that of decolonizing the minds of the people, generally; breaking the cocoon in the heads of some of us in order to make our minds more receptive of and adaptable to new ideas. On this particular task there is no turning back . . . in a country determined to build socialism like ours, the press must not only correctly inform the people of what is going on around them, but it must also act as a collective mobilizer, collective educator, collective inspirer, and an instrument for the dissemination of socialist ideas and the socialist ideology.[101]

This media approach described by Magome reflects TANU's larger approach to expertise and authority, often expressed through gerontocratic metaphors in which the state was a benevolent father charged with teaching and guiding a naïve and childlike population. Journalists who lived in urban areas where the newspapers had their headquarters were encouraged to write about rural development projects and ordered to refrain from writing anything that was critical of the implementation of government directives. To allow public commentary that was critical of the government, Prime Minister Rashidi Kawawa stated, would confuse the easily influenced peasants.[102] Reporters would be sent up-country to an Ujamaa village to report on a story for a day or two at a time before returning to the city, where they would compose a laudatory report of the progress they had seen in the rural Ujamaa villages.[103] This production process helped disseminate portrayals of rural villages as simple, apolitical, and socialistic communities.

This shift from urban to antiurban and from independent to state-owned newspapers became evident in a new style of reporting. As we've seen, exposing the bodies, sex lives, and movements of Dar es Salaam's women were preoccupations considered newsworthy by the media in the 1960s, and this aspect of urban journalism continued throughout the 1970s. In September 1970, a "roving reporter" for *Ngurumo*, one of the last remaining Dar es Salaam papers from the late colonial years, circulated through the neighborhoods of Ilala and Kariakoo to investigate rumors that a teenager named Dora Salimu had illegally terminated her pregnancy. Through interviews with neighbors, relatives of the accused, and the landlord of the rented room that Dora shared with several other young women at 9 Rufiji St., the reporter learned that Dora was a recent migrant to Dar es Salaam, having followed her father to the city after leaving school in the central Tanzanian town of Kondoa. Dora's neighbors and roommates told the reporter that in the days leading up to the alleged incident, many suspected that something was awry with Dora, who seemed physically unwell, and that the "house mother"—an older woman who acted as a surrogate mother to the "girl" tenants—had publicly accused Dora's lover of getting her pregnant. Both Dora and the young man had denied this charge, and Dora insisted to probing neighbors that she was suffering from a stomach illness. Neighbors told the reporter that, on the night in question, Dora had risen in the middle of the night and then stumbled outside in the dark to the public latrine. In the hours that followed, Dora suffered greatly from bleeding and abdominal pains, and after a spiced medicinal concoction failed to improve her condition, she was escorted to Muhimbili Hospital, where, nurses told the reporter, she was still being treated. Meanwhile, neighbors entered the latrine with a flashlight and called on the fire brigade to remove the lifeless body of a male infant who had been left there in the night. At the time that the story appeared in the paper, Dora was being treated at the hospital, and the police were planning to investigate whether the case constituted an illegal abortion, for which Dora would be prosecuted.[104]

Stories in this style appeared frequently in *Ngurumo*, from its first issue in 1959 through its last in 1974. The reporter was present in the unfolding of the story. His movements through the city and his interactions with a wide array of other urban residents were central to the telling of the story and served to establish his credibility. In many instances, reports like these followed up on local rumors of abortion, prostitution, and adultery, and the women featured in these stories were often identified by name, address, and physical description. It also often referenced their village of origin, signaling that these women were migrants who did not belong in the city and who were living in the city apart from an alternative moral universe of the village in which other community members might keep them in line. This story exemplifies the older mode of Dar es Salaam reporting for an urban public.

By comparison with this story, which appeared in the independently owned urban newspaper *Ngurumo*, consider a similar investigative report printed in *Nchi Yetu* (*Our Nation*), a monthly paper owned by TANU, in 1975. Chiku Abdallah wrote an exposé entitled, "What Kind of Life in Dar es Salaam?"[105] An illustration accompanying Abdallah's article depicts two figures: first, a stereotypically Westernized woman in a tight low-cut mini-dress that exaggerated her breasts and hips. The woman is depicted with blotchy skin, suggesting the ill effects of skin-lightening lotions.[106] The second figure in the illustration is an elderly man, wearing the traditional Swahili Islamic dress of a *kanzu* and *kofia* cap and gazing at the woman in apparent disgust and incredulity. The caption reads, as though an encapsulation of the man's thoughts, "This woman is among those aimless wanderers who reject a life of labor, and instead end up as hooligans and baby-killers."

Like the 1970 story of Dora Salimu that appeared in *Ngurumo*, the text of this report is animated by the reporter's movement through downtown Dar es Salaam and its adjacent neighborhoods of Kariakoo and Ilala, exploring markets, bus stops, and public streets. Yet unlike *Ngurumo*'s reporters, Abdallah remains at a distance from the objects of her gaze, portraying them as strangers. She encounters "beggars," "prostitutes," "abortionists," and "wanderers" in the city and directs the readers' imagination to the rural Ujamaa villages from whence they had presumably fled. Refusing the work of agriculture and returning to the city even after repeated government efforts to repatriate vagrants to rural areas, urban figures are labeled by Abdallah as people who chose to "live off of the sweat of others" as squatters in Dar es Salaam.

There are clear similarities between stories like Abdallah's and *Ngurumo* stories like the one about Dora Salimu. The male explorer, monitoring the activities of women on behalf of an imagined moral public, is present in both narratives, reporting to a broader public of concerned people. However, the intrusive presumption of intimacy in the earlier story, in which the observed is "one of us" and can be named, located in the city, and held accountable to a wider community, is now replaced with broader and more anonymous racial narratives. If in the earlier version the young woman deserved scrutiny and discipline because the observer and observed were members of the same intimate community of urban insiders, what made these women deserving of scrutiny and discipline was their perceived foreignness. In contrast with the investigative style of the earlier story, in which the author and reader are imagined as embedded in a single circumscribed moral universe of the neighborhood alongside landlords, tenants, relatives, and neighbors, Abdallah instead conjures a moral public of readers whose imagination encompasses the space of the nation and its collective vision of socialist villagization. Rather than familiarity, it is estrangement and incredulity that are invoked as a credible viewpoint. The reader is encouraged to view inhabitants of the city as through the eyes of an outsider, through the discerning and authoritative gaze of an elder man, such as the one in the image, shocked and betrayed by the behaviors of the nation's wayward sons and daughters.

In the urban narratives of *Nchi Yetu* and *Uhuru/Mzalendo*, the authority of the writer came not from a claim to possess the thorough and intimate knowledge of a participant in urban scenes, as in the highly sensationalized stories of *Ngurumo* and *Mwafrika*. Instead, authority came from the claim to an outside perspective that imagined the city in terms of a larger collective narrative of rural villagization. In media coverage of the cities, the reference point was often to unnamed rural communities, on whose behalf urban public intellectuals claimed to be acting and speaking. Editorial comments criticized "deviant" urban behaviors not in terms of urban sociability, but by invoking the betrayal of African rural values and communities. This political language defined the authentic citizen as disciplined and hard-working, fulfilled by modest rural lifestyles and relative poverty. Noncompliance with villagization directives was conflated with cultural and racial inauthenticity.

Those who created media images of deviant women in the party-owned press in the late 1960s and early 1970s used three strategies for portraying urban women as national outsiders. First, they interpreted certain practices of adornment—such as the wearing of wigs and hair-weaves and the use of skin-lightening cosmetics—as bodily artificiality and racial degradation to portray them as physically inauthentic. Second, they portrayed urban women as bad mothers who were a threat to social reproduction, incapable of producing legitimate offspring as future citizens of the nation. Third, they portrayed urban women as culturally incompetent, most often by describing them as incomprehensible or inept at speaking Swahili.

For example, a political cartoon that appeared in the newspaper *Uhuru* in December 1969 featured a husband and wife walking arm and arm, staring at an archetypal "modern" urban woman.[107] The woman being scrutinized possesses some of the key identifiers of delinquent femininity, according to the media iconography of the time: her skirt is short and her legs elongated. The woman, as is nearly always the case in these caricatures, is pictured carrying a purse, signaling her aspirations to economic autonomy in the city. Her hair is tied in a tall *kilemba*, or headwrap. By contrast, the wife in the image wears a *kanga*: a rectangular piece of fabric wrapped around the body, tucked under the arms, and her hair is braided close to her head, signaling racial authenticity and sexual modesty. She wears no shoes and does not carry a purse. The contrast in the adornment of the two women is telling. The miniskirt was associated with urban mobility and participation in a consumer economy, worn by women to work in offices or in spaces of leisure. The kanga, by contrast, was an item that was worn in the house or around the neighborhood and was associated with domesticity.

The wife says to her husband, "Why are you staring? Are you attracted to that woman's style?," and the husband replies, "Sadly, I do not speak her language. If I did, I would tell her that her clothing insults us." His comment "I do not speak her language," whether taken literally or figuratively, creates distance. By contrast, the wife's modest and "traditional" attire together with the couple's fluency in Swahili identify the husband and wife as Tanzanian nationals, and it is against this image of nationhood that this urban woman is made strange. As in many media depictions of this kind, the "strange" woman herself is silent and is perceived through the distancing eyes of people whose perspective the readers are presumed to share.

Caricatures of female migrants in the city, struggling to speak urban coastal Swahili as a second or third language and with an accent, reveal some of the complexities of Ujamaa rural romanticism. The emphasis on the telltale markers of rural origins suggests that urban women were perceived as threatening not because they became "urban," but because of what their presence in the city revealed about the rural: that village life was not as desirable or prosperous as politicians promised and that socialist villagization and modernization were not going according to plan. Rural people and their languages were celebrated, but only if they stayed put in rural areas, in Ujamaa villages. The scandal of these women was not about their urbanness, but about the fact that they were mobile and, according to Ujamaa spatial principles, ungovernable.

Portrayals of urban women as racially ambiguous in appearance, incompetent in Tanzania's national culture, and a threat to the nation's future generations naturalized the movements of militant men through the city as patriotic. These men could claim to act based on their cultural and perspectival alliance with rural areas and values. The TANU observer position combined older practices of policing female sexuality with narratives about racial insiders and outsiders so that perceived affronts to the gendered order of things could be recast in collective terms as affronts to the project of collective racial liberation. This made it ideologically possible for militant men to act punitively toward African rural female migrants in the name of decolonizing the African city. Paradoxically, African rural and racial authenticity became a language for punishing rural African women who made their way to the city.

This literary shift in how reporters wrote about the city and how they encouraged their readership to read the city coincided with attempts of TANU to manage public opinion and gain control over the city through a gradual privileging of intelligence gathering over service provision. TANU attempted to maintain surveillance over urban residences through the creation of the ten-cell system, first in urban neighborhoods and then throughout the country. Through this mechanism, TANU branches sought to keep track of what urban residents were up to and talking about. Similarly, Tanzania's government continued colonial-era requirements that all urban social and cultural groups register with the government, listing their members and activities. With the decentralization of government services, the municipal structure of urban government was replaced with a system in which many of the functions of governance were performed unofficially by the TANU Youth League, the militant branch of the ruling party, whose legal authority was never entirely clear or stable.[108] TANU closed down nightclubs and establishments that were deemed antithetical to national interests. The TYL also were deployed to prevent the growth of squatter settlements by tearing down new settlements as they were built. The TYL was often charged with policing the city, gathering intelligence that was seen as threatening to government officials,[109] and, most famously, attacking women deemed inappropriately dressed under the directives of Operation Vijana.[110] These practices of surveillance and the moral logic behind that gaze were made manifest in media portrayals of privileged patriotic observers surveying the city and its inhabitants on behalf of fellow outraged citizens.

For example, in a 1973 article published in *Nchi Yetu*, reporter Allen Mhije followed three women whom he witnessed getting off of a bus at the downtown bus stop of Dar es Salaam. The three young women had come from their homes in Mwananyamala, which at the time was one of the city's rapidly expanding squatter settlements. Mhije followed the *wasichana*, or girls, from the downtown bus stop into a nightclub called Margot's, a nightclub near the port known for its popularity among foreign sailors and adventure-seeking Dar es Salaam youth. In the nightclub, he watches the women dancing and speaking with men of other races, and he caricatures their attempts to speak broken English to European sailors. For Mhije, this was an intimate tableau of urban inequalities and sexual misconduct and simultaneously of a broader and enduring global imbalance between Africa and the wider world. As an author, he exposes a world in which, despite the rhetoric of racial equality, the nightclub scene still reveals hierarchies and inequalities persisting in the most intimate of acts. Mhije positions himself as a writer witnessing this on behalf of all other fellow Tanzanians.

In this narrative, the characters are divided into national outsiders and insiders. Mhije approaches one of the women for an interview. Drawing again on the trope of linguistic incompetence for describing urban migrant women, he emphasizes her accented and broken Swahili, betraying her up-country origins and lack of education. Mhije ends the story with an interview with an elderly male security guard at Margot's. Mhije approaches him by praising him for his age and wisdom and asking him, "As the Swahili say, to live long is to see many things . . . what can you tell me about these sisters and the environment here at Margot's?" The guard replies by denouncing his workplace as a den of Satan. The two men then are united, with the intended readership, in their righteous disapproval of the "girls." While the first part of the story narrates the movements and observations of a young man through the city as he pursues eye-catching women as they seek out male companionship in the nightclub, in the end, the story finds resolution when the reader perceives the scene through the eyes of Mhije and an elder male as they gaze in the same direction from the stance of indignant urban outsiders.[111]

Narratives like these, which appeared so frequently in Tanzanian newspapers in the 1970s, make visible the attempt to bring readers onto the side of the ruling party, making it possible to see the inhabitants of the city as foreigners and to render violence against them legitimate. These narratives were an attempt to teach the public a way of seeing the city and of linking TANU's antiurbanism with racial patriotism and male prerogatives. The observer was no longer an urban insider and participant, observing the city on behalf of other urban-dwellers. In these later versions, the observer is, in essence, the police. Concurrent with a shift away from the city and the aspirations of its residents was a shift in perspective, and a shift, to use Gyan Prakash's phrasing, in which stories were and were not possible about the city.

Conclusion

With the introduction of Operation Vijiji in 1973, Nyerere marked a shift in socialist policy from an open-ended voluntary movement to a coercive set of policies that sought to enforce villagization. During those same years,

TANU's relationship with the city also changed. Several policies marked a shift in its configuration of the relationship between city and village, including the declaration that villagization would be mandatory, the dissolution of Dar es Salaam as a municipal entity, the decision to shift the national capital from Dar es Salaam to Dodoma, and the demolition of Kisutu: one of the city's most vibrant squatter settlements and a hub of the urban informal economy. In naturalizing TANU's antiurban turn of 1972 through 1974, intellectuals drew on a longer historical dynamic of intergenerational struggles over the mobility, labor, and sexuality of youth that had been ongoing since the post–WWII years in response to the dislocations of capitalism and urbanization. These struggles were reanimated in the context of the global emergence in the 1960s of a rhetoric of Third World solidarity in which cities were understood to be sites of neocolonialism and rural areas were understood as sites of cultural authenticity and revolutionary potential. In this context, antiurban sentiment was recast as anti-colonial critique. The economic crisis of the mid-1970s that rendered urban modernity untenable made these arguments politically salient. Drawing on these multiple registers, TANU responded by attributing urban ills to the moral character of the urban population, recasting the city as a site of racial betrayal and the countryside as a site of authenticity. The only virtuous villagers were those who stayed put in their village. In this way, TANU promoted a political logic in which responsibility for urban inequality and poverty would fall squarely on the shoulders of urban Africans whose rightful place was in the village.

This transformation in how the ruling party represented the city reveals the decoupling of urban visions, citizenship, and claim-making from official nationalism. Yet in spite of this shift in TANU's relationship with urban migrants, the city of Dar es Salaam continued to stage other moral visions and other modes of urban citizenship. Paradoxically, the years of Ujamaa antiurbanism coincided with a flourishing of cultural production in the city of Dar es Salaam. The protectionism of Tanzanian products and the prohibition on consumer goods, entertainment, and media from outside Tanzania fostered a situation in which artists, intellectuals, and musicians had a protected market and a captive audience. Televisions were outlawed, and few people could afford private record players, which meant that people spent their evenings outside in public spaces. Despite the rise of antiurban sentiment as a powerful and ubiquitous moral political language, Ujamaa created the conditions for the rise of a new generation of city dwellers who elaborated an ethos of postcolonial

African citizenship based on the city and its networks. These competing urbanisms of the past can be found throughout the city's many "street archives."

For example, throughout Dar es Salaam today, one finds cassette-tape sellers who circulate through the city with glass aquarium-like cases on wheels like a wheelbarrow, filled with cassettes of music, much of which was recorded in the Ujamaa era at Radio Tanzania in the late 1960s and early 1970s and then pirated many times over. Urban migrants to Dar es Salaam in those years would have come to a city with a vibrant live music scene, with bands circulating through the city frequently, and music—though interrupted with frequent electricity cuts—was available to be heard in every neighborhood on nearly every night of the week. There were private bands and bands on the payroll of state institutions, parastatal companies, and workers' collectives. Songwriters gave voice to many of the experiences of urban life of the growing city of squatters. Additionally, the massive expansion of literacy rates over the Ujamaa years gave rise to a burgeoning subculture of underground fiction writers as well as to a rapidly growing reading public who would become a ready market for them in Dar es Salaam. In book stalls all around the city, in private collections, and in the basement of the National Library, one can find old, disintegrating Swahili pulp-fiction novellas and Christian prayer books and advice books, as well as old cultural magazines in the forms of film strips and comic books that became popular among writers in the early 1980s. The remainder of this book uses these "street archives" in order to excavate social networks that structured the city in the 1970s, some of which have endured and others that have since fallen away. The next three chapters of this book take us into some of these urban textual worlds.

CHAPTER 2

"All Alone in the Big City"
Elite Women, "Working Girls," and Struggles over
Domesticity, Reproduction, and Urban Space

In 1969, the Tanzanian writer Martha Mandao published her first book,
Peke Yangu Mjini, or *All Alone in the City*. Mandao was twenty-eight years
old at the time and was herself a recently arrived migrant in Dar es Salaam.
Published by the Ghana-based African Christian Press and subsequently
in Swahili translations by an Anglican publisher, the Central Tanganyika
Press, the text is advertised on the back cover as "a book for teachers,
nurses, and office workers—and for all who want to learn how to be strong
Christians when alone in the city." The book tells the story of Ani, a young
Christian woman who leaves her village and arrives in Dar es Salaam to
work in a modern office, but finds herself lonely and isolated in the city.
Over the course of the book, Mandao takes the reader through the city as
encountered by the young migrant—to the single room she inhabits in a
traditional Swahili six-room house with other tenants, the bus stop where
she waits for the agonizingly slow public transport to take her to work, to
the office, and out into the raucous commerce and sociality of the streets.
She faces the temptations of alcohol and dancing and bitterly envies the
wealth of her well-dressed female friends. She struggles to resist the in-
vitations of young attractive men who drive cars, eat out at restaurants,
and talk about politics. Having grown up in a community where everyone
was a member of the same Christian church parish, Ani must also adjust
to living in close quarters with non-Christians. Overwhelmed and lonely,
she receives counsel from her female neighbor Mama Rupia, a fellow
Christian. Mama Rupia becomes a mentor to the young Ani.[1] Mandao,
speaking through the character of Mama Rupia, advises the reader to find
peace by transforming her rented room into a spiritual and moral refuge,
disciplining her body, her mind, and her daily routines as a barrier against
the noxious influences of city life.

Figure 2.1 Cover artwork
of Martha Mandao's *Peke
Yangu Mjini*, published by
Central Tanganyika Press,
1972.

In the final pages of the book, Mandao guides her imagined readership of female nurses, teachers, and office workers through a series of
spiritual exercises. She recommends bible passages to go along with each
dilemma faced by the protagonist, Ani. Mandao composed prayers for her
female readers to recite alone in their rooms at night in the city, such as
the following:

> Dear Jesus, help me to be without fear, help me to cleanse my sins. Fill
> my life with the strength and love of the Holy Spirit. I thank you for
> the strength of my body and mind. Help me to use them well. I pray
> that you help me so that I can live with different kinds of strangers,
> and enable me to find friends that are suitable in the city. Stay with me
> Jesus so that I will never be alone again in my life in the city.

Mandao's book was one of many examples of advice literature composed
for the growing ranks of working girls in Dar es Salaam in the late 1960s

and early 1970s. In the years following independence from colonial rule, Tanzanian Christian organizations sought to expand their ministries to urban areas, and especially to the growing ranks of migrant youth in Dar es Salaam.[2] Literacy and the dissemination of Christian literature was a central part of this. Across denominations, parish leaders encouraged the formation of reading groups, especially for women, in which members would read and discuss the Bible and other texts on themes of conjugality, childrearing, and urban living. Christian bookstores and itinerant book-seller stands began proliferating in the city, and Christian presses stepped up the production of texts that would address contemporary challenges faced by African women. Women wageworkers were only ever a small fragment of the female population of the city and a small proportion of all the city's workers, and Christian women working in the formal sector were an even smaller proportion of the urban population. Yet despite their small numbers, a disproportionate amount of effort was directed at advising Tanzanian female wage workers on how they ought to live in the city. It is the literary construction of the working girl through advice composed for and about her that is the subject of this chapter.

Read as a street archive of the early Ujamaa-era city, the prayer guides, didactic novellas, newspaper advice columns, relationship advice books, and sex education pamphlets written for newly arrived migrant girls in the city reveal an emerging set of relationships in the city between middle-class educated women and poor and working-class "girls." For the former, the urban crisis was an opportunity to model themselves as reformers and define their position in the city through efforts to improve the lives of poorer women. Reformers and advice writers saw the working girl as a gateway into broader social and political change. In envisioning how she ought to live her life—what kinds of work she should do, where she should live, how she should spend her money, and what kinds of intimate relationships she should have—advice givers not only sought to affect the young women, but also sought to remake the city and their authority as reformers within it.

Yet this standpoint—similar to what Abosede George has called "the salvationist gaze"[3]—was not the only way middle-class women could engage with working women in the city. This chapter places this collection of advice texts into conversation with another source: a social survey produced by female university scholars and students from the University of Dar es Salaam in 1973 and 1974. Four graduate students at the University of Dar es Salaam—one European and three Tanzanians—researched and wrote the survey under the supervision of social-science professor Dr. Marja-Liisa Swantz. Rather than writing advice or prescribing behavioral solutions to the problems faced by women in the city, the students sought to report on what their lives were like, both in the workplace and in the neighborhoods where they lived, and to forge solidarities with the women in the process. I read this source in two ways: first, as data about the lives of working women in Dar es Salaam, and second, as another form of urban textuality.

As data about the lives of working women in 1970s Dar es Salaam, the survey data places the advice texts in a new light, for they reveal a vast array of domestic circumstances and creative conjugal arrangements that working women inhabited and shaped in the city. Whereas the Christian advice writers shared a vision of middle-class domesticity modeled on the self-contained, permanent nuclear family home as a vision of both spiritual and urban improvement, many of the women they sought to address and reform placed more importance on maintaining flexible familial arrangements, female social networks, and relative economic autonomy from spouses and domestic partners. Moreover, the kinds of household arrangements described in Christian advice literature were simply materially unfeasible for poor and working-class women in Dar es Salaam. The economic struggles of women workers to piece together a livelihood and a home in the constraints of 1970s Dar es Salaam reveals the distance between the worlds envisioned by advice givers and those of the women they were purporting to advise. Read alongside texts like Mandao's, this survey data brings into view the tension and power dynamics of this reformist relationship between author and audience, middle-class reformer and urban migrant.

At the same time, the survey and the field notes on which they are based are subjective texts revealing the intentions and positionality of the authors as social scientists and as products of a particular historical moment at the University of Dar es Salaam. The field notes of the authors and the papers they wrote based on their ethnographic research were steeped in the intellectual milieu of Marxism, underdevelopment theory, and radical participatory pedagogy in the model of Brazilian theorist Paolo Freire and the University of Dar es Salaam playwright and scholar Penina Muhando Mlama.[4] Like advice writers, the social scientists saw the potential to remake the city through the transformation of working women, yet for them, it would happen through the radicalization of working women as they became aware of the objective conditions of their labor, rather than through the adoption of a middle-class Christian habitus. Moreover, the flexible domestic arrangements that reformers defined as pathological appeared to the social scientists as having the potential to challenge patriarchal gender norms. The researchers conveyed their stance toward the women they studied not only in the content, but also in the form of the texts and the processes through which they were produced. While advice books, pamphlets, and newspaper columns modeled a relationship in which the author would cultivate and reform the reader, the university sociology students strove to find common ground by seeking to produce texts collaboratively with the women they were interviewing and observing. The process of producing the surveys was meant to inspire solidarities and incite political consciousness across the lines of class. The researchers saw in working women the potential for the students to build their own expert voice and to connect with a project of socialist urban citizenship despite their own openly acknowledged, comparative class privilege.

What these two bodies of advice literature reveal is a mode of authority and intervention crafted especially by elite, predominantly Christian migrant women in Dar es Salaam in the years following Tanzania's independence. What these texts do not reveal, however, is how readers read, used, and engaged with them. We cannot assume that readers interpreted texts in the ways that the authors intended. As Corrie Decker points out, readers—in her research, schoolgirls—actively develop and cultivate subjectivities through literacy, often interpreting and redeploying texts in new and unexpected ways.[5] Available evidence does not flesh out, in a satisfying level of detail, how female Christian readers in socialist-era Dar es Salaam responded to these texts, though it is likely that women who read advice texts about family life conducted their family lives in ways that diverged, or only selectively drew on, the models presented in Christian didactic literature.

Despite these limits, what both the advice literature and the survey do reveal is a moment at which the "working girl" became both a collective problem and a collective opportunity for various factions seeking social change in Dar es Salaam in the late 1960s and early 1970s. More than prescriptions for individual women and families, these different textual modes also reveal competing notions about how to organize urban space, and especially housing arrangements, for working-class women. Prescriptions for the lives of working girls were prescriptions for the city as a whole.

With the economic collapse and the antiurban turn in government policy, the preoccupation with female workers faded from public debate in the mid-1970s. Working-girl politics were the vision of a particular moment, occurring in the late 1960s and early 1970s, when changes in labor, gender relations, and the city were inextricably entwined. In the absence of livable wages and salaries, the "working girl" ceased to be a convincing symbol of either collective promise or danger.

Who Is the Working Girl? Demographic Shifts and Wage Work

In their study of the modern girl in the 1920s and 1930s, the Modern Girl Around the World Collective argues that "'girl' denoted young women with the wherewithal and desire to define themselves in excess of conventional female roles and as transgressive of national, imperial, and racial boundaries."[6] The postcolonial "working girl" in Tanzania and beyond became a site of intervention about two decades after the global emergence of the "modern girl," and in the context of decolonization, rapid urbanization, and the rise of African nation-states, she carried different historical burdens. The Tanzanian working girl bore the promise of the uplift of the nation, and she appeared, grinning and well dressed, in newspaper and magazine spreads featuring African female professionals, including typists, bankers, and flight attendants. A common topic in human interest stories, "working girl" features appeared not only in the pages of the glamorous and self-consciously cosmopolitan *Drum* magazine, but also in the ruling party papers and magazines, such as *Mzalendo* and *Nchi Yetu*. In the early years of decolonization, TANU's media outlets embraced the working-girl imagery as part of the iconography of a modernizing nation, alongside skyscrapers and infrastructural development projects. The salaried working girl held out the promise of making Africans collectively modern. A fashionable dresser, she signified the growth of consumer markets and urban leisure pleasures, and whenever she was featured in newspaper interviews, she was asked about her hobbies and dutifully reported that she enjoyed going to the cinema and dancing. The generic "working girl" was a diligent and professional worker and a product of the nation's growing educational system. As emblems of a modern consumer economy, a productive and educated workforce, and as symbols of the race, working girls indexed Tanzania's rising place in a global order.[7] For a brief period between the beginning of African socialist policies in 1967 and the economic crisis that went along with the catastrophic collapse of real wages beginning in 1974, the working girl became a key subject of political imagination.

The context for the rise of the working girl was the rise of salaried labor and expanding public-sector employment as a central plank of national socialist development in Tanzania. State programs to build an urban industrial economy and open urban jobs to women made it possible for some women migrants to find salaried employment in factories, particularly lower-status jobs like at the TANITA cashew nut–processing plant, where the labor was unskilled, the wages low, and the overwhelming majority of workers female.[8] In other factories, such as the textile factories where the wages and benefits were better, women made up a far smaller proportion of the workforce and typically occupied the lowest-skilled jobs. These coveted salaried positions were more significant symbolically than demographically in the creation of an urban vision. It was more common for women to work in the informal sector and as entrepreneurs, like earlier generations of Dar es Salaam women who were landlords and rented out rooms or who brewed beer and cooked food for urban working men. Women who were from the region and who had capital or access to local land could sell produce, raise chickens, or own a bar, for example. Those who came to Dar es Salaam from farther away, lacking durable local connections to agricultural producers, had more limited opportunities, purchasing items wholesale downtown and selling them in other parts of the city for a razor-thin profit margin. Among young unmarried women, the service sector was a common option. The work of barmaids and beer brewers could be particularly lucrative but particularly dangerous, as women in this line of work were often presumed to be sexually available and often faced harassment and problems of transport and sexual assault when working late at night.[9]

There was an enormous gap between the images of smiling women working in factories, as bank tellers, and as telephone operators and the realities of the lives of most women migrants to Dar es Salaam. For all the romanticism of the rural family in Ujamaa rhetoric, many people—especially women—came to the city to escape it. In the postcolonial years, the number of women who migrated to the city increased dramatically, and an increasing percentage of them were unmarried. Between 1950 and 1970, the percentage of female migrants who counted themselves as single increased from 13 percent to 33 percent. The main factor in the choice of young single women to migrate was vulnerability in rural areas.[10] Many women came to the city after a divorce had left them without access to the land and resources of their husband's family, while either personal or economic circumstances meant that their birth families were no longer able to provide for them. In other instances, the death of a parent made a woman responsible for the upkeep of her family. As the journalist Robert Rweyemamu found in his 1973 interview with teenage girls in the Kisutu squatter areas, some young women reported that they were in the city due to premarital pregnancies that were not socially recognized and that left young mothers socially isolated and economically vulnerable.[11] The young woman told him, "I am not here simply because I like to be here. I have been forced to come here. I had nothing else to do." Others migrated to the city as part of a strategy to improve the lot of their rural family by sending a portion of their income back home to their relatives.

Urban migration offered women the possibility of autonomy from rural patriarchal structures—many of which had been shored up under colonial indirect rule—or from the intense physical demands of agricultural labor. Most female urban migrants shared housing with relatives based on extended family networks, often initially relying on their brothers. In the city, some women reported, life was less physically taxing than in rural areas, yet at the same time, they felt increasing social anxiety as they entered the cash economy. Norms of respectability required that one appear in public wearing shoes and tailored clothing, rather than cloth wraps, and carrying a purse with money inside. Many felt pressure to dress in accordance with urban modes of respectability, sometimes going without food to save money so that they could afford suitable clothing.[12] They lacked the kinds of social safety nets that ideally may have been in place in their rural communities, and they faced periodic harassment from the police and the TANU Youth League if they were seen to be dressed inappropriately. While these urban sojourners were released from some of the gerontocratic and patriarchal structures of some of their communities of origin, once in the city, most continued to rely on relationships with men to access resources in the city, often living with male partners for whom they would provide domestic labor as a way of accessing housing and other basic necessities. The reliance of women on men often did not take the form of a single relationship with a permanent legally recognized husband, but was more often part of a flexible strategy of making temporary alliances. Celebratory images of working-girl self-sufficiency and panics over the threat of their increasing power masked deeper inequalities among women and the complexity of economic and domestic entanglements in the city.

At the same time as unmarried women were becoming a larger proportion of the urban population, the city was also becoming increasingly Christian. While one estimate suggested that Christians had made up about 1.5 percent of the population of Dar es Salaam in 1920, by 1974 they were estimated to be around 40 percent of the population.[13] The increasing prominence of Christian educated elites and the attempt of the church to articulate a place for Christians in the city went alongside an effort on the part of the Christian Council of Tanzania (CCT) to advocate for a shift in gender relations in the city. Throughout the mid-1960s, the CCT convened numerous conferences, bringing together bishops, prominent clergy members, government workers, and educators to discuss the role of Christians in the new nation and to make recommendations for Tanzania's policies on such issues as bridewealth, polygamy, the education of girls, and the organization of family life based on the nuclear-family model. As Christians were steadily making up a larger part of the population of the predominantly Muslim city, the 1960s saw a push among church leaders to build more parishes to minister to this growing urban population.

For their part, Christian migrants to the city attempted to establish community networks in their new environment. Various Christian organizations ran hostels for both long-term and short-term travelers to the city, and parish leaders organized choirs and reading groups for their members. Many dioceses also published newspapers. In the Lutheran newspaper *Umoja* (Unity), for example, essays addressed how new arrivals could live Christian lives in the environs of the city. They advertised the Lutheran Luther House Hostel in their pages as a place where Christians could stay in the company of likeminded people in familiar surroundings when they came to Dar es Salaam. In those same pages, they advertised *Sauti ya Njili*, the Lutheran radio station, as a way of keeping the community close-knit and within the same world of cultural references, despite the dispersal of communities between villages and the city.[14] Taken together, these spaces and texts shaped a kind of infrastructure of belonging for increasingly mobile urban Christians.

In 1975, Richard Stren observed that while TANU's core constituency in Dar es Salaam consisted mostly of Muslim property owners, those who had access to the most-skilled and highest-paying jobs in the new government bureaucracy after independence tended to be Western-educated Christian migrants. This disparity would lead to political tensions between the party ranks and the government bureaucracy throughout the

1960s and 1970s.[15] The girls' advice writers came from within the cohorts of educated Christian migrants who moved to the city to occupy the new modern professions of a nation that was Africanizing its workforce.

The Christianization of the city contributed to a change in the gender politics of TANU. As we've seen, many of TANU's earliest members were Muslim women in Dar es Salaam, such as Bibi Titi Mohamed, who was born and raised in the city. As an organizer for TANU, she forged a strategy of mass political mobilization based on engaging social and economic networks of urban women, largely made possible because of fairly flexible gender roles in Swahili society and female economic activity and mobility. She gathered support for the party among women's dance groups and beer brewers. As Susan Geiger has argued, this style of urban female sociability was a central advantage in TANU's organizing campaign in the urban areas.[16]

While critical to TANU's success in its early years, this style of urban female sociability and politics would largely fall out of the mainstream of TANU activism once the party was in power. Like the households and domestic architecture of the rising Christian African middle-class suburbs in Dar es Salaam, the models of womanhood promoted in development propaganda and in the Umoja wa Wanawake wa Tanzania (UWT), the women's wing of TANU, emphasized the nuclear-family ideal, salaried employment, and frugality. This model of female uplift signified a shift in TANU's gender dynamic and the erasure of a particularly robust form of urban community life from the political mainstream. Meanwhile, while the landlords and property owners that were caricatured as enemies of socialism were typically represented as Asian men or wealthy African big men, these representations hid the fact that many of the city's landlords were African women. As a divorced, semi-literate woman, without a husband's income and wealth to rely on, owning urban property and passing it on to her daughter was Bibi Titi Mohamed's plan for economic security in the future. In Dar es Salaam, shifts in the culture of TANU took shape through the Christianization of the city and the privileging of middle-class Christian gender roles over more prevalent regional social and kinship idioms.

The exclusivity of this vision was captured in the comments of a woman interviewed by Marja-Liisa Swantz and Deborah Bryceson in their survey of women cleaners in Dar es Salaam in 1973 and 1974. The women were asked their opinion about UWT. Their responses varied, ranging from those who considered themselves to be active members to those who were indifferent to the organization. Tellingly, some women commented that they felt excluded from the organization because they felt it was intended only for haughty wives of wealthier men. One woman expressed hostility toward the group, telling the interviewers, "The leaders do not like single women (she was a divorcé) only those who are married. . . . They always talk about their husbands and the single girls."[17] While this hostility was not universal and represents the views of only one individual, it signals the potential limits and tensions of a female activism that defined uplift based on a gendered order that was specific to Christian middle-class women.

The new ranks of "working girls" that were migrating to the city fit neither mode of domesticity and social life. As urban newcomers, they were not deeply embedded in the entrepreneurial and familial networks of the city. They did not own urban property and did not have access to resources such as agricultural products they could sell from their family's land nearby. This made it difficult for them to strike out as entrepreneurs. Yet as unmarried women, many having fled dire circumstances back home, they did not have the resources to set up the kind of nuclear family home promoted by Christian middle-class women, either. The question of how and where they should live in the city was both a problem and an opportunity for reformers.

Salvation for the Working Girl

Advice texts composed by mature women for an audience of younger women are a familiar literary mode in East Africa. One of the most famous and well-known Swahili literary classics is the mid-nineteenth-century poem "Advice of Mwana Kupona upon the Wifely Duty." The poem takes the form of advice to a young woman on the eve of her marriage, guiding her about how to perform the role of a submissive and sexually alluring wife.[18] Along the Swahili coast, songs performed by older women at the initiation rituals of younger women offered advice on how to cultivate the home and body in preparation for conjugal life. Historically, this role of the female mentor or sexual educator was institutionalized in the role of the *somo* or *kungwi*, which was a position taken by a nonrelative, often a respected older female slave.[19] Moreover, it was common in other parts of East Africa for grandmothers to play key roles in the conjugal education of girls.

From a different standpoint, Christian educators and publishers in Africa circulated moral parables and primers on domestic virtues throughout the twentieth century. These texts focus on homemaking rather than on sex. Some of the earliest books published in vernacular African languages were advice guidebooks about the keeping of house and home. In post-war Tanzania, widely circulating books included *Barua kwa Dada*, or *My Sister's Letters*, which took the form of advice from an older sister to a younger one, and Esther Kouene's 1953 series *Mama wa Afrika na Nyumba Yake*, or *The African Housewife and Her Home*.[20] These missionary texts were part of a longer history of missionary education in East Africa that linked female literacy with domesticity and spirituality. With independence, Christian intellectuals directed these pedagogical efforts to the task of national development. For educators, as for writers, the Christian writer sought to transform the reader through her text much in the same way that a mother teaches a child, so that, as Andreana Prichard has argued for Tanzanian Anglican female teachers, "the line between teaching, ministering and parenting was nonexistent."[21]

Building on these advice-giving genres, writers of the late 1960s and early 1970s turned their attention to a new category of citizen: female migrants in the city. The authors of this new literature were a small but influential group of missionary-educated Christian women who, due to their education and social connections with a growing class of African professionals, were well placed to shape urban spaces, institutions, and public discourses in Dar es Salaam. They were born in the period from the mid-1930s through the mid-1940s and had benefited from the colonial investments in female education provided for an elite minority as the state attempted to cultivate an African middle class following World War II. In the early years following independence, these women were in their twenties and just setting out on their careers. When envisioning their role in the new nation, they had the domestic education they had received in school as a model of modernization to draw upon.

These middle-class Christian women reframed the values of domesticity and companionate marriage in terms of Ujamaa ideologies of self-sufficiency and race pride as a way of extending notions of urban citizenship to include women in the city. Images of domestic harmony, frugality, and the moralizing effects of salaried employment fed into claims that public intellectuals would make on the socialist state on behalf of Tanzanian women. When addressing a national public, these intellectuals argued for the improvement of the status of women as a whole in the context of African socialism, extending the values of liberation from oppression and economic equality to the arena of gender. Yet when projected internally for an audience of fellow women, their visions of Ujamaa womanhood highlighted a notion of moral improvement in which educated elite married Christian women would educate and uplift their less fortunate urban working-class, and predominantly Muslim, sisters. By casting themselves in the role of redeemers of their wayward sisters, these women carved a role of authority for themselves as reformers of the depraved city.

In the late 1960s, the African working girl became one of the target audiences of a burgeoning genre of global Christian advice literature written by women. Alongside the more well known national literatures, such as those published by the Heinemann African Writers Series and those promoted through national cultural programs, African Christian writers and publishers proliferated in the 1960s as Christian communities sought to address the place of the church in newly sovereign African nations. Writers and publishers of Christian literature traveled for training in places like the All Africa Literature Center at the Mindolo Ecumenical Center in Kitwe, Zambia, an initiative to promote the writing, publishing, and dissemination of Christian literature across Africa. The Mindolo Ecumenical Center was founded in 1958 in the town of Kitwe on the Zambian Copperbelt through sponsorship from the World Council of Churches. Many prominent Zambian politicians and politicians' wives, including Betty Kaunda, wife of Zambian president Kenneth Kaunda, attended trainings there. Instructors offered courses to cultivate the Christian attitudes of a newly independent African elite, focusing on mineworkers and especially their wives. The Women's Training Center was the oldest established program, and the inculcation of a particular ideal of European Christian gender roles was central to their curriculum. The center fostered the training of women in homecraft and "helping women to adjust to the changed structure of family life in an urban area." Course topics included Christian Homemaking, Pan-African Women's Leadership, Homecraft for Refugees, and "Single Girls."[22] The faculty included Africans and Europeans, and they sought to breathe new life into older themes of Christian mission education in domesticity by combining them with discourses about national sovereignty and African respectability.[23] As James Ferguson points out, the flip side of these programs to offer women skills through courses in domesticity that would be relevant to lives in urban environments was that they also aimed at reforming the city, teaching women about their home lives, even though women were engaged in many other kinds of invisible economic activities in the city. Moreover, those who attended the Christian domesticity groups did not tend to have those kinds of nuclear families promoted in the courses, but rather a much wider, more flexible range of familial relations in their households.[24] Martha Mandao, the Tanzanian woman whose fictional portrayals of Ani opened this chapter, was a graduate of the All Africa Literature Center at Mindolo, and this influence is evident in her writings.

Taking on the ethos of decolonization, this Christian literature movement aimed to replace "the typical six-inch bookshelf, which . . . included *Pilgrim's Progress*, a book on hygiene published in 1927, a hymnal and a New Testament,"[25] with books on contemporary themes, composed in African languages, by Africans.[26] The church, many felt, needed to foster new young African writers to stay relevant. These books would not only help cultivate the Christian sensibilities of individual readers, but were intended to cultivate Christian communities, as well. The authors intended that their books be read and discussed in women's groups such as the *Chama cha Mama Wakristo* (Christian Women's Union), which was made up of female parishioners at the Anglican St. Alban's Church in Dar es Salaam.[27] The group was made up of women who were married and women who were engaged to be married. The syllabus combined Bible passages with Christian advice texts each week to guide discussions. Their group had a statement of purpose, which listed as its central goal the cultivation of Christian households in the city. Members encouraged each other to "make their houses like Nazareth," keep Bibles in their homes, and keep each other in check, giving each other advice and feedback, especially if one of their members ever fell behind in her standards of housekeeping and Christian childrearing.

Martha Mandao exemplified the push to make African Christian literature relevant to the changing worlds of postcolonial Africa, to cultivate new African Christian writers, and to address the growing moral crisis of urbanization. She was born in 1941 on the slopes of Mount Kilimanjaro. She completed secondary school a few months before Tanzania became independent and soon after went to study at Mwika Bible College, a Lutheran College in the Kilimanjaro region.[28] The Mwika Bible College was part of the broader Bible school movement in East Africa, which had the aim of educating lay teachers who would guide fellow parishioners in reading and interpreting the Bible in their daily lives, outside of Mass. One of the stated aims of the program at Mwika was to teach women parishioners in the modeling of Christian homes for fellow women.[29] After completing her course there, Mandao spent a year at the All Africa Literature Center at the Mindolo Ecumenical Center, followed by a final year of training in Christian literature at the Limuru Baptist Centre in Kenya. In 1967, the same year as the Arusha Declaration, she moved to Dar es Salaam like many young people, including her sister Anna, who worked as one of the directors of the Lutheran YWCA working-girl hostel. Like her sister, Martha also worked for the Lutheran Church as editor of their newsletter *Pwani na Bara*. She spent the next three years in Dar es Salaam, and during that time, she wrote the books *Peke Yangu Mjini* and *Ani Afungua Mkoba Wake*. In 1970, she returned to Moshi, married, had three children, and became a radio announcer for Sauti ya Injili, a Lutheran radio station where she hosted a Christian music program and a women's hour. But from 1967 through 1970, she was one of the Christian female intellectuals who sought to advise the working girl in the city of Dar es Salaam.

Alone in the City was published in English by the African Christian Press in Achimota, Ghana, in 1969 and appeared in 1972 in Swahili translation, through the Anglican Central Tanganyika Press, as *Peke Yangu Mjini*. She soon followed up her first book with a sequel, *Ani Opens Her Purse*, and its Swahili translation, *Ani Afungua Mkoba Wake*. Mandao's target audience was a female public made up of a growing community of middle-class Christian women who were coming to the city to work. She marketed the book toward "teachers, nurses, and office workers—and for all who want to learn how to be strong Christians when alone in the city."

Alongside training programs for new African Christian writing, a network of Christian community organizations also sought to build an infrastructure for the dissemination of Christian texts, especially in cities. The Christian Council of Tanzania (CCT), in conjunction with several Christian publishing houses, held workshops to train parishioners to become book evangelists, or colporteurs, in the publishing and dissemination of Christian books in Africa. These courses aimed to train booksellers who were committed Christians with a deep familiarity with the Bible who would keep up with all the Christian publications and could stock their bookstalls with books that were relevant to the lives of their potential customers.[30] Modest Belege, who was the manager of the Christian bookshop on site at the Msimbazi Center Catholic Hostel in Dar es Salaam throughout the 1960s and 1970s, attended one of these trainings held in Dodoma by the Central Tanganyika Press: a press that was run by the Tanzanian Anglican Church. There, he learned to target newly literate audiences of urban youth that were flooding the city with books on problems of sexuality, romance, and the family.[31] These books would also become curriculum for the classes on domesticity and family life offered at the Msimbazi Center, both for residents of the working girls' hostel and outside Christian youth who came to the center to enroll in classes.

Many of the advice writers came from within the ranks of educated Christian migrants who moved to the city to occupy the new modern professions of a nation that was Africanizing its workforce. Graduates of prestigious women's schools in the interior of the country, especially the Tabora and Loleza girls' schools, played prominent roles in defining elite womanhood in the public sphere of the new nation. Reforming and guiding female migrants was one of the key ways that a generation of educated women would build their careers. It was not just her poverty or vulnerability that made the working girl a target of intervention, but rather her contested and ambiguous status in the urban order of things.

In the 1960s, Christian literature traveled through transnational circuits, translated into multiple African languages through multiple publishing houses, and was sold at Christian bookstores and by "book evangelists" like Modest Belege. Many of the Christian books that found their way into Tanzania were first published in other Christian presses, such as the African Christian Press based in Achimota, Ghana, and Kitwe, Zambia, as well as the Daystar Press in Nigeria, and were then translated into Swahili and published with a Tanzanian press. Mandao's book first appeared in publication by the African Christian Press, a press that was started in the mid-1960s in Achimota, Ghana, alongside other titles on themes common to Christians living in growing African cities at the time, such as how to minister to Muslims, how to build modern Christian households and marriages, how to resist "superstitious" beliefs when living alongside pagans, and how to protect young women from the negative influence of friends and boyfriends. Tanzanian writers also published books that circulated beyond Tanzania to a larger community of Christian readers. Following their publication in Swahili with the Anglican Central Tanganyika Press, Mandao's two books were translated into multiple languages and published in numerous Christian publishing houses, including in Malawi, New Guinea, Argentina, and Côte d'Ivoire.[32] Much of this Christian literature of the 1960s was intended to model Christian responses to the perceived urban crisis in Africa and the global south.

In the 1960s and early 1970s, many books published by Christian publishers focused on the topic of how to have good marriages in the amoral godless milieu of the city. Some of these books were written by Tanzanian authors, while others were written in other African countries and then translated in Tanzania by local Christian printers, especially the Central Tanganyika Press. These books were available at bookstores such as the Anglican-owned Dar es Salaam Bookstore in downtown Dar es Salaam. They were also distributed through Christian hostels and sold by book evangelists at church bookstores for members. Christian women's reading groups would use the texts as guides for their weekly meetings and discussions.

The modernizing vision of Christian reformism overlapped with government media publications on women. For example, the writer Theresia Mshuza's "women's page" appeared regularly in the pages of the TANU-owned newspaper *Uhuru* from 1970 through 1972. She projected a reader who was young, urban, and working for her own money and positioned herself in relation to the reader in the form of a mentor, guiding working girls through the struggles of urban living and into proper forms of domesticity and respectability in the city. At the same time, she also saw herself as a spokesperson for the cause of working girls, advocating to a broader audience on behalf of working girls in the city.

Mshuza herself was an upwardly mobile professional and had migrated to Dar es Salaam during the early years of Tanzania's socialist era. She had been among the first cohorts of students to study at the journalism school at the Nyegezi Social Training Center, a Catholic institution run by the White Fathers since 1963 in Mwanza in northwestern Tanzania. In 1966, before becoming a columnist for *Uhuru*, Mshuza authored the women's page for the publication *Kiongozi*, the Catholic newspaper published in Tabora. In the pages of *Kiongozi*, her picture appeared next to her column, showing her with a broad smile and simple, modest, modern dress, and she addressed issues for upwardly mobile "girls" like her. What kinds of jobs might young female students do once they finish their studies? What kinds of qualities should ideal husbands have, and how could women keep their marriages alive after children were born? What kind of clothing was respectable, but also attractive and modern? She envisioned a kind of domestic harmony that was attainable through the cultivation of the body and the home. Speaking often in the imperative, she addressed her audience as female collaborators in a shared project of uplift, exclaiming "*Haya, shime!*" or "participate!"[33] When in 1970 she moved to Dar es Salaam and began writing the women's page for the ruling party paper *Uhuru/ Mzalendo*, she transformed her visions of modern Christian womanhood and family life into a critical lens through which to interpret the urban environment. Her work combined journalism and advice writing, and her main interest was in the plight of urban working girls, especially those in low-status and low-paying jobs.

Mshuza extended her message about female comportment outside of the home, however, and into the city's workplaces. She portrayed formalized salaried labor as a central plank of both the uplift of women and of the reform of the city and its ills. For example, she wrote a story on Dar es Salaam's female street cleaners, who were visible in public sweeping the streets and often subjected to taunts and jeers from passersby. Based on a series of interviews with the women, Mshuza uncovered the history of women's groups in the city who used to clean their own neighborhood as a kind of unpaid civic duty. She recounted how, in the early 1960s, the women approached the municipality asking to be hired to do this work on a piecework basis until, with a 1968 change in labor laws, they were hired as permanent employees with all the benefits of civil servants under the socialist wage-labor structure.[34] In another column, she explored the lives and work conditions of barmaids in Dar es Salaam, focusing on their mistreatment as sexual objects and their extremely low wages. Invoking the moral and historical language of racial violence that would be familiar to any African nationalist, she printed the comments of one barmaid who told her, "To be groped by every drunk in the place is the same as slavery."[35] The solution, Mshuza suggested, was to transform women from "barmaids" to professional beersellers and employees of the beer companies and bar owners for whom they worked. This would bring the service sector in line with other hourly wage labor professions and cultivate a sense of professionalism among the barmaids. Mshuza also wrote about the plight of women working the night shift in factories in Dar es Salaam, focusing attention on the challenges and concerns of women working there who were faced with a long commute home in the early hours of the morning. When they came home walking through the streets after their shift, they were thought of as delinquents for being out at night. They might be insulted or harassed by "hooligans" en route: an assault not only on their bodies and dignity, but also on the nation. These were respectable workers and nation builders, Mshuza argued, and it was a grave insult for them to be mistaken for immoral or unrespectable women.[36] In statements like these, while conveying a message of support for working women, she implicitly excluded certain kinds of work and urban belonging from her vision of female uplift. Her labeling of working women as *respectable* relied on the labeling of other kinds of women as undeserving of respect.

This body of Swahili literature about working girls, published during the early years of Ujamaa, shared a vision in which a self-styled mature and moral author dispensed advice to a vulnerable unmarried female. That advice presumed the primacy and desirability of Christian middle-class domesticity and the moral and cultural authority of the author.

University Students and Working Women

These aspects of the lives of women workers in Dar es Salaam appear in social-science research conducted by university intellectuals. Four University of Dar es Salaam social-science students, under the direction of professor Dr. Marja-Liisa Swantz, produced a survey of 252 women workers in Dar es Salaam in 1973–74. In 1973, students Hilda Ausi, Severa Mlay, Fatuma Macha, and Deborah Bryceson conducted research in the Urafiki textile factory and the TANITA cashew-processing factory. The student researchers entered the shop floor to observe working women firsthand. Severa Mlay, in her research at the TANITA factory, actually participated in the work of the factory alongside the women she was studying. In addition to observing the women at work, the students sought social connection with the women as well, inviting the workers into their homes and visiting them in theirs. A year after the study of factory workers, in 1974, the students conducted another study of women cleaners who worked in various offices in the city.[37]

The University of Dar es Salaam at that time was an international hub of leftist political thought, and these intellectual strands appear in the writing of the students. Inspired by thinkers including Frantz Fanon, Samir Amin, Issa Shivji, and Walter Rodney—the latter two were on the faculty—many students took a critical approach to the problems of postcolonial Tanzania through the analytic lens of neocolonialism and Rodney's theorizing of "underdevelopment."[38] In contrast with official TANU versions of socialism that emphasized the expertise of the ruling party and dismissed class struggle as anathema to authentic African socialism, the class analysis of scientific socialists was influential among many at the university. Many researchers at the university saw the goals of their research as indistinguishable from the goals of revolution and saw participatory, collaborative research as something that would break down the boundaries between university-educated intellectuals and the Tanzanian masses.[39] They had been trained to be critical and reflective about their position of relative privilege compared with the women, and they expressed a deep concern with wanting to break down barriers between them so that they could use their privilege to find new solidarities and political possibilities.[40]

In contrast with the Christian reformers and advice writers who saw marriage and domesticity as the antidote to urban life and its economic entanglements, the social scientists portrayed the flexibility of marriage and domesticity and the economic autonomy of women as having radical unrealized political potential. Commenting obliquely on the uplift advice of domesticity advocates, one student wrote: "The question for these women is not how to cook their food but how to get it to begin with, that is, how are they going to earn a decent living . . . the future of Tanzanian women does not lie in the direction of feminist careerism . . . neither does it lie in the emphasis on pride in homemaking. This supports the status quo and retrogressively dooms women to wallow in the home shut away from participation in the social trends of history."[41] Where the middle-class Christian reformers saw pathology, these researchers saw political possibilities. Rather than suggesting that single women needed to get married and join nuclear-family households, these UDSM students saw their flexibility as an asset that would be used to challenge patriarchy and inequality.

Though the published work on which the surveys were based, written by Bryceson and her supervisor, Dr. Swantz, avoided commenting on politics in the city, the student papers and notes reflected the academic world in which they were steeped, repeatedly referring to the women as "not yet conscious." They questioned whether they should socialize with the women they were studying by inviting them to their homes, pondering how that would affect the nature of the research, given that students had higher incomes than the women they were interviewing. They expressed the concern that, when the working women saw that the students had nicer houses and nicer possessions, the relationship might become material rather than genuine if the workers saw the student researchers as a potential source of wealth. "It is true," wrote two graduate students in their coauthored thesis, "that many workers not yet sufficiently politically conscious will be influenced by the ruling class ethos of acquisitiveness." After raising these concerns, however, they quickly rejected them and went on to posit, "A much more important question is how a worker becomes politically conscious. It is through the introduction of new ideas, that must come from a wide assortment of people, among them students and intellectuals." The students described the easy familiarity they gained with the women when they invited them into their homes. "We strove to participate in the fullest capacity allowable eager to exchange ideas with these women hoping we could awaken their political consciousness to their potential as women workers. In turn they helped us to get a more precise picture of the social trends in Tanzania, clearing away many mystifications we had believed to be true."[42]

In contrast with literature that would, in principle, reform or improve its female readers, these surveys were intended to be open and live texts that would circulate and be coproduced and continually augmented by women workers. Their research model echoed modes of literacy promoted by Paolo Freire, in which literacy and education would become a forum for critical thought and political engagement and, potentially, revolution.[43] Sensitive to the demands of workers and to the unequal relationships between workers and students, researchers sought to create a more egalitarian exchange between themselves and the working women by teaching adult literacy classes to them, and then using a portion of class time to conduct the research surveys. In this way, they grafted their research project onto the national literacy campaign. They encouraged the women enrolled in the courses to write about their own lives.[44] In turn, the surveys would serve a purpose: they would allow women to practice reading and writing and would potentially encourage a critical self-reflection on the part of the working women. "As literacy is gained," the students wrote in one of their coauthored papers: "[the women] will be their own spokesmen and as confidence in the justness of their struggle increases they will take action. This is not to say that they haven't begun—the restrictions of traditional attitudes within the new framework of neo-colonialism as experienced through living and working in the towns has caused a new Tanzania woman to emerge who views herself as independent of patriarchal marriage." The social survey, when produced, read, and circulated among women, was meant to bring about new kinds of political action. The student Severa Mlay went a step further and would later go on to organize a union in the Italian-owned cashew-processing factory where she completed her study.[45]

These two different collections of texts inspired by the problem of the working girl—Christian advice literature and the social survey—differed both in content and in the action they were meant to perform in the city. Compare, for example, Mandao's text with the social survey. Mandao's texts were intended to shape the reader, cultivating a Christian domestic habitus. The reader would learn to scan the urban landscape through the interpretive lens of selected passages from scripture, retreating from the city and reflecting on its conditions while alone in her room with a Bible, separate from other workers. She would protect her body and soul from those who would harm her and instead devote them to Jesus through her habits and the cultivation of private space. The text was meant as leadership and guidance. The social survey, by contrast, was meant as a catalyst. It was seen as collaboratively produced and interpreted by working-class women who would learn literacy from their university mentors, with whom they shared, it was presumed, a critique of patriarchy and capitalism. The very acts of reading and writing would have a radicalizing effect.

Yet despite the difference in their politics, the university feminists were perhaps more similar to the Christian writers than they would have proclaimed. Both modes of literary production intended to shape the behaviors of the women workers. In neither case were the texts only meant to convey content. The very modes of literacy they sought to cultivate conveyed an intention to shape urban communities. In both instances, women workers were seen as "not yet" modern and in need of intervention or transformation by an elite female educator.

Hostels, Houses, and "Little Houses": Making Space for the Working Girl

The story of Ani's struggles in the city as depicted in Mandao's didactic Christian novellas tells of Ani going out into city life, in the workplace, at the bus stop, out to restaurants and bars with friends, and being drawn into situations that threaten her Christian integrity. At the end of each struggle with her desires, she ends up in her home, with her books, her Bible, and her Christian mentor Mama Rupia, using her private room as a refuge from which to reflect on her life in the city. Mama Rupia encourages her to redirect her energy toward the home. She tells Ani, for example, when too much noise prevents her from resting, she should keep busy doing "little jobs here and there, like sewing," in the privacy of her home. Rather than venture out into the city's public spaces of leisure and consumerism, Ani learns to spend her time in productive self-improving activities centered on the home and the church. Cultivating the integrity of the home and the body was a way of domesticating the wilderness of the city.

Such a view of the city drew from a longer Christian mode of thinking about landscapes. For example, in colonial Africa, performances of competing modes of domesticity staged larger struggles over sovereignty, modernity, and race. Nineteenth-century and early twentieth-century British missionaries and Christian converts sought to separate themselves spatially and aesthetically from their non-Christian neighbors or from Muslims in heavily Islamic areas such as the Swahili coast through the domestication of the landscape and the performance of European domesticity.[46] Fences plotted in straight lines, gardens planted in straight rows, and the replacement of circular houses with rectangular ones signaled the cultivation of the earth, the family, the soul, a way of life, and an imagined community of Christian "civilized people."[47] In postwar African cities, the organization of domestic spaces was one way that colonial administrators sought to create productive African workers and families.[48] A number of scholars have understood colonial-era home-economics education as a form of cultural imperialism in which colonial states imposed Victorian British gender roles on Africa, denying African women the roles in public life that they had previously enjoyed.[49] Others have interpreted domestic education as a promise of collective economic uplift that Africans could seize in order to make claims on the state.[50]

In the context of the postcolonial African urban revolution, images of the cultivation of home spaces took on new meanings, especially among prosperous and well-educated African Christians, who were arriving in cities that they perceived as sites of economic promise but also of profound cultural pathology in need of domestication. Projected for outside audiences, these images of domestic oases in the city could be a form of political claim making. Antoinette Burton has argued that representations of domestic spaces in Indian literature performed political work, proclaiming the fitness of Indians to rule sovereign nations.[51] Projected outwards, images of domestic harmony suggest membership in a universal vision of modernity and civilization. Yet when projected inward toward working girls as "advice," working-girl literature was a way of cultivating individual behaviors that kept girls safe and separate from the temptations of the city. It contained implicit condescension toward the modes of domestic and sexual life that were far more common for Muslim, working-class, and poor women in Dar es Salaam. Advice literature and the forms of urban reform that were attached to it worked to entrench an exclusionary political vision in which Christian bourgeois domesticity was the primary criterion for urban citizenship.

Yet contrary to middle-class Christian assumptions, the urban environment was not an orderless wilderness, but a polyglot metropolis structured by multiple forms of domesticity. Swahili-style housing in Dar es Salaam is organized spatially in such a way as to be open to shifting household arrangements. The conventional Swahili house consists of six rooms, three on each side of a corridor with a courtyard in the back. When constructed of mud and wattle, walls could be punctured to add new doors or walled over or moved to accommodate different living arrangements. A door might open to the corridor where all members of a family unit would enter and share the space, or the room could be walled off from the corridor and have a door on the side of the house, allowing separate entrances into individual rooms if multiple families lived separately within the same home.[52] The size and shape of households were flexible and could be changed as conjugal relationships were made and dissolved. Relatives came and went as young people moved in with relatives to be closer to school or work or as inhabitants fostered the children of siblings or cousins, and rooms were often put aside and rented to tenants for extra income. Social life in Swahili households and neighborhoods tended to be segregated along gender lines, and domestic activities such as cooking and cleaning occurred in shared courtyards, where women congregated and socialized as they went about their work.

Cohabitation of a couple that had not undergone formal marriage rites was common in Dar es Salaam, and divorce was socially acceptable among coastal Tanzanians. Within couples, men and women were typically financially autonomous from one another, which made it relatively easy for women to leave their husbands when faced with abuse or marital strife. In the older forms of Swahili housing, the gendered order was such that women could integrate into urban space through familial ties, sexual relationships, or female social networks.

Reformers promoted monogamous companionate marriage as a goal of development, yet marriage arrangements were far from a straightforward matter in 1970s Dar es Salaam. Most women workers were migrants and formed sexual and familial bonds far away from kin. Moreover, with the rise in prices of bridewealth, the forms of socially recognized marriage that many young people had grown up expecting were increasingly difficult to attain. Urban dwellers responded creatively to these new conditions by composing new kinds of households. For example, many urban dwellers formed *ndoa ya kinyumba*, or "house marriages," which differed from a socially recognized marriage sanctioned by families through the exchange of bridewealth. The space the couple occupied together and the property that the couple shared in common were not part of rural inheritances or longer lineage arrangements, but were based on the urban home they shared and had fewer of the kinds of social checks and familial obligations that went along with the payment of bridewealth and the contract between families that such payments implied.[53] Men in this arrangement typically used their salaries to pay rent and some of the household expenses, such as food and clothing, while the female partner cooked and took care of the home. Often, these couples would have children, and despite the public outcry from some quarters against children born out of wedlock, these coparenting relationships were often chosen and intentional. Many women in the social survey reported that being unmarried did not diminish the value and personal satisfaction associated with motherhood, and in the long term, they found these relationships materially beneficial as a kind of social insurance in old age and an ongoing—even if legally unenforceable—claim on fathers of their children.[54] As Bryceson and Swantz reported in their 1973–74 survey of 252 women workers in Dar es Salaam: "There was no hesitation among divorcees to have more children. Only three of them did not want any more because they already had two, four and six children respectively which they thought was enough. Two of these women were using contraceptives after consulting the Umati family planning agency. They had not been allowed paid maternity leave without a marriage certificate."[55] The connotation of *ndoa ya kinyumba* was mostly negative. It invoked the conviction of many people that without bridewealth, young couples were unruly because their actions had no sanction by their husband and family. While its literal translation simply means "marriage of the house," a translation that includes the connotation might be "*merely* a marriage of the house" and not a proper, durable, socially recognized marriage.

More pejorative than *ndoa ya kinyumba* were *nyumba ndogos*, or "little houses," which referred to apartments or rooms paid for by married men to house their girlfriends or mistresses. These girlfriends appear frequently in fictional portrayals of urban life. In popular fiction, the sitting room of a young single woman with nice furniture or modern appliances, such as a refrigerator, is a coded way of telling the reader that she is inhabiting a nyumba ndogo, for it was widely assumed that there was no way that a single woman could expect to access such a standard of living on her own. Despite the pejorative connotations of *nyumba ndogo*, as well as the opposition of wives, some urban women found these arrangements preferable to marriage, as it allowed them a kind of mobility, freedom, and control over their time that they would not have enjoyed had they cohabited with a husband and been responsible for upkeep of the home and the needs of a full-time spouse.[56] Throughout the late colonial and postcolonial years, many migrants arriving in Dar es Salaam from various regions of the country found these arrangements a viable way of integrating into urban life.

In addition to these various arrangements between women and men, many households were composed not by a male and female couple and their children, but instead by multiple women of varying social status. Many working women living in Dar es Salaam in the 1970s had female economic dependents—sometimes a female relative—living in the home taking care of their children and the household while the female head of household worked for wages.[57] Though an extremely common practice in households in Dar es Salaam, it was virtually invisible in representations of the home that appeared in Christian literature or in the developmental iconography of TANU.

The images of Christian households promoted in advice literature were mapped onto shifts occurring in the urban landscape. Since the post–WWII years, new kinds of housing sprang up around Dar es Salaam alongside the typical six-room Swahili house. Built originally by the British Colonial Welfare Fund,[58] this housing was meant for African civil servants and their families. These government "quarter houses" were organized to preserve the privacy and functionality of the monogamous companionate marriage with children. Quarter houses typically consisted of four rooms divided into distinct functions, and each family had a small private verandah, latrine, and kitchen. These new houses and neighborhoods implied different modes of domesticity and gender. J. A. K. Leslie interviewed one inhabitant of quarter housing: a "married woman of the professional class" who explained her preference for living in a freestanding bungalow, away from the influence of neighbors. The woman described in detail a daily regimen that began with her rising before dawn to clean her house and make tea and breakfast for her husband. She would then go to her job as a schoolteacher and, upon returning home in the evening, would clean and iron clothes, tidy the house, and cook the evening meal. Speaking of her choice to live in a small detached government housing bungalow, she said, "We prefer to live in Quarters rather than a Swahili house, because there is room to spread yourself, and you don't get into bad habits from the other women; there is no noise or jostling, and you can keep the place clean."[59] She described a household division of labor in which her role was to manage the household budget, which her husband dictated to her. She explained that she must not leave the house and circulate in town without the permission of her husband. She compared her own domestic arrangement with the more flexible modes of marriage and cohabitation that were common in the city, claiming: "A proper marriage shows itself in both sets of parents knowing and approving it, with many witnesses present, all friends, a marriage for life. When people live together illicitly, there is less tolerance and a greater readiness to divorce. And when they quarrel they don't mind what they say and there is little mutual respect. Often it is those who have been married once that live together so." These new additions to the residential architecture of Dar es Salaam coincided with the increasing presence and influence of educated Christians in the city.

The National Housing Commission (NHC), which became the country's landlord with the implementation of socialism in 1967, built houses designed for nuclear families, privileging male breadwinners with their dependents in housing queues. The NHC carried out slum clearances in some neighborhoods and replaced the privately owned and constructed houses with newer models based on the same six-room Swahili layout, yet the NHC versions of those houses differed in that they were intended for single families, rather than for the kinds of flexible housing arrangements that allowed tenants to live alongside families. In the NHC versions of houses, the six rooms were divided and subdivided into different functions—sleeping, dining, sitting—and the backyards were enclosed, sometimes with taller walls with glass splinters embedded along the top, setting off the house from the rest of the neighborhood. In some versions, there was no central corridor dividing the house, eradicating the possibility of allowing different domestic units to live separate lives and occupy separate spaces and rooms of the same six-room house. The housing reinforced the ideal of familial intimacy between the people occupying the house.[60] Because they were constructed of cement, it was more difficult to repurpose the space through the movement of doors to different parts of the house.

For working women, or "girls," the politics of housing was particularly acute, as there was no housing especially suited for them. In 1966, a reporter for the TANU women's newspaper *Binti Leo* stopped by the offices of Kearsley's Travel Agency to interview one of their employees: a twenty-four-year-old woman named Pauline Joseph.[61] The daughter of coffee farmers in Bukoba in the far west of the country, she told the writer how much she enjoyed her life as a modern worker in Dar es Salaam. When asked about the biggest problems of urban life in Dar es Salaam, she answered: finding a place to live. The shortages of housing in the city, she told the reporter, led many young women to "ruin their lives." Single women in need of housing faced male landlords who assumed that sexual access was part of what they were owed by their female tenants. Voicing an opinion shared by many of her contemporaries, Joseph suggested that the solution was for the government to create more female hostels, where working girls could live cheaply without being harassed by landlords or being roped into sexual and romantic entanglements as a way of accessing housing. Pauline Joseph would go on to greater notoriety in later years as a target of Operation Vijana, when she would be arrested for wearing a miniskirt in public. In that instance, she would become a symbol of the struggle between ideas about modernity and cosmopolitanism and national culture: a story that Andrew Ivaska explores in detail.[62] Yet this earlier experience with housing shows a more banal struggle for the city faced by working women.

One article, entitled "On Housing and the Single Girl," described the challenges single women faced in the city. The NHC would not rent to them because they were not "family men" and were therefore a low priority for public assistance. In the new forms of housing meant for a new nation of modern urban workers, the nuclear family unit was the basis for access. At the same time, private landlords often would not rent to single women because they were seen as a threat to mainstream gender roles and expectations. Women were expected to contribute to the household not only through rent, but also in terms of their domestic labor, cooking, cleaning, and caring for children. Married women, it was believed, would contribute gendered domestic labor, helping to take care of the house and look after other tenants. Other landlords feared that single women would not fulfill these expected gender roles and, moreover, would bring unwanted sexual partners back to the house. Some women, such as a woman named Edna, told the reporter about a common practice of inventing fake husbands to attain public housing. Left without access to either NHC housing or private housing, where were working women to live in the city? The difficulty of placing the "working girl" in a gendered order of the city was echoed in the physical difficulty of placing her into urban space.

Figure 2.2 Residents of the Working Girls Hostel at the Msimbazi Center, Dar es Salaam. No date. Reprinted with the permission of the Msimbazi Center, Archdiocese of Dar es Salaam.

Many reformers and mainstream advocates of women's advancement feared that the housing shortage would lead women to rely on extramarital sexual and romantic relationships to access the city and its resources, living with boyfriends or "sugar daddies." A number of Christian organizations, the UWT, and individual philanthropists sought to address this need by creating "working girl hostels" in the city, where girls could access education and employment in the city while living under the supervision and tutelage of older women.

This setup was modeled on working-girl hostels in other parts of the world, including nineteenth-century London and other locations, often in the British Empire. Christian hostels in Johannesburg, while initially intended as training sites for girls in the kinds of domestic skills that would cultivate cohorts of domestic servants for white families, later came to serve modern African female workers, especially educated single women who needed housing in the city by the 1950s.[63] They were, in that sense, a version of colonial-era domestic-education courses, but repurposed for single women in the new nation who would be part of the Africanization of the urban workforce. Elite Christian women ran these hostels.

Dar es Salaam had several girls' hostels. In 1962 Swiss missionaries, with support from the Catholic Workers Movement in Switzerland, started the Msimbazi Centre hostel. This was the latest project of a group that, since 1955, had been financing around forty similar projects for the "spiritual and social formation of the workers" throughout Africa, Asia, and Latin America.[64] The hostel for working girls was part of a broader program at the Msimbazi Center that involved educational resources and a homecraft program teaching residents a domestic-sciences curriculum, including sewing, cooking, budgeting, and other topics common to women's Christian education. On a similar model, the Umoja wa Wanawake wa Tanzania (UWT), the women's branch of TANU, had a hostel on Uhuru Street, and its occupants tended to be educated single women in high-status positions. Maele Kushuma, who lived in this hostel when she first moved to the city to work as a nurse before getting married, describes the hostel population as made up of female nurses, teachers, and police officers: educated women destined for middle-class positions.[65]

Drawing on postwar ideals of developmentalism and a history of urban community centers, those who ran the hostels sought to cultivate spaces of self-improvement and education where urban migrant girls would learn to become salaried workers and eventually housewives. Toward this end, many of the hostels offered women's "self-help" classes for their residents. Since opening in 1962, the Msimbazi Center offered courses in literacy, homecraft, and "moral guidance" for girls, as well as marriage classes for Christian couples who planned to marry.[66] Hostel living was seen by many as an antidote to the problematic entanglement of sex, money, and urban resources for migrant girls, as well as a solution to the problems of pregnancy out of wedlock.[67]

Access to this source of housing and its added benefits was contingent on girls living according to the codes and rules of the hostels. Girls would be evicted for bad behavior, such as breaking curfew or engaging in "indecent" sexual activity. Residents in the hostels were expected to be models of African Christian womanhood.[68] Working girls had to be gainfully employed and could stay for up to two years in the hostel. They could not drink or smoke in the hostels, and if they became pregnant, they had to vacate their accommodations. Residents were reminded of their privileged place and encouraged to see themselves as models for other young women. For example, a note from a matron of the YWCA hostel, granting permission to a resident seeking to go home to visit her family on holiday, addressed the resident, "You may go on leave, as you asked me. I am sure you will be a good example to other girls who have not got a chance of staying in the Y.W.C.A. Hostel."[69]

While residents in the "working girl hostels" were meant to be good examples to their peers, the women who worked in the hostels were expected to play the role of spiritual and moral mentor. The female residents of the hostel would be overseen by a matron who would typically be an older female who embodied the ideals of Christianity and could model Christian homemaking. In the Catholic hostel at Msimbazi Center, matrons were female members of the clergy. Hostel matrons oversaw cooking, cleaning, and upkeep but also looked after the moral upkeep of the residents, acting as a kind of guide or mentor to the girls in their charge. These ideals are conveyed in a 1968 job description for the YWCA hostel matron for the Buguruni Kichwele center, which described the following responsibilities: "To develop and maintain a warm home atmosphere for students and working girls; to be available to listen and counsel in times of trouble; to develop and enforce hostel rules which are appropriate . . . to develop self-discipline as a preparation for independent living . . . and to plan a program for the 'recreational, educational and spiritual development of the residents.'"[70] The girls' hostel model of housing was one in which an older Christian female would provide mentorship for younger single women, like the Mama Rupia character in Mandao's books. This relationship was not without tensions. Young women often chafed at being evaluated on their behavior and at the accusations that they sometimes faced about their sex lives from the more conservative and less educated staff that ran the hostels. They complained that they were questioned about their sex lives and frequently accused of having self-induced abortions. Many young women in the city in such circumstances needed the housing, but resented having to live as junior dependents, kept under the surveillance and judgment of a supervisor.[71]

Christian advice books such as Mandao's can be read as a textual counterpart to these changes in the urban landscape, in which hostels were built for "working girls." Mandao envisioned these quotidian reforms in the spaces and habits of women as aspects of broader social change in urban life as a whole. In a section at the end of the book entitled "Jijini Kesho," or "The City of Tomorrow," she assured the readers that they were doing God's work in the city, gradually winning converts and Christianizing the city by cultivating their own bodies, minds, and homes and leading others to join them through their good example and their prosperity. This advice for urban "working girls" envisioned an urbanism that would start with them but eventually infuse the wider urban environment. In this way, Mandao continued a longer-term Christian missionary project, domesticating the urban wilderness with Christian values and practices. The hostels might be seen as a concrete spatial manifestation of this literary imagined community of mentorship between mature Christian women mentors and unruly and mobile young urban women. The advice texts and the built enclaves were mutually reinforcing.

Yet while the advice texts and urban domestic enclaves provide a glimpse into a vision of female uplift and an urban vision, they do not show us these texts and spaces in the rough and tumble of urban life. Glimpses from the historical record show that this view of salvation through domesticity was not universally shared or embraced as charity, but was instead hotly contested. For many, housing was not a privilege, but should instead be an entitlement of urban workers. For example, in 1974, thirty-five residents of the YWCA's downtown working girls' hostel protested an increase in their monthly rent. The residents, who were workers from various parastatal and public-sector jobs, argued passionately in a petition that no raise in rent was fair unless there was a commensurate raise in their salaries. They sent the petition to the president of the YWCA and to several of their employers: Mkurugenzi College of Business, the Bora shoe factory, the Natex textile factory, Twico wood industries, the National Development Corporation, and Dar es Salaam Motor Transport.[72] In contrast with the reformist mindset that saw working girls living in hostels as recipients of charity, the residents saw themselves as workers, and as workers, they were entitled to rent that they could afford with their salaries.

Motherhood, Contraception, and Sex Education for Urban Women

In 1970, Theresia Mshuza's regular "women's page" in the paper *Uhuru* appeared under the headline, "Why do so many marriages between urban workers break apart?" For this special story, Mshuza conducted interviews with male and female workers in three factories—the Tanganyika Textile Factory, the TANITA cashew-processing factory, and the Tanganyika Tegry plastics factory—and a Catholic priest. Padre R. P. Novatus from St. Joseph's Church lamented the freedom of young people in the urban environment who married without the sanction of their families and the church and ended their marriages whenever they chose. The workers generally expressed agreement with the priest and spoke with regret about the looseness of marriages based on material aspirations and cohabitation in the style of ndoa ya kinyumba, house marriages. Others commented about the temptations of urban life that took workers away from families in the hours after work and the difficulties of families living in close quarters in rented rooms alongside unpleasant or immoral neighbors rather than in stand-alone houses that would give privacy to working parents and their children. Several commenters bemoaned that women who worked for wages did not depend on their husband financially and so did not have the same bracing fear of being destitute after divorce that might otherwise keep women in line and keep a marriage together. Mshuza tells her readers that the only kinds of family recognized by God are ones in which children are raised by two married people. She urges readers to collectively seek to address these problems for the sakes of their children and the nation as a whole.[73]

Mshuza was an outspoken advocate of working women in Dar es Salaam, yet her vision of working-girl uplift presumed monogamous marriage and parenthood to be paramount. Yet, as we've seen, this domestic model was far from the reality of most working women. The University of Dar es Salaam sociology students discovered the slipperiness of concepts like marriage, family, and household when they attempted to collect basic demographic data about the women they were surveying. Many women who reported that they were legally married often did not live in the same household as their spouse, while many couples that lived and formed a household together over the long term were not legally married. The absence of marriage was no deterrent toward parenthood. Most women workers had children and were either divorced, married, or involved in some domestic arrangement other than legal marriage with a male partner. Others, rather than organizing their household around their relationship with a male partner, shared their salary or resources with another female who lived with them and cared for their child while they went to work. The survey found that the vast majority of women workers had children, often outside the context of legal wedlock. Single mothers hired domestic help in the home to take care of their children. These domestic workers would typically be an even younger, more economically marginalized female who would either work for a low wage or take care of children in exchange for being part of the household. Often, they were relatives of the female household head, recently arrived in the city and incorporated into the household as a dependent.[74]

Despite this complex reality, TANU embraced the nuclear-family ideal and made it the criterion for many of the benefits of its social-welfare programs. This approach to marriage is reflected in maternity legislation that was introduced in 1969. That year, Rashid Kawawa announced at TANU's annual meeting that all parastatal organizations would have to provide three months of paid maternity leave for married female workers, but that unmarried workers would not be eligible for the benefit.[75] Despite the frequency of divorce in coastal societies and the vast array of temporary household arrangements and definitions of what constituted marriage, the nuclear family became enshrined by the state as a model of citizenship and the criterion for access to resources and redistribution.

Biomedical contraception also first became widely available in Dar es Salaam in 1969, and its pathways through the city were shaped by these Christian middle-class conceptions of respectability. Throughout the socialist years, the Family Planning Association of Tanzania (UMATI) was the sole clearinghouse of biomedical contraception into Tanzania. The association started out as a small dues-paying membership organization in the late 1950s with mostly European and Asian members, and when it became an affiliate of the International Planned Parenthood Federation (IPPF) in 1969, UMATI received an influx of funding and resources, often in the form of various kinds of contraception. Christina Nsekela, a thirty-two-year-old mission-educated schoolteacher and mother of two, became the executive director of the organization. Soon after taking the helm of UMATI, she expanded the program by hiring a staff of Tanzanian female nurses to work in the clinics and as educators. Christina Nsekela, herself a graduate of the prestigious Christian Loleza Girls School in Mbeya and the wife of a prominent politician, composed a staff of female nurses who had also been educated in missionary and colonial government schools. In preparation for their duties, the nurses were trained to conduct medical examinations of their clients and to provide counseling to women about contraception, problems of fertility, and health and nutrition during pregnancy.

In practice, UMATI's staff consisted almost entirely of middle-class, Protestant, married mothers who were offering birth control and sex education to an urban female population that was predominantly Muslim and poor. The women they sought to serve were frequently divorced, single, or living in ndoa ya kinyumbas and other flexible domestic arrangements with children. UMATI offered these women a range of contraceptive technologies, including condoms and diaphragms, birth control pills, intrauterine devices, and in later years, injectables such as Depo-Provera.[76] Tanzania would first be introduced to modern forms of birth control by the middle-class, mission-educated married Christian women who had been hired by Christina Nsekela.

The public was deeply ambivalent about the work of UMATI. On the one hand, they were seen as modernizers with unique access to technology used by women in wealthier nations, yet on the other hand, many were suspicious about the intentions and effects of these powerful imported substances, particularly the birth control pill and injectable hormonal contraception. Rumors circulated in the city questioning the ties of UMATI to foreign donors. Critics cited examples of forcible sterilizations and medical testing imposed on African American women in the United States and on black Southern Africans living in apartheid South Africa and Ian Smith's Rhodesia. Some accused UMATI of being funded by foreign institutions and participating in racist population-control measures without local accountability.[77] Others thought of UMATI's nurses as naïve dupes of foreign population-control advocates. Still others accused UMATI nurses of being witches, nefariously seeking to make women infertile. This accusation drew on longer-term regional idioms that associated infertility with the work of witchcraft.[78] These rumors of population control led UMATI nurses, to the chagrin of some donors, to insist that their services must include help with both control of fertility and treatment for infertility.[79]

Like other advice givers in the Ujamaa-era city, UMATI workers attempted to establish their authority by linking their wisdom to tradition—in this case, to older intergenerational relationships between women. Christina Nsekela often made the case that young women in the city needed bio-medical sex education to keep themselves safe from the predations of older men in the city. Traditionally, she argued, this kind of education was provided by elder relatives, yet in the context of the modern city, young women lacked the moral mentorship of mothers and grandmothers at a crucial moment in their adolescence. Nsekela portrayed her role and the role of UMATI's nurses and sex educators as taking over the role that elder female relatives used to provide.[80] Nsekela explained in an interview with the TANU newspaper the *Nationalist*: "Women, especially, have been practicing family planning since time immemorial, using different local methods. The Family Planning Association has just modernized these methods. It has introduced what is safer, more effective and more suited to the type of life we lead. Did you know that one of the methods used in

Figure 2.3 A patient attends an UMATI clinic in Dar es Salaam in 1973. Reprinted courtesy of the Tanzania Ministry of Information.

the past was for a wife to live away from her husband for two years? Well, that won't suit modern families very well, especially those which are not polygamous."[81] Rather than introducing radically new practices and values, they claimed to be modernizing old familiar ones.

The nurses of UMATI took these messages with them into the streets of Dar es Salaam. Several times each week, members of UMATI's staff would go out together—two nurses at a time—and make arrangements with a neighborhood ten-cell leader to offer their services to residents in a particular location. They would park their mobile-van family-planning clinic near a school, tree, health clinic, or other landmark and receive clients and patients there.[82] Other institutions in Dar es Salaam and beyond found uses for family-planning services. For example, following the passage of the maternity bill requiring public employers to offer maternity leave to their female workers, managers had to grapple with meeting the cost of paying for maternity leave. Many of them hired UMATI educators, including Grace Mtawali, to come onto the shop floor and hold workshops on contraception and child-spacing.[83] Wearing their knee-length white nurse uniforms and driving around the city, the nurses—all of whom were women—epitomized modernity and mobility with all its potentials and pitfalls.

UMATI was the sole gatekeeper of powerful imported resources, managing the delicate boundary between democratic access and inclusion on the one hand and harmful overexposure to unregulated substances on the other. UMATI was at the center of controversy on multiple levels, from the personal to the geopolitical. These tensions came to a head in 1973 in a scandal when Nsekela announced UMATI's decision to remove Depo-Provera from the forms of biomedical contraception it would provide at its clinics. Developed by the Upjohn Corporation based in Kalamazoo, Michigan, Depo-Provera is an injectable form of hormonal birth control. Its effects last for three to six months, depending on the dosage. Depo-Provera was linked with several harmful side effects, including blood clots, breast tumors, and menstrual irregularity, and at the time, it was not clear to experts how reversible its effects on fertility were. The U.S. FDA repeatedly denied approval of the drug for manufacture and use as contraception in the United States throughout the 1970s and 1980s.[84] Yet while it was not made available in the United States, international organizations such as the IPPF distributed it as part of their aid programs, especially in locations in the global south in Africa, Asia, and Oceania. When UMATI announced that it would no longer distribute Depo-Provera, Tanzanian protesters accused the organization of trying to cover up an agenda of population control. Local government officials shut down several family-planning clinics throughout the country.

UMATI resumed its services again in 1974, but from then on under government supervision.[85] Because the Tanzanian Ministry of Health had previously avoided voicing a stance on the controversial topic of family planning, UMATI had been the sole provider of family-planning services. In 1974, in the wake of the scandal, the Ministry of Health changed course and began to offer family planning in government clinics. UMATI's staff would offer their services within that system while retaining their role as the sole importers of contraception.

The Depo-Provera scandal reveals some of the fault lines of struggles over urban women and families in Dar es Salaam. In the Swahili language press, critics accused UMATI of inciting young urban women to be promiscuous, bringing shame on their community. One of these critics, Rwehikira Bashome, penned several poems and editorials about the deleterious effects of contraception, linking birth control with sexual immorality:

. . . Who are the addicts?
Married Mothers?
Very few, ignorant of the dangers.

Unmarried mothers?
Yes, once bitten twice shy.
Schoolgirls, working girls with no families.
What do they plan?
Prostitution, destroying harmonious families,
Selling themselves to every man, the so-called girls . . .
. . . When wives now run away from husbands.
You call this family planning?

Though he was an outspoken critic of UMATI, Bashome shared with them an underlying set of judgments and assumptions about what constituted a proper family. In its rhetoric and policy, UMATI divided women into three types. First, the ideal candidates for biomedical birth control represented in all the propaganda and public presentations of the group's agenda were married mothers who would use contraception in consultation with their husbands to space their children according to calculations about the welfare of the nuclear family. Second, women who were single and childless, but who were presumed to be on a path toward companionate marriage and who would someday become mothers within that kind of domestic arrangement, would be denied access to contraception but would be given sex education to prevent pregnancy. These young women would be educated about the biology of fertility and warned about the influence of sugar daddies and boyfriends.

The third group consisted of women who had children but who were not married. These women would have access to contraception, though the justification was different for them than for the married women that were the projected ideal. Nsekela argued that although contraception was not intended for unmarried women, an exception would be made for "girls" who had already gotten pregnant out of wedlock, after an initial unplanned pregnancy had been brought to term. "Girls" who claimed to be in this situation, she explained to the public, would have to undergo a medical examination first to prove that they had in fact already given birth. UMATI did not want to be held responsible for making girls who had not yet had children infertile. Perhaps more crucially, UMATI would not be responsible for allowing girls to "go bad" in the city by removing some of the risks of sexual activity, but they would help rescue women who had already made such mistakes to prevent having future children out of wedlock.[86]

In this sense, married mothers were understood through the lens of family planning—health care centered on the agency of the fertile couple and their reproductive goals—while unmarried mothers were seen as targets of population control, an agenda of limiting the number of children that a society produces. Single women without children were understood in terms of risk, and sex education would guide them to becoming future married mothers in nuclear family homes rather than unmarried mothers in flexible domestic arrangements. In this respect, contraception, like sex education, was presented as a tool of urban social reform, modeled on the middle-class Christian nuclear family.

The content of sex education combined biomedical information about contraception and the reproductive cycle with developmentalist messages about the shape of modern African families. The pamphlets published by UMATI often featured illustrations contrasting families that used contraception with families that did not. Sometimes, the illustration representing the family that used contraception would be represented as smaller than the family that did not, but sometimes, the number of children in both families was the same. The most notable contrast between the families in UMATI pamphlets was not their size, but their wealth. Mothers who used contraception were depicted as attractive and "smart," with flawless skin and styled hair, wearing tailored clothes, shoes, and necklaces and carrying handbags. Their children were fully clothed in school uniforms and appeared smiling and well behaved. Mothers who did not use contraception had messy, unkempt hair, were barefoot, and wore a simple wrapped piece of fabric. Their children either wore ripped clothing or were naked and appeared to be crying. Through these family-planning and sex-education pamphlets, UMATI made the case that contraception, when used by married couples, would foster prosperous nuclear families and lift families out of the shame of poverty.

Perhaps the most widely circulated example of developmentalist sex education was a book called *Jando na Unyago*, by UMATI official Dr. Sifuel Mamuya.[87] The title, which translates as "circumcision and initiation," was meant to frame biomedical sex education as an extension of an older tradition whereby young people were initiated into adulthood through an education in sexuality and reproduction passed on by older generations. The book was disseminated across the city's family planning clinics, mobile family-planning van clinics, and bookshops. At its most basic, *Jando na Unyago* was an anatomical textbook, explaining in biomedical terms the reproductive system, the effects of puberty, pregnancy, and forms of biomedical contraception, and causes of infertility. Despite its seemingly tame developmentalist message, *Jando na Unyago*'s explicit reference to contraception and sexuality was deemed controversial by some members of TANU, and the book was banned by TANU in 1973. Local TANU officials threatened Dr. Mamuya and ordered him to hand over all of his copies to be burned, but the measure only made the book more popular. The book was banned a second time in 1976.

In Mamuya's book, as in many of the publications of UMATI staff and allies, biomedical knowledge was presented seamlessly as part of a curriculum about domesticity and marriage. In this way, modern biomedical sex education in Tanzania was expressed through the genre of Christian advice writing. Indeed, sex-education textbooks and Christian advice writing were overlapping genres, with overlapping publishers and authors. In addition to his work as a doctor on the board of UMATI, Mamuya collaborated with the Christian Council of Tanzania to form *Elimu ya Malezi ya Ujana* (EMAU)—Education in the Care of Youth—an organization that offered workshops and publications about Christian family living. In his book *Jando na Unyago*, Mamuya spoke in his capacity as a doctor and expert, advising his readers about anatomy, reproductive health, and biomedicine. Yet seamlessly interwoven into this content is advice about how to build permanent monogamous marriages and families. He instructed his readers to choose partners based on criteria such as good hygiene, sexual modesty, and emotional intimacy. He advised young people on how to balance the demands of bridewealth by a bride's family with the importance of choosing one's own marriage partner. He offered advice about child-spacing and the various forms of birth control appropriate to different stages in the life of a companionate nuclear-family marriage.

Like Christian advice writers such as Martha Mandao, the counsel provided by UMATI shared the model of the nuclear family as the only acceptable model of family life, and in this way, access to benefits came to be shaped by this perspective. The permanent companionate marriage was the only kind of arrangement that would be represented as a viable future for women and girls in Dar es Salaam, despite its relative scarcity as a lived reality among Tanzanian residents of Dar es Salaam. In that sense, biomedical contraception and sex education were mapped onto broader struggles over urban domesticity and respectability in Dar es Salaam.

Conclusion

Advice literature for urban women and girls reveals a moment of political and urban imagination in which salaried labor promised not only a new urban economic vision, but also the potential for the reworking of gender roles and domestic spaces. In crafting advice and infrastructures for working single women, middle-class Christian reformers including writers, hostel matrons, and nurses offered a vision of urban uplift in which the messy entanglements of sex, domesticity, and economic survival could be disentangled and reworked into neat, discrete nuclear-family households.

The texts and the kinds of reading publics they envisioned not only represented a particular set of values, but also cultivated spatial practices that emphasized the primacy and separation of the domestic sphere and depicted the social and economic entanglements of urban life as pathological. This spatial ethos is reinforced in the content of the texts, the modes by which they were produced and read, and spaces in which they are preserved. Tracing the pathways of Christian women's writing took me into walled urban enclaves, into the records of the girls' hostels, and into the libraries of Christian school campuses in Dar es Salaam.

This imagery of working-girl domesticity was based on the iconography of a rarified middle-class elite. Most urban women were neither fully economically autonomous, responsible for only their own upkeep, nor entirely and permanently dependent on a male breadwinner. Instead, most women had to pursue a flexible strategy toward domestic arrangements, becoming parts of households when necessary, but breaking free of them when the costs to their safety or well-being were too high. While workers like Pauline Joseph and the inhabitants of the YWCA hostel were able to make a case for themselves using the language of worker's rights and modernity, women who worked for the very lowest of wages or who were engaged in reproductive labor or who worked in the informal sector remained marginalized from such celebratory discourses of progress and uplift. For most urban women, the images of working-girl domesticity and sexuality promoted in advice literature were both culturally discordant and economically out of reach.

Whether one was more concerned about the danger or the potential of the working girl, the debate was dependent on an economy that could support worker salaries of both men and women. The ideal of the working girl whose mobility, sexuality, and income were both promising and threatening to the social order was a political possibility only at a time when she had economic agency. Theresia Mshuza's column appeared far less frequently from 1972 onward, and Martha Mandao left Dar es Salaam to work at an evangelical radio station in her hometown of Moshi in 1973, where she continued to produce programs about marriage and family life. Meanwhile, life continued to change for Dar es Salaam's working girls. In

1974, the right to maternity leave that in 1969 had been implemented for women workers who could provide a marriage certificate was extended to include unmarried mothers. That same year, the Tanzanian Ministry of Health incorporated family planning into its health infrastructure, making it available in government hospitals. Yet shortly afterward, economic collapse would render these various debates and social visions somewhat moot. Real wages in Tanzania declined dramatically beginning in 1974, as Aili Tripp has shown, and over the second half of the 1970s, it became increasingly impossible for Dar es Salaam residents to support themselves on government salaries.[88] As the economy declined and Tanzanian men and women left salaried employment in large numbers, and as the state adopted virulently antiurban policies over the course of the mid-1970s, the didactic literature of domesticity continued to appear occasionally in party newspapers, but without the same linkages to the politics of the working girl voiced by writers of the late 1960s and early 1970s. The material underpinnings of this vision were gone. Delinked from such material urban entitlements, the "women's page" advice about the keeping of house and home of later years would have less of that double-sided dynamic of advocacy on the one hand and condescension on the other. Instead, it would appear as though divorced from politics completely: a human-interest story, rather than the stuff of urban politics.

Meanwhile, durable forms of female economic activity and investment persisted quietly, neither as pathology nor as a radical movement, but as practical everyday urbanism. In their social survey, Swantz and Bryceson quoted one woman they interviewed:

> One woman boasted that her husband's wage was nothing in comparison to the thriving business she had selling tea, maandazi, coconuts, rice and beans since 1970. With an air of confident independence she declared "Whether he [her husband] is at home or with other women outside, I don't care. I have my own money and the house is mine." She was accumulating savings to buy a beer store in the near future.[89]

As the authors of the survey hasten to point out, this woman was exceptional in her success, prosperity, and confidence and should not be taken as an indication of the universal economic liberation of entrepreneurial women in the city. At the same time, her comment is indicative of a wide continuum of possibilities between dependency and economic self-determination. Her comment also illustrates how her income protected her from a potentially unreliable husband. While many reformers saw hostels, nuclear family homes, and monogamous marriage as salvation from the morally degrading entanglements of city life, for many women, the equation was precisely the reverse: city life, urban economic networks, and female networks could also be an additional form of security from the vicissitudes of the workplace, marriage, and the family.

CHAPTER 3

Dar after Dark
Dance, Desire, and Conspicuous Consumption
in Dar es Salaam's Nightlife

In 1975, the young singer Marijani Rajabu took the stage at Princess Hotel, a small but popular nightclub in downtown Dar es Salaam, and performed a new song called "Hanifa." Born and raised in the city, Rajabu was twenty years old and worked at the Urafiki parastatal textile factory in the year that "Hanifa" first was performed. He started singing in the dancehalls and nightclubs of Dar es Salaam while still a high school student and developed a reputation for songs depicting the pathos and predicaments of urban youth. Rajabu sang about gangsters, schoolgirls, workers, and especially urban women. "Hanifa" is the story of a young married woman who, unsatisfied with the standard of living provided by her husband, ventures out into the city and uses her feminine powers of seduction to seek "the good life," consisting of fashionable clothes and luxury food received as gifts from men.

The song "Hanifa" follows an archetypal format for Tanzanian dance band songs: the first half of the song features tightly orchestrated instrumentation while the vocalists sing in unison, building a story. Halfway through the song, there is an abrupt rhythmic shift coinciding with the climactic moment of the story: a feature of East African dance music known as the *chemko*, or the "boiling" part of the song. In "Hanifa," this shift occurs when her husband tires of her behavior and abandons her. The song's clave pattern then breaks into a more fluid rumba, and at that point, the audience members, who would have been standing near the walls listening or sitting at tables with their drinks, would flood the dance floor as the performers delivered the song's up-tempo refrain. The crisp vocal homophony of the first half of the song gives way to call and answer between lead vocalist, the backup singers, and the horn section. The backup singers start by chanting:

your father and your mother, together with your siblings;
your father and your mother, together with your siblings;
they too do not value you anymore;
they too do not value you anymore, Hanifa.

Rajabu's crisp nasal voice then emerges over the refrain, singing, "*oh bwana huna, hakutaki tena!*": literally, "you don't have a man / he doesn't want you anymore." But this literal translation fails to capture the full emotional range of the key phrase *huna*: a word that the backup singers and members of the audience shouted, as though punctuation to the end of each phrase. The phrase *huna*, "you don't have," or interpreted more often as "you've got nothing," was an insult that had particular resonance for young urban-dwellers in mid-1970s Dar es Salaam.

Rajabu performed the song "Hanifa" in the Princess Hotel, one of the more popular nightclubs among Dar es Salaam's young professionals. Like the establishments that became increasingly common in the downtown and Kariakoo neighborhoods during the 1950s, the nightclub portion of the Princess Hotel was located downstairs from a guesthouse, where many newly arrived migrants would stay when first arriving in the city.[1] The Princess Hotel served bottled beer and soda—prestigious consumer items—along with grilled meats and other foods associated specifically with commercial leisure, purchased and consumed outside the home. At the best of times, the government UDA bus service transported young people from the city's outlying squatter neighborhoods and suburbs into the downtown at night, but by the mid-1970s, shortages of petrol meant that getting to and from the Princess Hotel was a challenge for those who didn't live in the immediate vicinity. Those who had access to automobiles or taxis became immediately and visibly distinct from those who had to walk long distances. Young women often asked taxi drivers working the night shift to escort them to the door of the dancehall to help protect them from harassment, for in the area immediately outside, crowds of people would gather, including those who could not afford to get into the dancehall and those who had been kicked out or turned away by the bouncer. These people remained outside listening to the music and drinking *gongo* brew— homebrew alcohol—instead of bottled beer.[2] The setting of the dancehall itself revealed deepening distinctions in class and ability: between those with means and those who might be told, "huna!"

An astute observer of the rhythms of everyday speech, Rajabu would have heard the phrase *huna* in the city's commercial leisure spaces, where it was part of a lexicon of trenchant gendered banter. The writer Freddy Macha recalls the sting of this phrase, identifying it as an insult that was simultaneously economic and sexual. A woman would reject a man's advances saying, "huna," "*huna kitu!*" or "*huna bwalo lolote*,"[3] meaning, "you don't have a thing": in other words, "you cannot afford my company." For the thousands of young men who migrated to the city seeking paths to adulthood and economic agency unavailable to them in rural areas, positive social recognition required an income to distribute. A young man built his reputation by managing the multiple demands of generosity made by friends and lovers in the city, as well as meeting obligations to his relatives at home in rural areas. While many women had similar economic obligations, their reputations were more often based on the skillful navigation of these exchanges with men. By the mid-1970s, in the context of economic crisis, young migrants found that the obligations of gendered respectability were increasingly difficult to meet. In this song, the insulting "huna!" is addressed to a young woman, transforming an archetypal story about the economic pressures of manhood into a story about female greed, social vulnerability, and isolation, revealing the ever-present flip side of gendered exchange entanglements crafted in spaces of urban consumption.

This chapter examines the urbanism of dancehalls and nightclubs, using the texts of songs performed in them as an entry point into a moral lexicon of urban migrant youth in which consumerism, beauty, and sexual desire were inextricably bound together. In a time when everyday life in the city was shaped by severe shortages of basic consumer items, dense living quarters, and the routinized surveillance and harassment of youth in public spaces, in dancehalls young urban-dwellers could seek pleasure, sensuality, and social recognition for their style or generosity. Dancehalls staged the struggles through which urban youth experimented with new forms of social inclusion through the entanglement of sex, commodities, and reputation. Nightlife held key social significance for urban migrants to Dar es Salaam.

A precondition for the flourishing of this live music scene was the patronage of a number of musicians and venues by TANU and by parastatal organizations. A number of Dar es Salaam's most popular bands and nightclub venues were privately owned, yet most were sponsored either by government institutions, such as the police department, ruling party institutions, such as the TANU Youth League, or parastatal companies, such as the textile companies that would sponsor dancehalls and dance bands for the entertainment of factory employees. Even as the state retreated from the provision of resources and infrastructure for urban-dwellers, they continued to sponsor and maintain surveillance over music venues. State patronage helped to make live music a ubiquitous part of urban life, with the result of the emergence of music professionalism. There were more working musicians making a living in socialist Dar es Salaam than ever before. Virtually all city residents had music venues in their neighborhoods and within walking distance of their homes, making going out dancing a regular and relatively accessible feature of urban life. Finally, state protectionism against foreign imported forms of entertainment gave musicians a special role as artists and as public intellectuals in Dar es Salaam. At a time when television was still banned and items like record players and imported records heavily restricted, entertainment was sought outside the home in the city's spaces of commercial leisure.

Seen within the framework of the nation, urban dancehalls were sites of vital cultural struggle. The sponsorship of urban dance bands by government organizations and their incorporation into a project of national culture building occurred in metropolitan centers across Africa in the late 1960s and 1970s, from Bamako to Kinshasa to Dar es Salaam.[4] The archives of the ministries of culture in Tanzania reveal attempts to incorporate this popular cosmopolitan genre of music into a state-directed program of national culture and developmentalism.[5] Debates occurring in the pages of state-owned newspapers and magazines of the 1970s reveal how urban dancehalls also became sites of struggle over national culture as participants and onlookers debated the meanings of African authenticity, pan-African solidarity, and gender and generational roles.

Yet while debates in the media emphasized the politics of national identity, many song texts, such as "Hanifa," reveal a different cluster of themes, such as commodities, shame, pride, love, reputation, and poverty. Taking these collected song texts as a street archive of 1970s urban life, our attention is directed not toward the politics of national culture, but rather toward the intersecting circuits of migrants and of new forms of wealth and status that wove through the expanding urban landscape. At the same time as the headlines of newspapers across Africa displayed intense debates about youth culture and African respectability, below the surface, *among* youth participants in nightlife, intense and intimate struggles unfolded over the terms of social inclusion in the city and its networks.

While government policies may have been the preconditions for the vast expansion of nightclub and dancehall urbanism, the social significance of these venues far exceeded, and sometimes challenged, the Ujamaa vision of culture, pleasure, and consumer behavior. In contrast with the socialist ethos of bodily discipline, economic self-sufficiency, and the artistic authority of cultural authenticity, young migrants to Dar es Salaam participated in the crafting of an urbanism in which access to the city and its spaces was based on social networks made visible through consumer rituals and an ad hoc cosmopolitan look. Some young dancehall patrons celebrated their urbanism as part of a global pan-urban black aesthetic and a form of diasporic cultural solidarity.

For stage performers, consumers, and service workers in the venues, participation in nightlife was highly gendered, commoditized, and sexually charged. For the young urban man of 1970s Tanzania, his education in masculinity and sexual desire was bound up in the social obligation of men to distribute wealth and to facilitate urban mobility, paying for taxis, lifts in cars, tickets to enter the dancehalls, and even beauty products and dresses for the women that accompanied them out in public. Yet this ideology of masculine generosity also contained the risk of failure, shame, and social isolation. Female desire was bound up in an ethos of dependence on men for mobility through the city spaces—both literally in terms of transport and in terms of consumer items that secured their respectable participation in nightlife—while at the same time, participating in this social script of male generosity and female dependence meant that they struggled to maintain economic and bodily autonomy from young men.

The mocking "huna!" of Rajabu's hit song captures the precariousness of this dynamic. Those who aspired to be respected as men could be reduced to ineffectual boys by being told by women, "You have nothing!" Women accessed the trappings of the modern female consumer through men, and to mismanage the relationship was to risk public scorn in several overlapping registers: as a patriot, as a member of an urban moral community, and as a potential socially legitimate adult woman. Such missteps had high stakes, especially for women, and could result in social isolation and curtailed opportunities for participation in urban communities. In the second half of the 1970s, in the face of economic devastation, rising unemployment, and infrastructural collapse, this mutual vulnerability between young men and women was increasingly expressed as suspicion and antagonism.

Spaces of Performance

The song texts that shape this chapter are artifacts of life in the city in the 1970s. Yet while unique to the postcolonial city, as an expressive genre, socialist-era dance-band songs draw on longer traditions of East African performance. Songs like "Hanifa" were meant to provoke audience response and participation from audience members, who would make their approval or disapproval of the text's message known by shouting, singing along, or using physical gestures of the body. Dancehalls were spaces of dense communication and observation. Swahili performance idioms of competitive consumption and public morality informed dancehall cultures and performance idioms. The practice of making social commentary through song and dance performance has deep roots in East African traditions of competitive street poetry and dance, and with the commercialization of leisure and entertainment in the postwar years, these idioms made their way into nightlife in the form of competitive movement in groups on the dancefloor, often to the chagrin of self-styled modernizers who saw European-style dancing in heterosexual couples as a mark of civilization and uplift.[6] The social commentary of songs vocalized in the dancehalls often left the dancehall and became part of debates and conversations in the wider city in the form of what Jesse Weaver Shipley calls "detachable phrases" that take on lives of their own, connected to, but not fixed in, their original context.[7] Today in Dar es Salaam, excerpts from a hip-hop song may appear plastered on the side of a *daladala* bus or in the title of an editorial in the newspaper. In many of the city's dancehalls, the same group of young people would attend regularly, and audience members knew each other by name and reputation. Often, musicians would compose songs about particular women in the audience, especially women with whom the band members were, or wanted to be, romantically entangled.[8] More often, the songs would be intended as a reprimand or commentary on members of the audience in the style of a kind of public gossip. For example, the musician Muhiddin Maalim Gurumo, the lead singer of NUTA Jazz Band, explained to me the origins of the 1973 song "Mpenzi Ninakukanya," or "Lover, I'm Warning You!" This song addressed a young woman who gossiped about her boyfriend in public, spreading his private business around town, and the singer warns her that she would face consequences for her bad behavior and her lack of *heshima*, or respectability. Gurumo explains that the song was composed on behalf of a friend who complained about his girlfriend's tendency to gossip and talk about him with others. Gurumo and his bandmates performed the song in public in the working-class Buruguni neighborhood as a way of publicly embarrassing the woman for her behavior, perhaps evening the score or orchestrating a kind of public comeuppance.[9] Often, in these face-to-face communities, all those who were gathered at the neighborhood dancehall or nightclub would know the person to whom the song was referring.

Another example is the Marijani Rajabu song "Masudi," which, in the style of "Hanifa," tells a story about a known urban character: this time, an infamous gangster and hooligan. The song tells of Masudi's childhood years dropping out of school and disobeying his parents. It describes him as an antisocial character who desires solitude and who lives a life of crime, breaking into houses and stealing from neighbors. The refrain of the song warns the listeners, "Masudi, he's a gangster, if you pass him in the street at night, cross to the other side." When asked about this song today, some Dar es Salaam residents who frequented the Gateways dancehall where Rajabu played report that Masudi was a real person. According to lore, this song—performed by one of Dar es Salaam's most beloved singers of the time—publicly humiliated Masudi to the point that he came to a performance one night at Gateways, approached the stage, and ostentatiously tipped the band before prostrating himself toward the audience in a kind of public apology for his actions, asking to be forgiven and allowed back into the community.[10] Like Gurumo's song "Mpenzi Ninakukanya," the songwriter participated in, and shaped, the moral community by composing a song about another person known to the audience. It is impossible in retrospect to confirm the effect that these songs had on the people they were about, as the story about Masudi may be true, or it may simply be the stuff of urban legend. Yet these recollections do suggest the way that participants in the culture of dancehalls understood the role of songwriters as public moral authorities offering commentary on urban life as a way of participating in it and shaping it.

This performance idiom of public critique crosses genres in Swahili music and praise poetry. For example, the famous Zanzibar *taarab* singer Siti Binti Saad composed songs in the 1930s and 1940s criticizing colonial judges for delivering unjust rulings onto residents of the working-class Ng'ambo neighborhood of Zanzibar Town, while years later, Bi Kidude followed in her footsteps and composed taarab songs publicizing the plight of women, including compositions about women who were victims of rape.[11] While most songs drew on a sense of community morality, they were not always so altruistic. More commonly, songs used sexual innuendo to call out perceived promiscuity or snobbery. Singers competitively praised themselves and tore down their romantic rivals. In this way, performers sought to boost their own authority and reputation in ways that were reminiscent of older traditions of Swahili competitive street poetry. For example, the nineteenth-century poet Muyaka, who lived in Mombasa during a time of rapid economic change and instability in the city, performed poems lamenting his poverty, lambasting the uppity behaviors of the rich, and caricaturing the beautiful women who rejected him for his poverty. At other times, when he was doing well financially, he composed songs about himself, boasting about his riches, beauty, and stylish clothing and chiding onlookers for their jealousy. Many of the neighborhood dancehall poets of the 1970s grew up exposed to this, among other, performative traditions.

The directive of national culture promoted by postcolonial state patrons became one of the many inputs into a robust preexisting performance tradition. In the early 1960s, a Tanzanian band called Cuban Marimba performed in nightclubs and dancehalls of urban Tanzania a song called "Tulime Mashamba," or "Let Us Cultivate Our Farms." It was a light and upbeat-sounding song in the rhythmic style of Cuban *son*, yet the lyrics imparted a sterner message. The chorus went, "Mwalimu Nyerere has told all of us citizens to work together! Let's stop being lazy, and apply ourselves. Let's cultivate our farms: the economy of Tanganyika."

The young man behind the microphone was Salum Abdallah. His mother was a farmer from the Uluguru Mountains near Morogoro, and his father was a trader of Yemeni descent, with trade connections that extended throughout East Africa. Like his father, Abdallah was a traveler and cosmopolitan. He was a lover of South American music and as a teenager had run away to the Kenyan port city of Mombasa, where he attempted unsuccessfully to stow away on a boat to Argentina in pursuit of his dream of becoming part of the Buenos Aires music scene. When he became older, much to the chagrin of his devout father, Abdallah used his inheritance to open several nightclubs. He was known for cutting a stylish figure when riding his motorcycle through the streets of Kariakoo and between his home in Morogoro and Dar es Salaam. Though his mother came from a family of farmers, Abdallah had never farmed in his life, yet in the first half of the 1960s, before his untimely death in 1965, he would sing for crowds of urban youth in Dar es Salaam and Morogoro, delivering a rousing call: "Let us cultivate our farms!"[12]

This song told a story about a collective return to rural areas while precisely the opposite was happening all around him in the city streets. The very youth who were in the crowds listening to him perform songs about returning to the farm were the same people who had recently made the decision to flee their family farms and instead seek a life in the city. Meanwhile, outside the dancehalls where he played, young unemployed and underemployed youth were going home to villages by coercion rather than choice, as young unemployed people were frequently harassed or arrested for vagrancy, rounded up, and forcibly repatriated to rural areas. This dissonance between a myth of rural prosperity and the realities of mass urban migration was central to the urban experience of Ujamaa-era Dar es Salaam.

While songs like "Tulime Mashamba" performed allegiance to the socialist leaders of the ruling party and more broadly to the spirit of African independence, later songs about returning to rural areas from the Ujamaa era were about sadness at the difficulties of life in the city. For example, the 1970 song "Nafikiri kurudi," or "I'm Thinking of Going Back," a song performed by the Jamhuri Jazz Band, was more like a wistful dirge than a celebration of rural socialism.[13] The song was sung from the perspective of a young man who is searching for work, but can't find it, and barely manages to survive. He laments that he is tired of the hustle and that his rural family needs him. In other instances, songs were meant to chastise urban youth, especially women, on behalf of their peasant families. The Atomic Jazz Band's song "Veronica" sternly addressed a young woman for chasing "the good life" in the city and leaving her parents suffering without her household contributions in the village. Depictions of the rural, produced by and for young urban male migrants, were a lament about the experience of social failure. Though ostensibly about the countryside, these were songs about a distinctly urban predicament. In these songs, performers could be inoculated from censure by participation in a patriotic ritual, but they could do so from the standpoint of an urban popular intellectual.

Despite these contradictions, the nightlife of Dar es Salaam was in many ways a creation of the patronage of the national culture program. In this respect, Tanzania was similar to other postcolonial nations, in which the urban bands of the cosmopolitan colonial cities were reframed as national culture, singing praises of new national governments and national heritage

Figures 3.1 and 3.2
Dar es Salaam nightlife
in 1969. Reprinted
courtesy of the
Tanzania Ministry of
Information.

Figure 3.3 Dar es Salaam nightlife in 1969. Reprinted courtesy of the Tanzania Ministry of Information.

as a way of cultivating nationalist consciousness.[14] One of Nyerere's most famous statements about culture called for a reclaiming of African traditional cultures. He said in his 1962 inaugural speech, when laying out his plan for a national ministry of culture:

> When we were at school we were taught to sing the songs of the Europeans. How many of us were taught the songs of the Wanyamwezi or of the Wahehe? Many of us have learnt to dance the "rumba" or the "chachacha" to "rock and roll" and to "twist" and even to dance the "waltz" and the "foxtrot." But how many of us can dance, or have even heard of, the Gombe Sugu, the Mangala,' the Konge, Nyang'umumi, Kiduo or Lelemama? . . . It is hard for any man to get much real excitement from dances and music which are not in his own blood.[15]

Alongside "traditional" dance groups and ensembles, dance bands, many of which were sponsored by state organizations, were part of this terrain of national culture. The daily and weekly TANU newspapers reported on the dance bands as part of a developmentalist discourse of authentic modernization, promoting a kind of modernity rooted in authentic

Tanzanian culture. This attempt to recode these cosmopolitan urban musical genres as authentically African and to bring development and improvement to audiences is reflected in the newspapers of the ruling party and government, which featured regular articles about bands. The reporters described them as virtuous and praised them for having a salubrious effect on the nation's youth. For example, an article published by the government newspaper *Daily News* described a concert by the popular band Sunburst in 1973:

> Dressed in white Tanzanian shirts (without the collar) the "Sunburst" emerged on stage in professional style giving the enthralled fans a warming start with an instrumental beat. Then the man at the helm of the show, James Mpungu, introduced a series of self-composed songs employing the *kitoto* style, a dance tempo for the Wangoni of Southern Tanzania. Their first song in *kitoto* beats was *tuzingatie utamaduni wetu* (let us adhere to our culture), which sent the band fans in a dancing spree swarming the entire auditorium. James Mpungu who was the centre of attraction blew up a little whistle in traditional style doing the homestep accompanied by a blooming stage-dancing style. Other songs were called *enzi za utumani* (the age of slavery) and "black is beautiful." This is the new spirit, the spirit that motivates our youth to become Tanzanian and original.

Like Nyerere's urging of Tanzania to seek out music that was "in the blood," dance bands, many of which were sponsored by parastatals, took this up by inventing dance styles. In the previous description, Sunburst was described as reviving the kitoto dance of the Wangoni ethnic group and performing it for a national audience. Musicians responded to this directive by advertising new dance moves, such as *tetemea*—a dance that involved the rolling hip motions of the rumba with the feet and hips, while shaking the shoulders and arms, as though shivering from the cold. The *masika*, *kavasha*, and *sokomoko* were all dances that combined the basic steps of rumba with other gestures suggestive of "traditional" dances and given names in local languages to add to claims of authenticity. Mbaraka Mwinshehe's band Super Volcano had sixteen members, four of which were female stage dancers. They wore bell-bottoms and modeled their style after black international icons like James Brown and Angela Davis while modeling the new/old dance moves on stage to teach the audience members. This was a way of giving individual bands their own stamp, having crowds of followers that could perform their traditional dance. Super

Volcano's four "masika stage girls" taught *sululu, zolelanga,* and *zolezole* to packed dancehalls and nightclubs.[16]

Many bands also performed lyrics in a developmental idiom, intended to perform and cultivate patriotic values. In this respect, Sunburst's song, "Let Us Adhere to Our Culture" and Salum Abdallah's "Let Us Cultivate Our Farms" identified the musicians and the performance spaces as patriotic. This description of Sunburst in the government newspaper captured what Holston has called a larger dynamic of erasure and cultural reinscription in which African cultures would attempt to erase the colonial origins of cultural forms and reframe them as having African origins. As Kelly Askew points out, where earlier generations of Swahili musicians prided themselves as making cultural references to their worldliness and connections with the Indian Ocean world beyond the African coastline, in the realms of official culture, these connections were erased in favor of a pan-African aesthetic of black modern culture.

Sunburst, in addition to being praised for reviving the kitoto dance of the Wangoni and for imparting messages that would bring developmental ideals to the nation's youth, was popular among young people for its reputation of black cosmopolitanism. Two of their members were from abroad: one was African American and another West Indian, which added to their cosmopolitan credibility. In the 1970s, American PhD student Stephen Harvey interviewed band member James Kilema, who told him:

> We members of "Sunburst" are part of a new breed of citizens in Tanzania. . . . Our music attempts to blend all the traditional Tanzanian forms into a national style. But at the same time, because we are not an island of culture, our music must also blend with forms from around the world. In my band, for example, I have a trombone—no other group in Dar es Salaam has a trombone. And my trombone player is West Indian. Man, are you hip to West Indian music? It is African! Man, it is nothing but pure African! This man of mine, my brother from the West Indies—Jamaica, I think—can play his horn the way the Zaireans play guitar. He sings with his horn, man. My other brother is, like you, brother, from the states; a soul brother.[17]

This quotation conveys some of the overall excitement about black cosmopolitan cultures in Dar es Salaam. African American culture had multiple connotations in Dar es Salaam. As Ivaska points out, Dar es Salaam was a key node in internationalist circles, and many expatriate African Americans—including members of the Black Panther Party—relocated to Dar es Salaam in those years.[18] Yusuf Omari, a musician who played with the band Bar Keys, was born to migrants in Kariakoo in 1954 on New Street, then the center of TANU activism. He recounts the importance of African American cultural influences, both through the conduit of international black icons and through the presence of African Americans in the city. Omari was introduced to the music of James Brown and Mahalia Jackson by an African American couple in his neighborhood who belonged to the Black Panther Party.[19]

Members of the public contested this cosmopolitan iconography. James Brown was sometimes included in discussions of African cultural solidarity as a symbol of black pride, yet at other moments, he was derided by critics—especially older generations—as being materialistic and capitalist.[20] Debates in the pages of the Swahili press considered whether such music signified Afro-modernity or American cultural imperialism. They reflect a concern with seeking membership in the wider world beyond Tanzania, but in the form of a cosmopolitanism that included East African youth on favorable terms, rather than one that was based on exploitation.

The debates about the foreignness of dancehall aesthetics were, in a sense, abstract discussions about political loyalties, but they were also simultaneously about deeply personal politics of identity and the body. We get a glimpse of some of these more personal politics in a controversy over a popular new dance craze. In 1975, the international disco dance fad known as the "bump dance" made its way into the dancehalls and nightclubs of Dar es Salaam. Partners would bump their hips into the other dancers on the off-beats. Yet on the dance floor, the dance became more racy as partners grasped each other by the hips and made rotating movements or began bumping not only the hips, but also the pelvis and backside. The bump dance was part of the disco and soul music craze that was most popular in the upscale nightclubs downtown by the ports, like Etienne's, as well as the beachside discos on the coast such as Bahari Beach, which were the favored venues of more well-off youth, many of whom had access to outside capital or knowledge or whose parents worked in high-ranking positions in the government. In newspapers, the different upscale music venues ran advertisements with pictures of young people with Afros sporting bell-bottoms proclaiming, "Saturday night is 'bumping' night!"

The new dance craze sparked controversy in the pages of the ruling party newspaper *Uhuru*. In the mid-1970s, the Afro-Shiraz party in Zanzibar banned the dance, and in 1975, the Tanzanian mainland public debated whether TANU should do the same. The arguments that appeared on the "letters to the editor" pages in the weeks that followed were familiar: that it had no roots in traditional Tanzanian culture, that it mindlessly aped Western culture, and that it was sexually immodest.[21] In this respect, the critiques of the dirty dancing of youth had generic elements in which older generations lamented the loss of control over younger ones. Yet in the midst of these debates, another argument emerged defending bumping on the grounds that other traditional dances of Tanzania, such as the *sindimba*, a dance of the Makonde from coastal southeastern Tanzania, involved a similar motion of the hips. At times, the sindimba had also caused controversy when performed by national dance groups because its hip motions erotically simulated sexual intercourse, yet it was not as easily dismissed because it was widely recognized as "traditional" and therefore a component of national culture.[22] One writer argued that if the state were to outlaw bumping on the basis of its raw movements and its sexually suggestive nature, it would also have to ban sindimba and a number of Tanzania's traditional dances.[23] The *Uhuru* debate on bumping came to a close with a full-page essay on the topic, arguing that sindimba was fundamentally different from bumping because the former was a dance of oppressed people living under colonial rule, while bumping was a form of cultural imperialism.[24]

Like the controversies over miniskirts that played out in African cities throughout the 1960s and 1970s,[25] the outrage over bumping conflated controversy about sexual propriety with a critique of the broader forces of capitalism and racism. Karen Hansen points out in her essay about controversies over the miniskirt in Zambia that it was not nudity that was objectionable, for earlier in the century, women's near-naked bodies would have been socially acceptable. Instead, it was historical change, including the influence of missionary Christianity on discourses of national modernity, which would later render the exposure of flesh obscene.[26] Likewise, the suggestion of sex in the bump dance did not, on its own, make it controversial, and neither did its foreign aspect, as other forms of "foreign" culture did not provoke such controversy. What made imports like bumping and miniskirts register as obscene was their association with new forms of urban life and especially the commoditization of the sexual and social relationships of young urban migrants. Youthful liaisons in spaces of commercial leisure contributed to intergenerational tensions in which young people chose their own dance partners and presumably their own sexual partners. They created bonds of obligation through wages and other forms of currency they attained and exchanged for sex and companionship in the consumer spaces of the city. It was not sex that was offensive, but rather an eroticism associated with the exchange of commodities, commercial leisure, and intimate arrangements that were created outside of the bonds of bridewealth and legal marriage.

Beyond the debates over high and low culture and over traditional and modern culture, the controversy over sindimba and "bumping" reveals how dancehalls staged struggles over the meaning of sex and commodities in the city. While TANU discourse and patronage opened a forum for discussing traditions, modernity, and cultural authenticity, in certain moments, such as the 1975 dance controversy, those same spaces staged discussion of questions that were more pressing and intimate, such as whether youth sexuality was the prerogative of the community or whether it was something individuals negotiated as their own agents in an urban milieu. Song texts created in dancehalls by musicians and engaged by audiences reveal more intimate struggles among youth over matters of trust, wealth, and conjugality. To make sense of these struggles, we must look beyond the dancehalls and beyond the ruling party's attempts to control them and instead look out to the city of Dar es Salaam.

The Geography of Urban Nightlife

Urban nightlife in Dar es Salaam reflected the city's history of migration and expansion, as well as its history of segregation and social stratification.

West of the harbor is the central Mnazi Moja Park, which was originally mapped as a *cordon sanitaire* by colonial urban planners and which separated the predominantly African neighborhood of Kariakoo from the Indian and European zones on the other side. Kariakoo has long been a center of cultural, political, and economic life in Dar es Salaam and was home to a number of *dansi* clubs in the colonial period, including Ally Sykes's African Jazz Band and the Tanga Young Comrades Club. In later years, bands like the Dar es Salaam Jazz Band, Kilwa Jazz Band, and Western Jazz were based in small clubhouses in Kariakoo, where urban youth would come and attend their practices.[27] Also located in Kariakoo were venues where audience members could watch *taarab*: a Swahili music style influenced by musical traditions from Indian Ocean societies associated with pan-Islamic culture.[28] Ali Abbas, who grew up in Kariakoo in the 1950s and 1960s, remembers the neighborhood as a site of "two civilizations," referring to dansi culture and taarab culture, each with its own code of

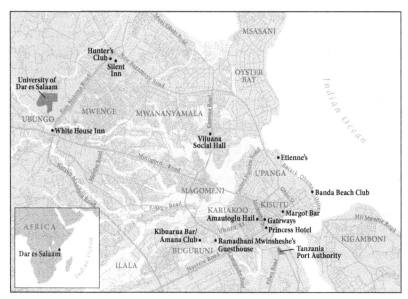

Map 3.1 Some of the popular dancehalls and nightclubs of socialist-era Dar es Salaam. Map by University of Wisconsin Cartography Laboratory.

conduct and dress.[29] These "two civilizations" also reflected two gender orders. In taarab, men and women watched performances—often very sexually suggestive—but were separated in different parts of the room, while in dansi, men and women danced together in pairs. The Mnazi Moja ground itself was the site of Arnautoglu Hall, opened in 1953 as one of the postwar community centers that were built in urban centers across the country in those years. During the day, classes were held at the center in topics such as literacy, childcare, cooking, and hygiene, while at night, the center raised funds by operating as a dancehall where local bands were invited to play.

Southwest of Kariakoo are the neighborhoods of Ilala and Buguruni: both popular working-class neighborhoods and hotbeds of TANU activity in the 1960s. Ilala was home to Ramadhani Mwinshehe's guesthouse and nightclub: the first African-owned nightclub in Dar es Salaam and a popular destination for working-class migrants and TANU supporters until around 1963, when Mwinshehe died and the place slowly declined. Mwinshehe's club was known for being an African establishment where a range of urban-dwellers, including mostly African male workers and their wives and girlfriends, would come to dance in the 1950s.[30] Samuel Machangu, another entrepreneur from Moshi and owner of several Dar es

Salaam nightclubs, was proprietor of the Kibarua bar in Buguruni, where the now-famous singer Muhiddin Maalim Gurumo used to play, wearing a tuxedo, with the Kilamanjaro Cha Cha band in the late 1950s and 1960s.[31] In Swahili, *kibarua* means casual day labor. Kibarua Bar was later taken over and run by the NUTA worker's cooperative and became known as the Amana Club.[32] The Kibarua Bar/Amana Club was an example of the many bars and dancehalls owned and run by parastatal companies and intended specifically for government workers. Unlike the commercial nightclubs that were open all night long, these parastatal worker establishments were set up to complement urban work rhythms, hosting dances only on weekend evenings and typically closing for the evening by around midnight. The parastatal companies acted as patrons to the musicians, paying them modest but regular salaries and providing them with musical instruments and a place to play.[33] These dancehalls were among the least expensive ones to attend, and they typically drew clientele from the neighborhoods where they were located, unlike the nightclubs out in the suburbs and in the city center to which young people would travel from throughout the city.

On the northeastern side of Mnazi Moja were two well-known dancehalls in multiple-story concrete buildings: Gateways and Princess Hotel. Gateways was located on the top floor of the Munir Mansion. The building also served as a hotel and guesthouse for out-of-town people, and its advertisements boasted having an elevator to take patrons to the top floor, where some of the town's most popular dances were being held by 1955. They served alcohol and meals of stewed bananas, chicken, chips, pilau, and skewered meats, and they featured live music acts. Gateways advertised in the English newspaper the *Tanganyika Standard*. By the 1970s, Gateways boasted musical acts from Zaire. A few blocks down, also overlooking Mnazi Moja, was the Princess Hotel: a small but popular nightclub started in the 1950s. By the late 1960s and throughout the 1970s, many of the town's notable young local celebrities and professionals spent weekend nights dancing to their famous house band the Safari Trippers, who were headed by the charismatic singer Marijani Rajabu. The band crafted an image of itself as a cultural broker, transmitting the music of the ancestors through the instruments and melodic structures of soul music.[34] Princess Hotel was where the song "Hanifa," from this chapter's opening scene, would have likely first been played for Dar es Salaam audiences.

Northeast of the Mnazi Moja nightlife, the nightclubs and dancehalls reflected the economy of the port, attracting a large clientele of sailors. The port leisure economy also brought with it prostitution and *magendo*, or black-market trade, often in fashion items and records. These downtown nightclubs were located in what was a red-light district between the port and the area of Kisutu, known for informal-sector enterprise, including *mama lishe* (female cooks), gongo brewers, and sex workers. This urban nightlife of Kisutu brought together local residents—those who made their living in the informal service industry—with both upscale clientele from abroad and professionals from the wealthier suburbs, who came for entertainment and then returned home by taxi in the evenings to their large and breezy residences in Upanga and Oysterbay.[35] It was also a neighborhood where men came to patronize the *madangaro*, or brothels. These nightclubs had a reputation for scandalous sexual behavior and dress and were often targeted by the TANU Youth League on their urban morality campaigns.

One of the most famous and infamous nightclubs in the port area was Margot's, which was started by a European Francophone woman in the 1950s.[36] Margot's became particularly controversial in the 1960s and 1970s, catching the attention of the TANU Youth League and urban journalists, who expressed outrage over the spectacle of African women soliciting foreign men. The clientele was a mix of local thrill seekers and foreign sailors, accompanied by African women and served by African wait staff. Margot's would later capture the imagination of investigative journalists and TANU Youth League activists, who saw in these urban leisure spaces an intimate tableau of an exploitative geopolitics. In the 1970s, Margot's was nationalized and converted into a cooperative nightclub of the TANU Youth League. Thereafter, its trade declined.[37]

Further out along the port, on the north side of the half moon–shaped harbor looking north out at the Indian Ocean rather than the bay, was the Banda Beach Club. This club was also associated with the local economy of the port and was another major site of police raids for prostitutes, dress-code violators, and young people attempting to stow away on boats with foreign sailors.[38] The tabloid writers for the newspapers *Ngurumo* and *Mwafrika* often frequented the Banda Beach Club in search of stories. Farther up the coast in the more upscale suburbs was Etienne's, a famous disco and nightclub started in the 1960s by a Greek expatriate, which soon became a popular destination for young urban professionals and the upwardly mobile. Etienne's featured bands such as Sunburst, who boasted of their ability to play American soul-music covers. Etienne's was one of the few places that, because of their connection with the trade at the ports, featured DJs playing records. The bar was in the lobby of a small hotel with a porch where guests sat on couches. The dances were usually held outside, in a clearing surrounded by large trees, with speakers hanging from the trunks and a stall off to the side selling grilled meat. In the mid-1970s, these upscale venues began to cater to the upper-class teenage audience, holding afternoon "boogies" (*mabugi*) for the well-to-do sons and daughters of high-ranking government civil servants.[39]

In the late 1960s, entrepreneurs began opening nightclubs and dance-halls in the outer suburbs. The club proprietors often sought to hire Congolese musicians from Kinshasa and Lubumbashi. This shift to the suburbs reflects a geographic decentralization away from Kariakoo, where Dar es Salaam's elite businessmen, religious leaders, and TANU founders were based. These growing suburbs were home to both a new educated migrant community as well as increasing, sprawling squatter communities. Up to that point, Dar es Salaam's nightlife had featured many African migrants from Kenya and from Southern Africa: Malawi, Zambia, Zimbabwe, and South Africa. In the late 1960s, Congolese music became a highly valued commodity. Many Congolese musicians, who developed their unique sound and guitar style as part of the sophisticated music infrastructure in Congo in the 1950s, fled after the assassination of Lumumba and continued to leave Zaire in the 1960s for cities throughout Africa and Europe, many seeking to escape violence and economic hardship under Mobutu's regime.[40] One of the most famous nightclubs was White House Inn in the far northwestern suburbs of Ubungo, where King Kiki used to sing with Orchestra Fouvette. Other bands that could boast the cosmopolitan appeal of Congolese musicians were Silent Inn and Hunter's Club in the northern neighborhood near the foot of the hill where the University of Dar es Salaam was located. Many of these migrant musicians, who had grown up playing in cabaret-style stage shows in Belgian Congo, featured stage dancing as part of the act.[41] The male musicians would move on stage in unison with their instruments while female stage dancers performed elaborate and often erotic choreographed dances, transmitting new dance fads to the audience members who would then perform them on the dance floor.[42]

The urban layout of dancehalls and nightclubs reveal the different kinds of cultural capital that were shaping urban citizenship in postcolonial Dar es Salaam. Throughout the era, a Congolese musical pedigree remained highly coveted, to the point that one writer complained about Tanzanian musicians affecting Congolese accents as a way of claiming prestige, associated simultaneously with cosmopolitanism and with African authenticity.[43] At the same time, many performers that received financial support from either TANU or a parastatal company also attempted to shape the urban leisure sector along the lines of national ideals about work and consumption. Young people often crossed over into these multiple spaces, going to their neighborhood dancehalls on some nights, while saving up the money and resources to go to the more upscale soul-music venues on other nights.

Inside the Dancehalls: Reputations, Patronage, and Work

The musicians who made a living or reputation in these establishments were almost all men, though they were often accompanied by female stage dancers who wore alluring costumes and performed choreographed dances in unison. For many urban migrant musicians, bands were a vital social and economic network, connecting members with other young men and with a patron, whether a state sponsor or a private entrepreneur. Many of the bands were associated with a government department and therefore had financial support through their employment, while other bands were privately owned.[44] Though independent of state organizations, privately owned bands needed a patron to have a home venue, as well as instruments and sound equipment, which could not be imported legally without government permission. The members of bands included more than musicians and dancers. Many young men were included with the band in less formal roles. For example, when Mbaraka Mwinshehe moved to Dar es Salaam for his music career, he took his "houseboy" from Morogoro with him. The young man worked running errands for the band until eventually he became a percussionist and started performing with them. This was typical for how these groups worked, forming patronage networks among young men and sometimes women. In addition to producing reputations through song lyrics and through fashionable dress, they were also establishing themselves as patrons, and while taking on many members into their social and economic network would seem to decrease each individual member's pay rate, it increased their prestige and reputation for largess.[45]

The musicians and dancers onstage were not the only ones performing. Dancehall youth built reputations, social networks, and romantic relationships through participation in consumer culture, while at the same time seeking release from the physical and cultural constraints of urban life. In the working-class residential areas, young people often found themselves perceived with suspicion. Despite popular fears that youth in the city were dangerously autonomous from the moralizing influence of their rural families, few actually lived apart from family networks. Many who arrived in Dar es Salaam looking for work or pursuing education stayed in housing with siblings, aunts, uncles, or other distant relatives who were already living in the city. Those who did not find space in a relative's home searched for rooms to rent with friends, often encountering landlords who were reluctant to rent to young bachelors. As we've seen, the challenges of finding housing were more pronounced for women, whose very place in the city was contested. Once housing was secured, the renter would live in close quarters with other tenants, often with two to four young men or women sharing a room mixed into a house with families and married couples that would share a common corridor, latrine, and cooking space.[46] In addition to maintaining a relationship with the landlord, urban youth were in constant contact with neighbors, with whom they shared the most intimate of spaces. Additionally, TANU established an increasingly visible presence in urban residential neighborhoods from the mid-1960s with its ten-cell system. As the city grew in population and neighborhoods became more crowded, TANU leaders, whose original base had been Dar es Salaam's urban population, began to plan for how they would maintain their influence and knowledge networks in the urban population as the city expanded. The purpose, according to TANU official Wilbert Klerruu, was to manage TANU's image among urban-dwellers, as well as to provide extra manpower and surveillance to assist the city council with problems of "hooliganism and delinquency."[47] The diffusion of the ruling party into neighborhoods through voluntary neighborhood authorities contributed to a sense of being watched by one's neighbors. In the context of a societal attitude of skepticism toward urban youth and of a national ideal of physical discipline and frugality, going out dancing offered a kind of bodily sovereignty and a kind of sensuality that was unique.

Yet while its appeal was based on its distinction from some of the harsh realities of everyday life, dancehall performances and experiences largely mirrored processes and pressures from the wider urban context. To stage a night out at the dancehall required preparations, the mobilization of social capital, and the ability to stretch one's limited income. Having the right clothing was necessary for going out dancing, and in this sense, the trade in secondhand clothing and in tailored approximations of cosmopolitan fashion was a kind of soft infrastructure, allowing mobility through the city.[48] The status of the band and of the venue depended on the way its patrons dressed. Bouncers at some of the more exclusive clubs turned away people who were not considered appropriately dressed.[49] By the early 1970s, men's favored attire included slim-fitting button-down shirts, platform shoes, and bell-bottom or tight "pipe" pants. Sometimes, it would include a fedora, gold chains, or a vest worn with no shirt underneath. Over the course of the 1970s, as the Tanzanian economy declined, these looks became more difficult to achieve. Secondhand items like these were banned from importation into Tanzania as part of the effort to make local textile industries self-sustaining, but these items remained socially valuable as part of the "soft infrastructure" of youth urban belonging. Secondhand clothing made it to Dar es Salaam through ports and other connections with Mombasa through Tanga, from Nairobi via Arusha, or from Zaire via Kigoma, and could be accessed and traded by the most savvy and connected of urban youth. As Freddy Macha recalls:

> To "be seen" was more important than anything else. Because the economy was restrictive, finding the right clothes and fashion was tough. So to be there you had to have the right stuff bought from dealers (*mitumba*) and guys from street corners. You had to show that you were "in tune." It was not like today where you just get stuff from Kariakoo or Samora Avenue. Those days you had to dig deep. I recall having to travel to Nairobi in Kenya just to get clothes. Or buying clothes from foreigners and even freedom fighters from South Africa and Zimbabwe. Going to a club meant, apart from music and sex, to show that you had managed to get in with the right regalia.[50]

While musicians performed on stage, audience members simultaneously performed for each other their capacity to access black-market commodities and create a sense of aesthetic bounty in the context of scarcity.

Having access to cosmopolitan fashions had more to do with the ability to call together the resources to make an appearance than with the performance of wealth or of ownership of these commodities. Most young people did not individually own a set of these "ready-made" clothes and had to pool their resources. As Telson Mughogho recalled of the difficulty of affording a pair of secondhand bell-bottoms, "You would often have three men, sharing one pair of pants among them."[51] A short story by Faraji H. H. Katalambulla, published in *Mwafrika* in 1964, describes a man going out and attempting to pass himself off as a well-paid civil servant, or *naizesheni*: a derivation of "Africanization," referring to Africans who inherited the well-paid jobs previously reserved for foreign employees of the colonial government. He narrates, "I wore a grey suit that I borrowed from my brother-in-law, Italian shoes that I borrowed from my brother, and a black tie from my uncle. I looked like 'naizesheni.' I carried off the outfit as though it were my own."[52] Many others who could not afford secondhand imports made use of well-skilled tailors, who made a cottage industry of approximating the ever-changing international styles with fabric that was available locally.[53]

Women's fashion changed from the early 1960s through the mid- to late decade. In the late 1950s and early 1960s, women's fashion emphasized mobility with knee-length dresses that were high-waisted with a flared A-line skirt. This was part of an aesthetic of health and physical fitness, allowing women to move around freely in dance.[54] For women attempting a cosmopolitan look in the 1970s, dresses became shorter and tighter around the hips, emphasizing the long, exposed leg and the movements of the hips and backside when dancing. One of the popular styles for dancehalls was a tight "mini" shift, worn with high heels and with a large kilemba, or headwrap, over the hair. This was a look that appeared in international advertising, such as in *Drum* magazine, where women appeared on the cover and in pictures in short skirts and high heels, legs exposed and shiny with lotions. Short dresses, along with hair oils and skin lotions, signified consumer culture, and some associated this look with progress, cleanliness, and hygiene.[55] To participate, then, required women to act as savvy, "up-to-date" consumers.

Although men and women participated in nightlife, they did so on different terms, reflecting both structural gender inequalities and an enduring, but malleable, ideology of male generosity and female dependence. At the height of the socialist period, an estimated 84 percent of men in Dar es Salaam worked in government jobs before the economic collapse that led to a mass exodus from salaried employment.[56] Most young men were workers, and their social lives and movements in the city's leisure spaces reflected their pay schedules. At the end of the month, the dancehalls were filled, and salaried workers felt both the exhilaration of a paycheck and the pressure of all of one's debts, financial, and social, being called in: hence the phrase *urafiki wa mwisho wa mwezi*, or "end-of-the-month friendship." Given that women increasingly filled the ranks of urban employment in the Nyerere years, they had spending power that, if not close to being equal to that of men's, was increasingly comparable with men, yet gender norms held that women should not spend money on commercial leisure and that women participated in nightlife through the men who paid their way. Working-class women interviewed by Bryceson and Swantz reported that they would only go out dancing or to the cinema if men paid for their entrance. Further, in newspaper debates about the use of hair-straightening beauty products, both young men and women argued that a woman should only use these items if her boyfriend or husband preferred her that way and that, in such a case, it was his responsibility to provide the necessary commodities.[57]

Much of what was being sold in the dancehalls was marketed toward young urban migrant male consumers and was being sold to them by female barmaids who, unlike their male clients, were not salaried workers with a minimum wage or benefits, but were part of the informal affective economy. One survey of 730 residents found that while women made up an estimated 28 percent of informal sector work as a whole, they constituted 75 percent of the service industry.[58] In contrast with older generations of Dar es Salaam women who had family ties in the region, who had invested in real estate over years of residence, or who had made a good living as beer brewers, women who worked as barmaids in dancehalls and nightclubs were among the most economically vulnerable people in Dar es Salaam. These were, by and large, women who lacked access to family land that would allow them to go into business for themselves as wholesalers of agricultural products. They lacked capital or real estate that would allow them to open their own establishments. Many of these women were long-distance migrants, working to support their families, sending money home to distant rural areas. At several junctures, groups of barmaids struggled to transform their jobs into more formalized professions, with minimum wages and protections. They drew on Ujamaa rhetoric of self-reliance, histories of exploitation, and the respectability of work in order to advance their position. In spite of these efforts, and without protections or a minimum wage or guaranteed salary, some women who worked in this sector combined waiting tables with sex work, which shaped the nature of the work even for those who did not.[59] As a waitress named "Asha Rajabu" explained to a journalist, whether or not they were available for sex, all barmaids and waitresses had to manage the presumption of male clients that they were sexually available.[60] Some of them invented fake boyfriends as a way of putting off unwanted advances.[61] Female service workers were often reliant on their male patrons, the nightclub owners, and musicians for both their income and for protection from violence. Many women slept in the venue after work to avoid the dangers of commuting home alongside intoxicated and aggressive male customers.[62]

While musicians and barmaids saw dancehalls as places to make a living in the city, the Tanzanian state attempted to use the patronage and surveillance of nightlife as a technique of governance. In addition to supporting some bands and social halls financially, they also used bands and venues as a way of policing urban space. In the mid-1960s, the coastal regional commissioner Mustapha Songambele hired up-country women and barmaids to act as undercover investigators in the nightclubs by the port to catch immoral women and prostitutes and report them to the police.[63] The Ministry of Culture renewed a colonial-era ordinance requiring all organized groups with more than ten members to register and obtain a license. A number of state officials saw bands as potential threats to the peace or as a front for illicit economic activity or political opposition. A letter from the Department of Defense to the head of the police stated, "These groups may be people who are threats to the peace of good citizens. Our office depends on your help so that, wither [sic] we register these groups or ban them, it is clear that they all cannot be musicians; some of them must be gangsters."[64] Archival traces like this one suggest the ways in which government ministers saw urban nightlife and culture as a strand of a broader concern with national security in an era of coup attempts and rapid unplanned urban expansion.

One of the urban spectacles most associated with struggles of ruling-party networks to exert authority and influence in the city was the members of the TANU Youth League patrolling the streets and commercial leisure venues as part of Operation Vijana, or "Operation Youth."[65] Following their 1968 ban on Western fashions and throughout the early 1970s, the TANU Youth League patrolled dancehalls and nightclubs to attempt to enforce the dress code, particularly in Dar es Salaam's downtown leisure establishments.[66] For participants in these campaigns, the impetus for policing the city came out of ideals that were explicitly gendered. Hamza Kalala, a musician and TANU Youth League member who played guitar with the TANU Youth League Jazz Band in uniform at the Vijana Social Hall, recalls how on several occasions, he physically restrained women who broke the national dress code, brandished a pair of scissors, and ceremoniously cut off their clothes. Located in the Kinondoni neighborhood, the Vijana Social Hall was one of several buildings given to the TANU Youth League by their ruling party patrons, and in the evenings, it functioned as a dancehall. Kalala described his approach toward the women as part of a patriotic prerogative of preserving sexual decency, saying that the women of the city needed to relearn a "traditional" sense of shame.[67]

The attack was meant to shame them by turning the exposure of flesh from something that conveyed power, mobility, and wealth into an experience of shame and powerlessness. If the exposure of flesh had been a sign of sophistication and privileged mobility and consumption, here the members of the Youth League were attempting to recode it as public humiliation and a reassertion of masculine power as a mode of patriotism.

The dramas of sociability in dancehalls reveal, in part, what Abdou-Maliq Simone calls an attempt to "spatialize an assessment of their life choices" as young people comported themselves in a way that reflected their patronage aspirations, whether seeking adulthood and authority based on a path laid out by membership in the ruling party or imagining economic (and gendered) personhood that went beyond the patronage system of the state through private patrons or social networks.[68] Young people who managed to appear as "cosmopolitan" signaled their aspirations to participate in an urban economy and to shape its moral and social manifestations. For members of the TANU Youth League, by wearing the party uniform and aligning themselves with arguments about the protection of national culture and respectability, they were demonstrating their loyalty to TANU's brand of racial nationalism and its sexual code and making visible their aspiration to advancement through the ruling-party apparatus.[69]

Commodities, Desire, and Sexual Risk

Dancehalls and nightclubs staged spectacles of conspicuous consumption through such displays as bottles of beer purchased and placed prominently on the table for all to see, difficult-to-attain secondhand ready-made clothes, and taxis pulling up to deliver patrons at moments when there would be spectators to witness a grand entrance.[70] This conspicuous consumption contrasted starkly with an Ujamaa consumer ethos of frugality and individual self-sufficiency.

As we've seen, Ujamaa rhetoric promoted a citizen ethos of material self-reliance, or *kujitegemea*: a concept that resonated at multiple levels. On a national level, Tanzanian self-reliance referred to economic and cultural autonomy from the outside world, narrated as a break with colonial-era dependency on wealthy Western nations. Kujitegemea gave vernacular philosophical meaning to the economic policy of import substitution. By producing their own food, construction materials, textiles, and other items, Tanzanians would, in theory, reduce their country's dependence on the outside world. Self-reliance also had meaning at the level of small communities. Ujamaa villages were envisioned as self-contained units, voluntarily taking up the challenges of villagization for the sake of their inhabitants and the greater vision of socialism at the national level, yet the rhetoric of kujitegemea meant that these communities were expected to sustain themselves without relying on resources or assistance from a central state.[71] They should produce for themselves, dig their own wells, build their own roads, and engage in their own development projects. They should be loyal to the state, but their participation should be voluntary, and they should not ask for anything in return from their government.

Within the Ujamaa view of the world, the individual consumer behavior and desire of Tanzanians was the lynchpin of these different scales, linking notions of cultural authenticity with the broader economic objectives of African socialism. As we've seen, the didactic literature produced and distributed by TANU through the literacy campaign of the mid-1970s associated the vices of greed and materialism with the economic impoverishment of the country as a whole. Mass literacy and education sought to discourage "frivolous" (feminine) desires for luxury items and cultivate a citizenry that would aspire toward a mode of development and self-improvement organized around the frugal nuclear family household. The individual who produced for herself, who did not desire more than her fair share, and who was responsible for her own survival was a patriotic individual. In one of his "Essays on African Socialism," first composed as a presidential address to the TANU National Conference in 1967, Julius Nyerere defined self-reliance for his fellow Tanzanians. "A self-reliant individual," he explained, "is one who co-operates with others, who is willing to help others and be helped by them, but who does not depend on anyone else for his food, clothing or shelter. He lives on what he earns, whether this be large or small, so that he is a truly free person beholden to no one."[72] To be free meant to have no debts or entanglements of obligation and to be generous toward others without expecting anything in return.

The archetype of the self-contained economic individual was part of the broader definition of African socialism as a system that was based not on class struggle, but rather on the natural communal predisposition of Africans in premodern societies. Nyerere famously stated, "I doubt if the equivalent for the word 'class' exists in any indigenous African language;

for language describes the ideas of those who speak it, and the idea of 'class' or 'caste' was non-existent in African society."[73] TANU political philosophy, articulated in texts published by ruling-party printers and distributed through the country's community centers and literacy classes, explained that greed and materialism were character traits of citizens who were, at best, self-hating Africans duped by foreigners and, at worst, race traitors. Such inauthentic behavior included waiters looking for tips from customers, African women who would only dance with men who wore imported clothes, African men who wanted to work in offices rather than work the land, or urban-dwellers who sought to live in multiple-story cement houses with corrugated iron roofs.[74] TANU's official political doctrine held that African socialists did not really desire these things. Africans were inherently self-reliant, hard-working, and egalitarian, and they preferred indigenous cultural products to foreign ones. Within Tanzania, the struggle for socialism and against capitalism and colonialism was articulated not so much as a class struggle as a struggle against racial and cultural inauthenticity.

In addition to economic autonomy, self-reliance implied bodily discipline. In a resource-poor country with an underdeveloped industrial infrastructure, it was the physical efforts of Tanzanians that would make the nation collectively independent of the outside world. This argument was sometimes bolstered by a strand of racial thought that held that Africans, unlike other races, were naturally hard workers, culturally predisposed to be hard workers and to live off their own sweat rather than the sweat of others. As we saw in chapter 1, TANU propaganda promoted the idea that anyone who did not perform physical productive work was potentially exploiting those who did work—the former were typically urban-dwellers and the latter were rural peasants—and that life pursuits that did not involve physically demanding labor were un-African.[75] This linkage between labor, productivity, and racial authenticity was at the core of Ujamaa antiurbanism. These debates about the body and its energies were extended to discussions of dancing and adorned youth bodies.

The core assumption that Africans were authentically socialistic and suited to manual labor was belied in part by the intensity with which the desires and habits of Tanzanian citizens apparently had to be disciplined and reeducated to align with socialist nation building. Fashion was one area of the luxury consumer economy that received a great deal of attention.[76] Designers created a "national dress" that was self-consciously non-Western, incorporating, for example, collarless Chinese men's shirts in the style of Mao's famous attire.[77] National dress also included, most noticeably, West African styles for women consisting of headwraps and flowing robes with open necklines and wide sleeves. These items were made in local fabrics from textile factories, and in some cases, the foreign origins of the designs were gently suppressed and replaced with promotional language that recoded them as authentic Tanzanian styles. In other cases, they were seen as remapping cultural solidarities away from the colonial relationship toward connections that emphasized cultural solidarities with other like-minded, especially African, nations.[78] This education of desire toward an authentically African aesthetic was linked to economic self-reliance. In addition to the valorization of self-reliance at the level of the nation, with consumers purchasing textiles made locally, urban Tanzanians were encouraged to value a new kind of aesthetic and a do-it-yourself mentality.

Fashion shows became a common form of fundraiser for women's organizations, such as the Umoja wa Wanawake (UWT), the women's branch of TANU, and the Family Planning Association of Tanzania (UMATI). They would feature young women modeling outfits sewn with cloth made in local factories from cotton grown in western Tanzania. These shows created an image of the nation, beauty, and the economy. Choreographers of fashion shows, self-consciously moving away from "foreign" terms like mini, bell-bottoms, and "soul shift," often attempted to give these fashions names that emphasized a political ethos; for example, in one such show various dresses were labeled "Uhuru" (freedom), "Ujamaa," "pambo la mwanadamu" (adornment of humanity), and "Afro Shiraz," the name of Zanzibar's revolutionary party.[79] At some of the fashion shows, the organizers would hire tailors to set up their sewing machines off to the side and to hold demonstrations, instructing people in the audience how to sew dresses in the patterns that they saw onstage.[80]

It was not so much what one wore as what one desired that was the real target of these campaigns. Propaganda produced by TANU explained that desires for foreign items were symptoms of a colonized mentality. The reeducation of desire implied a gendered order of things. Priya Lal demonstrates that the ideology of self-reliance was fundamentally gendered, based on the idea of women as defenders of the nuclear family households and men as militarized defenders of national borders.[81] This gendered order shaped ideologies of consumer desire. According to dominant political rhetoric, women tended to be materialistic and naïve and should stop insisting that family income be spent on dresses to show off to female friends, while men should stop spending money on tobacco and social drinking.[82] Instead, money should be saved, organized into a household budget, and used to create stable marriage households, which were self-contained microcosms of the larger self-reliant national economy. TANU intellectuals expressed frustration with the difficulty of instilling these values in urban youth, particularly women, whose unruly consumer desires not only were un-African and unsocialistic, but wreaked havoc on what the party was trying to promote as African socialist gender roles, rooted in the nuclear family and the self-contained household budget.

Ujamaa ethos framed economic autonomy, frugality, and physical discipline as authentically African while coding the global consumer culture and cosmopolitan pleasures as Western impositions. In its attempt to re-educate consumer desire, TANU's public intellectuals portrayed themselves as engaged in a heroic struggle against the superficial taste of its citizens for all things foreign. Tanzanians had to be taught how to be themselves and how to resist the pull of foreign standards of beauty and style. Yet debates over consumerism were far more complex, involving the profound entanglement of sex, social prestige, and conspicuous consumption.

In contrast with the ethos of individual economic autonomy, egalitarianism, and collective desires for homegrown "authentic" culture and commodities, Dar es Salaam's dancehall subculture—constituted through songs, social scripts, rituals, and the movement and adornment of the body—reveals an urban moral economy in which social networks and gendered identities were constituted and maintained through uneven material exchanges. Within the dominant Ujamaa narrative, this was understood as a distinction between traditional rural values and the Westernized decadence of urban life. However, the commoditization of sexual and romantic entanglements was neither a particularly urban problem nor a particularly new problem.

Anxieties over gender, sex, and money emerged as part of a more gradual commoditization of social and sexual relationships in East Africa over the course of the nineteenth and twentieth centuries. Marriage in East Africa has historically been negotiated between young men and older men as older men controlled the resources, such as land and cattle, that must flow between families to make marriage arrangements. Young men had to work for this access, whether through military service or physical labor performed in the farms and gardens of relatives, and through the cultivation of good relationships with elders.[83] At the same time, an intergenerational dynamic shaped fertility and sexuality as elders sought to control the reproductive capacity of younger women, whose ability to bear children within a legitimate family was a crucial component of the social bonds that would be made through marriage. As Lynn Thomas shows, the stakes of female fertility were extremely high and a source of great anxiety for parents, and the consequences of mismanaging female reproductive capacity were not simply dangerous for the young woman, but also for her community and family, who relied on these marital relationships and the multiple bonds of obligation they instantiated as the substance of community.[84] While there has been a great deal of regional variation in East and Central Africa in regard to accepted norms for sexual relationships before marriage, almost all shared a recognition of the importance of socially sanctioned children and families, secured through exchanges of wealth and labor.

The power balance in these intergenerational relationships has always been precarious, but these tensions were exacerbated in the nineteenth century with the extension and intensification of long-distance trade routes into East and Central Africa from the coast. Access to valuable imported commodities allowed men to bypass older social hierarchies and attain wealth, adulthood, and power through control and distribution of newly available commodities.[85] East African consumerism has historically been inextricably linked with the construction of gender in a way that was conveyed through an ideology of male generosity and female greed. Swahili speakers have long defined adult masculinity through a man's position as a distributor of wealth to dependents. Female mobility in Swahili cities and an ability to attend social events such as weddings required proper attire that was often secured as the gifts of a "generous" man, typically a husband or suitor. A woman's demand for commodities could shame a man for his inability to meet her needs. At the same time, she could be labeled greedy, reminded of her vulnerable position as an economic dependent, or even socially isolated, as men could lord their economic power over female dependents of different kinds.

These themes of gendered exchange were a theme in the nineteenth-century poetry of Muyaka. A number of his poems focused on the shame he felt when materialistic and greedy women mocked him for his poverty—a precursor to the insulting phrase "huna!" Yet this shaming could go in the opposite direction, too, as he demonstrates in another poem, which took the form of a taunt from a husband to a wife. In the narrative, the wife has disobeyed her husband, and so he refuses to buy her clothing so she can attend a wedding with her friends. She wants to go out and see her friends and participate in urban social life, but he mocks her, inviting her to go out and pick some rags off the trash heap. Without his generosity, the refrain of the poem harasses her: *"Utavaa Nguo gain?"* or, "What will you wear?"[86] This dynamic of female dependence on men for commodities that would allow them to move in public and attain social inclusion structured a range of different domestic arrangements on a spectrum that included marriage, concubinage, and slavery. Some historians have suggested that what distinguished slavery or concubinage from marriage was the nature of the exchange: in marriage, a man's gifts flowed not just to a woman, but to a larger familial network, in which the wife had kin to speak and act on her behalf.[87] These deeper regional histories of gender, slavery, and power lingered in the connotations of social danger associated with the exchange of gifts between romantically involved youth in the Ujamaa-era city.

In the colonial era, especially in the years following World War II, young men gained access to the cash economy through new opportunities to engage in trade and wage labor. At the same time, as educational opportunities expanded for both boys and girls, students spent more time away from home, forming bonds of friendship with members of their age set, which became increasingly important alongside intergenerational relationships. Young men, empowered by their increasing purchasing ability and autonomy, often opted for shorter-term romantic and sexual relationships before marriage.[88] East African youth began marrying at later ages, and this exacerbated already existing anxieties about fertility, particularly when it came to female students, who were delaying marriage and forming social relationships outside the watchful eyes of mothers and grandmothers. Pregnancies occurring outside communally sanctioned marriages had long been a concern of the relatives of girls and women of childbearing age. The conditions of urban life exacerbated these anxieties.

To an extent, the older ideology of male generosity harmonized with the ideal of the male breadwinner promoted by a colonial developmentalist agenda across cities in postwar colonial Africa.[89] Colonial policies and social-engineering endeavors were geared toward focusing men's material obligations on the nuclear family in order to create a stable urban working class.[90] Yet the "self-reliant" nuclear family household was only ever one possibility, and it was never the most common ideal in Dar es Salaam. As we've seen in the preceding chapter, flexible domestic arrangements and marriages remained common, and there were a wide variety of household arrangements involving, but not centered on, mutual economic dependence between a male and female partner who were not bound permanently through marriage. Terms like *ndoa ya kinyumba* and *nyumba ndogos* referred specifically to flexible domestic arrangements suited especially to the urban setting of Dar es Salaam.

How would young people manage these complex possibilities for material and sexual entanglement? This flexibility is part of what reformists were so concerned about. Theresia Mshuza printed a column devoted to the topic of "gift friendships": relationships in which unmarried boys gave gifts as signs of their affections to girls. The article warned girls not to accept such gifts, for, according to one commentator, while such friendships might be acceptable for *wazungu*, or Europeans, for Africans, the connections and obligations they implied were much deeper and difficult to disentangle and often involved sex. The developmentalist rhetoric of the self-contained nuclear family mapped unevenly onto these more fluid dynamics, which structured urban social relationships and spaces.

Participation in the gendered social order of the city required men to have money. An inability to purchase beers or tickets to the dancehall or to make an impressive appearance was a potential source of humiliation and social isolation. As one of the songs performed by the Atomic Jazz Band lamented:

The world these days is money, every thing is money,
To dress and to eat is money, oh, the world is money
Oh, the world is trouble if you don't have money!
You will lack everything, the women will flee from you.
Oh, the world is money.[91]

Men without money feared becoming socially invisible.

The ideology of female dependence, sometimes more cynically interpreted as female greed, was a trope in dancehall culture both in the expectations that men pay for the evening out and in song texts that comment on these gendered circumstances. That female desire for wealth was excessive and unreasonable was a truism in popular representations of women. Writers and performers represented urban African women as greedy, portraying their unruly desire for wealth and well-being as both emasculating to their male companions and threatening to the principles of Ujamaa.[92] This desire was understood as dangerous to the women themselves, and in the news coverage of the debate over the problem of schoolgirl pregnancies, the material desires of young women were widely understood to be the main culprit.[93] Schoolgirls were portrayed as unable to resist the desire to go to dancehalls, ride in automobiles, and wear nice clothing. Schoolgirls wanted to eat roasted chicken and chips and other commodified foods served and sold in the city's commercial spaces rather than cooked in the home. Such is the gendered stereotype of the song "Hanifa" that opened this chapter.

Women who chose to participate in nightlife had to walk a fine line. They were expected to look like "modern" women, displaying the trappings of international modes of beauty circulating through advertising and popular culture. Some of the dancehalls enforced dress codes. The more upscale ones turned away those who appeared at the entrance wearing "traditional" clothes, but even without these restrictions, many women felt that "modern" clothing was socially necessary for participation in nightlife. Cosmetics and clothing were, for women, part of a "soft infrastructure" that allowed them to participate in the gendered cycles of exchange that constituted urban belonging. At the same time, desire for these commodities was widely pathologized in public political discourse, described by some as self-hatred and racial betrayal. Those who aspired to look modern engaged in debates: just how short could a skirt be before one could be accused of betraying one's racial respectability?[94] Young women and men debated: what was the difference between fashioning one's hair to look "modern" and fashioning one's hair in order to look European, Asian, or Arab?[95] Often, participants in debates on newspaper editorial pages explained women's consumer choices by attributing them to men's desire, turning accusations of female race betrayal back on men who, they argued, spoke loudly about African authenticity while themselves leaving their respectable authentically African wives neglected at home and seeking pleasure in the company of miniskirt-wearing beauties.[96]

The gendered meanings of urban luxury consumption are captured in the term *kisura*: a Swahili word referring to a fashionable and attractive young urban woman.[97] The term is used to describe others rather than an identity embraced by those it described. The figure of the kisura reflects some of the gender anxieties and moral strivings of young people in the city. Neither strictly derogatory nor flattering, *kisura* connotes the pleasure and desirability of female consumerism, yet connotes superficiality and surfaces as well, capturing the precariousness and pleasure of commoditized beauty. Literally, *kisura* can be translated as "little face," suggesting the centrality of surfaces and appearances to her place in urban life. The word *kisura* signals a concern with appearances. Kisura are consumers of "up-to-date" fashions. They wear makeup, they use skin products and hair oils, and they wear "modern" fashions: particularly short dresses and skirts. They move easily through urban space, their movements facilitated by the money of men who buy them drinks and give them gifts. *Visura* (the plural of *kisura)* are admired for their beauty, consumer savvy, and respectability as sophisticated urbanites. When the famous Southern African singer Dorothy Masuka came to perform in Tanzania in 1962, she was described affectionately in the local paper as a kisura.[98] To be a kisura was to stage a public performance, whether literally on stage and in front of cameras or in one of the many spaces of public spectacle in the city. Like the international "modern girl" of the 1920s and 1930s,[99] the kisura drew on aesthetic influences from elsewhere and made them resonate in local registers.

In popular images, the kisura is always an unmarried female, signifying the pleasures of urban consumerism rather than the potentials of marriage or family. She is portrayed occupying spaces of public consumption rather than the household. *Kisura* has ambivalent connotations: on the one hand, connoting desire and pleasure, and on the other, signaling a threat to the family and the nation.[100] Portrayals of visura reflect a broader tendency in popular discourse to juxtapose the consumer pleasures of urban life with the virtues of family life. Visura were accused of luring men's money away from them, diverting the resources away from their children and families. They were themselves unmarried and had no children—kisura was in many ways the foil of motherhood and what was portrayed as patriotic femininity—and in this way, posed a threat to the family.

If wearing national dress was a way of publicly demonstrating patriotism and attempting to establish a claim to state patronage networks, the cosmopolitan fashion displayed by women who appeared in the mode of the kisura also signified an alternate cycle of exchange and mode of belonging. Out of these objects and exchanges, young people produced gendered identities. In the late 1960s and 1970s, the Jamhuri Jazz Band performed the song "*Shangazi Naomba Taiti,*" or "Aunty, Lend Me Your Tight Skirt," in dancehalls around Tanzania. They sang, in a mid-tempo rumba, "*Aunty, lend me your tight skirt so I can look beautiful when I go out dancing tonight; and then, maybe I'll return tomorrow with a shilling.*" At the bridge, the song breaks into a section in which the vocalist sings a capella as the instrumentalists keep time on the down beats:

Oh mama-shangazi, lend me your boots,
and maybe I'll return tomorrow with a shilling;
oh mama-shangazi, lend me your head scarf,
and maybe I'll return tomorrow with a shilling;
oh mama-shangazi, lend me your shoes,
and maybe I'll return tomorrow with a shilling.[101]

The woman who is the protagonist must borrow the proper garments to participate in a night at the dancehall and begin the cycle of exchange that secures her inclusion. If she successfully pulls off the right look—a tight skirt and top, with a tall headwrap on her hair and high-heeled shoes—she would be appropriately dressed and allowed into the dancehall, where she would socialize and dance with men. If all went well, she would attract a male companion, who, in his attempt to woo her and dance with her, would give her a monetary gift.

For some women, participation in urban nightlife potentially offered a kind of liberation, but one that was precarious. Some women, including those whose needs were not met in socially recognized marriages, found romance and the urban consumer economy to be a place where they could attain status and financial survival.[102]

At the same time, this position also carried substantial risks: a harsh reality captured in a song written by Mbaraka Mwinshehe, entitled "Pole Dada," or "Sorry Sister." The song begins with a story about a girl who is widely loved until one day, when her lover scorns her. After that, all her other potential lovers want nothing to do with her, and she is left isolated by her bad reputation. In the second half of the song, the singers alternate lines, singing:

Now you will not get tickets to the cinema, (oh, sorry sister!)
New soap, who will buy it for you? (oh, sorry sister!)
Now you won't get a ticket to see dance music (oh, sorry sister!)
Now nice oil and face powder, how will you get it? (oh, sorry sister!)
Now to buy shoes, who will buy them for you? (oh, sorry sister!)[103]

These lines, sung out in dancehalls in Dar es Salaam, Morogoro, Tanga, and other Tanzanian cities, are suggestive of how female participation in consumer pleasures was mediated through their relationships with men. Far from autonomous self-reliant individuals, men and women constructed a popular urbanism based on exchanges and entanglements, placing both in positions of mutual vulnerability.

Figure 3.4 Mbaraka Mwinshehe Mwaruka entertaining a crowd, no date. Reprinted courtesy of the Tanzania Ministry of Information.

For migrant youth in Dar es Salaam, the deep entanglement of consumerism, sexuality, and gift exchange made dancehalls and the activities that happened in them dense with social significance and potential risk. This is what made nightlife so controversial to onlookers, who feared not merely sexual impropriety, superficial materialism, or cultural inauthenticity, but also the very real threat of social ruin for their children. In dancing, drinking, forming relationships of obligation and indebtedness through sex and money, young people were dealing with real power.

Conclusion

In socialist Dar es Salaam, dancehalls and nightclubs were unique sites of pleasure and release. They emerged as vital urban cultural institutions due to a combination of factors, including an expanding urban migrant population, state patronage of the arts, and policies of protectionism that restricted the importation of foreign cultural goods, which allowed live music venues to compete favorably with other forms of entertainment. At the same time, these urban venues staged broader intersecting struggles over Ujamaa and urban citizenship, enacted through song texts, consumer rituals, and the adornment of the body. While Ujamaa doctrine modeled a national economy that was made up of individual, autonomous, and self-sufficient consumers of locally produced commodities and aesthetics, the urban youth economy, by contrast, was based on exchanges and distributions that had multiple meanings. Out of these exchanges, young urban sojourners crafted notions of prestige, gender, and sexuality.

By the 1970s, songs like "Hanifa" that explored the risks of consumer desire and the precarious balance between socially productive exchange and mutual vulnerability became a dominant social script in nightlife. Popular portrayals of sites of commercial leisure, which in an earlier era connoted modernization and uplift, increasingly warned of the dangers of uneven exchanges and the illegitimate or disastrous social relationships that might result. The script of male generosity and female dependence and the precariousness of that dynamic became strained in the context of economic crisis. The dynamic of gender roles negotiated through material exchange endured over time, yet in the context of economic scarcity, it morphed into the language of gender antagonism. Male generosity was recast as either poverty or corruption and female dependence as greed and promiscuity.

Yet despite deepening gender tensions, these relationships and all their constitutive exchanges remained crucial to an expanding migrant urbanism. In a city under siege from economic collapse, self-reliance was a luxury few could afford.

CHAPTER 4

Lovers and Fighters

Pulp-Fiction Publishing and the Transformation
of Urban Masculinity

Armed with the most dangerous weapon of half-education they demand
cards, which would make them members of a class to which they think they
belong. With anger they keep on spitting poisonous saliva like rabid dogs,
and frenzily snarl at every car passing by. Walking idly in the streets they
go round counting stories of skyscrapers and knock at every door looking
for jobs. They are furious. They are furious because they feel they have been
cheated by the "Pariah Literati." They feel they are being bullied by politicians and government officials, some of whom have lower standards of
education. —Euphrase Kezilahabi

We were called writers of *riwaya pendwa* (popular novels). Sometimes I accepted it, sometimes I thought it wasn't true, because I thought, for example, my work *Mpenzi* was a very serious work. You know! So we were rebel-
lious and we banded together like some rebels. . . . As far as I was concerned,
my writings reflected the challenges and the dilemmas and the thinking of
the youth. Especially the youngsters who had been educated in the Nyerere days and who had a certain vision and certain dreams. So I think I was
angry; sometimes I think I was trying to preach. Of course, I attempted to
thrill people, and this and that, but I think generally, it reflected the kind of
challenges, dilemmas, dreams that young people at that time had. Of that
class, especially those of us who had just finished high school. Didn't have
some type of employment, hadn't gone to college, were hustling you know
with life, both women and men . . . those things were real, those were real,
those were real, those were real. Yeah. —Kajubi Mukajanga

Economic crisis and austerity pummeled denizens of Dar es Salaam in
the late 1970s and the early 1980s. From the mid-1970s onward, the value
of real wages steadily collapsed, making it impossible for workers to support themselves and families through their take-home pay. The state had
begun to retreat from its role as service provider in the city and instead

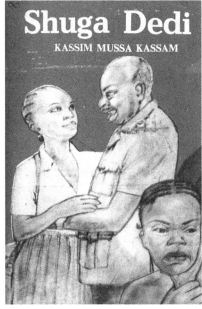

Figure 4.1 Cover artwork for Kajubi Mukajanga's novella *Tuanze Lini?*, written in 1975, published by Grand Arts Promotion in 1983.

Figure 4.2 Cover images from Kassim Musa Kassam's 1984 novella *Shuga Dedi*, published by International Publisher's Agency.

Figure 4.3 Cover artwork for A. E. Musiba's 1980 novella *Kikomo*, published by Continental Publishers.

invested its energies in cracking down on the economic activities of the urban poor. Tanzania's planned economy was not meeting the needs of urban residents. During these years, basic food items were scarce and difficult to come by in the city, and every day people had to queue at a cooperative store, sometimes for hours, in hopes of being able to purchase a bag of rice or flour or a tube of toothpaste.

Paradoxically, this time of great material scarcity was also the heyday of a thriving underground pulp-fiction industry. These novellas were written in the style of romance novels and crime thrillers. In these books, readers would encounter glamorous characters, including beauty queens, spies, kung fu fighters, detectives, motorcycle gangs, and criminal masterminds, ensnared in kidnappings, airplane hijackings, coup plots, mysterious suicides, and car chases. At the same time, for all their fantastical elements, the stories unfolded in recognizable locations in Dar es Salaam, in the streets, buses, squatter neighborhoods, and beachside hotels and nightclubs, where young male heroes used their knowledge of the city to solve crimes, defeat villains, and win recognition.

They were written in a colloquial style of Swahili, and the stories unfolded in recognizable locations in Dar es Salaam. They ran from around 75 to 150 pages in length and had titillating cover artwork featuring scantily clad women, kung fu fighters, and villains lying in pools of blood.

In a context of scarcity, we might think of romance and thriller novellas as nonessential luxury items, and yet they were widely available in bookstalls and from individual sellers throughout the city at a time when many basic commodities, such as soap, sugar, and rice, were scarce and sometimes impossible to find. They were priced at about one-tenth of the cost of imported books in English, and three to four times as much as one ticket for a night at one of the less expensive worker cooperative dancehalls.[1] A consumer could purchase one or two of these novellas for about the same cost of buying the daily newspaper for a month or two, depending on the newspaper.[2]

These books were written, published, and disseminated by a network of young migrant men in Dar es Salaam. The networks of young male pulp-fiction writers who circulated through Dar es Salaam started writing their own pulp-fiction novellas and publishing and selling them in the underground economy of a city that increasingly found itself in an economic downward spiral. These small publishing companies had names and reputations, but no legal address or real estate in the city. For their mobility, semi-legality, and apparent informality, these young men were labeled by literary elites "briefcase publishers." This publishing industry in fantasy novellas thrived at the height of economic collapse, scarcity, and censorship in Tanzania and virtually disappeared within a few years after the end of African socialism. Paradoxically, the briefcase publishing industry declined during a time associated with the liberalization of the economy and an increased cultural permissiveness as censorship measures and restrictions on foreign imports were lifted. This chapter draws on about two hundred of these novellas and reads them as a street archive of the late Ujamaa-era city.

In the first of the two epigraphs opening this chapter, Euphrase Kezilahabi, a university professor with a PhD from the University of Wisconsin–Madison and a reputation as Tanzania's most internationally celebrated novelist, described the "briefcase publishers" for an academic audience in Germany. Despite his condescension toward these "snarling" and "angry" young men, he links the literary projects of these writers with their material circumstances in the city of Dar es Salaam, walking the streets, observing material inequality, simultaneously aware of the promise of urban life in the city and of their exclusion from it. Their relationship with the city was material in another sense, as well. The creation of an underground publishing industry under a regime that sought to control both the material production and content of art and entertainment required an intimate knowledge of the city and the cultivation of social and economic networks. At a time when access to paper and ink was highly restricted, individual ownership of a typewriter virtually unthinkable, and printing largely in the hands of a highly bureaucratic, inefficient, and unwieldy system of state-owned printing presses, one had to know not only one's audience, but also financial patrons, owners of stationery stores, and people in the printing factories that could be bribed. One also had to know where and how to get pilfered paper and know bookstall hawkers, itinerant newspaper sellers, typists with office jobs, and truck drivers who could deliver gunny sacks full of paperbacks to other locations throughout the country. For both the briefcase publishers and their critics, the work of pulp-fiction publishing was both literary and material.

For all their use of fantastical elements, the briefcase publishers created fictional heroes who resembled themselves, for the protagonists in the stories were almost all young urban migrant men. These novellas documented the difficult choices of young men, portraying the temptations to participate in illicit black-market trade, the emasculating experience of urban poverty, the struggle of the urban migrant to manage the obligations to rural families, and the search for romantic love. Likewise, the authors themselves—all young migrant men in Dar es Salaam—crafted their genre and their industry out of the informal economic arrangements of a city in collapse and transition. In this sense, the quests of young protagonists in the novellas for adulthood and recognition in the urban environment replicated the production process of the novellas themselves.

Recent work by scholars including Gyan Prakash, Elliott Colla, and Jennifer Robinson has recognized the portability of international genres like crime thrillers and their potential as a form of social intervention or critique.[3] Writers of noir fiction, Prakash observes, describe the urban environment in such a way as to offer a diagnosis of social ills. In this way, pulp-fiction literature can offer an alternative view of the city that departs from texts produced by more conventional archives, such as police reports, newspapers, and other mainstays of municipal archives. As a city under assault from economic decline and infrastructural collapse following the oil shocks of the mid-1970s and then the 1979 war with Idi Amin and an urban population simultaneously marginalized and antagonized by a repressive one-party state, Dar es Salaam's pulp fiction offers a way of reading the city from a different standpoint than officialdom. Yet while some aspects of crime thrillers—plot lines, character types, and aesthetics—might be portable and universal, the meaning of authorship and readership and the mode of producing and disseminating fictional texts cannot be taken as a universal.

Written from the standpoint of young male migrants in Dar es Salaam, the novellas present a crime counternarrative of the city. While the dominant political discourse of Ujamaa valorized the rural peasant and attributed societal problems to the criminality of urban migrant youth, the pulp-fiction novellas shifted blame elsewhere. Like the "angry young man" of British new-wave literature and Indian cinema of the 1970s and the Mexican detective fiction of the post-1960s La Onda movement in Mexico City, the male protagonists created by the briefcase publishers were lower middle class and working class, and they valorized their experiences of injustice and frustration as a lens into the broader evils facing urban society.[4] The young male protagonists sometimes engaged in immoral activities, but they did so in the pursuit of a greater moral good.

In addition to offering windows into the perspectives of a network of writers, pulp-fiction novellas are also artifacts of urban life. The briefcase publishers were simultaneously a literary movement and a social and economic network created by newly arrived young men in a rapidly changing city. Both in form and content, the novellas reveal the processes by which newly arrived migrants invested in forms of urban masculinity characterized neither by the expectation of regularized wage labor and reliable state infrastructure nor by forms of prestige and security that were possible in the rural areas of their birth, but instead by the improvised construction of networks, credentials, and reputations. To be a briefcase publisher was to be a maker of stories, but that was only one of the skills involved. To be a known and successful briefcase publisher required the ability to produce a social network, prestige, and recognition and to be materially involved in the city and its informal-sector economy. The production process was not beside the point, nor something to be hidden to let the individual artistic voice come through unadulterated: instead, it was central to the artistry and mode of communication and something to be displayed and embedded in the text. For these authors, to write and publish stories about Dar es Salaam was not to stand back and comment on urban life: it was to *make* urban life itself.

Fiction as "Development"

The underground pulp-fiction industry departed in many ways from Tanzania's socialist cultural mission. Its portrayals of the city and its glamorous inhabitants certainly departed from official perspectives on, and diagnoses of, the ills of urban life. Moreover, they embodied a different relationship between author and audience: while TANU texts sought a pedagogical relationship with the reader, in which the knowledgeable author would educate and enlighten the ignorant reader, the authors of the briefcase novellas were more like tricksters, who sought to surprise, impress, and titillate.

Yet at the same time, the briefcase publishers were able to flourish in part because of socialist educational and literacy programs. As we have seen in chapter 1, mass literacy was one of the most celebrated accomplishments of the Ujamaa era. More than just a skill for the economic development of the public, literacy was linked with the creation of modern national citizens. For Nyerere, literacy was central to national goals. In a 1965 speech given at the opening of the Printing Works and Books Warehouse in Arusha, Nyerere said:

> Too often in our society, a person who sits down to read is accused of being lazy or being unsociable. This attitude we must change. When we

get to the position where a man and his wife sit together in the evening, each reading or reading to each other, and when children are encouraged to learn out of school by reading books which are easily available, then we shall have made a big break-through in our development.[5]

Yet the literate Tanzanians conjured in Nyerere's speech did not resemble the average urban Tanzanians of 1965. The readers in his vision lived as a two-parent nuclear family in a self-contained home that was quiet and free of distractions; yet in Tanzania, the self-contained nuclear-family home was the exception rather than the rule and was typically confined to the Christian middle class. The family Nyerere envisions presumably worked and went to school during the day and had free leisure time in the evenings, which they would spend on self-improvement through reading; yet much of the informal-sector labor engaged in by the urban population did not fit into the industrial work-day rhythm he describes. According to Walter Bgoya, who became the director of the Tanzanian Publishing House (TPH) in 1972, only 3.9 percent of the population used electricity in their homes; and with the oil crisis, fewer people could afford to spend their income on lighting with paraffin lamps. Most urban homes were not places that were conducive to the kind of literate spectacles that Nyerere put forth as a symbol of modernity.[6]

Nyerere also envisioned a publishing infrastructure that would provide books for this domestic scene, yet at the time of his speech, all paper used for printing books had to be imported from abroad at great expense to Tanzanian publishers. The only paper that was produced in the country was of a lower quality, used for industrial purposes such as the production of paper sacks and cardboard boxes. Books in English or produced by foreign companies were far too expensive for most Tanzanians to purchase.[7] The vision of a literate population was also a view of a society that was economically and infrastructurally self-sufficient. This image of literacy captured hopes not only for the cultivation of the individual habits of modernity, but also aspirations toward collective economic advancement.

The history of the novel and fiction writing in East Africa is linked with histories of modernizing ambitions of the colonial state, missionary communities, and nationalist intellectuals, who, in the post–WWII years, saw literacy and fiction reading in particular as a form of modernity, civic virtue, and development for Africans.[8] Tanzanian writers had read fiction in English in school, and in the 1950s, Tanzanians began writing novelistic fiction in Swahili, in newspaper serials published by the colonial Ministry of Information. The East African Literature Bureau (EALB), which disseminated books throughout East Africa from its base in Nairobi, was founded in 1948 as part of this broader colonial mission to promote literacy and modernization among urban Africans through affordable books published in English and in a number of African languages. The EALB not only published books reflecting "modern" themes such as hygiene, frugality, companionate marriage, and education, but also recognized tradition as a fundamental part of African modernity and so published a number of "tribal histories" intended to inculcate a sense of national identity and history.[9] The target audience of these texts was the upwardly mobile educated middle-class African, who might have a stake in the late colonial status quo. The idea was to create an African variant on universal modern themes and genres. The EALB had a branch in Dar es Salaam that endured throughout the 1970s until the collapse of the East African Community in the mid-1970s. The first generation of Tanzanian crime thrillers, including those written by Edi Ganzel, Jumaa Mkabarah, and Elvis Musiba, were published there in the early 1970s.

Nyerere built on these late-colonial institutional foundations, but directed literacy toward the ends of political liberation and African socialism through what he called an Adult Education Revolution, spearheaded in 1972.[10] In cities and towns across the country, new libraries were opened and older colonial era ones revamped and stocked with school textbooks, TANU publications, and English language novels. In addition to promoting childhood literacy through a growing public school system, TANU used its community centers as bases from which to launch a campaign of adult literacy, often deploying young people from the TANU Youth League to travel to the countryside and teach literacy at adult-education centers. TANU produced books and pamphlets on a range of development-themed topics, including guides on how to produce a household budget, self-help books on how to care for infant children, and "tribal histories." They were published in language intended to be accessible to beginning and intermediate readers of Kiswahili. Tanzania in the late 1960s and early 1970s was one of the world's poorest nations, yet state officials reported that they had raised the national literacy rate from a mere 10 percent at independence in 1961 to 61 percent in 1974.[11]

The Tanzania Publishing House (TPH), which was one of the central institutions of the adult-education revolution, was originally founded in 1966 when the British publishing company Macmillan approached the Tanzanian state directly and negotiated a deal in which they would partner with the National Development Corporation to become the major publisher of Tanzania's educational and commercial print materials.[12] In the late 1960s and early 1970s, the Tanzanian Publishing House had a monopoly on publishing all of the materials for the Tanzanian Ministry of Education, as well as a large number of Kiswahili novellas. This collaboration between Macmillan and the Tanzania Publishing House collapsed with a scandal in 1972, when Macmillan was accused of overcharging the Tanzanian government for its services.[13] In response, the ministry pulled all of its publications and moved to self-publish all of its materials on its own printing presses. The loss of business was devastating to the Tanzania Publishing House, and soon afterward, Macmillan withdrew, and the company faced extreme financial difficulty. It was at this point that Walter Bgoya was made director.[14] Under his leadership, the TPH publications attained a new and invigorated social mission.

Bgoya's approach to publishing was shaped by his years as a student and activist. He spent the early 1960s as an exchange student at the University of Kansas, where he was involved in student activism against racial discrimination. When he returned to Tanzania in 1965, he joined the TANU Study Group: a reading group that met weekly to read about and discuss the political issues surrounding ongoing African anti-colonial liberation movements.[15] As we've seen in chapter 1, under the leadership of Walter Bgoya, the Tanzania Publishing House published the English-language scholarly works of internationally acclaimed socialist thinkers from the University of Dar es Salaam, including Issa Shivji and Walter Rodney. They also published Swahili translations of works by Frantz Fanon and Kwame Nkrumah, as well as biographies and memoirs of freedom fighters such as Murray Chiume, the Malawian political exile who had been a TANU organizer in the 1950s.[16] As head of the TPH, Bgoya maintained connections with African American activists, leading to a temporary collaboration with the African American publishing company Drum and Spear, who set up a shop temporarily in Dar es Salaam in the early 1970s.[17] Bgoya and his allies saw Swahili literature as a tool for raising political consciousness and fostering African cultural autonomy from Europe.

As part of the literacy campaign, the Tanzanian state, in conjunction with intellectuals from the University of Dar es Salaam, promoted the writing, publication, and dissemination of novels in Kiswahili. Cultural policymakers and university intellectuals saw literacy as an indispensable skill for a modern citizenry, and more importantly, they believed that the content of an emerging national literature would work to cultivate the habits and sensibilities of national citizenship in its Tanzanian readership. As the cornerstone of this effort, the Tanzanian Publishing House began publishing and disseminating Kiswahili novellas. They were typically published on cheap, thin paper, ran between sixty and 120 pages long, and, in contrast with imported books in English, were affordable to a significant segment of the urban population. They were sold throughout the city's many bookshops. The majority of these novellas told stories about urban migration, describing either the descent of the urban migrant into poverty, criminality, or prostitution or their redemption when they returned to rural areas to join an Ujamaa village.[18] Advocates of this literature labeled it "development fiction."

While TPH political publications under Bgoya explored questions of African liberation by looking outward toward a wider pan-African and socialist global community, the novellas looked inward, attempting to cultivate the habits of mind of African socialists. They published many of the primers used for teaching adult literacy, offering lessons about frugality and hard work. The books were marketed as a kind of moral education and improvement, and the back covers often published summaries describing the books in terms of the moral lesson being offered. For example, *Penzi la Dawa* (*Love Medicine*), a novella about a poor urban migrant woman who becomes jealous at the spectacle of her friends' wealth and subsequently becomes wealthy herself by seducing married men and swindling them out of their money, has the following description printed on the back: "*Penzi la Dawa* is a good story that shows the danger that can result from a man with a family going around town outside of his marriage. This writer shows examples of this kind of behavior and especially the bad family relationships in the home and the results that befall the wife and children."[19]

The descriptions on the backs of books privileged the moral lesson, or *mafundisho*, that the book imparts. This educational description of the fiction reflects the business strategy of many writers and publishers of the time, who aimed not to sell books directly to consumers, but rather to the educational officers who would then arrange to have that book assigned in schools and adult-education centers.[20] Like the primers produced through Kivukoni College and used to teach literacy, the TPH novellas were created largely for the state intermediaries—those who considered themselves "fighters of ignorance"—who would choose the books based on what they thought would help to enlighten and uplift the Tanzanian masses living in their districts.

Literacy, then, implied a particular kind of public that reproduced the expertise and authority of the state. The networks of education, of the publication of the books, the spectacles of reading in public, and the intended effect of the content of books on readers solidified an idea of citizenship that operated through the ruling-party hierarchy. This program of mass literacy and the publishing infrastructure to which it gave rise made possible unintended consequences, as well.

Given the narrowly defined mission of the Tanzania Publishing House, a number of Tanzania's fiction writers found a more conducive publishing environment and a larger publishing infrastructure in Nairobi. While Tanzanian publishing outlets were incorporated into the developmentalist model, Nairobi had several newspapers and publishing houses that published on matters of culture and urban life for the purpose of entertainment. Edi Ganzel and Jumaa Mkabarah, who went on to become among Tanzania's most popular crime-thriller writers, got their start publishing their stories as serialized fiction in the Nairobi newspaper *Taifa Weekly*.[21] In the early 1970s, many of these writers, whose work did not fit the vision of the Tanzanian Publishing House, sent their manuscripts outside Tanzania to companies based in Nairobi and imported them back to Tanzania to be sold to a Tanzanian audience.

Other writers published their work with the East African Literature Bureau (EALB), which was still in operation in the 1970s. The writer Jumaa Mkabarah was one of the editors of the Dar es Salaam branch. Mkabarah was born in 1946 and educated in the town of Muheza in the Tanga region, first in Arabic at an Islamic school and later in English and Swahili at a mission school, and had been publishing his stories in East African newspapers since his teenage years. When he finished his studies, he moved to Dar es Salaam to work in the Tanzania office of the EALB. As an editor, Mkabarah worked to recruit writers who would become some of Tanzania's most popular fiction writers, including Edi Ganzel and Elvis Musiba, who published their first novels with EALB, along with Maurice Sichalwe, or "Kashkash," who wrote the *Mitaani na Kashkash* series for the newspaper *Mwafrika*.[22] The first generation of writers who would become the briefcase publishers got their start in this commercial publishing sector, which was linked with the literary scene in Nairobi and the older modernizing vision of late colonial publishing.

Despite this auspicious start, by mid-decade, Tanzania's publishing sector began to shrink drastically. International publishers such as Longman and Macmillan had initially come to Tanzania in hopes of making a profit as the producers of school textbooks and other texts for the new nation, but by the 1970s, these companies had closed down their local Dar es Salaam branches. Additionally, the prices of paper and ink rose. The collaborative relationship between Dar es Salaam popular-fiction writers and Nairobi publishing houses declined in 1976, with the collapse of the East African Community and the subsequent closing down of the flow of commodities and people across the border between Kenya and Tanzania.[23] When Tanzanian writers lost their access to the Nairobi publishing scene, Tanzania's development-fiction apparatus held a monopoly on publishing. It was in these conditions that young writers started their own alternative publishing industry.

The Briefcase Publishers: Reputation and Male Friendship in the Making of an Industry

Like the famous Onitsha Market Literature of Nigeria several decades earlier, the briefcase publishers arose in a context of rapid rural–urban migration and rising literacy rates, and their publications focused on themes of urban modern life.[24] The years following the collapse of the East African Community saw an explosion of small independent publishing companies in Dar es Salaam. More notable among them were John Simbamwene's Jomssi Publications, Hammie Rajab's Busara Publications, Edi Ganzel's Tamasha Publications, Jumaa Mkabarah's Utamaduni Publications, and Kajubi Mukajanga's Grand Arts Promotion. These companies started out as small-scale operations, run out of the homes of individuals, families, or groups of friends, or out of stationery shops whose main business was in office supplies. Most of these endeavors were short-lived, with a few friends getting together to produce a novella or two and then close, yet others, such as the Press and Publicity Center, Jomssi Publications, and Grand Arts Promotion, endured for decades as publishing institutions in Dar es Salaam's literary landscape. Based on his study on publishing and literacy in Tanzania, University of Dar es Salaam sociology professor C. S. L. Chachage reported that, by 1978, there were at least eighty small-scale independent publishers operating in Dar es Salaam.[25] The publishers sought to keep overhead costs low, and so rather than selling out of Dar es Salaam's many bookstores and sharing a cut of the profits with the owners, the writers more often sold their wares directly to consumers.

Young writers peddled their books out of briefcases on the streets and in marketplaces and through networks of newsstands and informal book-stalls, earning them the nickname "briefcase publishers."

If the characteristics that made writers successful in this industry were literacy and education, an urban and cosmopolitan standpoint, and entre-preneurialism, the briefcase publishers should have counted numerous women among their ranks. Literacy and education rates in Tanzania were raised dramatically in the 1960s through the 1980s, for both women and men. Women wrote and published in other genres, as we've seen in earlier chapters, whether in the mode of a Christian advisor, or a journalist em-ployed by the state or party newspapers, or in the developmentalist mode of an educator. Many of the most prominent writers in the development-fiction genre, published by the Tanzania Publishing House, were women, as were many of the most celebrated writers in residence as faculty at the University of Dar es Salaam. In their novellas, short stories, and plays, ed-ucated elite women such as Penina Muhando, Martha Mvungi, and Zainab Mwanga wrote eloquently on the themes of women's emancipation, gen-der violence, and economic vulnerability. Moreover, from the late 1960s onward, women migrated to Dar es Salaam at higher rates than men, reversing the gendered dynamic of the colonial years. Finally, while most salaried government jobs were reserved for men, women were the central players in many informal-sector industries in Dar es Salaam.

Yet the briefcase publishers were men, and not women. What made briefcase publishing an industry of, and *riwaya pendwa* (popular novels) the genre of, young male urban migrants?

At the start of their publishing careers, the briefcase publishers were recent school-leavers in their late teens to mid-twenties. Kajubi Muka-janga completed the romance and crime thriller *Tuanze Lini (When Shall We Begin?)* when he was eighteen years old, Charle Ndibalema's *Nimeponzeka (I Was Sacrificed)* was published when he was seventeen, and John Sim-bamwene's *Mwisho wa Mapenzi (The End of Love)* when he was twenty-two. Edi Ganzel was publishing serial detective fiction in newspapers in Nairobi by the age of twenty-one and published his first novella, *Ndoto ya Mwendawazimu (The Dream of a Crazy Person)*, when he was twenty-five.[26] In the early 1970s, the major pulp-fiction novella writers were John Simbamwene, Edi Ganzel, Jumaa Mkabarah, Hammie Rajab, and Elvis Musiba, and by the end of the 1970s, a new generation of writers includ-ing Kajubi Mukajanga, Ben Mtobwa, Jackson Kalindimya, and Agoro

Anduru joined their ranks. These writers were all born between 1946 and 1949, with the exception of Hammie Rajab, the oldest of them, who was born in 1940 and acted as a patron to the younger writers, and Kajubi Mukajanga, the youngest, who was born in 1957.

The earlier generation of briefcase publishers had been educated in the colonial education system, were secondary students at the time of Tanzania's political independence, and were young educated men of around twenty years old at around the time of the Arusha Declaration. The later generation had been students in the early years of African socialism, and their education had been infused with the optimism and critical engagement that characterized the movement of pan-African socialism. Hammie Rajab and Kajubi Mukajanga, the oldest and youngest of the briefcase publishers respectively, had a notoriously close friendship, spending most of their time together. Their friendship and collaborations acted as one of the connecting threads between these two distinct generations of writers.

The briefcase publishers shared in common the experience of urban migration in the era of Ujamaa villagization. Though born and educated outside of Dar es Salaam, all would go on to live and write about life in Dar es Salaam. As outsiders in the city, none of them could boast connections to the older forms of urban authority such as religious authority or real estate or through deep-rooted social networks. These writers had secondary education, and many of them had been accomplished as students, but none had been able to secure admission to the prestigious University of Dar es Salaam. Instead, most of this cohort of men had pursued further vocational training and worked as civil servants during the early 1970s. Of the briefcase publishers, Hammie Rajab had perhaps the most varied job experience prior to becoming a writer and publisher. He studied in Mombasa to become a mechanic in 1960, and later, when he returned, he worked as a mechanic for the railway and eventually became railyard foreman. He got his start writing articles for the cooperative railway magazine *Sikio*.[27] After leaving a career as a mechanic, Hammie Rajab had a brief stint working for the Tanzanian Film Corporation, writing didactic scripts for the government film company, before moving from Morogoro to Dar es Salaam, into the Kariakoo neighborhood, in 1974. Jumaa Mkabarah, as we've seen, became an editor with the East African Literature Bureau after leaving his studies. John Simbamwene worked for the national library service and was twenty-two when his first novel came out. Elvis Musiba, who studied accounting in Nairobi, went on to work in the office of the TAZARA railroad. Mukajanga worked for the state-owned Tanzanian Airlines, a job he eventually left to pursue writing and publishing full-time. Though endowed with education, employment, and high expectations, their experience of urban life was one of frustrated ambitions. They were part of the urban working class that watched the value of their salaries decline by 83 percent over the final years of Ujamaa. They were part of a larger group that left government jobs en masse during those years.

Far from the hilly suburbs of the University of Dar es Salaam, where professors discussed classical Swahili poetry, theorized the role of literature in socialism and development, and sought to standardize the Swahili language, Dar es Salaam's new men of letters met in each other's rented rooms during the day to read each other's manuscripts and work out plot lines until evening, when they would head over to the bars and beer-brewer stalls to continue the conversations into the night. Hammie Rajab's apartment in Kariakoo became one of the central nodes in the social network. They would write their first drafts by hand in a notebook and then bring it to a secretary—typically a female acquaintance, who had highly coveted access to a typewriter through her office job—and that friend would type up the manuscript after hours at work. After receiving the typed manuscript, the author would show it to the other writers, mark up the typed manuscript, and then make another handwritten copy based on the changes. The secretary would make a final copy and would enlist an illustrator to design the cover artwork.

Most briefcase publishers were financed by a patron who would give loans to the writer to publish the book and then take a cut of the profits.[28] Some patrons would take on several young writers, and in the absence of legal agreements, there was often an undercurrent of suspicion in these dealings. When it came time to print the books, the briefcase publishers had two options. The first option was to take their manuscripts to one of Dar es Salaam's few small privately owned printing presses, whose main trade was in producing stationery or Islamic texts. One of the most prominent of these Asian-owned Islamic print shops was the Nayani Bookstall, located on the corner of Mkunguni and Nyamwezi streets in Kariakoo, which financed the emergence of several well-known briefcase publishers, including Hammie Rajab and Kajubi Mukajanga.[29] One of the fears of briefcase publishers was piracy, as they often only had one handwritten or typed manuscript at any given point in the process and no enforceable legal agreement securing their right to their material. It was in their interest to get a product to market quickly before pirated copies became available and outran their own supply, and so speed and efficiency were often privileged over quality in terms of editing. When working with the small printing shops that sometimes financed these endeavors and sometimes simply printed their manuscripts, the briefcase publishers feared getting swindled. For example, as several writers explained, they feared that after putting in an order with the printer for 3,000 copies of the book, the shop owner would then print an extra 1,000 to sell on his own, without the knowledge of the author.[30] This led many of the writers to produce their own, albeit unenforceable, copyright stamps in their books, forbidding readers from making copies without the permission of the author. Many of the briefcase publishers sought to dispense with these small print shops altogether and publish their own books through other means.

The second option available to the briefcase publishers was to take their manuscripts to one of the parastatal cooperative printing presses. To go through the parastatal printing presses—either Printpak or KIUTA—entailed a different kind of risk than working with the small private print shops. Due to chronic shortages of materials, especially paper, and internal inconsistencies in the running of the factories, the official turnover time for even a small print job would typically range from eighteen months to four years.[31] In addition to the immediate financial strains this put on the publishers, by the time a manuscript was printed, the initial buzz about a new novella would have likely died down, and its cultural references to films and celebrities might be out of date. For this option to work well, the briefcase publisher needed a connection inside the print factory that could, for a fee, push his manuscript to the front of the queue.

In either scenario, the final product was typically between 75 and 150 pages long, printed on thin paper folded in half and held together with staples at the seam.[32] Briefcase novellas typically had an initial print run of between three thousand and ten thousand copies, and the books by the more popular authors would typically sell out in less than a month.

The briefcase publishers distributed copies to newspaper stalls and street-corner book vendors around the city, often spending time at the bookstalls, chatting about their books with potential buyers in an attempt to sell more copies. They would negotiate arrangements with drivers and send gunnysacks filled with copies of their novellas on lorries and buses headed upcountry to be sold by vendors in other markets, hoping that based on the strength of their relationships, either the unsold books or the money paid for them would find their way back to them in the city a few weeks or months later. Often, the writers themselves would circulate through the city selling their own books directly to customers. Once purchased, the books would continue to circulate among readers. M. M. Mulokozi, a professor at the University of Dar es Salaam who conducted research on reading and publishing in Dar es Salaam while he worked for the Tanzania Publishing House in the second half of the 1970s, cited the popularity of these novellas among young male school-leavers in the city. He explains that copies of books would be traded among friends in the neighborhood, circulating until the copy, printed with low-quality thin materials to begin with, was worn down.[33] The writer Mukajanga adds that he believes that a large percentage of his readership were women, and especially young housewives, who would approach him on the street and comment on his book, either to praise or chastise him or to advise him on what to write in his next novella. "One book would be read," he explained, "by several people in the household, and also on the street. Especially books bought by women. They would pass it from one person to another, one person to another, one person to another . . . so the book would be read by anywhere between four, five to ten people before it was completely run down. So very few homes you would go to and find that kind of shelves, you know, bookshelves; no, you would find a copy of *Mpenzi* in the kitchen."[34]

As briefcase publishing replaced the larger publishing houses that had their roots in late colonial developmentalism, the task of writing novellas went from being perceived as a middle-class profession to being something more improvisational: part of a more diverse repertoire of skills and cultural capital. This change marked a generational shift between the earliest generation of pulp-fiction writers, who had come of age in the late 1960s and who had become invested in the idea of a literary scene that would produce a modern East African literary canon, and a later generation, for whom publishing fiction was part of a broader urbanism. Jumaa Mkabarah was part of the earlier generation of writers and was a patron to younger writers, connecting them with publishing opportunities in Dar es Salaam.

In 2013, as we sat in chairs in the shade in his hometown of Muheza, he spoke of his days writing for the East African Literature Bureau, remarking that in those days, he could expect royalties and a modest advance for his work. He estimated that he would earn around 3,000 Tanzanian shillings for the initial print run of a novella in 1973. To demonstrate what this meant in material terms, Mkabarah explained, "A *bati* (a single corrugated iron sheet) was 800 shillings."[35] That Mkabarah would remember and communicate the value of his past earnings through the measure

Figure 4.4 The writer Jumaa Mkabarah near his home in Muheza in 2013. Photograph by author.

of urban real estate and specifically bati is telling, for, as we saw in the opening image of chapter 1, a house with a bati roof was one of the most prominent symbols of the modernizing aspirations of urban Africans in Tanzania's era of decolonization.

While writing was, for some select members of Mkabarah's generation, a middle-class profession that could literally put a roof over one's head and allow entrance into a particular kind of urban respectability, to be a briefcase publisher was not a profitable endeavor, nor did the young men who created this trade expect it to be. This was not a literary movement of middle-class breadwinners, but of mostly single urban male renters and squatters. These writers were usually broke, barely breaking even for all of their efforts. The payoff was in gaining a reputation, or "*jina fulani*"—a name.[36] "We were basically hustlers," said Kajubi Mukajanga. "But everyone knew us, and that was good."[37]

For this new generation of writers, reputation was the most important kind of currency. The creation and valorization of urban reputations differed from notions of authority and prestige in the East African rural communities from whence Dar es Salaam's urban migrants came, where the right to "be heard" at public gatherings was acquired by becoming a categorical adult with property and resources to disperse to junior and female dependents. At the same time, it also differed from state developmentalist ideas about authority, in which ruling-party designations of expertise and authority were what bestowed the right to speak for the greater good, in public. Whereas the novellas of the Tanzania Publishing House advertised on the back covers in the developmentalist mode with lessons about how the story would improve the morality and knowledge of the reader, the novellas published by Rajab, Mkabarah, Mukajanga, and Ganzel had on their back covers boasts about the skill and social network of the storyteller. For example, the back cover of Edi Ganzel's novella *Kitanzi* contains the following text: "Hammie Rajab was reading it on a plane, and got so caught up that he flew to Kigali instead of his intended destination at Msamvu! He'll never make fun of Ganzel again! Geranija was reading it on the daladala and forgot to get off, and as a result, was charged a higher fare. Jumaa Mkabarah started to read the book while shaving, and forgot to finish shaving the second half of his beard. Now he is walking around with half a beard!"[38]

The briefcase novellas were commodities, marketed directly to consumers rather than to educational officers, and they wooed the reader with the promise of escape and pleasure rather than seeking to improve the reader. The texts were supposed to be escapist to the point where a reader should be able to be on a bus and forget her surroundings. At the same time, the texts on the back covers of books convey the attempt of the writer to build a reputation through the praises of other notable young men. In addition to displaying the praise of other writers on the back covers, the briefcase publishers dedicated their books to their friends who were writers and staged cameo appearances of both fictional characters from other books and sometimes the authors themselves in the novellas. They were marketed as products of a particular urban milieu.

The briefcase novellas were both about, and productive of, male friendship. Consider, for example, a passage from Ben Mtobwa's *Dar es Salaam Usiku*, or *Dar es Salaam by Night*, conveying the perspective of a female character, Rukia, who is out at a nightclub. Published in 1990, after the heyday of briefcase novellas had passed and shortly before Mtobwa's death,

Figure 4.5 Hammie Rajab, posing on the cover of his 1982 novella *Ama Zao, Ama Zangu*. Rajab self-published this novella with his company, Busara Publications.

Figure 4.6 The back cover of Hammie Rajab's novella *Ama Zao, Ama Zangu*, which includes a summary of the book, images of the author posing, and words of praise from Edi Ganzel and K. R. Wibbo.

a stray paragraph in the novella expressed affection and nostalgia for the social networks of writers in the city:

> The table was now occupied by five men. One of them, Rukia recognized. Wasn't that Sam Kitogo? Yes, isn't that the stout young man, the writer of books? And that one, isn't that Hammie Rajab? Rukia had never met him, but she didn't need to be told. His face was recognizable from his books and magazines. Without a doubt, that must be Kajubi Mukajanga, because he and Hammie never left each other's sides. Those others . . . that one maybe Nicco ya Mbajo . . . and that one could be John Rutayisingwa. Rukia saw the barmaid approach them to take their order. Kitogo said something that made the barmaid laugh. Hammie said something that made her giggle. Now, she was stroking Kitogo's beard. And when she left to go fetch their beers, her gait was different. She tossed and swayed her ass. The writers laughed and toasted their glasses.[39]

Years later, writers describe, with great affection, their coconspirators in their attempts to publish their stories. As the previous passage implies, the intense and close friendship between Kajubi Mukajanga and Hammie Rajab, despite their age difference of around twenty years, was well known even beyond their immediate social circles. The friendship between Hammie Rajab and his childhood friend Edi Ganzel was also well known. The two published a book together in the form of an epic poem about the defeat of Idi Amin, called *Kipigo cha Fashisti Iddi Amin Dudu*.[40] Friends and relatives recall that when Ganzel's excessive drinking led him to financial difficulty, Hammie often helped him with loans and with publishing opportunities.[41] When asked how they became writers, briefcase publishers describe their education and their literary and cinematic influences, but place equal or more emphasis on the process of arriving in the city, seeking patronage, and becoming part of the social network of other briefcase publishers. Theirs was a social and economic role as much as it was an artistic one. The writers often thanked their financial patrons in the acknowledgments to their books.

As an urban archive, the books themselves are artifacts of male sociability, conveying not only the story within them, but also the social networks and mobility required to produce that story. The success of a briefcase publisher emerged out of an interdependent relationship between urban knowledge, reputation, and mobility. The book was not merely the end goal or product, but was also an object or amplifier that fed into a social process that would continue. The book concretized reputation and urban knowledge, displayed one's networks, and moved though the city in much the same way as its authors and fictional characters did.

This relationship between reputation, social networks, and mobility was gendered, as the characteristics that created positive recognition for young men had different connotations and consequences for women. As the previous passage suggests, writers made their networks visible in public spaces, such as nightclubs and bars and street corners, or in the homes of young men. While the mobility of men—both physical and social—was celebrated as a sign of Afro-modernity and collective progress, for women, such ease of movement was widely interpreted as a broader sign of social decline, promiscuity, and the negative effects of westernization.[42] The ability of the briefcase publishers to produce and "move" a novella and the heroism of the protagonists of the novellas themselves were based on an ability to move through urban space and to be seen and known. By contrast, narratives of female mobility and visibility, produced by men and women writers alike across different genres, were markedly different. For example, Martha Mvungi's powerful short story published by the University of Dar es Salaam literary magazine *Darlite* describes a girl of little means who leaves school in rural Njombe to follow a lover to Dar es Salaam. Once there, her lover abandons her in the city with no money or social connections. The story describes her desperate struggle to get back home again, with only a few shillings in her possession. The protagonist must rely on the driver of an oil truck making a delivery from the port to Zambia on the Tanzam highway. The author conveys her protagonist's terror at what she is agreeing to when she gets on the truck, noting his larger physical stature and insisting that he only drive her as far as her money is worth so that she does not owe anything.[43] Stories about hijacking planes, detectives moving throughout the city to investigate crimes, men moving on foot and on motorcycles around the nightclubs of the city resonated with a particular and embellished fantasy that valorized male mobility. By contrast, whether sympathetic to the women as victims or critical of them as vamps, portrayals of female mobility in the city connoted dependence, vulnerability, and sexual danger.

For young aspirant men, having mobility, reputation, and urban knowledge fed into something socially productive and produced something of value. This was not the case for women, who expressed themselves and sought status and recognition in genres other than urban pulp fiction.

The novellas, as artifacts and tools of the production of reputation, reveal how a new generation of young migrant men invested in an urban identity and new forms of authority that were distinct from the kinds of prestige that their fathers and grandfathers would have sought in their rural homes and from the kinds of prestige earlier generations of migrants to the city in post–World War II years of state building attained through stable wage labor. It was not just the content of the novellas, but these new kinds of public authority, cultural capital, and urban masculinity that elite observers like Kezilahabi, quoted in the opening of this chapter, found potentially threatening.

Inside the Novellas: Lovers and Fighters in the Socialist City

Just as the briefcase publishers sought recognition and adulthood and status, so too did the protagonists of their novellas. The briefcase publishers placed urban aspirant male youth at the center of their dramas, sometimes as proxies in pursuit of political and economic liberation.

The writers were self-consciously anti-imperialist. They borrowed popular-culture stereotypes of male heroes and recast them in dramas of African liberation.[44] Perhaps the most well known example of this is the spy Willy Gamba, the hero of Elvis Musiba's serial novels. Willy Gamba is a twenty-four-year-old Tanzanian man and a major player in the nightclub scene at Dar es Salaam. He is loved by women and admired and envied by all for his impeccable style, and when he is called to duty, he works protecting Africa from its enemies, fighting on the side of freedom fighters from FRELIMO against Portuguese spies, helping to find assassins responsible for the deaths of South African freedom fighters, or protecting Tanzania's natural resources from nefarious foreign diamond smugglers.[45] Similarly, Joram Kiango, the dapper hero of Ben Mtobwa's series of novellas, spends his days undermining foreign plots against the Tanzanian government. Often, these political loyalties were expressed in a less overt way, such as when Sipekta Beneza of Jumaa Mkabarah's *Marehemu Susanna* (*Dearly Departed Susanna*) comments to his partner how much better life is in Dar es Salaam since the departure of colonialists.[46] Mukajanga's controversial novella *Mpenzi*, a highly critical piece about the Tanzanian military police, begins with epigraphs quoting both Mao Zedong and Agostinho Neto, the first president of Mozambique, positioning him within an international politics of socialism and anti-imperial struggle.[47]

Though fully aligned with a mainstream anti-imperial political perspective and despite borrowing heavily from international popular cultures, the politics of the briefcase publishers were Dar es Salaam–centric. They shared with development fiction the imperative of male heterosexual virility as a pillar of nationalism, but they also represented the demands and grievances of a new generation of young men. By the late 1970s, a generation of writers had been educated to aspire to the promises of a liberated Africa under the banner of African socialism. Students graduating from the best high schools were versed in the writings of African writers from around the continent, as well as African American writers, and in the ideas of Marx and Mao. They expected to enter a society in which their talents would be used, in which they would be able to earn a salary, support a family, and have a voice in society. By the mid-1970s, it was becoming increasingly clear that these expectations would not be met, or at least not easily or for most people. It was these frustrations about the challenges of attaining adulthood that were at the heart of this literary movement.

The plotlines of most briefcase novellas are driven by the modern aspirations of sympathetic young men. Much like the men who were doing the writing, the protagonists of pulp novellas are young urban migrants, typically between the ages of eighteen and twenty-five, with education, though typically not at the highest levels. Many of them appear to us in the novellas reading newspapers and books and writing letters. As modern men, they seek monogamous relationships and communicate their emotions and desires to their female lovers through handwritten love letters. They smoke cigarettes, go out dancing, and pay special attention to how they dress and to how their lovers dress, favoring cosmopolitan, yet respectable styles. They refer to themselves and their companions as *watu wa kisasa*, or "up-to-date people,"[48] a label that often refers to their aspirations more than to an attainable reality. It is this aspiration, and the challenges of attaining it, that drive the plot.

Physical mobility is also central to the novellas. Young men in the fiction move around the city on motorcycles or in cars—or else looking jealously at those cars, which they describe in precise language like, "He was driving a 1600 SSS."[49] The narrators piece together the stories by following the movements of cars that were seen circulating around Dar es Salaam, driven by powerful elites: Datsun 1600s, Peugeot 504s, Volvos, Land Rovers, and, of course, Mercedes Benzes. Much like the imagined social universes of connections of male migrants at the time, the characters also move between rural and urban areas around Tanzania, traveling on trains and buses and negotiating the demands of their rural relatives. In some cases, the protagonists move across national borders, participating in liberation struggles of other African nations or, in some cases, smuggling.[50] More often, though, it is the villains who fly on Boeing 747s, whether as secret agents of imperialist forces, hired assassins, or as diamond and gold smugglers. The novellas derive their momentum through the characters' search for love, prosperity, or justice, their mobility from village to city and back again, and their travels across national boundaries.

The material iconography of the novellas portrays Dar es Salaam as a site of promise, sexual dangers, and frustrated ambition. The Benzes of wealthy men and the motorcycles of heroes and villains move quickly and efficiently through the city, to the posh hotel lobbies and nightclubs of the city, while buses and public transit grind slowly through the city's disintegrating roads. Wealth often has a hidden meaning, as a meal of chicken and chips—the quintessential urban food consumed in public—signals the illicit relationship between a young woman and her older, wealthier male lover, while a woman's sitting room filled with furniture often signals the gifts of a man in exchange for sexual favors.

Briefcase publishers drew inspiration from a variety of international genres, including crime-thriller films and pulp-fiction paperbacks, particularly the detective novels of James Hadley Chase, Ian Fleming, and Peter Cheyney, which had been available in Tanzania in bookshops and libraries since the 1950s.[51] Moreover, the character development and relationships in the novellas covered similar moral and topical terrain as the South African *Drum* magazine's East Africa edition published in Nairobi and disseminated across East Africa, especially the relationship and advice columns, which displayed the plight of young lovers from throughout Anglophone Africa and their struggles over questions of how to be modern and African in matters of love and sex. Though banned in Tanzania in 1972, *Drum* remained clandestinely popular among young readers in Dar es Salaam.[52]

Even more influential than these publications, and more controversial in the eyes of critics, were films.[53] Musiba's Willy Gamba, for example, a spy and man of international mystery modeled in the style of James Bond, traveled around Africa on behalf of the government, fighting imperialist spies, diamond smugglers, and other enemies of Africa; using excessive violence when necessary; sleeping with beautiful women; and weaving his way between allies and double-agents.[54] Mkabarah and Anduru told stories about criminals and their victims using the format of courtroom drama. With the exception of Musiba's Willy Gamba series, the detectives tend not to be the main characters, but when they appear, they dust for fingerprints to catch the culprits, drive around in police cars, and keep elaborate files on criminals: aspects of police work that writers saw in films and not in Dar es Salaam precincts. Writers drew on scenes from so-called spaghetti western films, such as, for example, in Elvis Musiba's *Kufa na Kupona*, in which the thug who attacks the hero Willy Gamba is described as looking like "Cowboy Cuchillo," the bandit Cuchillo Sanchez from the 1960s films of Sergio Sollima. Ndibalema's novel includes car chases, gun shoot-outs, and a gang of villains dressed like cowboys,[55] while Ganzel's criminal gangsters ride motorcycles, hijack planes, and get into shoot-outs with the police. Later, many novels featured young protagonists who studied or were fans of the martial arts.[56] Kassam's and Mukajanga's novellas feature young hip male protagonists, who are kung fu experts and who are able to defeat wealthy villains, despite their poverty, using their physical and mental training.

Intellectuals from the university lamented the influence of foreign capitalist films on local audiences, with good reason.[57] Given the weakness of Tanzania's homegrown film industry, Hollywood films had the potential to dominate the market over Tanzania's fledgling state-produced industry. University intellectuals and conservative observers alike lamented the negative influence of Bollywood films on Tanzanian youth, who could be seen holding hands outside the movie theaters. Such behavior was seen both as indecent and frivolous. Yet at the same time, young people who drew inspiration from these genres did not simply produce local copies of these foreign genres, but reconfigured them in Dar es Salaam in a way that allowed them to break with developmentalist conventions of authenticity and state authority and used them to say new things about the city and the place of young migrant men within it.[58] While they did not have the resources to make films that could compete with Hollywood and Bollywood, they could produce fiction.

Crime thrillers proved a particularly compelling genre for briefcase publishers seeking to stage their stories in Dar es Salaam. In crime thrillers, a genre spread throughout the globe through Hollywood film and print paperback novels, the audience witnesses the crime from the perspective of the criminal. Crime thrillers, according to Martin Rubin, resemble adventure stories and films in that the events are shocking and out of the ordinary; yet whereas in adventure stories, the effect of surprise and suspense is achieved through setting the story in exotic locations, the appeal of thrillers is that they occur in familiar, local settings in the city.[59] Whereas classic detective novels, in the style of Sir Arthur Conan Doyle, portray an otherwise bucolic world disturbed by a singular crime, crime thrillers and the related genre of noir fiction, by contrast, portray the city itself as a world in moral upheaval and disarray.[60] The source of the suspense is not the mystery of a crime that was committed in the past, but rather the question of what is going to happen to the criminals, the victims, and those charged with bringing the criminals to justice. The city itself is a site of suspense and uncertainty, and the mood is cynical.

As a city under assault from state disinvestment, economic decline, rapid unplanned growth, and widespread antiurban sentiment, Dar es Salaam of the 1970s provided a compelling new setting for the international genre of the crime novella and the urban decay and cynicism that were its trademarks. Through the interactions of detectives, criminals, victims, and urban youth, Swahili crime-thriller writers, including Edi Ganzel, Hammie Rajab, John Simbamwene, and Elvis Musiba, provided critical readings of the urban landscape, its moral meanings, and the causes of urban crime.

Rajab's *Ufunguo wa Bandia*, or *The Counterfeit Key*, tells the story of Sami Kiama, a twenty-five-year-old petty thief in Dar es Salaam, and his girlfriend, Atende. The couple has a young child together, but because Sami's father cannot help him to pay bridewealth to her family, they cannot marry. Meanwhile, Atende's father sees Sami as a hooligan and withholds his blessing. Sami gets a government job, but finds the pay too little and too infrequent, and he becomes a thief so he can support his lover and their daughter, both of whom he loves dearly. A tribute to their dire material circumstances, they name their daughter Sina, or "I do not have."

At the outset of the novella, Sami is only a small-time crook, stealing here and there and then disappearing into the crowded streets of Kariakoo before the police can catch him. His life takes a turn when Boni, an infamous criminal who has served jail time, invites Sami to participate in a larger burglary of the Ismaili Jamat Khana mosque: a highly visible Dar es Salaam landmark. The name *Boni* evokes the slang "boni town," or "born in town," referring to a lifelong urban-dweller with deep knowledge of the city and a cynical ability to prosper, by hook or by crook. At first, Sami hesitates at the offer, knowing that this task would involve much more risk and potential violence than the petty crimes in which he was so skilled. Yet he also sees the possibility of a better life. He tells Atende: after this robbery, we will finally be able to get married. Atende is thrilled at the idea of finally attaining this marker of respectability and supports him.

All of this personal detail is conveyed near the beginning of the novella. The majority of the pages are spent elaborating Sami's movements through town in the planning of the robbery, scoping out the scene of the crime, hiring a tailor to make phony police uniforms, bribing the security guard at the mosque into giving him the key so that he can make a copy, committing the robbery with his three co-conspirators, and murdering a witness before finally getting caught by Inspekta Sindi: the detective that makes an appearance in many of Rajab's crime novellas. Like the other novellas, we see the crime unfolding from the perspective of the criminal, and we learn that Sami experiences economic pressures familiar to most young migrants in Dar es Salaam. The sense of suspense comes not from solving a mystery, but rather from knowing and empathizing with Sami, the criminal, and wondering if he will cope with the challenges posed by life in the city. Sami is caught in the end and charged with burglary and with the killing of the security guard. As he is being taken to jail, he thinks despairingly of Atende and Sina, his would-be family, left to fend for themselves in an unforgiving city.[61]

Collectively, the briefcase publishers as a literary movement presented the city through the eyes of a male protagonist, the way it would have been encountered by a young male newcomer, seeking to create social and economic bonds with other migrants while away from one's closest kin networks. For example, John Simbamwene's 1971 novel *Mwisho wa Mapenzi*, or *The End of Love*, tells the story of Patrick, a young urban migrant to Dar es Salaam who becomes a murderer in the course of his struggle to attain urban belonging, love, and marriage. Though he has managed to secure a government job, he is an outsider in the city and struggles to make connections that will allow him access to housing and to women. Patrick laments that, as a newcomer, he is lost in the city. After becoming discouraged when his boyhood lover is married off to an older, wealthier man of her parents' choosing, and after suffering at the hands of conniving and clever coastal Swahili women, including the philandering wife of his landlord and another neighbor named Hadija, he finally meets Rosey—a self-proclaimed "modern girl" who likes to be up-to-date and who shares his aspirations to modern migrant respectability. But his neighbor Hadija, who is jealous of their love, kills her. Patrick, in despair, stabs Hadija in a Dar es Salaam alley at night and escapes onto a ferry to Zanzibar just as he sees the detective, Inspekta Fog, arriving on the scene.

Patrick, like Sami Kiama, becomes a criminal not because of an inherent hooliganism, or because of unbridled lust for wealth or sex, or because of a character flaw reflected in his choice to leave the rural areas. To the contrary, Patrick is a hardworking student and a respectable government employee who seeks the modern and no longer supportable ideal of the male breadwinner. It is the struggle in the city and his frustrated desires for love and stability that lead him to murder.[62] The briefcase publishers recast urban problems of crime, poverty, unemployment, and promiscuity as obstacles to proper manhood rather than as problems caused by delinquent youth and their unruly desires.

The writers made their most overt political critiques through the romance genre. Romance stories offered more overt criticism of urban inequality, deploying, in the words of Cole and Thomas, "ideologies of love to elaborate generational and cultural distinctions and claim political inclusion."[63] By creating sympathetic portrayals of young lovers and of the obstacles put in their way by urban authority figures and rural parents, writers expressed ideologies of love within a more mainstream dichotomy of modernity and backwardness while appropriating aspects of Ujamaa ideology by posing romantic love as the opposite of capitalistic "greed." Through the urban romance, set amid the uneven urban landscape of Dar es Salaam, writers like Kajubi Mukajanga and Jumaa Mkabarah mounted a defense and celebration of the urban male youth migrants, expressed through stories of love. The male protagonists in the novellas believe in and are guided by romantic love. The heroes suffer for the sake of romantic love.[64] They give their lovers gifts, take them out on the town, and lose their jobs over them;[65] they betray their rural families and follow their lovers to the city;[66] they withstand abuse and torture from their romantic rivals.[67] For many young men writing novellas, romantic love not only marked the protagonists as modern and emotionally authentic, but also offered an ideological justification for youth claims on autonomy, opportunity, and urban space.

The novellas contrasted modern progressive urban "lovers" with conservative rural relatives. This theme of intergenerational tension spoke to the experiences of many urban youth in the Ujamaa era. Most urban-dwellers continued to have links to their rural families, and most urban squatters in Dar es Salaam claimed that they still had access to land in the rural areas where their relatives lived.[68] The potentially fraught nature of these relationships between young urban migrants and the rural communities they left behind was dramatized in late Ujamaa-era novellas, largely in the form of struggles over family, sexuality, and reproduction. In many of the novellas, the modern protagonists face pressure from controlling and "traditional" parents. For example, Jumaa Mkabarah's 1974 novella *Kizimbani*, or *On the Witness Stand*, tells the story of the young Rosa, who is found dead in her lover's bedroom. The lover, Joseph Gapa, is poor and comes from a family of little means, which is why Rosa's family rejects him as *mshenzi* or "uncivilized person," despite the fact that he is hardworking and virtuous. After Rosa's death is made public, Rosa's father viciously attacks Joseph with a machete, but in the end, we learn through a note left by Rosa that the young woman had committed suicide after learning that her father had forbidden her from marrying the man she loved. Joseph Gapa is proved innocent in court and is carried out of the courtroom on the shoulders of the crowd: a hero of love and youth. Meanwhile, the traditional father, motivated by materialism, pays the ultimate price for his backward thinking: the death of his child.[69]

Briefcase publishers and their predecessors helped to recast romantic love as a masculine and patriotic virtue, in contrast with the materialistic desires of female and Asian characters, who were often used as foils of the heroic young men in the novellas. At a time when austerity and discipline were heralded as central components of Tanzanian manhood, the desire for wealth was not acceptable in moral discourses of manhood.[70] The ideal man of Ujamaa narratives was supposed to welcome poverty, physical labor, and a life of austerity. While urban women were widely portrayed as motivated by a desire for wealth and the trappings of modernity, such characteristics were unacceptable for a sympathetic male protagonist. In Tanzanian literature of the 1960s and 1970s, female greed was a common theme that transcended genres, also appearing often in nationalistic patriotic texts, from the Arusha Declaration to the propaganda texts of TANU, which blame female desire for clothing and other luxuries as a drain on men and a cause of the poverty of their families. In this respect, the briefcase novellas reproduced mainstream gender ideologies.

The aspirations of young men are thwarted in the novellas, not only by infrastructure, but also by the greed and materialism of urban women. In a number of stories, it is the sight of a sitting room filled with nice furniture that tempts a young woman to give up a life of virtue and resort to prostitution so that she can attain the same luxuries herself. Indeed, often in the novellas, the sight of a woman's sitting room filled with nice furniture signals that she is a prostitute.[71] Wealthy bureaucrats take their girls from their poverty-stricken neighborhoods in Kisutu and Manzese to their luxurious mansions. The visible display of wealth is portrayed as a problem of youth masculinity in which young men must either go to extreme and often illegal lengths to please a demanding woman or be insulted and impoverished through exclusion, loneliness, and isolation. This was part of a much larger discourse about the city in which problems of sexual immorality and schoolgirl pregnancy were blamed on the materialistic desires of young women.[72] In pulp fiction, female characters, like other villains in the urban criminal underworld of Dar es Salaam, were foils used to frame the articulation of masculine heroes of the fictionalized city. In contrast with greedy women and corrupt older men, the young men in Swahili pulp fiction are moved primarily by love and the desire to support a family and to be an adult.[73] The desire for romantic love was associated with a respectable and even admirable desire for adulthood, while the desire for wealth is displaced onto the female lovers.

In recasting the city as a site of male romance, young writers intervened in some of the most intense debates of the Ujamaa-era city. The concerns of the main characters of the novellas paralleled public debates about the same issues: namely, debates about what kinds of adults and families would enjoy the benefits of modern citizenship. The briefcase publishers were producing them at a time when there was a great deal of controversy about marriage, sexuality, and childrearing in the press and on the floor of Parliament. Public intellectuals and politicians debated whether polygyny should remain legal, whether the government should regulate bridewealth payment, whether youth could marry without the permission of their parents, whether unwed mothers should be allowed maternity leave from their jobs, and whether female students should be allowed to continue their studies after becoming pregnant.[74] While one dominant strand of political discourse blamed urban ills on the lust and unruly material desires of urban youth, who were in need of moral reeducation, the thrust of these novellas was to shift the blame from male and female *wahuni*, or "hooligans," to the hardships imposed on youth by an older generation and a corrupt system. Many of the novellas, for example, feature young women killing themselves or resorting to adultery because their parents married them off to men for money and family arrangements instead of love.[75] In the novellas women could be conniving vamps, but they could also be tragic victims.

An aesthetic of heterosexual virility runs through the briefcase novella. The texts fixate on bodies, especially the erotic pairing of young, healthy, athletic bodies, as a way of creating a case for conjugal arrangements that privileged young sexually potent men, rather than their elders who had more resources to distribute. The novels describe young bodies that desire each other, but are kept apart by the injustices and inequalities of life in the city. The desirable female characters are described in physical detail, with emphasis on their small waists, round backsides, and ample breasts, smooth and healthy dark skin, and natural hair. Rejecting the skin-lightening creams and cosmetics that signaled the global valorization of whiteness, the desirable women of the novellas were coded as authentically African either through their sexual modesty and "traditional" appearance or through being black, proud, and cosmopolitan, wearing clothing that signaled their modern aspirations and their participation in a pan-urban cultural aesthetic. But most of the sensual bodily descriptions are reserved for the male protagonists in the stories. Their wiry, thin, and muscular athletic builds are described in detail and celebrated, as is their fashion sense. The male heroes take pride in their ability to cut an impressive figure, wearing leather shoes, bell-bottoms, and button-down shirts and vests in the city's spaces of leisure, where their physical endurance and dexterity are on display. The sexual potency and physical vitality of these young men is contrasted with the obesity and slowness of elder wealthy men who pursued younger women with their conspicuous wealth. The coming together of two young, athletic, desiring bodies, whose promise is of social reproduction, provides an erotic momentum to the briefcase-novella narratives.

Writers like Rajab, Mkabarah, and Ganzel wrote about the struggles of young men to start families and attain adulthood by dramatizing their conflicts with conniving women and "backward" elders; by the late 1970s, a young generation of writers expanded on this theme with the development of one of the most infamous archetypal villains in Kiswahili popular literature: the sugar daddy. The sugar daddy is an old or middle-aged man who uses his wealth to take advantage of young women, typically schoolgirls, for sex. They prey on young girls who are physically repulsed by them, but who are desperate for money, for rides in cars when public transit is unreliable, and for food when they are hungry. The sugar daddy was a symbol of decadent masculinity, wasted female sexuality and health, and the misuse of wealth and power. Physically, he is fat and balding and has little energy for youthful pursuits, like dancing. He spends time in the leisure areas of the city—restaurants, bars, and upscale dancehalls—and drives around town in an expensive car. In these novellas of urban crime and violence, the sugar daddy is often held up as a foil for urban youth.

The sugar daddy and urban male youth were created as physical opposites. In contrast with physically fit young men who play soccer or practice kung fu, who wear the latest fashions in secondhand clothes that accentuate their thin athletic bodies, and who comb their hair into fashionable Afros, sugar daddies are soft and overweight from eating luxury foods, like chicken and chips, and from moving around the city in expensive cars, rather than walking.[76] Young men look elegant through their cosmopolitan savvy and creativity; sugar daddies simply have money and can adorn themselves with illicit finery. Perhaps the most striking distinction drawn between sugar daddies and urban youth is that, while the young urban male protagonist is motivated by romantic love, the sugar daddy acts out of a wild and uncontrolled lust. In the novellas of this new generation of writers, the sugar daddy, rather than out-of-control youth sexuality, is the cause of the city's moral ills, such as unwanted pregnancies and botched illegal abortions, and is responsible for the ruin of the nation's youth. In this way, by deploying the sugar daddy, the briefcase publishers offered a crime counternarrative of the city of Dar es Salaam.

Shifting Masculinities and Frugal Cosmopolitanism

Taken together as an archive of urban life, the novellas—particularly those published in the late 1970s and early 1980s—elaborated an urban ethos of frugal and ad hoc urban cosmopolitanism. Such an ethos was both socialist—frugality was also a central value of Nyerere's theorization of Ujamaa—and subversive in that its heroes were young urban men: the very citizens who were the foil of Ujamaa notions of patriotism.

An earlier generation of writers who came of age in the 1960s had faith in law and in the government's ability to deliver collective prosperity. These writers included men like Edi Ganzel, Jumaa Mkabarah, and Elvis Musiba, who made their living publishing serial fiction in the newspapers and novellas for the East African Literature Bureau from the late 1960s throughout the 1970s. Take, for example, the opening lines of Edi Ganzel's novella *Faili Maalum*, or *The Special Files*: "My name is Onda. Stoni Simi Onda. S.S.O., if you like. I earned the rank of Major in the Army and in the Police after proving that I was gifted, and that I was not afraid to lose my life defending my country and its patriots. On the street, they call me 'shushuu.' I have a .38 pistol and authorization to use it against any 'pig,' of any race, anywhere, any time. If you are one of them, pray that you never meet me."[77]

For these earlier writers, respectable manhood could be attained within notions of citizenship and legality laid out through official state channels. By contrast, the writers who came to Dar es Salaam and got their start during the years of economic collapse of the late 1970s celebrated a different kind of masculinity. For example, Kassam's novel *Joto la Fedha* features Chikwanda: a young Dar es Salaam man who is hired to help rescue the kidnapped daughter of a wealthy Arab man. The villains of the story reflect Ujamaa-era stereotypes. The main character is a capitalist who wants to own urban property "in order to spit on those below him."[78] This caricature echoes those expressed in TANU's propagandistic *Unyonge wa Mwafrika* parables that played on the radio and circulated as pedagogical pamphlets. The novel, like others in the genre, also features diamond smugglers and other enemies of African sovereignty and socialism. Chikwanda is poor in material terms. He lives in a rented shabby room. Yet unlike the heroes of development fiction, he is deeply connected with the social networks of the city, gleaning information from detectives, prostitutes, businessmen, and service workers. He is a skilled practitioner of kung fu, and his discipline and skill allow him to defeat well-armed men with more resources than he.[79] Moreover, despite his material poverty, he leaves the house looking stunningly elegant, in fashionable clothes. "To see him so dressed," the narrative proclaims, "you would never believe he lives in such a shabby place in the Mchafukoge neighborhood."[80] Like other heroes of pulp-fiction novellas, he is able to pull off a good look, privileging his outward appearance and presentation of the self in public over accumulation in the home and private sphere. This too contrasts with development fiction, which saw urban consumerism as a waste of the nation's resources and instead focused on the home.[81] This theme—of elegance, style, and skill, in the face of scarcity—resonated with Ujamaa ideals of discipline and self-sufficiency, yet recast them in an urban context as a form of fashion bricolage.

No writer did more to place romance pop novellas as a form of political critique and as a manifesto of urban youth manhood than the writer Kajubi Mukajanga. His first, which he wrote in 1975, told the story of a young man who, in order to be with the woman he loved, had to fight against corrupt, wealthy, and older male criminals who had seduced his beloved with their wealth. In the end, his reward for defeating the corrupt and wealthy older men is marriage to the woman he loves.[82] Later in his career, Mukajanga became one of few writers who wrote novellas with female protagonists, typically depicting their abuse at the hands of older men. In another novel, *Kitanda cha Mauti*, or *Bed of Death*, a young woman plots and carries out the murder of an older wealthy man by luring him home with her before stabbing him in his sleep. We later learn her motivations: the man had impregnated her when she was a student, and years later, she tracked him down to kill him in revenge, before then poisoning herself and the child.[83]

His later, extremely controversial though less popular series of novels *Mpenzi* pushes his critique further, only this time, he takes on abuse within state institutions. The books portray the rape and sexual abuse of women by the military police while they are performing their national service. After the main character in *Mpenzi I*, Shangwe, is abused by a soldier, the author asks his readers the hypothetical question: is it any wonder that young women hate all men? This book, though different from the more fantastical pulp-fiction crime and romance novels of his peers, builds on a central underlying theme of the Dar es Salaam pulp-fiction literary movement: young men who seek love and status and feel that they are prevented from finding it because of the sins of older generations. Young men are unfairly vilified because they are put into the same category as exploitative older men.

The sugar daddies and other exploiters are always distinct from the young aspiring urban men that are the heroes. Mukajanga makes this explicit in his poem "Logic." He writes:

When I put on a big bugaloo / Dirty and literally made up of patches
And tight slim-fit shirts / That are torn and without buttons,
When I wear long hair / That is combed only when God is happy,
When I enter the cinema and dance halls / At night
By forging and jumping over the wall / It is all hooliganism.
But when you, An age mate of my father,
Delude my sister, Confusing her with your Datsun,
And hypnotizing her / By showing her bundles
Of one hundred shilling notes, And then using her
And making her pregnant / Then, like the coward you are,
Eluding her / So that you are clear
To hunt for others, / It is not hooliganism.
That is logic.[84]

In this poem, the city that Mukajanga imagines is not one of hooligan youth with no sense of obligation to their nation, but rather a site where greedy and immoral men act in ways that rob young men of their chances to become adults. In a world where there is no clear path to a prosperous and respectable future, men have to create and improvise their way.

Taking on the perceived greed, hypocrisy, and physical repulsiveness of sugar daddies, the conservatism and backward thinking of rural elders, and the materialistic greed of their female age-mates, young men made the case that, in a modern society, it was they who were best suited as sexual and romantic partners of young women. The writers transformed anxious public discussions about schoolgirl pregnancies from a focus on female suggestibility or male hooliganism to a debate about modern African manhood and the failures of an older generation to meet their obligations toward youth. The effect of these narratives was to argue that sexual and romantic relationships with young women were a prerogative of young urban manhood. It was a celebration of youthful black masculinity that was based, in part, on access to women's bodies.

Writers like Mukajanga and Kassam depicted urban masculinity through an aesthetic of frugal cosmopolitanism. This ethos shared many of the citizenship ideals of African socialism. They were frugal. They battled imperialist enemies of Africa. They were self-sufficient, and they sought elegance not through individual wealth, but through knowledge and skill. They articulated an urban socialist ethos and reframed the struggle of socialism from the perspective of the city.

Conclusion

From the late 1970s and the early 1980s, dozens of pulp-fiction novellas, published in the interstices of Dar es Salaam's economy, both circulated through the city and depicted the circulations of characters through the city. The pinnacle of this literary movement seemed to occur right at the moment of the most severe economic scarcity, in the early 1980s, following the war with Idi Amin's Uganda. Pulp-fiction novellas continued to appear on newsstands and in markets across the city during the final years of socialism. Some of the censorship measures that had been set into motion in earlier years were scaled back in the final years of socialism, and many of the briefcase publishers sought to branch out into other ventures, including the publication of several newspapers and cultural magazines. Mukajanga started publishing *Wakati ni Huu*, Hammie Rajab started pub-

lishing *Busara*, and Ben Mtobwa published *Heko*. These magazines focused on culture and the arts and were staffed by the same networks of
young men who had made up the briefcase publishing industry. These
magazines advertised new novellas published by the briefcase publishers,
as well as the booksellers and print shops that were part of their network.

The magazines, staffed by former briefcase publishers, became a
gateway for future public intellectuals and newsmakers. The famous Tanzanian political cartoonist Godfrey Mwampembwa, known as Gado, got
his start publishing political cartoons in Kajubi Mukajanga's *Wakati ni
Huu* when he was a teenager in Dar es Salaam before going on to become
one of the most well known syndicated political cartoonists in East Africa.
By the end of the 1980s, the briefcase publishing industry had largely disappeared. Hammie Rajab went from being Dar es Salaam's most prolific
pulp-fiction novelist to being a prolific screenwriter and director for television and film until he passed away in 2011. Mukajanga received a scholarship and attended university at the University of Toronto and upon his
return to Dar es Salaam became a journalist. He is currently the head of
the Tanzanian Media Council. Ben Mtobwa died in 2008; his collaborator,
Jackson Kalindimya, became a journalist and now writes for the newspaper *Nipashe*. Elvis Musiba became a prominent businessman involved
in a variety of entrepreneurial endeavors, while Jumaa Mkabarah and
Edi Ganzel—in particular, the older generation of writers—struggled to
scrape together a living after the opportunities in the briefcase publishing and its networks dried up. When I met him in 2013, Jumaa Mkabarah
was living in his birth village of Muheza, a small town in the foothills of
the Usambara Mountains, several hours northwest of the city of Dar es
Salaam.

The opening of Tanzania's markets under Ali Hassan Mwinyi allowed
for the importation of popular cultural forms, particularly television, that
had previously been banned. Paper and ink were imported. The state no
longer claimed control over print media, and independently owned tabloid newspapers and magazines proliferated. One might expect that these
events would lend themselves to a new era of thriving for the briefcase
publishing industry, yet the opposite appears to have been true.

The literary movement of the briefcase publishers was made possible
in the distinctive conditions of the socialist era, with all of its repressions
and possibilities. Television and popular entertainment magazines had
been banned, and though the intention of these restrictions was to
protect an official state version of national culture, these restrictions

simultaneously provided protectionism for a vibrant urban informal-sector entertainment industry. Additionally, Tanzania's highly successful literacy campaign helped create a nation of readers, thus producing an audience for pulp-fiction novellas. Literacy rates declined after the Adult Education Revolution ended, as did the broad embrace of fiction reading as a form of developmental virtue. The developmentalist mode of literacy sought to create a kind of reading public that was disciplined into socialist modes of citizenship and primed to receive education from state-appointed educators, yet practices of literacy and writing exceeded the boundaries of the state vision and created the conditions for a different kind of literary culture. Neither resistant nor compliant with the state's modernizing project, the briefcase publishers, the publics they created, and their literary imagination were an unintended product of Ujamaa's development vision.

The literary movement of the briefcase publishers confirms that rather than a rapid decisive shift from a state-controlled to a free-market system and the rise of an informal sector, Dar es Salaam's urban economy had been gradually becoming unmoored from state control throughout the 1970s as the state became increasingly unable to pay salaries that could reproduce an urban working class. City residents forged other economic possibilities alongside the state project of African socialism. At the same time, this forging of economic communities was connected to the elaboration of new modes of identity, sociability, and public life for a generation of recent urban migrants. The rise of the briefcase publishers reveals experimentation with conceptions of authority and creativity in the city. Building off a late colonial and early postcolonial model of artistry that embraced a universalizing vision of African nationalist modernity—a model that was supported through colonial and donor-funded institutions and staffed by young men like Jumaa Mkabarah—by the end of the 1970s, to be an artist meant something different. Moving away from the individualistic ideal of the author whose creativity was conveyed through the texts they wrote, artistic talent and authority for the briefcase publishers were inseparable from the ability to chart a path in the city through urban networks and to use that ability as a point from which to constitute a public and a reputation.

Though fantastical and thrilling, there was a kind of cynicism and realism to the briefcase novellas in that both the novelists and the fictional protagonists they created, to attain validation and recognition, had to instigate movement of the self and of objects through a city that threw up obstacles to urban circulation and to these projects of male self-realization. The ways that the young lovers and fighters of Ujamaa-era pulp fiction sought to attain adulthood resembled the production process of the novellas themselves in that they required the deft negotiation of social networks and the mobilization of materials in times of economic constraint. As a literary movement, the briefcase publishers created an aesthetic, language, and ethos of urban manhood that valorized improvisation, integrity, and elegance in spite of intense scarcity, and against the odds.

CHAPTER 5

From Socialist to Street-Smart
A Changing Urban Lexicon

The relationship TANU had with the city of Dar es Salaam shifted dramatically over the course of Tanzania's socialist experiment. In the early days following Tanzania's national independence, politicians envisioned the fate of a modernizing Dar es Salaam as synonymous with the fate of the nation, yet by the end of the first decade after independence, TANU's spokespeople began to portray a city whose existence was at odds with the goals and populist rural values of Ujamaa rhetoric. In the early 1970s, the state set into motion its retreat from the city of Dar es Salaam, disinvesting from the city and its infrastructure, dissolving its municipal political structure and launching a campaign to recast the urban areas as the foil of the nation. By the end of the socialist years, the shared narrative of a collective future that had been forged between nationalist visionaries and urban aspirants had fallen away, and the trajectory of the city and of the nation seemed to run separate and parallel to one another.

By the early 1980s, Dar es Salaam's inhabitants had given the city a new moniker: Bongoland, or "brain-land," for the Swahili word for *brain*, *ubongo / bongo*. This coinage had two meanings: first, it was an affirmative recognition of the kinds of people who survived and thrived in Dar es Salaam, as it required bongo or brains to make a life in the harsh economic and infrastructural conditions of the city. Its second meaning was that Dar es Salaam was the powerful brain of the nation, shaping, instigating, and directing what happened elsewhere. With the label *Bongoland*, popular urbanists reclaimed the city in spite of the state's rejection of Dar es Salaam in the name of rural African socialism. Bongo was initially a countercultural ethos, carrying the suggestion that urban-dwellers had to rely on their own creativity and intelligence—their brains—to survive at a time when conventional forms of authority, such as the state or rural patriarchal leadership, proved absent or unreliable. In contrast with ruling-party promises and platitudes about which measures would lead to collective prosperity, young people with bongo believed that they had a more realistic and appropriately cynical perspective on what contemporary life was like for everyday people. As African socialism lost its viability as a language of claim making, the term *Bongoland* recast Dar es Salaam, once again, as a kind of synecdoche of the nation and its uneasy place in the world economy. Yet in this new context, the connotation of the city was quite different from what it had been in the early modernizing years following Tanzania's independence.

Bongo was an East African variant of popular responses across the globe to economic reconfigurations in which flexibility and economic improvisation became a requirement of urban life. Young people in cities across the global south developed a new vocabulary to describe what it meant to live in these changing circumstances, simultaneously reflecting both a shared economic predicament and regional differences in the moral and ideational resources that people used to make sense of that predicament. In India, for example, young people began to valorize *jugad*, a term that, in its literal translation, refers to the improvisational act of making do with what is on hand. In more recent years, Indian youth have recast jugad as an entrepreneurial economic ethos as well as a kind of euphemism for activities that might otherwise be seen as illicit.[1] In Kenya, informal-sector work is known as *jua kali*, or "hot sun," referring to the kind of work that one performs without the official sanction of legal permission signified by a semi-permanent address and a roof over one's head. Instead, workers make their living while fully exposed to the hot sun.[2] In Abidjan, Côte d'Ivoire, in the 1980s, young people began to define a range of legal and illegal economic activities in contrast with formal wage labor simply as "business."[3] In Zimbabwe, in response to economic collapse and unreliable currency, youth speak of their ability to zigzag (*kukiya-kiya*) through the city in the absence of a straight and predictable path to economic security.[4] In the 1990s in post–civil war Angola, urbandwellers in slums and squatter settlements innovated a new dance called *kuduro*. Literally "hard ass," the dance and lyrical genre valorize toughness and an ability to withstand hardship. As Marissa Moorman argues, the movements suggest an ability to bend, adjust, and make one's body flexible in response to unpredictable and seemingly impossible situations.[5] While the act of improvisation itself might be understood as mere survival and a condition of powerlessness, the linguistic labeling of these activities suggests something more: an ethos, a claim to moral legitimacy, and the potential for critique. The words innovated to describe these new urban experiences reflect the shared resolve to make a home and a moral logic within spaces and experiences of displacement.

Emerging during a time of global economic transformation and dispossession, bongo was part of the universal global shift in how young people thought about urban livelihoods, yet it is also a distinctly East African ethos. Its moral valence is rooted in longer regional intellectual traditions, including the sources and offshoots of Ujamaa political philosophy.[6] However, despite sharing some common origins, Ujamaa and bongo have nearly opposite political connotations: the former valorized tradition, socialism, rural living, and the family unit, while the latter celebrates immediacy, entrepreneurialism, city life, and the abilities of the individual. How did bongo emerge as a dominant moral and populist idiom alongside Ujamaa: an ideology that, in many respects, seems to be its opposite?

Drawing together common keywords from the disparate street archives explored in earlier chapters, this chapter tracks the transformation of the vocabulary of urban citizenship among the migrant communities of Dar es Salaam. It reveals a changing relationship between modes of urban belonging and promises of collective national prosperity as each became unmoored from the other over the course of the socialist era into its aftermath in the 1980s. During the late socialist era, the ethos of bongo conveyed a subversive connotation and contained the possibility of critique, as urban residents' boasts of "using their brains" to survive a harsh social order implicitly called out the widespread failures of the state and powerful men to provide support, dignity, and adulthood for a new generation of youth. Yet that critical edge was dulled in later years as politicians, businesspeople, and members of the media incorporated and domesticated bongo as a mainstream discourse of liberal economic citizenship in the mid- and late 1980s.

African Socialism in Dar es Salaam

In spite of having one of the most antiurban political regimes on the planet, socialist-era Tanzania fostered the growth of a vast city of migrants and the creation of new forms of urban community. The expanding space of the city was an opportunity for urban migrants to achieve notoriety and to create new moral publics. The TANU Youth League men on patrol invoked a collective vision of a virtuous rural peasant society on whose behalf they observed and punished the sins of the city's wayward country daughters to justify their movements through the streets, nightclubs, and squatter settlements. In acts of intimidation and violence against women, they could see themselves as righteously intervening in the city on behalf of an imagined rural peasant whose honor they were protecting. For the generation of middle-class Christian women writers, parishioners, and reformers who arrived in Dar es Salaam in the early days following independence, the city was a site of moral danger to be domesticated through the cultivation of Christian homes, households, and routines that were safely walled off from the perilous sexual and economic networks of the city. Social scientists, activists, and intellectuals from the University of Dar es Salaam, animated by global leftist politics and hungry to apply their thinking about social justice beyond "the hill," saw the city as a site of potential radicalism and social change. Through ethnographic work in the city, some students sought connection and solidarity across the boundaries of class and education—and for some, race—while at the same time seeking to incite working-class women to collective social action. In dancehalls, nightclubs, and bars, young lovers and revelers used the commodities and global style repertoire available to them to create spaces of elegance and pleasure distinct from the bodily regimes of austere socialist virtue, while songwriters cultivated their authority as neighborhood intellectuals by articulating moral norms for how lovers and friends should treat one another. Pulp-fiction writers produced an infrastructure of reputation and social recognition based on urban male sociability. The stories that they penned and sent into circulation through the city's reading public solidified into a crime counternarrative of the city that shifted blame for societal ills from young urban men to the systemic injustices that excluded them from paths to respectable adult manhood. Taken together, the various urbanists that emerged in the socialist-era city of Dar es Salaam reveal overlapping moral idioms and histories that gave shape to a complex urban fabric.

The history of this urbanism did not occur within city limits, for it came into being in the minds and aspirations of people who came from elsewhere. The popular African urbanists that appear in these pages were born and had most of their schooling in rural areas before coming to the city as young men and women. They moved to Dar es Salaam in their teens or early twenties during the global trend toward urbanization that began in the 1950s and accelerated steadily throughout the 1960s and 1970s. Most of them had some Western education, either at missionary schools or later, at the newly expanding government schools of the late colonial and early postcolonial developmentalist era. Their literacy and their expectations of social mobility distinguished them as a cohort, positioning them as influential figures for a new era in the life of the city.

A generational shift distinguishes those who came to Dar es Salaam in the early years of Ujamaa and those who came in the late years following the economic and political conurbations of the early and mid-1970s. Those who arrived in the city in the 1960s had been born in the post–World War II era of "stabilization," and they expected to forge a life within the structure of wage-labor employment and a modernizing city.[7] As urban intellectuals, they sought to make the city in that image as a model of postcolonial citizenship. The city, for them, was one site in a broader vision of modernity and African national sovereignty. By contrast, a later generation of urban popular intellectuals had been born in the 1950s and had been children during the early years of African socialism. They were steeped in its ideological principles, and they shared many of their predecessors' expectations of modern life, yet they arrived in the city at a time when the state was in the process of abandoning its earlier promise of modernization, infrastructural investment, and salaried jobs. As authors of popular texts that would circulate through the city, this later generation of urban sojourners strove to make moral and political sense of those disappointments. In doing so, they interpreted the postcolonial condition from their vantage point in the city streets.

Similar kinds of urban-based artists and intellectuals emerged simultaneously in other African cities, from Lagos to Bamako to Accra to Kinshasa, in the 1960s and 1970s.[8] Through the development of state patronage systems for musicians, writers, and artists, new national governments attempted to incorporate and redirect the city's popular intellectuals into systems of national culture making. Later, these artists would, by and large, drift away from those state patronage systems in the face of state collapse and retreat and, eventually, privatization. Ryan Skinner describes this transformation in the role of public intellectuals particularly well in his study of the emergence and changing role of *artistiya* in Bamako, Mali.[9] In this sense, Dar es Salaam's socialist-era urban intellectuals exemplify a kind of urbanism and a mode of city building that is indicative of processes that were happening across the continent in the postcolonial era. This book argues that the work of these popular intellectuals constitutes a vital form of city building. It argues that many of their creations became part of the human capital and infrastructure of postcolonial cities in the era of rapid and unplanned urbanization that occurred throughout the global south.

At the same time, while Dar es Salaam in many respects resembles other cities in the postcolonial global south, its circumstances were also unique. One factor setting it apart from other cities was the protectionism of its socialist policy. Restrictions on imports meant that foreign popular-culture forms, including film, music, and literature, were scarce. Because the state and its enforcement mechanisms were weak, popular-culture forms made their way over porous borders in spite of efforts to prevent it, yet such items were difficult to come by and had great prestige. Though censorship was part of the policy of African socialism,[10] the experience of Tanzanians was of scarcity and partial exposure, rather than ignorance of the outside world. This meant that many cultural producers who had access to imported circuits of culture became brokers and interpreters of these cultural forms, giving them new iterations and resonances in various city spaces. For the most part, artists and intellectuals did not have to compete with television, or with records purchased and played on private gramophones, or imported dime novels from elsewhere. Instead, they improvised distinctive Dar es Salaam genres of their own that borrowed from these other forms and produced and recast them for a mass African audience. In this way, a creative person in socialist-era Dar es Salaam with something to say enjoyed the unique privilege of a captive audience. TANU intellectuals like professors L. A. Mbuguni and Gabriel Ruhumbika from the University of Dar es Salaam spoke vehemently about the need to combat the deleterious effects of foreign cultural influences like James Brown songs and Bollywood romance films on the youth of Dar es Salaam by replacing imports with more productive forms of socialist and nationalist culture,[11] yet the partial success of the attempt to restrict imports had the unintended consequence of creating a market for alternative local versions.

TANU's role as patron of the arts and as a sponsor of socialist national culture had the unintended consequence of giving rise to numerous cultural offshoots in urban popular culture, often with themes and messages that were irrelevant, or sometimes anathema, to the state's cultural mission. As part of an effort to build national sentiment, state branches and parastatal cooperatives formed and financed many of the dancehalls and nightclubs of the 1970s.[12] This system provided patronage to musicians, but at the same time, the spaces they created also staged confrontations between the TANU Youth League and cosmopolitan youth. Even if the musicians and dancers were hired under the pretense of promoting patriotism, discipline, and esprit de corps among government workers, they also provoked debates over money, sexuality, and the meanings of urban life. Controversies over dance steps or Western fashions circulated out of the dancehalls and into the newspapers, magazines, and novellas. These were vital public spaces in part because of limited options for self-expression and pleasure in a time of scarcity. Inadequate housing conditions and unreliable transport to take people elsewhere, either within the city or beyond, also contributed to the shapes of neighborhood audiences.

Similarly, in the realm of fiction, during the very same years that urban-dwellers struggled to access basic items like sugar, cooking oil, and soap, they could find thousands upon thousands of copies of pulp-fiction novellas available on newsstands. The state infrastructure of literacy and education made possible a large and voracious reading public in Dar es Salaam. Though the mass literacy campaign cultivated citizens' skills, it was less successful in molding citizens' appetites. Literacy classes taught in factories and community centers made possible an audience for pulp fiction and newspaper reporting on cities. The explicit intention of such campaigns had been to craft a modern rural population receptive to state propaganda. Yet many rural people left the villages, and their urban-centric view of the postcolonial predicament was an unintended consequence of these investments. In his promotion of mass literacy, Nyerere did not intend to foster the growth of an underground urban pulp-fiction industry, yet at the same time, the underground pulp-fiction industry could not have existed without the investments of the state.

Finally, the absence of a robust official vision or plan for urban prosperity allowed intellectuals a great deal of freedom to craft their own visions. The state was weak and could not succeed in actually preventing rural people from moving to the city, nor could they prevent the flourishing of a black-market economy. While in some socialist contexts, heavy-handed government restrictions led to insurgent underground art and politics, such as with *samizdat* literature in the Soviet Union, this was not the case in Dar es Salaam.[13] Tanzania's popular urban intellectuals did not reject socialism or Tanzanian nationalism, but instead recast their predicament from an urban standpoint. It was only in the 1980s when the socialist project began a phase of total collapse that writers became overtly critical of the state.

In all these ways, the city of migrants was both a problem and an opportunity. It was an expanding space for improvising new urban infrastructures constructed out of people and connections and texts. In seeking to understand urban life in this context, this book has focused neither on urban planners with the authority to shape physical space and impose their vision on others nor on the spontaneous, ephemeral subaltern urbanism of anonymous masses.[14] Tanzania's experiment with rural-based socialism, paradoxically, gave rise to new kinds of actors: urbanists for whom the city was both a problem and an opportunity to remake moral community. While these different textual genres that emerged in the city reveal very different perspectives about how one should, and could, craft a meaningful life in the city, at the same time, they reveal a shared set of preoccupations. Dar es Salaam's sojourners of various persuasions asked how to reshape respectability and community using the material trappings of a disintegrating city and especially how conditions of scarcity could lead to new configurations of money, sex, household, and the self. In such circumstances, how did one make social relationships and communities durable and concrete?

Ujamaa Urban

The relationship between Ujamaa thought and urbanism was a creative tension, rather than a contradiction. Some of the moral vocabulary of Ujamaa resonated with aspects of the urban experience and was taken up in selective ways by popular urbanists. As Ferguson points out, African socialism was based largely on regional idioms of morality in which the production and exchange of wealth were understood as being "inseparable from social relations."[15] Nyerere argued that Africans were naturally socialistic and did not desire more wealth than their neighbors. The idea of familyhood—the literal meaning of the word *Ujamaa*—suggested that the relationship between the head of state and citizens was based on a set of moral obligations toward collective prosperity and social reproduction, in much the same way that a male household head would be responsible for the well-being of his dependent kin.[16] These ideas were rooted in the history of the region, though not only in rural communities. These concepts were also foundational to the older cultures of Swahili cities dating back several centuries. The moral logic of circulation and distribution is captured in proverbs passed over generations of Swahili-speakers, such as the proverb *mali bahili kula duda*, or "the wealth of a miser is eaten by worms."[17] Wealth, in other words, should not be accumulated in the hands of an individual, but should rather be deployed to perform work and build connections between people. The flip side of this ethos was a kind of racial caricaturing between Indians and Africans in Dar es Salaam, in which Indians might portray the tendency to spend money in public as fiscally irresponsible, while Africans portrayed Indians as antisocial and greedy: stereotypes that became especially prominent in the colonial era.[18] Similarly, the proverb *baniani mbaya, kiatu chake dawa*, or "the Indian is evil, but his (nice) shoes are medicine (desirable)," simultaneously conveys a racial caricature and a moral question: how should one act in situations in which the source of wealth might be morally questionable, yet the wealth itself is desirable, or in some circumstances, needed?[19] One of the defining elements of East African moral political discourse was a recognition that wealth had moral and social origins, yet the flip side of this rhetoric was that people often relied on racial caricature to denounce economic injustice.

While Nyerere's iteration of Ujamaa drew on these older moral idioms concerning the social meaning of wealth and its circulation, the idea that Africans were not competitive or acquisitive was a modern innovation. This argument about the naturally egalitarian proclivities of Africans has less in common with regional moral idioms originating in precolonial Africa than with a post-abolitionist and missionary-era ideology, in which Europeans made the condescending argument that "detribalized" Africans needed to be protected from cities where Arabs and Asians would inevitably dominate them. This idea about African communalism was replicated in colonial Dar es Salaam through paternalistic policies that allowed Indians, but not Africans, to own property.[20] One need only look, for example, to the history of female property ownership and entrepreneurialism in Swahili cities,[21] and to long traditions of competitive consumerism, gift exchange, and feasting in East Africa,[22] to find examples that contradict the racial rhetoric that Africans are inherently socialistic in the ways Nyerere imagined. In promoting egalitarianism as inherently African and coding property ownership, consumerism, and competition as non-African characteristics, Ujamaa rhetoric selectively suppressed vital aspects of African urbanism, much as colonial predecessors had.

Perhaps an even more jarring innovation in Ujamaa rhetoric was the idea that Africans should embrace poverty. Nyerere's call for his fellow Tanzanians to see themselves as citizens of a poor country was in many ways a realistic and materialist assessment of Tanzania's position in the world and in part a vital critique of the persistent and devastating structural legacies of colonialism. Yet for everyday Tanzanians, poverty was

more than a geopolitical and economic condition. Poverty had deep social and personal meaning in East African moral thought. Wealth was
what allowed people to become full adults with the rights to participate
in public debate and decision making. As Derek Peterson articulated in
his description of central Kenya, "Poverty shut men's mouths, making
them socially inconsequential."[23] Wealth not only bolstered individuals
and families, but was also the substance of respectability and social relationships and one of the central building blocks of adulthood. A Swahili
proverb that claims, *Mkata hapendi mwana*, or "a poor man loves not his
child,"[24] conveys the notion that parental love could only become productive and socially viable when it took material form through the provision
of gifts and material security for one's offspring. When Nyerere called
on Tanzanians to heroically embrace their poverty, he was speaking to a
people who feared, at a personal level, that to be poor was to be socially
inconsequential.

Nyerere argued that one of the tools for fighting poverty, both collectively
and individually, was self-reliance, or *kujitegemea*. Yet while kujitegemea in
the postcolonial socialist context connoted the power of self-determination,
it was also closely related to social isolation: a condition that, historically,
had been especially dangerous for women. For centuries, the prospect
of being separate from social networks, without access to the resources
of husbands, fathers, or sons, has been an extremely precarious position for women in East Africa.[25] These dependencies took shape through
gender norms. Aspects of this moral language continued to inform how
men and women identified each other in cities, such as, for example, when
a woman went to a dancehall and made it known who had paid for her
ticket, or bought her clothing, or paid for her beauty products so that
men received recognition and praise for their provider roles.[26] Whether
one was talking about a nation, a village, a family, or an individual, self-
sufficiency, for Nyerere, connoted the ability to chart one's own destiny
and to be immune to the exploitation of wealthy and powerful nations
and entities, yet Dar es Salaam's newcomers were sensitive to the fact
that empowered self-sufficiency was on a spectrum with the devastation
of social isolation.

Nyerere's socialist philosophy portrayed the Ujamaa village as a reflec-
tion of precolonial egalitarian communal values and the city as the site
of foreign influence. Within this broader narrative, those who left their
rural villages and came to the city were abandoning traditional, socialistic, and authentically Africans ways of life in favor of pursuing foreign

lifestyles and aspirations. Yet a closer examination of the popular urbanism of the era reveals urban-dwellers acting and thinking in some ways that would have been familiar to precolonial East Africans. In investing in urban social networks and amassing "wealth in people" in the radically new circumstances of the city, they drew on older values and strategies. Contrary to the political rhetoric of the time, urbanism drew on a wellspring of older ways of thinking, while it was the Ujamaa ideology of African authenticity and the invention of the egalitarian African village that was the true innovation, and it was formed in a distinctly global historical context.

An Ujamaa Urban Lexicon

Across the various texts produced in Ujamaa-era Dar es Salaam, certain terms appear frequently and take on special significance in discussions about the moral legitimacy and illegitimacy of the city and the lifestyles of its inhabitants. These words and phrases constitute a lexicon of urban belonging: an Ujamaa urban lexicon. I draw here on the work of Nancy Rose Hunt, who reframed scholarship on colonialism in Africa through her concept of "a colonial lexicon." Challenging the idea of a colonial encounter that is based on a dichotomy of oppressors and resisters, she defines "colonial lexicon" as an open-ended and shifting vocabulary that is not imposed by hegemonic political authorities or produced in protest by workers or the lower classes, but is rather a list of terms that is produced and negotiated collectively, in the messy entanglements of colonial life. Over time, the lexicon comes to include new elements that circulate through colonial spaces and that can include terms from multiple languages from both local contexts and global circuits that pass through colonial spaces.[27] Extending this analytic insight to the polyglot and rapidly changing city of postcolonial Dar es Salaam reveals an urbanism that has been historically shaped through the incorporation of new elements and through contestations over new meanings of older elements.

Many of the keywords that had moral resonance for Dar es Salaam's residents had to do with buildings and real estate. Descriptions of *nyumba*, or houses, often contained deeper political meanings and underlying tensions between ruling party rhetoric and popular idioms of urban belonging. As we've seen, the TANU leader Bibi Titi Mohamed emerged out of an urban milieu in which owning urban real estate was a common aspiration and an especially important source of income and security for women. By the time of the Arusha Declaration of 1967, however, there were few figures more roundly caricatured in state propaganda than urban landlords.[28] For example, a poem published in the TANU-owned newspaper *Uhuru* in 1970 models a conversation between a husband and wife in which the husband shares his vision of owning houses to rent to tenants in the city and the wife attempts to convince him that such behavior is contrary to the aims of socialism. In the end, the wife heroically chooses loyalty to TANU and leaves her recalcitrant husband, proclaiming:

> Goodbye, sir, goodbye, I will not change my resolve
> I do not want a capitalist husband; I'd prefer a life as a widow
> The Arusha Declaration is my pride; it will nurture life.
> The Arusha Declaration forbids exploitation.[29]

Commenting on houses and the furniture contained within them became a way of signaling tensions and overlaps between competing economic moralities in the city. Whether one accessed housing through the government, a private landlord, a relative, or a lover, and whether one did so as a single renter or a family, talking about houses was a way of probing what kinds of urban community were morally acceptable. "Modern" houses with cement walls, corrugated metal roofs, and furniture inside were both desirable and suspect, depending on one's gender and marital status. In the developmentalist imagery of a modern middle class, furniture connoted a respectable and socially recognized marriage and the construction of a stable urban household unit. However, for urban-dwellers who did not live in legally recognized marriages, furniture raised questions about the origins of wealth. For example, Ani—the protagonist in both of Martha Mandao's Christian girls' advice books *All Alone in the City* and *Ani Opens Her Purse*—notices a couch and tables and a separate room for a bed in the home of her friend Kise when she goes for a visit. Ani wonders how her friend attained such material comforts, and eventually she deduces Kise has an older, wealthier boyfriend who is keeping her in a nyumba ndogo.[30] Likewise, in popular pulp-fiction literature, one of the signals of an illicit sexual relationship was for a woman to have furniture in her sitting room, for it was assumed that the furniture inside was part of what a single woman was given in exchange for sex.

Houses and furniture became part of the moral language of urban-dwellers in part because they indexed social investments. How one assembled such a space was a narrative about one's social connections and community. The story of one's house and furniture was a story about the social and sexual terms on which one inhabited the city.

While stories about houses and furniture revealed how one established economic permanence in the city, modes of transport revealed social relationships and inequalities through the lens of mobility. In one of the opening scenes of the didactic Tanzania Publishing House novel *Penzi la Dawa* (*Love Medicine*), the protagonist waits on the agonizingly slow public transportation to travel to her friend's house. On the way back home, she observes the potholes in the roads and the movement from a neighborhood in which the bus glides easily across the tarmac past modern illuminated houses where people have electricity and furniture in their sitting rooms, to the area where she lives, where the smooth tarmac gives way to dilapidated dirt road. The city goes dark as they enter the part of the city that does not have electricity, and she hears the buzz of mosquitoes because they have entered an area without proper drainage. Witnessing this through the window of the bus, she recalls the nice furniture and other comforts of her friend's home, and thinks to herself, "We are the same in color only. We could not be more different."[31] Though both young women are African and black, the bus ride through the city reveals the failures of African socialism to render them equals.

Moving along slick tarmac or the rough dirt roads of most of Dar es Salaam was part of a popular idiom for understanding citizenship in the city. Official images of public transportation promised mobility through the city, yet these images were increasingly incredible, especially when the oil shocks of the mid-1970s ground the buses to a halt, and when the waiting lines at the bus stops wrapped around city blocks. Meanwhile, popular novellas projected fantasies of male mobility in the form of airplanes, motorcycles, and cars—the Datsun 1600, Peugeot 504, Volvo, Land Rover, or Mercedes Benz—as an image of empowerment in which Dar es Salaam residents joined a faster and more modern world order. These various Ujamaa-era images of mobility speak to a debate about who could move through the city and who could not; who was immobilized or stuck and who could escape.[32] To be mobile was to have power. Images of slow buses or of walking long distances either because the buses are not running or because the fare is unaffordable are images that convey frustrated desires and ambitions in multiple registers. Images of buses and Benzes and other vehicles of mobility, from airplanes to shoes, was one of the ways urban migrants held up Ujamaa promises of collective progress against a congested and slow-moving urban landscape that revealed a different story.

The unevenness of mobility in the city revealed fissures not only of class, but also of gender. Like buses and Benzes, purses (*mikoba*) were also a potent symbol of mobility in the socialist-era urban lexicon. Political cartoons of "westernized" urban women show them wearing miniskirts and high heels and carrying purses. The title of Martha Mandao's second Christian guidebook for girls is entitled, *Ani Opens Her Purse*. As the central metaphor of the book, the money that goes in and out of Ani's purse registers Ani's movements through the city and the moral choices involved in such circulations.[33] Middle-class reformers such as the newspaper columnist Theresia Mshuza saw transportation as a necessity for full female citizenship. Women who lived in squatter settlements, off the paved roads and designated bus routes, had to walk on roads too narrow for buses to travel. Especially when walking at night, this infrastructural unevenness might cause them to be mistaken for prostitutes rather than respectable women who were working for the nation in formal employment.[34] The repeated distinctions between respectable and unrespectable modes of urban habitation were part of the logic of claims to female urban citizenship.

Images of transportation and mobility threw into stark relief urban inequalities and the inextricable entanglement of sex and money. Scandalous stories of sugar daddies would typically commence when a girl is walking to school and is offered a ride in a car with an older man. Sugar daddies were often called *wabenzi* for the ill-gotten wealth that allowed them to drive a Mercedes Benz. Like the caricatures of wealthy politicians whose swollen bellies signify their consumption of wealth at the expense of others, the sugar daddy's corpulence indicates that he has taken more than his share of society's resources.[35] In Swahili, the sugar daddy was sometimes called *kizito*, or a heavy or weighty person. He is physically similar, in a grotesque and ironic way, to the body of a *mjamzito*: a pregnant woman. In some ways, the sugar daddy was part of the broader iconography of corpulence in which a politician's large belly was seen to signal corruption and a tendency to "eat" the wealth of the people,[36] while the large belly of a schoolgirl was a sign of sexuality gone tragically awry. The ubiquity of the sugar-daddy figure in popular-cultural forms of the 1970s signaled changes in household and family economies. As Lynn Thomas has argued, the threat of the sugar daddy was the twentieth-century iteration of a longer debate about who would control female sexuality and benefit from its productive rewards.[37] As a popular political idiom, the sugar-daddy figure reflects the durability of deeper regional moral ideas and the deep dilemmas raised as African individuals, families, and communities grappled with new forms of wealth and accumulation in a rapidly changing urban context.

The sugar daddy offended and scandalized people for similar reasons to the bump dance and miniskirts. What made these things offensive was not their association with sex, but rather their suggestion of a kind of sexuality and conjugality forged from within the milieu of one's urban social, sexual, and economic connections. The sugar daddy, like city life more broadly, suggested reproductive capacity wasted on what were perceived as temporary arrangements rather than invested in something more solid, permanent, and collective, such as life in the rural village of one's birth. Devoid of land, ancestral claims, and deep familial ties of obligation, such sex was obscene and socially destructive.

As a popular villain figure, the image of the sugar daddy was made to perform political work. Depending on who was speaking, the invocation of the sugar daddy could express a critique of female materialism and greed, of traditional forms of masculinity and polygamy, or of the selfishness and corruption of powerful men. More broadly, authors deployed the sugar daddy to critique social conditions in postcolonial Africa in which traditional forms of social bonds and obligations were distorted in the context of mass urban migration. According to the authors of these representations, girls were drawn to sugar-daddy relationships because of disparities of wealth. While the sugar-daddy character and his relationship with socially vulnerable girls was seen as particularly heinous, sugar-daddy relationships were on a spectrum with other more acceptable relationships. For example, many girls formed "gift relationships" with boys and men to access the resources of urban life—transportation, food, and clothing—especially if their parents could not provide material security. When Christian middle-class reformers warned about the dangers of "gift friendships," they were not simply being prudes, but were commenting on the social meaning of wealth in which gifts created mutual indebtedness.[38] For many women, housing, public transportation, and, most importantly, wage labor from a government job were alternatives to these more dangerous and sexually charged entanglements. The tension between exchange and autonomy was built into the very landscape and its architecture. Hostels were built with walls around them and strict curfews, in part based on the perceived need to protect girls from such exchanges in the city. In the view of many socialist-era urban intellectuals, public urban infrastructure was a potential form of gender uplift, rendering women's and girls' dependency on powerful men unnecessary. However, the communities formed within the walls of the compounds did not provide a viable substitute for the webs of social exchanges that stretched beyond.

In this view of the world, relationships between urban girls and sugar daddies were the opposite of a functional state-based citizenship. Often, in popular novels, the culmination of destructive relationships between sugar daddies and schoolgirls was illegal abortions and infanticide, which were also key terms in a lexicon of urban citizenship.[39] Exposing abortions in the city had long been a mode of "realist" newspaper reporting on urban life.[40] Though portrayed as a distinctly modern urban ill, abortion has a longer history in East Africa in which it is seen as a social ill, but one that is sometimes necessary for the preservation of socially recognized persons and families.[41] Recast in the context of the postcolonial city, stories about secret abortions raised new debates about what kind of family or legitimate unions might be possible. Drawing on older idioms for discussing legitimate and illegitimate social relationships and bonds, in postcolonial Dar es Salaam, abortion became a condition of, or metaphor for, urban life.

This urbanist lexicon reflects a shared concern that the circulation of money should be orchestrated to promote productive rather than exploitative interactions and a respectable gendered order. Discussions about seemingly innocuous topics such as nyumba ndogos, Mercedes Benzes, or furniture invoked a broader question: should one seek belonging and security in urban social and sexual networks or from the forms of citizenship offered by the state? How urban-dwellers answered that question changed over time. A state-led urban citizenship seemed possible in the early Ujamaa years for many writers and intellectuals. Yet this vision became less tenable in the years between 1972 and 1974 as the state took an authoritarian and distinctly antiurban turn. Thus, at precisely the same time as TANU took over newspapers and began to increasingly portray the urban poor as criminals, pulp-fiction novellas did precisely the opposite: they became more cynical about authority, elders, and the moral authority of the legal system and valorized migrant youth as heroes of a homegrown urban ethos. As the economy began to collapse and the state retreated from its earlier visions of urban investment, those other social forms and moral economies not only endured, but became even more indispensable.

The Collapse of African Socialism

Despite displaying a wide range of perspectives, the various urban texts of the socialist era share a single conundrum: the extent to which urban citizenship might come from a regularized relationship with the state through amenities like wage labor and public housing and the extent to which it would be based on the circulation of money, work, sex, and reputation, which create bonds of obligation between people. Contrary to policy, state socialism never became the dominant economic or social mode of life in the city and was always one of many moral economies, yet the relationship between state patronage and other kinds of urban belonging would have different stakes and moral weight by the later years of socialism. By the early 1980s, Tanzania's economy was in free fall. In the context of the economic decline and the collapse of socialist programs, the state pursued two particularly repressive policies: Operation Nguvu Kazi and Operation Economic Sabotage. Inaugurated in 1983, Operation Nguvu Kazi, "Operation Hard Work," otherwise known by its euphemistic title "Human Resources Deployment Act," required local government officials to ensure that all citizens were performing "productive" work. Each district office was required to create and maintain an "employer register" that would keep track of all citizens and the type of work they performed. Tanzanian citizens were required to carry identification cards showing proof of employment. In theory, those who did not work would be rehabilitated, retrained, or transferred to an Ujamaa village to do agricultural labor. In practice, however, Operation Nguvu Kazi was a severe intensification of earlier policies going back to the colonial era, and most interventions simply took the form of urban residents being arrested, repatriated to rural areas, and left without resources. In the initial sweep in Dar es Salaam, 5,724 residents of Dar es Salaam were rounded up and brought to screening centers. Soon after, the detainment of the urban unemployed or those suspected to be unemployed was nearly a daily occurrence.[42] Operation Nguvu Kazi was a dramatic culmination of the erroneous belief, promoted in TANU propaganda, that the failures of socialism and the problems of the city could be attributed to the idleness and behavioral shortcomings of citizens.

That same year, the government also enacted Operation Economic Sabotage: a policy that was intended to crack down on illicit trading that occurred outside of the system of government cooperatives. As part of the
effort to enforce the policy against black-market trade, or *ulanguzi*, the Tanzanian Broadcasting Corporation established a radio program that invited
people to call in and report on their neighbors for possession of contraband items, contributing to an environment in which people lived in suspicion and fear of their neighbors.[43] Virtually everybody participated in
the black-market economy—it was practically impossible not to. Yet with
the government crackdown against ulanguzi, many Tanzanians lived in
constant fear of being caught. Social scientists T. L. Maliyamkono and
Mboya S. D. Bagachwa recall buses running empty because people were
afraid of being searched at checkpoints for contraband. Children, they recall, got into the habit of shouting "karibu!" or "welcome" loudly when
any visitor was at the door to alert their parents, giving them time to
hide, if necessary. People buried precious items such as televisions and
banknotes underground, and those who possessed motorcycles and cars
tried to find places away from the home to store them. Yet it was not only
luxury items that were confiscated in the Operation Economic Sabotage
campaign, but cooking oil, soap, toothpaste, corrugated iron sheets, textiles, and secondhand clothes: items that had become the basic trappings
of respectable urban citizenship for Dar es Salaam's denizens.

Together, Operation Nguvu Kazi and Operation Economic Sabotage
signaled government antagonism of the forms of urban life that had been
sustaining the city in the context of economic decline and the absence of
a strong state. Aili Tripp estimates that, during the final days of Ujamaa,
a formal salary would support a family of six for only four to six days
out of the month. The rest of a family's income would have to come from
elsewhere.[44] For urban-dwellers, this time period was experienced as an
absurd contradiction: it was literally impossible to survive in the city if
one followed the letter of the law.

Ben Mtobwa captures some of the economic and moral dynamics of
this predicament in his 1984 novel *Pesa Zako Zinanuka*: "Your Money
Stinks." It tells the story of Kandili Maulana, a destitute orphan who
manages to pull himself out of dire poverty through his wits. When, as a
young adult, he finally gets a job, he learns that his boss is participating
in a major black-market operation in which an international conglomer-
ate of businessmen seeks to steal a (fictional) drug called Oxton, which

would cure a deadly disease affecting poor children. Rather than making it available to Tanzanian children, the corporate villains instead sell it on the international black market. Unable to resist the promise of material prosperity, Kandili becomes involved in the scheme. He later learns that he has a long-lost son through his childhood lover, and in a tragic irony, he learns that his son has died of the very illness that would have been cured by Oxton. An orphan himself, he has now unwittingly participated in an economic scheme that led to the death of his own son.

In the end, Kandili's co-conspirators are arrested, and once in jail, the criminal masterminds behind the Oxton scheme are imprisoned alongside virtuous young hawkers who had been arrested for petty economic crimes, such as selling loose cigarettes to support their families.[45] In this poignant scene, Mtobwa portrays a gap between how the late-socialist state defined criminality and legality and the ideals of equality and familyhood that were at the heart of Ujamaa philosophy.

Ben Mtobwa was a briefcase publisher, and as was customary, the back cover of his book explains something about the intentions of the author. He invokes the proverb "no money smells" and identifies its suggestion that money circulates free of the moral stain of its origins. He then explains his rejection and reversal of that principle in his book title, *Pesa Zako Zinanuka*: "Your money stinks." He explains to his readers that his intention is to place society under a microscope and to look without fear at the injustices and pain of the contemporary world. In contrast with his other books, which promised to make the reader surprised, delighted, and shocked, Mtobwa promises to move the reader to tears by laying bare a tragic reality.[46] Mtobwa sold this book alongside other books in the Kariakoo market each week.

Ben Mtobwa was born in 1958 in Kigoma on the western border of Tanzania and began writing fiction while he was a secondary school student. In Dar es Salaam, he worked with Jackson Kalindimya publishing the magazine *Heko* and running their small publishing company, Heko Publications. Mtobwa and Kalindimya were a new generation of writers who arrived in Dar es Salaam right at the end of the Ujamaa years and who were writing about a society in collapse. While earlier generations had been more oblique in their portrayal of political issues, in the very final years of African socialism, particularly in 1983 and 1984, several writers began to write works that were more overtly critical of political conditions. Jackson Kalindimya, who came to Dar es Salaam from his home in Shinyanga in his late teens in the late 1970s and collaborated with Ben

Mtobwa, described how the conditions of Dar es Salaam led him to become a writer:

> My first ideas were inspired by what life was like at that time. First, there was scarcity of items here in Dar es Salaam. . . . I was among those people who would chase down the trucks that were transporting things like bread; we would chase them down in the traffic to buy things in order to get them, and things like that. . . . Back then, there were restrictions such that it was necessary to have special knowledge in order to get food or bread; you had to get things on the black market back then. At that time, while people were trying to get these things, many police officers were not trustworthy. They could really mistreat people. They would steal things from people; other times, they could make false accusations against people; things that weren't good. Also, because of these conditions, it pushed lots of young people to take on the behaviors of thieves and gangsters. Now, for this behavior of the police, all of these things, I saw them and it made me want to talk about it. I saw how things were not good with the police. The police would sometimes not even enforce the word of the courts. Then and there, I decided to write books about detective work; *my own private detective work*, which would be done without using the police, and finally catch the true criminals.[47]

In the final days of Tanzania's socialist experiment, urban-dwellers like Kalindimya and Mtobwa reflected on conditions of scarcity but also of irony. In other words, it was literally impossible to live one's life according to the rules. To live in the city during such a time was to be defined as criminal for existing during a time in which, officially, it was impossible to exist. As Jackson Kalindimya expressed, people had to decide for themselves where the line between legality and criminality was drawn. If earlier heroes in pulp fiction were faced with a struggle against evil sugar daddies and backward elders, now, youthful protagonists were less straightforwardly heroic. In the early 1980s, there was a proliferation of male characters in pulp fiction who embodied this position of legal ambiguity.[48] Compared with male protagonists in earlier fictional works, these young men were more cynical.

This new literary mode of cynical realism appears across popular fiction. Recall, for example, that Sami Kiama—the hero of Hammie Rajab's *Ufunguo wa Bandia*—is a government employee who takes on a life of crime because his salary does not allow him to support his daughter and girlfriend. It is the urban condition itself, rather than the young man, that is on trial. In Amina Ng'ombo's *Heka Heka za Ulanguzi*, or *Activities of the Black Market*, two young men in Dar es Salaam describe the various tricks they use to hide their poverty so that nobody can tell that they are hungry or poor. Maliyatabu comes to the city and meets a friend, Begamoja. Maliyatabu, whose name means "trouble money" in Swahili, feels great relief when he discovers that he is not the only one who cannot live on his salary, and finds comfort in his friend, who shares tips on how to survive. Begamoja explains that bus fare on the UDA,[49] the public transport system, would take up his entire salary if he paid it, leaving nothing left over for food, shelter, and other expenses, so rather than pay, he ducks and dives into the crowd, avoiding the eye of the bus conductor to avoid being asked for the fare. At other times, he doesn't want to be seen walking to and from work because girls laugh at him and mock his poverty, perhaps telling him "huna!," so instead, he loiters downtown, pretending to be "window shopping" until after dark, when he can walk home without being seen. Last, he confides to Maliyatabu that rather than eating full meals, he eats *ugali* with "maji ya bizari": that is, stiff cornmeal porridge flavored with curry powder and salt, but no meat or vegetables. Maliyatabu, who had felt shame and confusion at his inability to survive in the city, is reassured by Begamoja. "This is the norm, bwana!" Begamoja tells him. "Don't see people dressed well and think that they are satisfied and successful. Really, they have nothing but troubles!" The trick was artifice. Urban elegance was increasingly about crafting a public persona and elegance in the context of scarcity.[50]

In popular literature in the 1980s, authors began writing stories featuring heroic characters whose elegance came not from wealth, nor from hard work, but instead from intelligence.[51] By suggesting a moral rubric for the economic life of the city that differed from how the state defined criminality and legitimacy, pulp-fiction novelists of the city of the late socialist era produced an urban socialist counternarrative to the antiurban discourse and policy of the socialist state.

Dar es Salaam as a Brain

By 1985, Ujamaa officially was declared over with the stepping down of Julius Nyerere and the inauguration of Ali Hassan Mwinyi, who would become popularly known as *Mzee Ruksa*, or Mr. Permissiveness, for his apparent laissez-faire approach to the economy. This was an era described by contemporaries with the word *magzi*, or a changes," that went along with the liberalization of the country's economy.[52] In 1986, Tanzania entered into its first agreement with the IMF and implemented an ambitious Structural Adjustment Policy in an attempt to spur the stalled economy. The sale of government parastatal companies, massive layoffs from government jobs, and the shrinking of the public sector led to widespread unemployment in the city, and economic disparities took visible shape in the simultaneous proliferation of skyscrapers and shantytowns spread across the skyline of the city: an aesthetic juxtaposition that captured the polarizing futures of the post-socialist city.

One might expect massive layoffs and austerity measures to lead to urban upheaval and social protest, yet, as Aili Tripp points out, most urban-dwellers responded to the official end of Tanzania's socialist era with indifference.[53] In fact, the shift from a society ostensibly organized around the principles of socialism to a society in which the state would abnegate responsibility for urban lives was not experienced as a contradiction. In material terms, urban-dwellers had long stopped relying on the state and made their living and their city in the informal sector. Similarly, though they may have embraced certain images and philosophical principles of Ujamaa, doing so had not prevented them from developing a more relevant, robust language of urban belonging that had little to do with—and in many ways contradicted—Tanzania's socialist project.[54] Both socialism and its collapse required Dar es Salaam's inhabitants to practice self-reliance. For urban-dwellers, the end of the regime did not mean having to build a new society from scratch. It meant a continuation and transformation of urban processes and moral principles that had already started to take shape in the socialist-era city. State socialism and the principles of Ujamaa had constituted one entangled thread in the fabric of East African urbanism.

The opening of Tanzania's markets during the Mwinyi years allowed for the legal importation of foreign goods and popular cultural forms. Many of those who had been briefcase publishers broadened their publishing endeavors to start publishing humor and entertainment magazines featuring short stories, advertisements, and human-interest news stories.[55] They still made use of their networks and notoriety, advertising the books of their fellow publishers and praising each other's work to boost each other's reputations. With the loosening of censorship to allow privately owned newspapers from 1992 onward, the number of independently owned tabloid newspapers and magazines increased dramatically.[56] Similarly, while the briefcase publishers were cultural gatekeepers who profited from their ability to stage kung fu and cowboy stories in local Dar es Salaam locations, now people could watch foreign films much more easily in their living rooms on their VCRs and televisions. In 1993 and 1994 respectively, the government liberalized radio and television regulations, leading to a massive influx of foreign images and popular music. This opening of the entertainment market was detrimental to the livelihood of local musicians, who now had to compete with imported forms. Parastatal organizations began to cut bands and workers' social clubs from their budgets, while bars and restaurants could simply display televisions playing foreign music videos instead of purchasing equipment and hiring live bands to compose songs and offer their own interpretations and reworkings of foreign styles. In these new circumstances, the role of the popular urban intellectual changed. *Mageuzi* presented new opportunities for artists to experiment with new mediums. Hammie Rajab, for example, went into the television industry and became one of the most prolific producers of Tanzanian films and telenovellas up until the time of his death in 2011. At the same time, the captive audience created by socialist-era protections was lost. Consumers now had direct access to the products of the outside world without these migrant artists and intellectuals acting as mediators and translators.

It was in the midst of these changes that Dar es Salaam residents began to refer to *bongo*: an urban ethos valorizing the kind of creativity and street-savvy one needs to survive in a precarious economic urban environment. Musicians played a central role in popularizing the term and giving it content, and in the 1980s, postcolonial Tanzania became home to one of the most vibrant and prolific hip-hop genres on the continent: *bongo flava*. Alex Perullo describes bongo as an ethos of creativity and of the valorization of the ability of youth to adjust to precarious and unpredictable circumstances and of proclaiming their agency in spite of living in a recognizably unjust world.[57] By contrast, Koen Stroeken argues that bongo-flava rappers take a cynical view of society, criticizing the powers that be—whether local or foreign politicians or businessmen—but including themselves in that critique as a way of neutralizing its effect and protecting themselves, implicitly accepting that they too must participate in the world as it is.[58] Like Ujamaa's vision, bongo imagined an awareness and critique of a shared experience of global inequality, yet in the post-socialist era, survival and victory against the odds were no longer a collective process, but rather an individual one. One resigns oneself to circumstances and seeks to rise above them, against the odds.

When it emerged, the ethos of bongo was defined in contrast with other moral terms: namely, *jasho*, or sweat, and *ujanja*, or cleverness. Jasho has long been an important moral metaphor in East African political language. In the late colonial years, nationalist thinkers described exploitation with the metaphor of sweat. They posed critical questions about wealth and distribution, asking who had the right to benefit from the sweat of others. The metaphor of sweat became a way of mapping race onto material differences. Racial caricatures of Arabs, Asians, and European colonizers drew on images of these various groups profiting from the sweat of Africans, sometimes depicted in cartoons with people literally sucking the sweat off African bodies through straws.[59]

Ujamaa rhetoric made use of the metaphor of sweat, as well, valorizing physical labor in the agricultural sector as the key component that would create wealth and liberate Africa from colonial underdevelopment. The moral promise of virtuous sweat was that Africans themselves would benefit from their own effort, rather than creating surplus value for outsiders. The novelist Mkabarah captures this idea when he describes the idyllic socialist village as a place where "every person lives off of their own sweat."[60]

If in Ujamaa rhetoric using one's jasho was a virtuous way of producing value associated with rural labor, a less virtuous source of wealth was *ujanja*: cleverness. In the late colonial and early postcolonial era, the word *mjanja*—or "clever person"—implied someone who was superficial or sneaky. For example, TANU Youth League member Fundi Mussa wrote an editorial in the newspaper *Mwafrika* in 1963 denouncing Dar es Salaam youth ujanja as meaningless, especially compared with the deeper, more authentic intelligence of rural communities.[61] Clever urban migrants produced nothing but could sustain themselves through their relationships with others. For example, kisura, "pretty girls," were often described as "clever" for their ability to squeeze money out of men,[62] all the while shirking their duties as potential mothers, farmers, and guardians of the rural homestead. In Kassim Chande's 1984 novella *Kazikwa Yu Hai*, the narrator distinguishes between *wajanja* and *wajinga*, or "clever people" and "idiots." Wajanja are "those who get themselves lots of money and become rich by using any tactics that they know, while idiots are those like me: our condition is of poverty. Money for us is like a matter of bad luck."[63] Ujanja was the foil of both rural wisdom and urban middle-class respectability. For urban middle-class educated elites in Dar es Salaam, *ujanjaujanja* was a derogatory expression used to describe the ways that people in the informal sector made a living and prospered: not with "legitimate" or formal education and salaried labor, nor with virtuous sweat, but with mere clever tactics.[64]

In contrast with these moral concepts, urban youth used the term *bongo* to describe themselves. Bongo does not carry the negative or duplicitous connotations of *ujanja*. The kinds of improvisation and hustle that many considered to be pathological were accepted by an increasing number of people as what one was simply expected to do in the city. Rather than a critique, bongo, in a sense, can be seen as an acceptance—if grudging and even cynical—of the conditions of urban life. AbdouMaliq Simone describes the postcolonial urban predicament as one in which urban-dwellers must always be on the lookout for the next possibility, keeping all options open. The discourse of ujanja blames urban-dwellers for being opportunistic, trying to get an unfair advantage over others without doing the necessary work. By contrast, the ethos of bongo understands brains as a necessity and a skill and, in a sense, suppresses the question of what is fair and unfair.

Embedded in discussions of sweat and brains is a running commentary on economic change over time. In speaking of the dancehalls and nightclubs of the socialist era, Fatuma Mdoe describes a time when people used to dance *bila jasho*: without sweating.[65] Now the owner of her own cafe in a sleepy section of the city of Tanga on the northeast coast of Tanzania, Mdoe spent decades working as a barmaid in a number of dancehalls and nightclubs in Dar es Salaam and Tanga from the 1960s through the 1980s. Like Mdoe, musicians and dancehall denizens looking back on the Ujamaa era and the years preceding it described with great fondness a style of music and dancing that they describe as bila jasho, and it is also a commentary on the times. In recollections of the past, they invoked a kind of graceful, civilized, self-controlled movement of the body to appear effortless. They contrasted that with a caricature of how young people in Dar es Salaam appeared to them in the 2000s. They described popular youth dance, including bongo flava, as a kind of frenetic flailing of limbs: a desperate and aimless expenditure of energy. When young people danced, they appeared to older generations as though they were working hard, sweating. It appeared less like pleasure than the release of desperate and libidinous anxiety. When city people like Fatuma Mdoe talk about a past in which people danced bila jasho, they describe a contemporary world where cleverness is now elevated to the status of "brains" and the possibility of earning a living through honest jasho is remote. That energy and effort—that sweat—is now expended elsewhere, in the realm of pleasure and leisure, and with a purpose and end goal that appear distant, inscrutable, and impossible to satisfy.

In a post-socialist context, popular intellectuals and politicians alike revalorized qualities that earlier generations of public intellectuals considered low-class, basic, or even criminal. To be mobile and flexible, scanning the urban landscape for opportunities, was, in an earlier era, associated with hooliganism, or *uhuni*. It was associated with aimlessness, promiscuity, and cultural inauthenticity.[66] To be endlessly mobile and flexible was, in the eyes of critics, to lack commitments and integrity. Many of those same behaviors that caused a moral panic in the late colonial era, and that were criminalized in the Ujamaa years, would later become part of the ethos of bongo. To move through the city, and between village and city, without a predictable plan for the future is not hooliganism, but an ability to make use of opportunities. The kinds of mobility and openness that had once been seen as a lack of rootedness and purpose could now be recast as a strategic openness. The ethos of bongo is about not only living with instability, but being at home in that condition, embedded in the realities of the city. If the Ujamaa ethos emphasized bodily discipline and austerity, bongo sacrificed the body and instead valorized the brain.

Though associated with the opening of markets, the end of African socialism, and the entrenchment of Dar es Salaam as a cultural and economic center of the country, much of the bongo ethos emerges out of a longer history of social life and urbanism in the city. Yet at the same time, the changing global economic context gave bongo a starkly different political meaning. In Ujamaa rhetoric, the self-reliant individual was simultaneously a microcosm and metaphor of the larger social units, from the family, the village, the nation of Tanzania, and the continent of Africa, all of whom were seeking autonomy in their respective registers of an inegalitarian world order. Like Ujamaa philosophy, the ethos of bongo also privileges self-reliance, but rather than seeing the self-reliant individual as a microcosm of society, she is instead seen as someone who acts in response to state failure and vulnerability. A citizenry who could not rely on the socialist state had to rely on themselves. In this sense, to embrace an ethos of bongo, to give it a label and ontological status, was to create a language of critique. One relies on one's brains not as a choice, but first and foremost because of a larger failure, and to proclaim bongo is to make visible that failure.

The ethos of bongo lost some of that critical potential with the economic liberalization of the 1980s, when the state no longer claimed responsibility for providing collective prosperity through rural socialism. With the reimagining of Dar es Salaam as Bongoland, self-reliance was no longer linked with the expectation of decolonization and a revolution against the ills of unjust global histories. The language of historical entanglement and visions of accountability on a global scale were not part of the conversation, and bongo went from being the scrappy, defiant, ad hoc response of the dispossessed to a mainstream expectation of all citizens. Seen within a longer historical context, bongo appears as an acceptance and depoliticization of, and desire for partial mastery over, persistent conditions of vulnerability.

Conclusion

> Somewhere down the line, a city is a bit like . . . a gigantic group of clut-
> tered books. But a writer or artist has a way of making sense of it, of under-
> standing how it is catalogued. The catalog lives in the writer's head. Only if
> you write will the city-catalog be expressed. If you don't, it slips into chaos.
> —Sarnath Banerjee

In 1968, Tanzania's new National Library, the Maktaba Kuu ya Taifa, opened its doors to the public in downtown Dar es Salaam.[1] Architect Anthony Almeida, one of Tanzania's only licensed architects at indepen-dence, explained that the key architectural feature of the Maktaba Kuu was its prominent external front staircase descending from an elevated main entrance outward in both directions, so that it would be the first thing a person on the street would see when encountering the building. Colonial-era libraries, Almeida explained to an interviewer years later, tended to have a design that was exclusionary and fortress-like when viewed from the street. The typical front entryway of such an institution would be narrow and closed off, appearing like a passage into which only the educated elites were allowed. By contrast, this new national library with its outer staircase would allow Tanzanians on the street to see their fellow citizens moving in and out of the library, conveying the ideal of collective participation and literacy.[2] The library, one of the prominent landmarks demonstrating the mark of the postcolonial state on central Dar es Salaam, was designed not only to be a repository for books and a location of research, but also to be a spectacle of mass literacy at the cen-ter of the nation's capital.

Today in the public reading rooms of the Maktaba Kuu ya Taifa, one finds a respite from the noise and heat of the city, where students in school uniforms work on their homework at long wooden tables. Elderly men and women read the Tanzanian newspapers, which are bound at the seam with long wooden poles and hanging from racks. Yet it seems that library patrons rarely venture into the sparsely stocked book stacks. Most of the library holdings are kept in the basement, which is not open to the general public.

I first visited the Maktaba Kuu in search of newspapers and policy documents from Dar es Salaam in the 1960s and 1970s. Yet I soon found that targeted searches do not work well for this kind of library. The main finding device is an outdated card catalogue, a looming wooden cabinet with cards inside organized by subject, author, and title of the kind that my generation learned to use in elementary school in the days before library cataloguing moved online. On the shelves, books and newspapers are arranged in such a way that is only vaguely suggestive of a larger sequence. I would approach a member of the staff with a request for a specific issue of a newspaper such as *Uhuru*, for a date range during which I knew there had been an event of historical interest, but more often than not, no one would be able to find issues of the newspaper from the specific dates I had requested. Sometimes, it was because the library's collection was sparse and incomplete, and in other cases, the issue may have simply been unfindable, having perhaps been perused once and never returned to the shelf. It became clear that if I was going to make use of this vast store of historical documents, my approach was going to have to change.

Over the years between 2008 and 2015, I made a habit of spending time in the library basement. Eventually, rather than asking the librarians to locate specific books or newspapers, I asked for permission to browse instead, to see what items I might find that I would not think to ask for, and so the library staff generously allowed me to roam around the basement collections. Over the years since I've been conducting research in Dar es Salaam, I've spent many of my days sifting through the shelves, making lists of holdings and reading items produced in the Ujamaa era, conducting what would become a kind of makeshift historical exploration of Swahili mass literacy.

Like all national libraries, Tanzania's Maktaba Kuu ya Taifa offers insight into a nation-state's preoccupations and identity. The collection of texts on the shelves raises questions about the intersections of literacy and politics. What did various intellectuals think Tanzanians should read and write about? What kinds of textual inroads into the Tanzanian population did mass literacy allow from outside national borders? What kinds of ideas did Tanzanians themselves seek to communicate with each other, beyond their face-to-face communities through the printed word? What kinds of literary works were translated into Swahili, and by whom? What kinds of reading publics have been called into being over the course of Tanzania's literary history?

The collection of texts in the Maktaba Kuu provides a partial answer to these questions. One shelf holds Swahili translations of the works of thinkers including Frantz Fanon, Karl Marx, Booker T. Washington, and Bertolt Brecht and biographies of Vladimir Lenin, Mao Zedong, and Kwame Nkrumah, published by the Tanzanian government in collaboration with foreign press agencies in Moscow, Beijing, and London.[3] Another group of shelves contains the agronomy textbooks and sociological surveys produced by the University of Dar es Salaam. Another series of shelves holds copies of the magazines published by Tanzania's burgeoning professional associations in the 1960s, during the era of working-girl politics and the promotion of the African modern family as a national ideal. There are also numerous shelves filled with books about health and hygiene, about matters such as deworming and lice, and a noticeable concentration of Swahili translations of books and pamphlets about family planning. There are FAQ guides to various forms of biomedical contraception and pamphlets about child nutrition and cooking food for children, produced by various development organizations, including the IPPF and USAID. Christian lifestyle books offering advice on marriage and courtship, premarital sex, and urban temptations such as dancing addressed young African Christians in newly independent African countries. Many of these texts are Swahili translations of books first published by Christian publishers in Nigeria, Ghana, Côte d'Ivoire, or Malawi, revealing a wider imagined community of African postcolonial Christendom that transcended national boundaries.[4] Another shelf section holds the didactic plays meant to be staged in rural areas, written by University of Dar es Salaam scholars in the genre that Tanzanian playwright and professor Penina Muhando Mlama calls "development theatre." Piled high and falling apart in the back corner are pulp-fiction novellas by the likes of Hammie Rajab, Elvis Musiba, and Eddie Ganzel, with brightly colored cover artwork featuring kung fu fighters, guns, motorcycles, and scantily clad women. The back covers, with their self-referential network of young men writing blurbs for each other, reveal a community of entrepreneurial writers and self-publishers. Taken together, the library basement and its collections are a kind of composite map of some of the competing and entangled genres of collective address that have shaped Tanzania's public sphere in the twentieth century.

The basement of the Maktaba Kuu preserves a cross section of Tanzania's textual landscape at the convergence of two events: the expansion of mass literacy and the uncharted growth of the city beyond the parameters of state investment and surveillance. The texts reveal a changing relationship between the postcolonial nation and the city. As Louise Young has argued, the kinds of textual sources that are left behind about various urban pasts are not random, but instead reveal diverse trajectories of national development and engagement with global capitalism. "What one city archive possesses in abundance," she observes, "is nowhere to be found in another."[5] For example, some cities might have meticulously archived police records, while others have an abundance of independent newspapers, literary zines, or real-estate documents. Sometimes, the absences of particular kinds of sources reveal modes of governance. Ananya Roy argues that the absence of a master plan documenting property claims in Calcutta both demonstrates a lack of government accountability and neglect of the urban poor, while simultaneously revealing a systemic flexibility and extralegality that makes the lives of poor people possible.[6] For both Young and Roy, the relationship between urban texts and city life is not a straightforward matter of documentation of the city and its past. Texts, as well as the absence of texts, are a constitutive element of urban history, culture, and governance.

In a related approach to the relationship between official texts and the territories they are meant to represent, Ann Laura Stoler has urged scholars of colonial history to read "along the grain" of European colonial archives to reveal the structures of power that inhere in processes of documentation and preservation practiced by colonial states. Although *Street Archives and City Life: Popular Intellectuals in Postcolonial Tanzania* has explored sources outside of the archives created by nation-states, I have drawn on Stoler's insights by reading along Dar es Salaam's textual grain as a method of historical inquiry. The absences and presences are telling. There is a relative dearth of detailed government plans and maps of 1970s Dar es Salaam. Moreover, government control and censorship of the urban media meant that much of the urban reporting for the era was propagandistic and reflected an antiurban bias. Yet at the same time, the city fostered an abundance of popular unofficial texts produced in the city: for example, pulp-fiction novellas, published, sold, and read in the city, described, albeit in the form of fiction, the very urban spaces that are largely "unmapped" from the perspective of the state. This unevenness, with all of its empirical gaps, is not so much an obstacle as a clue.[7] While Dar es Salaam's textual landscape reveals very little in the way of official documentation of urban spaces and populations and, relatedly, suggests a lack of accountability and regularized communication between the state and the urban public, it reveals an abundance of texts, produced by and for urban sojourners, that actively address an urban population and seek new forms of urban spatial arrangement.

By thinking of these texts as street archives, this book has made the case that popular texts—both written and nonwritten—and their authors and audiences are part of a city's temporally layered human infrastructure. In doing so, this book has built on the work of scholars who have theorized infrastructure, especially in cities in the postcolonial global south. Brian Larkin has defined infrastructure as the "totality of both technical and cultural systems that create institutionalized structures whereby goods of all sorts circulate, connecting and binding people into collectivities."[8] AbdouMaliq Simone has shown, for example, how knowledge of Arabic and the practices of Sufi orders allow some Muslims to move through the world into new urban spaces because they are able participate in a widely distributed, yet intimate, community.[9] Style and dress can serve a similar purpose as soft infrastructure, as dress codes maintain the boundaries of institutions, allowing some people, but not others, access to particular spaces.[10] Linguistic competency facilitates some modes of mobility and entrance into spaces, whether in a female-dominated courtyard where a regional mother tongue is spoken or a global institution in which English is the lingua franca. In his work on colonial Indonesia, Rudolf Mrázek has referred to "language as asphalt."[11] Infrastructure, then, might include bridges and roads, title deeds, passports, and sewer systems, but also immaterial forms of cultural capital, such as reputation, skills, and knowledge, that allow people to move through, and participate in, cities and their economies.[12] Literacy, as a skill and a component of a "cultural system," can be understood as one part of urban infrastructure, for mass literacy and the circulation of reading material facilitates the mobility of ideas and discourses from authors to audiences.

To consider the historical textuality of the city is to investigate how people have addressed each other, making, breaking, and refashioning bonds of dependence, and to investigate the processes through which popular urbanists have fostered concrete commitments and connections out of conditions of precariousness, economic crisis, and marginalization. The textual worlds that crisscross through the basement of the Maktaba Kuu and the many other spaces of the city map Tanzania's changing relationship with Dar es Salaam during the socialist era. Over the course of the 1970s, the trajectory of the city became separate from that of the nation of Tanzania as the state withdrew urban investments and urban text makers defined new ways for narrating meaningful lives in the city. Perhaps paradoxically, this time of economic decline and of government neglect of the city was simultaneously a time of great urban creativity and imagination. After TANU abandoned earlier modernization plans, dissolved Dar es Salaam's municipal status, and actively attempted to redirect bodies away from cities into rural areas, visions of urban lives and futures continued to emerge from the grassroots, in dancehalls, six-room Swahili houses, bookstalls, working girls' hostels, and churches. By the 1980s, when Tanzania was pressured to accept austerity measures imposed by the International Monetary Fund in the name of structural adjustment policies, urban people had already begun to retreat from their expectations of the state, having already forged modes of belonging, connection, and dependence rooted in the city and its networks. As Aili Tripp has shown, by the time this restructuring was imposed on Tanzanian communities, the economic activities of urban-dwellers had long been separate from state-directed activities.[13] Just as Dar es Salaam residents diversified their economic strategies, in the collective imagination as well, the socialist vision of Nyerere was only one of many moral, political, and textual communities in which urban-dwellers were entangled.

As millions of young people across the African continent began seeking their lives in urban areas in the years following decolonization, the promises of national liberation projected in the 1960s were thrown into stark relief by the material visible realities of the city. While in the global north, the mobility of capital decoupled from national governments led to what Saskia Sassen has labeled the era of "the global city," in places like Tanzania and in much of Africa and the global south, the limits and failures of national sovereignty following on the heels of colonial infrastructural underdevelopment were experienced as urban neglect that necessitated new urban formations.[14] The cities of the former colonies, decades earlier seen by colonial and early postcolonial policymakers as laboratories of modernity and development, were now seen by Western experts as harbingers of a global crisis, threatened by a so-called population bomb and by the increasing informality of economic and social relations.[15] For urban intellectuals across the African continent, these tensions between modernization promises and the material inequalities of the city gave friction and substance to new kinds of cultural expression. Drawing on a vast and temporally deep repertoire of ideas about wealth, gender, and social connection, the urban moral language of the 1970s emerged where regional long-durée idioms of morality and economy intersected with global material and economic histories of the continent. African migrants in the 1970s had to face questions about how to create viable selves and futures, making sense of the city and its "catalogue," to use Sarnath Banerjee's phrase. In doing so, they not only represented the city, but created new modes of urbanism.

Unlike stories of nations, coups, or political regimes, city stories do not easily lend themselves to heroes or villains or to beginnings and endings. Cities are composed of entanglements, contingencies, repurposed circuits, and sedimented layers. The ad hoc realism characteristic of city stories is a grounded, material contrast to utopian narratives of technocratic solutions to deep historical injustices and to dystopian images of the aimless suffering of a historyless people inhabiting a "planet of slums." City stories revealed in the textualities of the street reveal how collective aspirations toward futures of dignity, security, and moral meaning are not produced out of whole cloth, but more often are cobbled together with the debris of what remains from the multiple overlapping pasts, in the joys and struggles of the quotidian present.

Notes

Introduction

1. Over the course of socialism, the city of Dar es Salaam grew from a population of about 272,000 to about 1.3 million.

2. The phrase *kutafuta maisha* entangled both material meanings and philosophical connotations. At one level, it refers to "making a living," in the sense of searching for an income. As Jamie Monson has shown, socialist-era workers on the TAZARA railroad described the work as part of kutafuta maisha, encompassing both a life course and a livelihood. Felicitas Becker, in her work on poor women in coastal East Africa in the years after the abolition of slavery, describes kutafuta maisha as working for a living in public spaces, in contrast with the respectability and status associated with the practice of female Islamic seclusion. In postsocialist Arusha, Brad Weiss shows how the phrase *kutafuta maisha* includes a recognition of the struggle of doing so in the context of systemic poverty, and, in this sense, the phrase might be seen to include an implicit critique of economic conditions. Andreasen and Agergaard state that migrants to Dar es Salaam describe that migration to the city as "kutafuta maisha." In the context of postcolonial Dar es Salaam, kutafuta maisha combines these personal and economic connotations. It typically refers to income-generating activities, the migration from rural to urban areas in search of such opportunities, and the attempt to forge a personal sense of respectability, accomplishment, or status through those activities. See Jamie Monson, *Africa's Freedom Railway: How a Chinese Development Project Changed Lives and Livelihoods in Tanzania* (Athens: Ohio University Press, 2011), 114; Felicitas Becker, "Female Seclusion in the Aftermath of Slavery on the Southern Swahili Coast: Transformations of Slavery in Unexpected Places," *International Journal of African Historical Studies* 48, no. 2 (2015): 229; Brad Weiss, "Thug Realism: Inhabiting Fantasy in Urban Tanzania," *Cultural Anthropology* 17, no. 1 (2002): 102; Manja Hoppe Andreasen and Jytte Agergaard, "Residential Mobility and Homeownership in Dar es Salaam," *Population and Development Review* 42, no. 1 (March 2016): 101.

3. Priya Lal, *African Socialism in Postcolonial Tanzania: Between the Village and the World* (Cambridge: Cambridge University Press, 2015), 37.

4. For additional examination of TANU antiurbanism, see Emily Callaci, "'Chief Village in a Nation of Villages': History, Race and Authority in Tanzania's Dodoma Plan," *Urban History* 43, no. 1 (2015): 96–116.

5. For further analysis of Nyerere's predicament, see Andrew Coulson, *Tanzania: A Political Economy* (Oxford: Clarendon, 1982), especially chapters 18 and 19. For a broader global context to the Tanzanian experience, see Odd Arne Westad, *The Global Cold War: Third World Interventions and the Making of Our Times* (Cambridge: Cambridge University Press, 2005).

6. Jeffrey Ahlman, *Living with Nkrumahism: Nation, State, and Pan-Africanism in Ghana* (Athens: Ohio University Press, 2017); Stephan Miescher's "'Nkrumah's Baby': The Akosombo Dam and the Dream of Development in Ghana, 1952–66" *Water History* 6, no. 4 (2014): 341–66.

7. Walter Rodney, *How Europe Underdeveloped Africa* (London: Bogle L'Ouverture Publications, 1972).

8. Julius Nyerere, *Ujamaa: Essays on Socialism* (Dar es Salaam: Oxford University Press, 1968).

9. Two recent monographs document the history of the villagization programs of Tanzania's socialist era; see Lal, *African Socialism*, and Leander Schneider, *Government of Development: Peasants and Politicians in Postcolonial Tanzania,* (Bloomington: Indiana University Press, 2014).

10. Richard Stren, "Urban Inequality and Housing Policy in Tanzania: The Problem of Squatting," in *Research Series* (Berkeley: Institute of International Studies, UC Berkeley, 1975); Andrew Burton, "The Haven of Peace Purged: Tackling the Undesirable and Unproductive Poor in Dar es Salaam, ca. 1950s–1980s," *International Journal of African Historical Studies* 40, no. 1 (2007): 119–51; Andrew Ivaska, *Cultured States: Youth, Gender and Modern Style in 1960s Dar es Salaam* (Durham, NC: Duke University Press, 2011), chapter 2.

11. Garth Myers and Martin J. Murray, "Introduction: Situating Contemporary Cities in Africa," in *Cities in Contemporary Africa*, ed. Garth Myers and Martin J. Murray (New York: Palgrave Macmillan, 2006), 3–7.

12. AbdouMaliq Simone, *For the City Yet to Come: Changing African Life in Four Cities* (Durham, NC: Duke University Press, 2004), 169.

13. Keith Hart, "Informal Income Opportunities and Urban Employment in Ghana," *Journal of Modern African Studies* 11, no. 1 (1973): 61–89.

14. Paul Ehrlich, *The Population Bomb* (New York: Ballantine, 1968); Matthew Connelly, "To Inherit the Earth: Imagining World Population, from the Yellow Peril to the Population Bomb," *Journal of Global History* 1, no. 3 (2006), 299–319.

15. Emma Tarlo, *Unsettling Memories: Narratives of the Emergency in Delhi* (Berkeley: University of California Press, 2003).

16. R. H. Sabot, *Economic Development and Urban Migration* (Oxford: Clarendon, 1979), 48.

17. World Bank, *World Development Report 1994* (New York: Oxford University Press, 1994), 222–23.
18. African Development Bank Group, "Tracking Africa's Progress in Figures" (Tunis: African Development Bank, 2014).
19. The major historical works on Dar es Salaam in recent years include Andrew Burton, *African Underclass: Urbanisation, Crime and Colonial Order in Dar es Salaam* (Oxford: James Currey, 2005); Andrew Ivaska, *Cultured States* (Durham, NC: Duke University Press, 2011); James R. Brennan, *Taifa: Making Nation and Race in Urban Tanzania* (Athens: Ohio University Press, 2011); and James R. Brennan, Andrew Burton, and Yusuf Lawi (who also edited a collection of essays on the city), *Dar es Salaam: Histories from an Emerging African Metropolis* (Dar es Salaam: Mkuki na Nyota, 2007).
20. On Ujamaa, see most notably Leander Schneider, *Government of Development*, and Lal, *African Socialism*.
21. Raymond Williams, *The Country and the City* (New York: Oxford University Press, 1973).
22. Ananya Roy, *City Requiem, Calcutta: Gender and the Politics of Poverty* (Minneapolis: University of Minnesota Press, 2003); Swati Chattopadhyay, *Representing Calcutta: Modernity, Nationalism and the Colonial Uncanny* (London: Routledge, 2005); Abidin Kusno, *Behind the Postcolonial: Architecture, Urban Space and Political Cultures in Indonesia* (London: Routledge, 2000); and James Ferguson, "Country and City on the Copperbelt," in *Culture, Power, Place: Explorations in Critical Anthropology*, ed. James Ferguson and Akhil Gupta (Durham, NC: Duke University Press, 1997), 137–56.
23. This book is not the first to examine binary portrayals of city and country in Nyerere's political philosophy; see Ivaska, *Cultured States,* especially the introduction.
24. Monika Krause, "The Ruralization of the World," *Public Culture* 25, no. 2 (2013): 233–48.
25. There is an expanding literature that explores the politics of national culture production in postcolonial Africa. In addition to Ivaska, *Cultured States,* see also Kelly Askew, *Performing the Nation: Swahili Music and Cultural Politics in Tanzania* (Chicago: University of Chicago Press, 2002); Andrew Apter, *The Pan-African Nation: Oil and the Spectacle of Culture in Nigeria* (Chicago: University of Chicago Press, 2005); Mary Jo Arnoldi, "Youth Festivals and Museums: The Cultural Politics of Public Memory in Postcolonial Mali," *Africa Today* 52, no. 4 (2006): 55–76; Ryan Thomas Skinner, "Cultural Politics in the Post-Colony: Music, Nationalism and Statism in Mali, 1964–75," *Africa* 82, no. 4 (2012): 511–34; and Jay Straker, *Youth, Nationalism and the Guinean Revolution* (Bloomington: Indiana University Press, 2009).
26. Karin Barber, "Popular Arts in Africa," *African Studies Review* 30, no. 3 (1987): 14.
27. My thinking on intermediate figures builds on the work of Nancy Rose Hunt on "colonial middle figures"; Hunt, *A Colonial Lexicon: Of Birth,*

Medicalization and Mobility in the Congo (Durham, NC: Duke University Press, 1999).

28. Steven Feierman, *Peasant Intellectuals: Anthropology and History in Tanzania* (Madison: University of Wisconsin Press, 1990).

29. The term *informal sector* was first coined by anthropologist Keith Hart in 1973, based on his work in Accra, Ghana; Hart, "Informal Income Opportunities and Urban Employment in Ghana." For more recent evaluations of the term, see Karen Tranberg Hansen and Mariken Vaa, "Introduction," in *Reconsidering Informality: Perspectives from Urban Africa,* (Uppsala: Nordic Africa Institute, 2004), 7–20; Ananya Roy and Nezar AlSayyad, *Urban Informality: Transnational Perspectives from the Middle East, Latin America, and South Asia* (Lanham, MD: Lexington Books, 2004); Deborah James and Elizabeth Hull, "Introduction: Popular Economies in South Africa," *Africa* 82, no. 1 (2012): 1–19. In Tanzania, see Aili Tripp, *Changing the Rules: The Politics of Liberalization and the Informal Urban Economy in Tanzania* (Berkeley: University of California Press, 1997).

30. Tanzanian literacy rates rose rapidly from a mere 11 percent at independence in 1961 to 79 percent at the end of the socialist era; H. S. Bhola, *Campaigning for Literacy: Eight National Experiences of the Twentieth Century* (Paris: UNESCO, 1984), 149.

31. See several works by Judith R. Walkowitz, including *City of Dreadful Delight: Narratives of Sexual Danger in Late-Victorian London*, Women in Culture and Society (Chicago: University of Chicago Press, 1992); "The Indian Woman, the Flower Girl and the Jew," *Victorian Studies* 42, no. 1 (1998): 3–46; and *Nights Out: Life in Cosmopolitan London* (New Haven, CT: Yale University Press, 2012).

32. Teresa Pires do Rio Caldeira, *City of Walls: Crime, Segregation, and Citizenship in São Paulo* (Berkeley: University of California Press, 2000), and Martin J. Murray, *City of Extremes: The Spatial Politics of Johannesburg* (Durham, NC: Duke University Press, 2011).

33. Murray, *City of Extremes,* chapter 2; Ferguson, *Expectations of Modernity: Myths and Meanings of Urban Life on the Zambian Copperbelt* (Berkeley: University of California Press, 1999); and Achille Mbembe and Sarah Nuttall, "Introduction," in *Johannesburg: The Elusive Metropolis*, ed. Achille Mbembe and Sarah Nuttall (Durham, NC: Duke University Press, 2008).

34. Louise Young, *Beyond the Metropolis: Second Cities and Modern Life in Interwar Japan* (Berkeley: University of California Press, 2013).

35. Gyan Prakash, *Mumbai Fables* (Princeton, NJ: Princeton University Press, 2010).

36. Joanne Rappaport and Thomas B. F. Cummins, *Beyond the Lettered City: Indigenous Literacies in the Andes* (Durham, NC: Duke University Press, 2012).

37. Weiss, "Thug Realism."

38. Barber, *The Anthropology of Texts, Persons and Publics* (Cambridge: Cambridge University Press, 2007).

39. I am inspired here by Derek Peterson's definition of "creative writing," which refers not to artistic merit, but instead to the ways in which quotidian forms of writing and reading are socially productive; see Peterson, *Creative Writing: Translation, Bookkeeping, and the Work of Imagination in Colonial Kenya* (Portsmouth, NH: Heinemann, 2004), and Peterson, "The Intellectual Lives of Mau Mau Detainees," *Journal of African History* 49 (2008): 73–91.

40. Simone, *For the City Yet to Come*; Sasha Newell, *The Modernity Bluff: Crime, Consumption, and Citizenship in Côte d'Ivoire* (Chicago: University of Chicago Press, 2012); Alex Perullo, *Live from Dar es Salaam: Popular Music and Tanzania's Music Economy* (Bloomington: Indiana University Press, 2011); and Jeremy L. Jones, " 'Nothing Is Straight in Zimbabwe': The Rise of the *Kukiya-Kiya* Economy 2000–2008," *Journal of Southern African Studies* 36, no. 2 (2010): 285–99.

41. Frederick Cooper, *On the African Waterfront: Urban Disorder and the Transformation of Work in Colonial Mombasa* (New Haven, CT: Yale University Press, 1987).

42. Jane Guyer, "Introduction," in *Money Struggles and City Life: Devaluation in Ibadan and Other Urban Centers in Southern Nigeria, 1986–1996*, ed. Jane L. Guyer, LaRay Denzer, and Adigun A. B. Agbaje (Portsmouth, NH: Heinemann, 2002).

43. Simone, "People as Infrastructure: Intersecting Fragments in Johannesburg," *Public Culture* 16, no. 3 (2004): 407–29.

44. Cooper, *On the African Waterfront*.

45. Jean Allman, "Phantoms of the Archive: Kwame Nkrumah, a Nazi Pilot Named Hanna, and the Contingencies of Postcolonial History Writing," *American Historical Review* 118, no. 1 (2013): 129.

46. Most famously, James C. Scott, *Seeing Like a State: How Certain Schemes to Improve the Human Condition Have Failed* (New Haven, CT: Yale University Press, 1998).

47. Baz Lecocq and Erik Bähre, "The Drama of Development: The Skirmishes behind High Modernist Schemes in Africa," *African Studies* 66, no. 1 (2007): 1–8.

48. Roy, *City Requiem, Calcutta*.

49. Daniel Magaziner and Alexei Yurchak have made a similar argument about the lives of artists in apartheid South Africa and the Soviet Union respectively; see Yurchak, *Everything Was Forever, Until It Was No More: The Last Soviet Generation* (Princeton, NJ: Princeton University Press, 2005), and Magaziner, "Two Stories about Art, Education and Beauty in Twentieth-Century South Africa," *American Historical Review* 118, no. 5 (2013): 1403–29.

Chapter 1: TANU, African Socialism, and the City Idea

1. "Tumpe Kura Zetu Mwl. Nyerere," *Ngurumo*, September 21, 1965.

2. On the desire for cement houses, see Julius Nyerere, "The Arusha Declaration Ten Years After" (Dar es Salaam: Government Printer, 1977), 29–31. On

TANU's changing relationship with labor unions, see Andrew Burton, "Raw Youth, School-Leavers and the Emergence of Structural Unemployment in Late-Colonial Urban Tanganyika," *Journal of African History* 47 (2006): 363–87.

3. Nyerere, "Arusha Declaration Ten Years After."

4. Issa Shivji, "Tanzania—the Silent Class Struggle," in *Socialism in Tanzania: An Interdisciplinary Reader*, ed. John S. Saul and Lionel Cliffe (Nairobi: East African Publishing House, 1973), 304–40.

5. Raymond Williams, *The Country and the City* (New York: Oxford University Press, 1973).

6. Jonathan Hyslop, "Gandhi, Mandela and the African Modern," in *Johannesburg: The Elusive Metropolis*, ed. Achille Mbembe and Sarah Nuttall (Durham, NC: Duke University Press, 2008), 119–36.

7. James Ferguson, "Country and City on the Copperbelt." In *Culture, Power, Place: Explorations in Critical Anthropology*, ed. James Ferguson and Akhil Gupta, 137–56 (Durham, NC: Duke University Press, 1997).

8. Ananya Roy, *City Requiem, Calcutta: Gender and the Politics of Poverty*, Globalization and Community (Minneapolis: University of Minnesota Press, 2003).

9. J. A. K. Leslie, *A Survey of Dar es Salaam* (London: Oxford University Press, 1963).

10. James R. Brennan, *Taifa: Making Nation and Race in Urban Tanzania* (Athens: Ohio University Press, 2011), 49.

11. W. T. Casson, "Architectural Notes on Dar es Salaam," *Tanzania Notes and Records* 71 (1970): 181–84; Alex Perullo, "Rumba in the City of Peace: Migration and the Cultural Commodity of Congolese Music in Dar es Salaam, Tanzania, 1968–1985," *Ethnomusicology* 52, no. 2 (2008): 196–223; Askew, *Performing the Nation* (Chicago: University of Chicago Press, 2002); Mark Horton and John Middleton, *The Swahili: The Social Landscape of a Mercantile Society* (Oxford: Blackwell, 2000); and Derek Nurse and Thomas T. Spear, *The Swahili: Reconstructing the History and Language of an African Society, 800–1500* (Philadelphia: University of Pennsylvania Press, 1985).

12. Andrew Ivaska, *Cultured States: Youth, Gender and Modern Style in 1960s Dar es Salaam* (Durham, NC: Duke University Press, 2011).

13. Such an apparent contradiction, Glassman argues, is not at all contradictory: nativisms are not local, but are universalizing and circulate globally; Jonathon Glassman, "Creole Nationalists and the Search for Nativist Authenticity in Twentieth-Century Zanzibar: The Limits of Cosmopolitanism," *Journal of African History* 15, no. 2 (2014): 229–47.

14. Casson, "Architectural Notes on Dar es Salaam,"181–84.

15. For a far more subtle and detailed breakdown of this policy, see Brennan, *Taifa*, 21–34.

16. Brennan, *Taifa*, 152–53.

17. Brennan, *Taifa*, 152–53.
18. N. J. Westcott, "An East African Radical: The Life of Erica Fiah," *Journal of African History* 22, no. 1 (1981): 85–101.
19. In both cases, African intellectuals inverted these ideas to perform new work for them in Dar es Salaam. As Brennan points out, the Gandhian slogan calling for the British to quit India would be recast as a call for Indians to quit Africa. Similarly, Aggrey's claim that Africans could be self-sufficient within a colonial system would eventually be reworked to claim that Africans could be self-sufficient without colonial rule. On Dar es Salaam intellectuals and their engagement with James Aggrey and Booker T. Washington, see Brennan, *Taifa*, 120–25.
20. Emily Callaci, "Dancehall Politics: Mobility, Sexuality, and Spectacles of Racial Respectability in Late Colonial Tanganyika, 1930s–1961," *Journal of African History* 52, no. 3 (2011): 365–84; Derek Peterson, *Creative Writing: Translation, Bookkeeping, and the Work of Imagination in Colonial Kenya* (Portsmouth, NH: Heinemann, 2004); Justin Willis, *Potent Brews: A Social History of Alcohol in East Africa 1850–1999*, Eastern African Studies (Oxford: James Currey, 2002); Burton and Hélène Charton-Bigot, eds., *Generations Past: Youth in East African History* (Athens: Ohio University Press, 2010); and Shula Marks, "Patriotism, Patriarchy and Purity: Natal and the Politics of Zulu Ethnic Consciousness," in *The Creation of Tribalism in Southern Africa*, ed. Leroy Vail (Berkeley: University of California Press, 1989), 215–40.
21. Andrew Burton and Gary Burgess, "Introduction," in *Generations Past: Youth in East African History*, ed. Andrew Burton and Hélène Charton-Bigot (Athens: Ohio University Press, 2010), 8; Richard Reid, *War in Pre-Colonial Eastern Africa: The Patterns and Meanings of State-Level Conflict in the Nineteenth Century* (Athens: Ohio University Press, 2007); Willis, *Potent Brews*, 50–60; Reid, "Arms and Adolescence: Male Youth, Warfare and Statehood in Nineteenth-Century Eastern Africa," in *Generations Past: Youth in East African History*, ed. Andrew Burton and Hélène Charton-Bigot (Athens: Ohio University Press, 2010), 25–43; and Stephen J. Rockel, *Carriers of Culture: Labor on the Road in Nineteenth-Century East Africa* (Portsmouth, NH: Heinemann, 2006).
22. Glassman, *Feasts and Riot: Revelry, Rebellion, and Popular Consciousness on the Swahili Coast, 1856–1888* (Portsmouth, NH: Heinemann, 1995); Holly Hanson, "Queen Mothers and Good Government in Buganda: The Loss of Women's Political Power in Nineteenth-Century East Africa," in *Women in African Colonial Histories*, ed. Susan Geiger, Nakanyike Musisi, and Jean Marie Allman (Bloomington: Indiana University Press, 2002), 219–36; Meredith McKittrick, "Forsaking their Fathers? Colonialism, Christianity and Coming of Age in Ovamboland, Northern Namibia," in *Men and Masculinities in Modern Africa*, ed. Stephan Miescher and Lisa Lindsay (Portsmouth, NH: Heinemann, 2003), 33–51.

23. Shane Doyle, "Premarital Sexuality in Great Lakes Africa, 1900–1980," in *Generations Past: Youth in East African History*, ed. Andrew Burton and Hélène Charton-Bigot (Athens: Ohio University Press, 2010), 237–61.

24. Derek Peterson describes the creation of "ethnic patriotisms" through a process by which, in postwar East Africa, "men came to feel themselves responsible for women to whom they were not directly related" and came to define the political community that would seek to discipline women in terms of an ethnic "fatherland"; Peterson, *Ethnic Patriotism and the East African Revival: A History of Dissent, c. 1935–1972* (New York: Cambridge University Press, 2012), 3–4.

25. Michael Schatzberg tracks these patriarchal metaphors across the African continent in his *Political Legitimacy in Middle Africa: Father, Family, Food* (Bloomington: Indiana University Press, 2001).

26. Karen Tranberg Hansen, "Dressing Dangerously: Miniskirts, Gender Relations and Sexuality in Zambia," in *Fashioning Africa: Power and the Politics of Dress*, ed. Jean Allman (Bloomington: Indiana University Press, 2004), 166–85; Ivaska, *Cultured States*; Alicia Decker, *In Idi Amin's Shadow: Women, Gender, and Militarism in Uganda* (Athens: Ohio University Press, 2014), 63; Cyprian Kambili, "Ethics of African Tradition: Prescription of Dress Code in Malawi 1965–1973," *Society of Malawi Journal* 55, no. 2 (2002): 80–99; Peterson, *Ethnic Patriotism and the East African Revival*.

27. R. H. Sabot, *Economic Development and Urban Migration* (Oxford: Clarendon Press, 1979).

28. Erica Fiah, "Money and Its Effect upon the African," *Kwetu*, June 7, 1942, 42; italics are mine.

29. "Proposal for Control of Africans in Dar Es Salaam Township," 1942–44, TNA Accession 61 File 443/1; "Detribalization," 1955–61, TNA Accession File 481, 2/9; "Dar es Salaam District Office Annual Reports," 1921–30, TNA; and Report on "Detribalization Among Africans," 1949, TNA 37520.

30. See, for example, Frederick Cooper, *On the African Waterfront: Urban Disorder and the Transformation of Work in Colonial Mombasa* (New Haven, CT: Yale University Press, 1987), and Jane Parpart, "Wicked Women and Respectable Ladies: Reconfiguring Gender on the Zambian Copperbelt, 1936–64," in *"Wicked" Women and the Reconfiguration of Gender in Africa*, ed. Dorothy Hodgson and Sheryl McCurdy (Portsmouth, NH: Heinemann, 2001), 274–92.

31. On the Haya Union, see Luise White, *The Comforts of Home: Prostitution in Colonial Nairobi* (Chicago: University of Chicago Press, 1990), 103–19, and Peterson, *Ethnic Patriotism and the East African Revival*, 34 and chapter 7. For example, the files of the Usambara Union (*Umoja wa Usambara*) from 1948 through 1953 reveal great concern on the part of parents over young migrants to the city of Tanga; TNA 493 6/15. In response to young people migrating to the coast, *Mhola Ziswe*, the paper from Tabora, no. 27, Sep-

tember 1953, 7, in the article "Vijana wa Leo Msiache Jadi Zetu," urges the Nyamwezi community to prevent young people speaking Kiswahili in the place of Kinyamwezi.

32. The attempt to cultivate female virtue and ethnic endogamy through traditional dance was not unique to colonial Tanzania; see, for example, Shula Marks, "Patriotism, Patriarchy and Purity," 215–40.

33. Benjamin K. Aaron, "Vyama Vya Wanayamwezi: Majibu," *Mambo Leo,* April 1935.

34. Aaron, "Vyama Vya Wanayamwezi: Majibu."

35. Kenda Mutongi, *Worries of the Heart: Widows, Family and Community in Kenya* (Chicago: University of Chicago Press, 2007), 144–47.

36. Mutongi, *Worries of the Heart,* 26.

37. James Brennan has argued that control of female sexuality and criticism of interracial relationships was one of the main discursive arenas in which racial identification solidified in Tanzania in the 1940s; Brennan, "Realizing Civilization through Patrilineal Descent: The Intellectual Making of an African Racial Nationalism in Tanzania, 1920–1950," *Social Identities* 12, no. 4 (2006).

38. Callaci, "Dancehall Politics," 365–84.

39. J. A. K. Leslie, *Survey of Dar es Salaam.*

40. John Iliffe, *A Modern History of Tanganyika* (Cambridge: Cambridge University Press, 1979), chapter 15.

41. Susan Geiger, TANU *Women: Gender and Culture in the Making of Tanganyikan Nationalism, 1955–1965* (Portsmouth, NH: Heinemann, 1995); Brennan, "Youth, the TANU Youth League and Managed Vigilantism in Dar es Salaam, Tanzania," *Africa* 76, no. 2 (2006): 221–46. For an analysis of claims to urban real estate based on race, see Brennan, chapter 4, "Between Segregation and Gentrification: Africans, Indians and the Struggle for Housing in Dar es Salaam, 1920–1950," in *Dar es Salaam: Histories from an Emerging African Metropolis,* ed. James R. Brennan, Andrew Burton, and Yusuf Lawi (Dar es Salaam: Mkuki na Nyota, 2007).

42. Brennan, "Youth, the TANU Youth League and Managed Vigilantism in Dar es Salaam, Tanzania," 227–29.

43. Brennan, *Taifa,* 143.

44. Brennan discusses these policies and their role in racial politics in "Between Segregation and Gentrification," 126–31.

45. Geiger, TANU *Women,* chapter 2.

46. Martin Sturmer, *A Media History of Tanzania* (Peramiho: Ndanda Mission Press, 1998), 74–76. For an interview with Robert Makange, see also Hubert Temba, "Looking Back through the Time Tunnel: Makange; Once Feted as 'Prison Graduate,'" *Daily News,* January 4, 1975.

47. Ivaska, *Cultured States,* 30.

48. Hadji Konde, *Press Freedom in Tanzania* (Arusha: Eastern African Publications, 1984).

49. Ronald Aminzade, *Race, Nation, and Citizenship in Post-Colonial Africa: The Case of Tanzania* (New York: Cambridge University Press, 2013), 53 and 109.

50. For a more detailed elaboration of the concept of racial respectability, see Lynn Thomas, "The Modern Girl and Racial Respectability in 1930s South Africa," *Journal of African History* 47 (2006): 461–90; and Callaci, "Dancehall Politics," 365–84.

51. For example, Omar Bawazir, "Mitaa ya Tanga, na Bratha Bawazir," *Mwafrika*, March 21, 1964; Sukari, "Naitklab ya Mwanza Yanipeleka Mbio," *Mwafrika*, May 2, 1964; and Peter Kagisa, "Kampala ni Mji wa Anasa," *Mwafrika*, May 2, 1964.

52. See Ivaska, *Cultured States*, 200–205.

53. Laura Fair, "Drive-in Socialism: Debating Modernities and Development in Dar es Salaam, Tanzania," *American Historical Review* 118, no. 4 (2013): 1077–1104; Lawrence Mtawa, "Maktaba Kuu ya Taifa Itatufaidia," *Nchi Yetu*, November 1969; Majengo Mapya, "Mjini Dar es Salaam," *Nchi Yetu*, August 1969; Majengo Mapya, "Mjini Dar," *Nchi Yetu*, December 1970; S. Mkandawire, "Majengo Mapya Mjini Dar," *Nchi Yetu*, January 1971; "Mecco Ad," *Mzalendo*, July 16, 1972; and "Toleo Maalum: Kariakoo Market," *Mzalendo*, December 7, 1975.

54. H. I. Kundya, "Bahari Beach Hotel: Kuna Harufu Ya Kiujamaa," *Nchi Yetu*, December 1970; John Siliya, "Hoteli Ya Namna Ya Pekee," *Nchi Yetu*, February 1971; and Richard Mngazija, "Hoteli Ya Kisasa Yenye Asili Ya Kiafrika," *Uhuru*, December 3, 1973.

55. The paper *Nchi Yetu* had a regular series called, "Majengo Mapya Mjini Dar es Salaam," or "New Buildings in Urban Dar es Salaam," from 1969 through 1971.

56. Publications of this sort include *Dar es Salaam Medical Journal*; *Tatejo* (teacher's journal); *Habari za Posta* (for workers in the postal service); *Tanzania Police Journal*; *Habari za Mwadui* (for employees of diamond mines); *Tanzania Engineers*; *Tanesco News* (for employees of the parastatal electrical company); and the *Civil Servants Magazine of the United Republic of Tanzania*.

57. "Obtain a Plot for your Own House," *Civil Servants Magazine of the United Republic of Tanzania*, no. 4 (November/December 1965).

58. Askew, *Performing the Nation*; Laura Edmondson, *Performance and Politics in Tanzania* (Bloomington: Indiana University Press, 2007).

59. These projects are showcased in the monthly publication of the Ministry of Education, *Nchi Yetu*.

60. National Museums of Tanzania, *Maelezo ya Kijiji cha Makumbusho* (Dar es Salaam: Printpak Tanzania, 1966).

61. Two recent works provide a more nuanced historical account of the African socialism in Tanzania; see Priya Lal, *African Socialism in Postcolonial Tanzania: Between the Village and the World* (Cambridge: Cambridge University Press, 2015); and Leander Schneider, *Government of Development: Peasants*

and Politicians in Postcolonial Tanzania (Bloomington: Indiana University Press, 2014).

62. See Lal's discussion of the "continental repertoire of African Socialism," in *African Socialism in Postcolonial Tanzania*, 37.

63. Frantz Fanon, *The Wretched of the Earth*, trans. Constance Farrington (New York: Grove, 1963), 185. In addition to being disseminated in English in East Africa, this text appeared in at least two Swahili translations: Franz [sic] Fanon, *Viumbe Waliolaaniwa,* trans. Gabriel Ruhumbika and Clement Maganga (Dar es Salaam: Tanzania Publishing House, 1978); and *Mafukara ya Ulimwengu*, trans. Ahmed Yusuf Abeid, 1977.

64. Fanon, *Wretched of the Earth*, 61.

65. Fanon, *Viumbe Waliolaaniwa*, and Fanon, *Mafukara ya Ulimwengu.*

66. For an analysis of Tanzania's Ujamaa program in the broader context of the Third World political imagination, see Vijay Prashad, *The Darker Nations: A People's History of the Third World* (New York: New Press, 2008), 191–203.

67. George T. Yu, *Africa's China Policy: A Study of Tanzania* (New York: Praeger, 1975).

68. G. Thomas Burgess, "Mao in Zanzibar: Nationalism, Discipline and the (De) Construction of Afro-Asian Solidarities," in *Making a World After Empire: The Bandung Moment and Its Political Afterlives*, ed. Christopher Lee (Athens: Ohio University Press, 2010), 196–234.

69. Nyerere, "Ujamaa: The Basis for African Socialism," in *Ujamaa: Essays on Socialism*, 11.

70. Lal, *African Socialism in Postcolonial Tanzania*, 33.

71. For nuanced understandings of "tradition," see especially Thomas Spear, "Neo-Traditionalism and the Limits of Invention in British Colonial Africa," *Journal of African History* 44 (2003), 3–27.

72. Glassman, *War of Words, War of Stones: Racial Thought and Violence in Colonial Zanzibar* (Bloomington: Indiana University Press, 2011).

73. For example, the radio series *Unyonge wa Mwafrika*, printed and distributed as a literacy primer, contained parables attributing, for example, the desire to own urban real estate or work in an office job as elements of a "slave mentality," imposed on Africans by Arab slave traders.

74. Callaci, "'Chief Village in a Nation of Villages': History, Race and Authority in Tanzania's Dodoma Plan," *Urban History* 43, no. 1 (2015): 96–116.

75. In his highly influential *Seeing Like a State: How Certain Schemes to Improve the Human Condition Have Failed*, James Scott argued that Ujamaa villagization was an example of a highly centralized, top-down, and scientific program of "high modernism"(New Haven, CT: Yale University Press, 1998). For an in-depth critique of this idea, see Lal, *African Socialism in Postcolonial Tanzania*.

76. Schneider, *Government of Development,* 134–35.

77. Richard Stren, "Urban Inequality and Housing Policy in Tanzania: The Problem of Squatting" (Berkeley: Institute of International Studies, University of California, 1975).

78. Stren, "Urban Inequality and Housing Policy in Tanzania," 1975; Stren, Mohamed Halfani and Joyce Malombe, "Coping with Urbanization and Urban Policy," in *Beyond Capitalism vs. Socialism in Kenya and Tanzania*, ed. Joel Barkan (Boulder, CO: Lynn Rienner, 1994), 175–200.

79. See chapter 3 of this volume.

80. Marie-Ange Goux, "Public Housing Policies: Decentralization, Government Policies, and the People's Solutions," in *From Dar es Salaam to Bongoland: Urban Mutations in Tanzania*, ed. Bernard Calas (Dar es Salaam: Mkuki na Nyota, 2006), 99–124.

81. "Wasichana Wetu," *Uhuru*, April 15, 1969; "Wazazi Wetu Hufurahia Mavazi Ya 'Mini' Na 'Michinjo,'" *Uhuru*, April 15, 1969.

82. Decker, *In Idi Amin's Shadow*; Kambili, "Ethics of African Tradition."

83. Ivaska, *Cultured States*, chapter 2.

84. Andrew Burton, "The Haven of Peace Purged: Tackling the Undesirable and Unproductive Poor in Dar es Salaam, ca. 1950s–1980s," *International Journal of African Historical Studies* 40, no. 1 (2007), 119–51.

85. Iliffe, *East African Doctors: A History of the Modern Profession* (Cambridge: Cambridge University Press, 1998), 207.

86. Callaci, "'Chief Village in a Nation of Villages,'" 99–116.

87. Ivaska, *Cultured States*, 29.

88. Ivaska, *Cultured States*, 56–57.

89. Examples by female authors of novellas with this formula of rural ruin followed by female uplift in Ujamaa villages include Ndyanao Balisidya, *Shida* (Nairobi: Foundation, 1975); Bi. S. Abubakar, *Haki Ya Mtu Haipokei* (Peramiho: Benedictine Publications Ndanda-Peramiho, 1981); Martha Mvungi, *Hana Hatia* (Dar es Salaam: Tanzania Publishing House, 1975); see also Abdul Baka, *Salome* (Dar es Salaam: Tanzania Publishing House, 1972).

90. Mvungi, *Hana Hatia*.

91. "A Guide to the Operation of Literacy/Adult Education Programme in Tanzania," n.d.

92. "Tanzania Adult Literacy Adult Education Programme," report produced by J. M. Rutashobya, Adult Education Coordinator, Ministry of Community Development and National Culture, Dar es Salaam, n.d.; Melville J. Herskovits Library of African Studies, Northwestern University, Evanston, IL, vertical files.

93. Z. J. Mpogolo, *Functional Literacy in Tanzania* (Dar es Salaam: Swala, 1980).

94. See chapter 4 of this volume.

95. Z. J. Mpogolo, *Functional Literacy in Tanzania*.

96. S. K. Msuya, *Mazungumzo Ya Usiku* (Dar es Salaam: Tanzania Publishing House, 1978).

97. Williams, *The Country and the City*.

98. Msuya, *Mazungumzo Ya Usiku*, back cover.

99. Lila Abu-Lughod, *Dramas of Nationhood: The Politics of Television in Egypt* (Chicago: University of Chicago Press, 2005).

100. Sturmer, *Media History of Tanzania*.

101. Guido Magome, "The Press and Socialism," *Daily News*, April 26, 1972.

102. This was, in part, in response to an opposition newspaper launched by Oscar Kambona in a failed coup attempt from exiled in London; Graham Mytton, *Mass Communication in Africa* (London: Edward Arnold, 1983). This approach to development resembles what Lila Abu-Lughod calls "developmental realism," which encourages a faith in authority and defines grievances of the marginalized as moral shortcomings; Abu-Lughod, *Dramas of Nationhood, The Politics of Television in Egypt* (Chicago: University of Chicago Press, 2004), chapter 4.

103. These reports appeared frequently in *Nchi Yetu* and *Uhuru*. For a description of how students were expected by the government to write about Ujamaa, see Zakia Hamdani Meghji's essay "Sisterly Activism," in *Cheche: Reminiscences of a Radical Magazine*, ed. Karim Hirji (Dar es Salaam: Mkuki na Nyota, 2010).

104. "Alijifungua: Mtoto 'Aingia Chooni,'" *Ngurumo*, September 26, 1970.

105. Chiku Abdallah, "Maisha Gani Haya Jijini Dar es Salaam?" *Nchi Yetu*, April 1975.

106. Miniskirts and skin-lightening creams and cosmetics had been banned by the TYL in 1969; Ivaska, "Anti-Mini Militants Meet Modern Misses: Urban Style, Gender and the Politics of 'National Culture' in 1960s Dar es Salaam, Tanzania," *Gender and History* 14, no. 3 (2002): 584–607.

107. The quality of the image was too low to be reproduced in this book. It appeared in *Uhuru*, December 4, 1969, 5.

108. Schneider, "The Maasai's New Clothes: A Developmentalist Modernity and Its Exclusions," *Africa Today* 53, no. 1 (2006): 101–31.

109. Brennan, "Youth, the TANU Youth League, and Managed Vigilantism in Dar Es Salaam," 234.

110. Ivaska, "'Anti-Mini Militants Meet Modern Misses'"; Hansen, "Dressing Dangerously," 104–8.

111. Allen Silver Mhije, "Kulikuwa na Nini Margot?," *Nchi Yetu*, November 1974, 32.

Chapter 2: "All Alone in the Big City"

1. Martha Mandao, *Peke Yangu Mjini* (Dodoma: Central Tanganyika Press, 1969).

2. Many of these issues were raised at conferences and workshops. For an example of this, see the Tanganyika Rapid Social Change Study conference proceedings from a 1964 meeting: *The Church Meets Life in the Town* (Dar-es-Salaam: s.n., 1964).

3. Abosede George, *Making Modern Girls: A History of Girlhood, Labor, and Social Development in Colonial Lagos* (Athens: Ohio University Press, 2014).

4. Penina Muhando Mlama was a professor of theater at the University of Dar es Salaam. Her work on "development theater" emphasized rural theater productions as spaces where local participants would develop a critical consciousness of their society and give voice to new political possibilities. In later years, she reflected on this approach in her book *Culture and Development: The Popular Theatre Approach in Africa* (Uppsala: Nordiska Afrikainstitutet, 1991).

5. Corrie Decker, "Reading, Writing, and Respectability: How Schoolgirls Developed Modern Literacies in Colonial Zanzibar," *International Journal of African Historical Studies* 43, no. 1 (2010): 89–114.

6. Modern Girl Around the World Research Group, "The Modern Girl as Heuristic Device: Collaboration, Connective Comparison, Multidirectional Citation," in *The Modern Girl Around the World: Consumption, Modernity, and Globalization* (Durham, NC: Duke University Press, 2008), 9.

7. Laura Bier makes this point in her essay about portrayals of women in the Egyptian press; see Bier, "Feminism, Solidarity and Identity in the Age of Bandung: Third World Women in the Egyptian Press," in *Making a World after Empire: The Bandung Moment and Its Political Afterlives*, ed. Christopher Lee (Athens: Ohio University Press, 2010), 143–72.

8. Research Notes and Data for 1973/1974 Social Survey of Dar es Salaam. Marja-Liisa Swantz, Deborah Bryceson, Hilda Ausi, Severa Mlay, and Fatuma Macha.

9. M. A. Bienefeld, "The Self Employed of Urban Tanzania," in DS *Discussion Paper* (Brighton: University of Sussex, 1974).

10. R. H. Sabot, *Economic Development and Urban Migration* (Oxford: Clarendon, 1979).

11. Robert Rweyemamu, "In a Hive of Activity Where Night Is Hell," *Daily News*, February 11, 1973.

12. Marja-Liisa Swantz and Deborah Fahy Bryceson, "Women Workers in Dar es Salaam: 1973/74 Survey of Female Minimum Wage Earners and Self-Employed," in *University of Dar es Salaam Research Paper No. 23* (Dar es Salaam: University of Dar es Salaam, 1974), 1–35.

13. William B. Anderson, *The Church in East Africa, 1890–1974* (Nairobi: Uzima, 1981), 155–56.

14. See the publication *Umoja*, May 1964–December 1970.

15. Stren, "Urban Inequality and Housing Policy in Tanzania: The Problem of Squatting," in *Research Series* (Berkeley: Institute of International Studies, University of California, 1975), 90.

16. Susan Geiger, TANU *Women: Gender and Culture in the Making of Tanganyikan Nationalism, 1955–1965* (Portsmouth, NH: Heinemann, 1995), chapter 2.

17. Marja-Liisa Swantz and Bryceson, "Women Workers in Dar es Salaam," 27.

18. Alice Werner and William Hichens, *The Advice of Mwana Kupona upon the Wifely Duty from the Swahili Texts* (Medstead, Hampshire: Azania Press, 1934), 49–51.

19. Margaret Strobel, *Muslim Women in Mombasa, 1890–1975*. Corrie Decker has examined the relationship between colonial sex education and these regionally rooted traditions of sex education in her article "Biology, Islam and the Science of Sex Education in Colonial Zanzibar," *Past and Present* 222 (February 2014): 215–47.

20. Additional titles include Margery Pelham-Johnson, *Binti Leo Kwake* (Nairobi: Eagle, 1950); Isabelle Victorine Frémon and Sister Mwuguzi, *Mdoe na Mama Yake: Mashauri katika Kuwalea Watoto Wadogo* (London: Sheldon, 1951); and St. Clair Hamilton and Archer Wallington, *Maarifa Yawapasayo Mama Katika Kutunza Watoto Wao* (London: Sheldon, 1943).

21. Andreana Prichard, *Sisters in Spirit: Christianity, Affect and Community Building in East Africa, 1860–1970* (East Lansing: Michigan State University Press, 2017), 304.

22. Denis M'Passou, *Mindolo: A Story of the Ecumenical Movement in Africa* (Lusaka: Multimedia, 1983), 85.

23. Loretta Kreider Andrews and Herbert D. Andrews, "The Church and the Birth of a Nation: The Mindolo Ecumenical Foundation and Zambia," *Journal of Church and State* 17, no. 2 (1975): 191–216.

24. James Ferguson, *Expectations of Modernity: Myths and Meanings of Urban Life on the Zambian Copperbelt* (Berkeley: University of California Press, 1999), 172.

25. Ferguson, *Expectations of Modernity*, 91.

26. Frederick Rex, "Africa Literacy and Writing Centre," *International Review of Missions* 49, no. 193 (1960): 91–94.

27. Chama cha Mama Wakristo, *Msaada kwa Viongozi* [Women's Mother's Union], *Guidelines for Leaders,* St. Mark's Center Archive, Dar es Salaam.

28. Martha Mandao, personnel file, Redio Sauti ya Injili, Moshi, Tanzania.

29. Carl J. Johansson, "The Bible School and the Church," *International Review of Mission* 45 (1956): 396–400.

30. Report of the Evangelical Literature Fellowship of East Africa, October 30, 1973, St. Mark's Center Archive, Dar es Salaam.

31. Interview with Modest Belege, Msimbazi Center, Dar es Salaam, July 27, 2015.

32. Marthe Mandao, *Seule dans la Ville* (Abidjan: Centre de Publications Evangéliques, 1974); *Ani y la Ciudad* (Argentina: Editorial Mundo, 1975); *Zowawa za m'tauni* (Blantyre: CLAIM, 1973); *Umoyo wa m'tauni* (Blantyre: CLAIM, 1973); and *Ani I stap wanpis long biktaun* (Madang, Papua New Guinea: Kristen Press, 1976).

33. In the earlier issues of *Kiongozi*, she published under the name "Theresia Mahunda," perhaps indicating that she married during this time; see *Kiongozi*, August 1, 1966–February 15, 1968.

34. Theresia Mshuza, "Kwa Uvumilivu Huiweka Mitaa Safi," *Uhuru*, August 28, 1971.

35. Mshuza, "Tusidharauliwe Katika Kazi," *Uhuru*, January 16, 1971.

36. Mshuza, "Mtindo Wa Wanawake Kufanya Kazi Usiku Unahitaji Marekebi-sho," *Uhuru*, February 12, 1972.

37. Research Notes and Data for 1973/1974 Social Survey of Dar es Salaam. Marja-Liisa Swantz, Deborah Bryceson, Hilda Ausi, Severa Mlay, and Fatuma Macha.

38. See Walter Rodney, *Walter Rodney Speaks: The Making of an African Intellectual* (Trenton, NJ: Africa World Press, 1990).

39. See, for example, accounts of the spirit of engaged activism at the University of Dar es Salaam in memoirs such as Rodney, *Walter Rodney Speaks*, 37–43; Marja-Liisa Swantz, *In Search of Living Knowledge* (Dar es Salaam: Mkuki na Nyota, 2016), 143–49; John S. Saul, "Radicalism and the Hill," in *Socialism in Tanzania: An Interdisciplinary Reader*, ed. John S. Saul and Lionel Cliffe (Nairobi: East African Publishing House, 1973); and Mlama, *Culture and Development*. See also selections in Karim F. Hirji, ed., *Cheche: Reminiscences of a Radical Magazine* (Dar es Salaam: Mkuki na Nyota, 2010).

40. On the issue of university women's solidarity with peasant and working women, see Mlama and especially Zakia Hamdani Meghji's essay "Sisterly Activism," in Hirji's edited volume *Cheche*.

41. Bryceson, Mlay, Macha, and Ausi, University of Dar es Salaam, research notes, 1973–74.

42. Bryceson, Mlay, Macha, and Ausi, University of Dar es Salaam, research notes, 1973–74.

43. Mlama, *Culture and Development*.

44. Marja-Liisa Swantz, *In Search of Living Knowledge*, 148–49.

45. Marja-Liisa Swantz, *In Search of Living Knowledge*, 149.

46. Nancy Rose Hunt, "Colonial Fairy Tales and the *Knife* and *Fork Doctrine* in the Heart of Africa," in *African Encounters with Domesticity*, ed. Karen Tranberg Hansen (New Brunswick, NJ: Rutgers University Press, 1992), 143–71.

47. Jean Comaroff and John Comaroff, *Of Revelation and Revolution*, vol. 2, *The Dialectics of Modernity on a South African Frontier* (Chicago: University of Chicago Press, 1997), chapters 3 and 6.

48. Luise White, "Separating the Men from the Boys: Constructions of Gender, Sexuality and Terrorism in Central Kenya, 1939–1959," *International Journal of African Historical Studies* 23, no. 1 (1990): 1–25.

49. This argument was made, most famously, by Ifi Amadiume in chapter 8 of *Male Daughter, Female Husbands: Gender and Sex in an African Society* (London: Zed, 1987).

50. For example, Lisa Lindsay shows how people seized on the notion of the breadwinner to get better wages; Lindsay, "Working with Gender: The Emergence of the 'Male Breadwinner' in Colonial Southwestern Nigeria," in *Africa after Gender*, ed. Catherine Cole, Takyiwaa Manuh, and Stephan Miescher (Bloomington: Indiana University Press, 2007), 241–52. James Ferguson sees visions of housewives baking cakes in kitchens not as cultural

imperialism, but as economic "expectations" of a prosperous future and a global economic modernity that would include Zambian mineworkers and their families; Ferguson, *Expectations of Modernity*, chapter 5.

51. Antoinette Burton, *Dwelling in the Archive: Women Writing House, Home and History in Late Colonial India* (Oxford: Oxford University Press, 2003).

52. Geiger, *Tanu Women*; Dick Vestbro, *Social Life and Dwelling Space: An Analysis of Three House Types in Dar Es Salaam* (Stockholm: Ordfront, 1975).

53. In Zimbabwe, women involved in such relationships of cohabitation with men without the payment of bridewealth came to be called "mapoto women," with that form of marriage known as a mapoto marriage; Chipo Hungwe, "Putting Them in Their Place: 'Respectable' and 'Unrespectable' Women in Zimbabwean Gender Struggles," *Feminist Africa*, no. 6 (2006), 33–47.

54. Research Notes and Data for 1973/1974 Social Survey of Dar es Salaam. Marja-Liisa Swantz, Deborah Bryceson, Hilda Ausi, Severa Mlay, and Fatuma Macha.

55. Bryceson, Mlay, Macha, and Ausi, University of Dar es Salaam, research notes, 1973–74.

56. Liv Haram, "'Prostitutes' or Modern Women? Negotiating Respectability in Northern Tanzania," in *Rethinking Sexualities in Africa*, ed. Signe Arnfred (Uppsala: Nordiska Afrikainstitutet, 2004), 7–34; Margrethe Silberschmidt, "Masculinities, Sexuality and Socio-Economic Change in Rural and Urban East Africa," in *Re-Thinking Sexualities in Africa*, ed. Signe Arnfred (Uppsala: Nordiska Afrikainstitutet, 2004), 233–50.

57. Bryceson, Mlay, Macha, and Ausi, University of Dar es Salaam, research notes, 1973–74.

58. Vestbro, *Social Life and Dwelling Space*, 38.

59. J. A. K. Leslie, *A Survey of Dar es Salaam* (London: Oxford University Press, 1963), 90–92.

60. Vestbro, *Social Life and Dwelling Space,* chapter 4.

61. "Geraldine Auliza Maswali," *Binti Leo*, August 1966.

62. Andrew Ivaska, *Cultured States: Youth, Gender and Modern Style in 1960s Dar es Salaam* (Durham, NC: Duke University Press, 2011), chapter 2.

63. Deborah Gaitskell, "'Christian Compounds for Girls': Church Hostels for African Women in Johannesburg, 1907–1970," *Journal of Southern African Studies* 6, no. 1 (1979): 44–69.

64. Reverend Father Lucas, "Msimbazi Community Centre, Dar es Salaam," paper presented at the conference "The Church Meets Life in the Town," Dar es Salaam, Tanzania, May 14–21, 1964 (Dar es Salaam: Tanganyika Rapid Social Change Study, Commission "C," 1964).

65. Interview with Maele Kushuma, December 21, 2010, Dar es Salaam.

66. Anderson, *The Church in East Africa, 1840–1974.*

67. Mrs. H. R. Kasambala, "Help for Unmarried Mothers," *Nationalist*, April 12, 1969.

68. "Working Girls Hostel Rules for Ghana Avenue Branch," Folder "Reference Copies," YWCA Dar es Salaam headquarters archive.
69. "Y.W.C.A. Hostel Ghana Avenue, Leave Permission," Folder "Reference Copies," YWCA Dar es Salaam headquarters archive.
70. "Job description for matron, 1968 Hostel (Buguruni)," YWCA Dar es Salaam headquarters archive.
71. "On Housing and the Single Girl," *Nationalist*, December 4, 1967.
72. "Residents Y.W.C.A. Hostel, to President Y.W.C.A., June 6, 1974," Folder "Rais wa Chama," YWCA Dar es Salaam headquarters archive.
73. Mshuza, "Kwa Nini Ndoa Nyingi Kati Ya Wafanya Kazi Katika Miji Huvunjika," *Uhuru*, August 15, 1970.
74. Research Notes and Data for 1973/1974 Social Survey of Dar es Salaam. Marja-Liisa Swantz, Deborah Bryceson, Hilda Ausi, Severa Mlay, and Fatuma Macha.
75. "New Deal for Maternity Women from July 1," *Nationalist*, June 6, 1969.
76. UMATI, *Umati Story: From Family Planning to Sexual and Reproductive Health*, ed. UMATI (Dar es Salaam: UMATI, 2005).
77. For example, see "Umati Chief Explains Ban on Injection," *Daily News*, July 19, 1973; "Tanga Suspends Umati Activities," *Daily News*, July 27, 1973; Rwehikira Bashome, "Contraceptives Are Evil to Our Society," *Sunday News*, April 22, 1973; and Benjamin Mkapa, "Mrs. Nsekela Talks to Ben Mkapa: Umati Does Not Want to Control Birth Rate," *Daily News*, February 19, 1973.
78. Interview with Grace Mtawali, December 26, 2010, Dar es Salaam; Lloyd Swantz, *The Medicine Man among the Zaramo of Dar es Salaam* (Uppsala: Scandinavian Institute of African Studies, 1990).
79. Interview with Christina Nsekela, December 6, 2010; interview with Amy Mfinanga, January 3, 2011, Moshi; interview with Maele Kushuma, December 21, 2010, Dar es Salaam.
80. "Sex Education in Schools," *Nationalist*, June 6, 1970.
81. "Family Planning," *Nationalist*, October 11, 1969.
82. UMATI, *Umati Story*; interview with Christina Nsekela; interview with Amy Mfinanga, January 3, 2011, Moshi, Tanzania; interview with Maele Kushuma, December 21, 2010, Dar es Salaam.
83. "Tandau visits UMATI Offices," *Daily News*, October 5, 1972; interview with Grace Mtawali, December 26, 2010, Dar es Salaam; UMATI archive, file TR/Murg/Hosp; UMATI archive file TR/Seng/Hosp; interview with Dr. Sifuel Mamuya, January 3, 2011, Marangu, Tanzania.
84. Wendy Kline, *Bodies of Knowledge: Sexuality, Reproduction and Women's Health in the Second Wave* (Chicago: University of Chicago Press, 2010), 97–125.
85. Emily Callaci, "Injectable Development: Depo-Provera and the Mapping of the Global South," forthcoming.
86. Mshuza, "Likizo za Uzazi Bila Malipo Kwa Wasioolewa," *Uhuru*, August 21, 1971.

87. Dr. S. J. Mamuya, *Jando Na Unyago* (Nairobi: East African Publishing House, 1973); Juma Penza, "Tanu Bans Books," *Daily News*, June 5, 1976.

88. Aili Tripp, *Changing the Rules: The Politics of Liberalization and the Informal Urban Economy in Tanzania* (Berkeley: University of California Press, 1997), 38–44.

89. Marja-Liisa Swantz and Bryceson, "Women Workers in Dar es Salaam," 22.

Chapter 3: Dar after Dark

1. Interview with Elias Kasore, September 9, 2009, Dar es Salaam; "Kisura Kamwibia Mhisani—Jela miezi 4," *Ngurumo*, April 10, 1965, an article describing the fighting that sometimes broke out between young women staying there.

2. Interview with Sagaya Hussein, October 19, 2008, Dar es Salaam; interview with Hassan Ngoma, April 9, 2009, Tanga; interview with Telson Peter Mughogho, January 21, 2009, Tanga.

3. Freddy Macha, correspondence with author, December 21, 2008; Projectus Ruttaigwa, "Huna Dada," *Daily News*, March 24, 1975.

4. Ryan Thomas Skinner, *Bamako Sounds: The Afropolitan Ethics of Malian Music* (Minneapolis: University of Minnesota Press, 2015); Bob White, *Rumba Rules: The Politics of Dance Music in Mobutu's Zaire* (Durham, NC: Duke University Press, 2008); Nate Plageman, *Highlife Saturday Night: Popular Music and Social Change in Urban Ghana*, African Expressive Cultures (Bloomington: Indiana University Press, 2013); and Thomas Turino, *Nationalists, Cosmopolitans and Popular Music in Zimbabwe* (Chicago: University of Chicago Press, 2000).

5. Kelly Askew, *Performing the Nation: Swahili Music and Cultural Politics in Tanzania* (Chicago: University of Chicago Press, 2002).

6. Gregory Barz and Frank Gunderson, eds., *Mashindano! Competitive Music Performance in East Africa* (Dar es Salaam: Mkuki na Nyota, 2000); Terrence Ranger, *Dance and Society in Eastern Africa, 1890–1970: The Beni Ngoma* (Berkeley: University of California Press, 1975); Stephen Harvey Martin, "Music in Urban East Africa: A Study of the Development of Urban Jazz in Dar Es Salaam" (PhD diss., University of Washington, 1980); and Emily Callaci, "Dancehall Politics: Mobility, Sexuality, and Spectacles of Racial Respectability in Late Colonial Tanganyika, 1930s–1961," *Journal of African History*, no. 3 (2011): 365–84.

7. Jesse Weaver Shipley, *Living the Hiplife: Celebrity and Entrepreneurship in Ghanaian Popular Music* (Durham, NC: Duke University Press, 2013).

8. Interview with Steven Hiza and Zigi Saidi, January 25, 2009, Tanga, Tanzania.

9. Interview with Muhiddin Maalim Gurumo, Dar es Salaam, November 11, 2008; NUTA Jazz Band, "Mpenzi Ninakukanya," *Zanzibara*, vol. 3, *Ujamaa, the Sound of 1960s Tanzania*, Buda Music 860142, 2007.

10. Interview with Ismaili Issa Michuzi, Dar es Salaam, September 9, 2009.

11. Laura Fair, *Pastimes and Politics: Culture, Community, and Identity in Post-Abolition Urban Zanzibar, 1890–1945* (Athens: Ohio University Press, 2001), chapter 4.
12. Jumaa R. R. Mkabarah, *Salum Abdallah: Mwanamuziki Wa Tanzania* (Dar es Salaam: Taasisi ya Uchunguzi wa Kiswahili, Chuo Kikuu cha Dar es Salaam, 1975).
13. Jamhuri Jazz Band, "Nafikiri Kurudi Shamba," Jamhuri Jazz Band 1970/71, PKLP 101, 1971.
14. Askew, *Performing the Nation;* Skinner, *Bamako Sounds*; Plageman, *Highlife Saturday Night*; White, *Rumba Rules*.
15. Julius Nyerere, "President's Inaugural Address," in *Freedom and Unity: A Selection from Writings and Speeches, 1952–65* (Dar es Salaam: Oxford University Press, 1966).
16. Cosmas Mfaume, "Super Volcano: Kipindi Cha Kwanza Cha Mafanikio," *Mzalendo*, July 14, 1974.
17. Stephen Harvey Martin, "Music in Urban East Africa: A Study of the Development of Urban Jazz in Dar es Salaam" (PhD diss., University of Washington, 1980), 77.
18. Andrew Ivaska, *Cultured States: Youth, Gender and Modern Style in 1960s Dar es Salaam* (Durham, NC: Duke University Press, 2011).
19. Interview with Yusuf Omari, June 15, 2009, Dar es Salaam.
20. Ivaska, *Cultured States*.
21. Hussein Ziki, "Kuzuia Bumping ni Uamuzi wa Busara," *Uhuru*, March 4, 1971, 11; Zahra Abdurazak Mussa, "Vijana bado wanaiga mitindo mibaya Zanzibar," *Uhuru*, September 4, 1975, 5; Juma R. Mchelenga, "Bumping," poem, *Uhuru*, August 20, 1975, 8; and Peter S. Mokiwa, "Utamaduni wa Wapi?," poem, *Uhuru*, September 9, 1975, 8.
22. Laura Edmondson, "National Erotica: The Politics of 'Traditional' Dance in Tanzania," *Drama Review* 45, no. 1 (spring 2001): 153–70.
23. Charles Simbira, "Bumping ni Mtindo wa Kuridhisha," *Uhuru*, May 3, 1975, 11.
24. "Bumping na Sindimba," *Uhuru*, October 4, 1975, 3.
25. Ivaska, *Cultured States*, chapter 2.
26. Karen Tranberg Hansen, "Dressing Dangerously: Miniskirts, Gender Relations and Sexuality in Zambia," in *Fashioning Africa: Power and the Politics of Dress*, ed. Jean Allman (Bloomington: Indiana University Press, 2004), 166–85.
27. On jazz band clubhouses, see Tadasu Tsuruta, "Popular Music, Sports and Politics: A Development of Urban Cultural Movements in Dar Es Salaam, 1930s–1960s," *African Study Monographs* 24, no. 3 (2003): 203–5. On the groups of youth who gathered at band practices, interview with Bakari Majengo, February 11, 2009, Magomeni, Dar es Salaam.
28. "Habari za Miji: Kufunguliwa kwa Tanga Young Comrades Club," *Mambo Leo*, August 1932, 166.

29. Interview with Ali Abbas, May 14, 2009, Kariakoo, Dar es Salaam.
30. Advertisement for Ilala Restaurant and Guesthouse, *Afrika Kwetu*, January 1952; interview with Bakari Majengo; see Callaci, "Dancehall Politics."
31. "Municipal Council Liquor Licensing Board," *Tanganyika Standard*, September 4, 1963; interview with Muhiddin Maalim Gurumo, November 11, 2008, Dar es Salaam.
32. Interview with Taabu Ramadhani (former waitress from Amana Club), June 21, 2009, Dar es Salaam.
33. I learned this through interviews with musicians; see also report entitled, "Music General," 1971–74, TNA 622/M 3.
34. A. Likoko, "Sokomoko na Safari Trippers," *Nchi Yetu*, May 1974, 16.
35. A number of articles appeared in the Tanzanian press in the 1970s talking about the sex trade in Kisutu; for example, S. Rweyemamu, "Kisutu Yahatarisha Maisha ya Watu," *Uhuru*, January 14, 1974; and "Dar Mbili Ndani ya Jiij Moja," *Uhuru*, April 14, 1973. For a discussion of Kisutu "slum writing" by Tanzanian journalists, see chapter 2 of this volume.
36. Richard West, *The White Tribes of Africa* (London: Jonathan Cape, 1965), 40–41.
37. A. Mhije, "Kulikuwa na Nini Margot?" *Nchi Yetu*, November 1974.
38. There were a series of stories about police raids on Banda Beach in the paper *Ngurumo* in 1964 and 1965.
39. Interview with Yusuf Omari and Abraham Kapinga, June 15, 2009, Sinza, Dar es Salaam. For a story that describes the setting of Etienne's, see Mpufu Katojo, "Someone You Can Count On," *Daily News*, August 19, 1973.
40. For a study of Zairean musicians in Dar es Salaam, see Alex Perullo, "Rumba in the City of Peace: Migration and the Cultural Commodity of Congolese Music in Dar es Salaam, Tanzania, 1968–1985," *Ethnomusicology* 52, no. 2 (2008): 196–223.
41. Interview with Kikumbi Mwanza Mpango (Kingi Kiki), January 5, 2009, Dar es Salaam.
42. Some places, like Stereo Bar in Temeke, advertised their remote location as a desirable quality, saying that their secluded location prevented prostitution and other urban ills from bothering their "respectable" patrons.
43. Hadji Konde, "Trouble Ahead of Our Music Copycats: Kinshasa's 150 Bands Close Down," *Sunday News*, April 25, 1976. On the prestige of Congolese music, see Perullo, "Rumba in the City of Peace," 296–323.
44. Perullo, *Live from Dar Es Salaam: Popular Music and Tanzania's Music Economy* (Bloomington: Indiana University Press, 2011), chapter 2.
45. Interview with Amne Mbaraka Mwinshehe, December 3, 2008, Dar es Salaam.
46. J. A. K. Leslie, *A Survey of Dar es Salaam* (London: Oxford University Press, 1963); Dick Urban Vestbro, *Social Life and Dwelling Space: An Analysis of Three House Types in Dar es Salaam* (Stockholm: Ordfront, 1975). Though published in 1975, this research was based on observations in 1966.

47. "Discipline and Unity Drive: Residents in Ten Houses Form 'Cell,'" *Nationalist*, November 6, 1964, 8. More research is needed on the everyday realities of life in these neighborhood arrangements.

48. Women interviewed by Bryceson and Swantz report that the necessity of clothing was one of the greatest sources of stress and pressure in urban living.

49. Interview with Ibrahim Hamisi Mtumwa, June 1, 2009, Dar es Salaam; P. P. Kasembe, "Mavazi Kwenye Ngoma Zetu za Dansi," *Mambo Leo*, August 1961; and Peter Lienhardt, "Introduction," in *Medicine Man (Swifa ya Nguvumali)* (Oxford: Clarendon, 1968), 16–18.

50. Freddy Macha, correspondence with author, December 21, 2008.

51. Interview with Telson Peter Mughogho, January 21, 2009, Tanga.

52. Katalambulla, "Nilipata Kisura 'Naizeheni' Lakini Mwisho Nikanunua 'Pijo,'" *Mwafrika*, February 26, 1964, 3.

53. Lawrence Gwakisa, correspondence with author, September 4, 2009; Fidelis Tungaraza, correspondence with author, September 8, 2009. On skilled Dar es Salaam tailors, see Theresia Mshuza, "Mavazi na Wakati ya Kuyavaa," *Uhuru*, September 19, 1970.

54. Callaci, "Dancehall Politics."

55. "Letter to the editor," *Drum*, March 1971.

56. Margrethe Silberschmidt, "Masculinities, Sexuality and Socio-Economic Change in Rural and Urban East Africa," in *Re-Thinking Sexualities in Africa*, ed. Signe Arnfred (Uppsala: Nordiska Afrikainstitutet, 2004), 233–48

57. Marja-Liisa Swantz and Deborah Fahy Bryceson, "Women Workers in Dar es Salaam: 1973/74 Survey of Female Minimum Wage Earners and Self-Employed," in *University of Dar es Salaam Research Paper No. 23* (Dar es Salaam: University of Dar es Salaam, 1974); "Tuwe Wa Kisasa," *Nchi Yetu*, October 1966.

58. M. A. Bienefeld, "The Self Employed of Urban Tanzania," in *IDS Discussion Paper* (Falmer, Brighton: University of Sussex, 1974).

59. Judicate Shoo, "Why Barmaids Turn to Prostitution," *Daily News*, December 17, 1972.

60. Asha Rajabu, "Tabia Mbaya Ya Wanywaji Pombe," *Mzalendo*, October 22, 1972.

61. Interview with Fatuma Mdoe, March 27, 2009, Tanga; interview with Telson Peter Mughogho, January 21, 2009, Tanga.

62. Interview with Taabu Ramadhani, June 21, 2009, Dar es Salaam.

63. "Kutekenyana Mabar Hakutavumilia—Songambele," *Mwafrika*, June 10, 1963.

64. M. G. N. Manzi, Wizara ya Usalama Nchini, to Mkuu wa Polisi, TNA 622/M/3/22/16.

65. For a history of the TANU Youth League, see James Brennan, "Youth, the TANU Youth League and Managed Vigilantism in Dar es Salaam, Tanzania," *Africa* 76, no. 2 (2006): 221–46.

66. Ivaska, *Cultured States*.
67. Interview with Hamza Kalala, August 10, 2009, Tanga.
68. AbdouMaliq Simone, *For the City Yet to Come: Changing African Life in Four Cities* (Durham, NC: Duke University Press, 2004), 3; see also James Ferguson, *Expectations of Modernity: Myths and Meanings of Urban Life on the Zambian Copperbelt* (Berkeley: University of California Press, 1999), 82–122.
69. Interview with Lucia Matewele, April 21, 2009, Tanga.
70. With respect to placing bottles on the table for conspicuous display, Sasha Newell describes a similar phenomenon in contemporary Abidjan; Newell, *The Modernity Bluff: Crime, Consumption, and Citizenship in Côte d'Ivoire* (Chicago: University of Chicago Press, 2012).
71. Priya Lal, "Self-Reliance and the State: The Multiple Meanings of Development in Early Post-Colonial Tanzania," *Africa* 82, no. 2 (2012): 212–34.
72. Julius Nyerere, *Ujamaa: Essays on Socialism* (Dar es Salaam: Oxford University Press, 1968), 151–52.
73. Nyerere, "Ujamaa—The Basis for African Socialism," in *Ujamaa: Essays on Socialism*, 11.
74. TANU, *Vitabu Vya Darubini: Unyonge Wa Mwafrika* (Dar es Salaam: East African Publishing House, 1970), 29–31. An editorial In the TANU monthly magazine *Nchi Yetu* criticized women who would not date or dance with men who wore locally produced clothing, preferring instead men who wore second-hand imports; "Kutoka Kwa Mtengenezaji," *Nchi Yetu*, May 1971.
75. TANU, *Vitabu Vya Darubini*.
76. Tanzanian bottled beer, meant to replaced imports, was another luxury item coded as part of nation-building consumer culture; Justin Willis, *Potent Brews: A Social History of Alcohol in East Africa 1850–1999*, Eastern African Studies (Oxford: James Currey, 2002).
77. TANU intellectuals often disputed that the shirts were modeled after the Chinese style; see "Wamejidanganya Waliosema Mtindo Huu Ni Wa Kichina," *Nchi Yetu*, December 1970, 26.
78. Hilda Mamlay, "Vazi La Taifa Ni La Heshima Kwa Mama Wa Tanzania," *Nchi Yetu*, March 1968.
79. Peter Ndila, "Mitindo Ya Kitaifa," *Nchi Yetu*, August 1970.
80. Vincent Mtambo, "Vazi La Kitenge La Pendeza," *Nchi Yetu*, August 1969.
81. Lal, "Militants, Mothers and the National Family: Ujamaa, Gender and Rural Development in Postcolonial Tanzania," *Journal of African History* 51, no. 1 (2010): 1–20.
82. S. K. Msuya, *Mazungumzo Za Mchana* (Dar es Salaam: Tanzania Publishing House, 1973).
83. Willis, *Potent Brews*.
84. Lynn Thomas, *Politics of the Womb: Women, Reproduction and the State in Kenya* (Berkeley: University of California Press, 2003).
85. Jonathon Glassman, *Feasts and Riot: Revelry, Rebellion, and Popular Consciousness on the Swahili Coast, 1856–1888* (Portsmouth, NH: Heinemann,

1995); Holly Hanson, "Queen Mothers and Good Government in Buganda: The Loss of Women's Political Power in Nineteenth-Century East Africa," in *Women in African Colonial Histories*, ed. Susan Geiger, Nakanyike Musisi, and Jean Marie Allman (Bloomington: Indiana University Press, 2002), 219–36; Meredith McKittrick, "Forsaking Their Fathers? Colonialism, Christianity and Coming of Age in Ovamboland, Northern Namibia," in *Men and Masculinities in Modern Africa*, ed. Stephan Miescher and Lisa Lindsay (Portsmouth, NH: Heinemann, 2003), 33–51; and Jeremy Prestholdt, *Domesticating the World: African Consumerism and the Genealogies of Globalization* (Berkeley: University of California Press, 2008).

86. M. Abdulaziz, ed. and trans., *Muyaka: 19th Century Swahili Popular Poetry* (Nairobi: Kenya Literature Bureau, 1979).

87. In Swahili history, Margaret Strobel, *Muslim Women in Mombasa, 1890–1975* (New Haven, CT: Yale University Press, 1979).

88. Shane Doyle, "Premarital Sexuality in Great Lakes Africa, 1900–1980," in *Generations Past: Youth in East African History*, ed. Andrew Burton and Hélène Charton-Bigot (Athens: Ohio University Press, 2010), 237–61.

89. For a history of "the breadwinner" ideal in Nigerian history, see Lisa Lindsay, "Domesticity and Difference: Male Breadwinners, Working Women, and Colonial Citizenship in the 1945 Nigerian General Strike," *American Historical Review* 104, no. 3 (1999): 783–812.

90. Frederick Cooper, "Industrial Man Goes to Africa," in *Men and Masculinities in Modern Africa,* ed. Lisa Lindsay and Stephan Miescher (Portsmouth, NH: Heinemann, 2003), 128–37; Lindsay, "Domesticity and Difference," 783–812; and Andrew Burton, "Townsmen in the Making: Social Engineering and Citizenship in Dar es Salaam, c. 1945–1960," *International Journal of African Historical Studies* 36, no. 2 (2003): 331–65.

91. Atomic Jazz Band, "Dunia Ina Tabu," *Dunia Ina Tabu/Dada Tabia Zako Mbaya*, Saba 7–39, 1971.

92. For example, the theme of female greed leading to the betrayal of rural communal principles is explored in novellas, including Abdul Baka's *Salome* (Dar es Salaam: Tanzania Publishing House, 1972). See also the didactic adult-education pamphlet about the need for husbands and wives to make household budgets and particularly for women to spend money on their families rather than on clothing, in S. K. Msuya, *Mazungumzo za Mchana*. For more on the theme of female greed in Ujamaa-era fiction, see chapter 4 of this volume, as well as the excerpt of the song "Hanifa" quoted at the beginning of this chapter.

93. For example, S. Rweyemamu, "Hatu ya Kufukuza Wasichana Shuleni Yafaa Irekebishwe," *Uhuru*, January 30, 1974.

94. Theresia Mshuza, "Mavazi na wakati wa kuyavaa," *Uhuru*, September 19, 1970.

95. "Tuwe wa Kisasa," *Nchi Yetu*, October 1966, 16.

96. Letters on this theme appeared frequently in the letters to the editor pages: for example, H. S. Mkoga, "Vazi Fupi Litadumu," *Uhuru*, April 15, 1970, and B. A. Kaninka, "Vazi Fupi Kudumishwa na Vijana," *Uhuru*, May 11, 1970.

97. For a discussion of *kisura*, see Ivaska, *Cultured States*, 200–205.

98. "Yakutana na Kisura Dorothy Masuka," *Mambo Leo*, February 1962, 14–15.

99. The Modern Girl around the World Research Group, *The Modern Girl around the World: Consumption, Modernity and Globalization* (Durham, NC: Duke University Press, 2008), 4–5.

100. Two scholars have been particularly influential to my interpretation of *kisura*: Lynn Thomas in her discussion of the "modern girl" and Jennifer Cole in her exploration of the distinction between *tanora* and *jeunes* in contemporary Madagascar; Thomas, "The Modern Girl and Racial Respectability in 1930s South Africa," in *The Modern Girl around the World*, and Jennifer Cole, "Fresh Contact in Tamatave, Madagascar: Sex, Money and Intergenerational Transformation," in *Generations and Globalization: Youth, Age and Family in the New World Economy*, ed. Jennifer Cole and Deborah Durham (Bloomington: Indiana University Press, 2007).

101. Jamhuri Jazz Band, "Shangazi Naomba Taiti," *Zanzibara*, vol. 3, *Ujamaa, the Sound of 1960s Tanzania*, Buda Music 860142.

102. Interview with Fatuma Mdoe, March 27, 2009, Tanga; interview with Taabu Ramadhani, June 21, 2009, Dar es Salaam.

103. Morogoro Jazz Band, "Pole Dada," *Choyo Uache*, Polydor POL 7–051, 1970.

Chapter 4: Lovers and Fighters

Epigraph 1: Euphrase Kezilahabi, speaking at an academic conference in Germany. His address appears in "The Swahili Novel and the Common Man in East Africa," in *The East African Experience: Essays on English and Swahili Literature, 2nd Janheinz Journal of African Historyn-Symposium*, ed. Schild (Mainz: Verlag, 1980), 78–79.

Epigraph 2: Interview with Kajubi Mukajanga, June 8, 2013, Dar es Salaam.

1. This is based on estimates from advertisements in the newspaper the *Daily News* and *Wakati ni Huu* in 1982, which advertise novellas selling for between 30 and 40 Tanzanian shillings. Going to see Urafiki Jazz Band cost 8–10 shillings, as did going to see a movie at one of the cinemas. See also "Paying Dearly for Books," the *Daily News*, March 1982, for the cost of imported books, estimated at 330–350 shillings.

2. In the mid-1970s through the mid-1980s, newspapers ranged in cost from around 50 cents to 2 shillings, depending on the newspaper. This estimate is based on the price printed on the newspapers *Uhuru*, *Mzalendo*, the *Daily News*, and the *Sunday News*.

3. Gyan Prakash, "Imagining the City, Darkly," in *Noir Urbanisms: Dystopic Images of the Modern City*, ed. Gyan Prakash (Princeton, NJ: Princeton University Press, 2010), 1–16; Jennifer Robinson, "Living in Dystopia: Past, Present and Future in Contemporary African Cities," in *Noir Urbanisms: Dystopic*

Images of the Modern City, ed. Gyan Prakash (Princeton, NJ: Princeton University Press, 2010), 218–40; and Elliott Colla, "Anxious Advocacy: The Novel, the Law, and Extrajudicial Appeals in Egypt," *Public Culture* 17, no. 3 (winter 2005): 417–43.

4. Stephen Lacey, *British Realist Theatre: The New Wave in Its Context 1956–1965* (London: Routledge, 1995); Ilan Stavans, *Antiheroes: Mexico and Its Detective Novel*, trans. from Spanish, Jesse H. Lytle and Jennifer A. Mattson (Cranbury, NJ: Associated University Presses, 1997); Sangita Gopal and Sujata Moorti, "Introduction," in *Global Bollywood: Travels of Hindi Song and Dance* (Minneapolis: University of Minnesota Press, 2008), 2; Koushik Banerjea, "'Fight Club': Aesthetics, Hybridisation and the Construction of Rogue Masculinities in *Sholay* and *Deewar*," in *Bollyworld: Popular Indian Cinema through a Transnational Lens*, ed. Raminder Kaur and Ajay J. Sinha (Thousand Oaks, CA: Sage, 2005), 63.

5. Julius Nyerere, "The Importance and Pleasure of Reading," speech at the opening of the Printing Works and Book Warehouse, Arusha, 1965, in *Nyerere on Education*, vol. 2, ed. E. Lema, M. Mbilinyi, and R. Rajani (Dar es Salaam: E. and D., 2006), 22.

6. Walter Bgoya, "Books and Reading in Tanzania." Paris: Unesco, 1986.

7. Bgoya, "Books and Reading in Tanzania."

8. For more on this project of developmentalism, see Andrew Burton, "Townsmen in the Making: Social Engineering and Citizenship in Dar Es Salaam, C. 1945–1960," *International Journal of African Historical Studies* 36, no. 2 (2003): 331–65.

9. Andrew Ivaska, "Negotiating 'Culture' in a Cosmopolitan Capital: Urban Style and the State in Colonial and Postcolonial Dar es Salaam" (Ph.D. diss., University of Michigan, 2003).

10. See chapter 1 of this volume.

11. Bgoya, "Books and Reading in Tanzania," 39–41. Though it is widely accepted that literacy rates dramatically improved in Tanzania after independence, the exact numbers here may reflect the bias of Tanzanian officials. Literacy, in these numbers, refers to literacy in Roman script for reading Kiswahili—or English. Significantly, literacy in Arabic script, which many Tanzanian Muslims would have attained through Quranic schooling, is not taken into account in these numbers. UNESCO estimates that literacy rates rose from 33 percent at the beginning of the socialist program to 79 percent by its end in 1986; H. S. Bhola, *Campaigning for Literacy: Eight National Experiences of the Twentieth Century* (Paris: UNESCO, 1984), 149.

12. Bgoya, *Books and Reading in Tanzania*.

13. Article in *Daily News*, July 26, 1973.

14. Article in *Daily News*, July 26, 1973.

15. Bgoya, "From Tanzania to Kansas and Back Again," in *No Easy Victories: African Liberation and American Activists over a Half-Century, 1950–2000* (Trenton, NJ: Africa World Press, 2008), 103–6.

16. M. W. Kanyama Chiume, *Dunia Ngumu* (Dar es Salaam: Tanzania Publishing House, 1969), as well as a translation of the works of Kwame Nkrumah, *Harakati Ya Kitabaka Katika Afrika* (Dar es Salaam: Tanzania Publishing House, 1974).

17. Seth Markle, "'Book Publishers for a Pan-African World': Drum and Spear Press and Tanzania's Ujamaa Ideology," *Black Scholar* (2008), 16–26.

18. For example, see Abdul Baka, *Salome* (1972); Emmanuel Mbogo, *Giza Limeingia* (1980); Kapombe Mnzava, *Usiku Wa Mbalamwezi* (1979); S. K. Msuya, *Mazungumzo Ya Usiku* (1978); B. R. Nchimbi, *Penzi La Dawa* (1974); Ngalimecha Ngahyoma, *Huka* (1973); and Cuthbert K. Omari, *Barabara Ya Tano* (1973).

19. B. R. Nchimbi, *Penzi la Dawa* (Dar es Salaam: Tanzania Publishing House, 1974).

20. C. S. L. Chachage, "The Tanzanian Publishing Industry," Occasional Paper (Kingston, UK: University of Hull, 1994), 56–60. For example, the back cover of J. Ngomoi's *Ndoto ya Ndaria* promised, "This book is suitable for teaching *Ujamaa* literature in secondary schools. The writer of this book, Ndugu Ngomoi, is starting a new wave of development writing in Swahili literature."

21. This observation is based on the full run of *Taifa Weekly* in 1968.

22. Interview with Jumaa Mkabarah, Muheza, Tanzania, June 17, 2013.

23. For the impact of the border closing on the Nairobi-based East African Literature Bureau and the East African Publishing House, see Chachage, "Tanzanian Publishing Industry," 50–56.

24. For Onitsha market literature, see Emmanuel N. Obiechina, *An African Popular Literature: A Study of Onitsha Market Pamphlets* (Cambridge: Cambridge University Press, 1973).

25. Chachage, "Tanzanian Publishing Industry," 58–59.

26. The birthdates and birthplaces of the writers are stated in their author biographies printed on the backs of their books.

27. Clemence Merinyo, "Hammie Rajab: Msanii Mzoefu, Mchapakazi, Mkomavu," *Wakati ni Huu* 1, 1982.

28. For example, the Dibwe brothers—Salum Dibwe, a.k.a. "Lemmy Special," and Subira Salum Dibwe, a.k.a. "Zanta de Gaste"—financed several publications. In the introduction to his book *Kazikwa Yu Hai*, or *Buried Alive* (Dar es Salaam: Southern Publications, 1984), the writer Kassim Chande thanks his patrons: "Many thanks to Ndugu Subira Salum Dibwe (Zanta-De-Gastor) and Ndugu Mwalomi Salum Dibwe (Reminy) for their help with the conditions and finances necessary for me to succeed in publishing of this book and for their sharing in its distribution." The Dibwe brothers published their own novels, as well.

29. Interview with Kajubi Mukajanga, Dar es Salaam, June 8, 2013; interview with Farid Hammie Rajab, Dar es Salaam, June 10, 2013; interview with Jumaa Mkabarah, Muheza, Tanzania, June 17, 2013. Advertisements for

Nayani Bookstall appeared in the pages of *Hamasa*, which was the popular arts magazine published by Kajubi Mukajanga in the early 1980s.

30. Interview with Kajubi Mukajanga, Dar es Salaam, June 8, 2013; interview with Farid Hammie Rajab, Dar es Salaam, June 10, 2013; interview with Jumaa Mkabarah, Muheza, Tanzania, June 17, 2013; interview with Jackson Kalindimya, Dar es Salaam, June 11, 2013.

31. Bgoya,"Books and Reading in Tanzania."

32. The process was described in interviews by several writers, including Jackson Kalindimya, Dar es Salaam, June 11, 2013; interview with Farid Hammie Rajab, Dar es Salaam, June 10, 2013; and interview with Kajubi Mukajanga, Dar es Salaam, June 8, 2013.

33. Interview with M. M. Mulokozi, June 6, 2013.

34. Interview with Kajubi Mukajanga, Dar es Salaam, June 8, 2013.

35. Interview with Jumaa Mkabarah, Muheza, Tanzania, June 17, 2013.

36. Interview with Jackson Kalindimya, Dar es Salaam, June 11, 2013.

37. Interview with Kajubi Mukajanga, Dar es Salaam, June 8, 2013.

38. Back cover of Edi Ganzel, *Kitanzi* (Dar es Salaam: Utamaduni, 1984).

39. Ben Mtobwa, *Dar es Salaam Usiku* (Nairobi: Mkuki, 1998), 24.

40. Hammie Rajab and Edi Ganzel, *Kipigo Cha Fashisti Iddi Amin Dudu* (Dar es Salaam: Tamasha, 1979).

41. Interview with Stanley Ganzel, Dar es Salaam, June 5, 2013.

42. Joshua Grace, "Heroes of the Road: Race, Gender and the Politics of Mobility in Twentieth Century Tanzania," *Africa* 83, no. 3 (2013): 416, and Emily Callaci, "Dancehall Politics: Mobility, Sexuality, and Spectacles of Racial Respectability in Late Colonial Tanganyika, 1930s–1961," *Journal of African History* 52, no. 3 (2011): 365–84.

43. Martha Mlagala, "Was It an Illusion?" *Darlite*, 1970, 34–38.

44. Rajab and Ganzel, *Kipigo cha Fashisti Iddi Amin Dudu.*

45. Elvis Erastablus Musiba, *Kufa na Kupona* (Dar es Salaam: East African Literature Bureau, 1974); *Kikosi cha Kisasi* (Kilimanjaro, 1979); and *Kikomo* (Dar es Salaam: Continental, 1980).

46. Jumaa Mkabarah, *Marehemu Susana* (Dar es Salaam: Utamaduni, 1974); the Joram Kiango novels of Ben Mtobwa include *Lazima Ufe Joram* (Dar es Salaam: Heko Publications, 1983); *Dimbwi la Damu* (Dar es Salaam: East African Publications, 1984); *Tutarudi Na Roho Zetu?* (Dar es Salaam: Heko Publications, 1987); *Najisikia Kuua Tena* (Dar es Salaam: Tanzania Africa Publications, 1984); *Joram Kiango, Mikononi Mwa Nunda* (Dar es Salaam: Heko Publications, 1986); *Salamu Toka Kuzimu* (Dar es Salaam: Heko Publications, 1987); and *Malaika wa Shetani* (Dar es Salaam: Heko Publications, 1988).

47. Kajubi D. Mukajanga, *Mpenzi* (Dar es Salaam: Grand Arts Promotion, 1984).

48. For examples of novellas whose protagonists make a real point of this, see Agoro Anduru, *Kukosa Radhi* (Dar es Salaam: Press and Publicity Center,

1983); and John Simbamwene, *Mwisho wa Mapenzi* (Dar es Salaam: Longman, 1971).

49. Musiba, *Kufa na Kupona*.

50. For example, the novellas of Musiba, including *Kufa na Kupona* (1974); *Kikosi cha Kisasi* (1979); and *Kikomo* (1980). See also H. C. M. Mbelwa, *Donda Ndugu* (Dar es Salaam: Tanzania Publishing House, 1973).

51. C. S .L. Chachage, "Tanzanian Publishing Industry." See also Anthony Olden, "For a Poor Nation a Library Service Is Vital: Establishing a National Public Library Service in Tanzania in the 1960s," 421–45.

52. For more on *Drum*, see Kenda Mutongi, "'Dear Dolly's' Advice: Representations of Youth, Courtship, and Sexualities in Africa, 1960–1980," *The International Journal of African Historical Studies* 33, no. 1 (2000): 1–23.

53. See, for example, M. Sikawa, "Is It Time Tanzania Banned These Western Films?" *Daily News*, January 24, 1975, on the scandal of young lovers showing affection in public after seeing Western films. For a discussion of attempts of town elders to ban cinema in colonial Dar es Salaam, see Burton, *African Underclass: Urbanisation, Crime and Colonial Order in Dar Es Salaam* (Oxford: James Currey, 2005), 75.

54. Musiba, *Kufa na Kupona; Kikosi cha Kisasi; Kikomo; Njama* (Dar es Salaam: Continental Publishers, 1981).

55. Charles Ndibalema, *Nimponzeka* (Dar es Salaam: Longman, 1970).

56. For examples of kung fu in pulp fiction, see Kassim M. Kassam's *Joto la Fedha* (Dar es Salaam: Kobe, 1982); Simbamwene, *Dogodogo Wanitesa* (Morogoro: Jomssi, 1982). Less overtly, W. E. Mkufya's protagonist in *The Wicked Walk* (Dar es Salaam: Tanzania Publishing House, 1977) is a fan of Bruce Lee. Mukajanga went on to publish a biography of Bruce Lee in Kiswahili: Kajubi Mukajanga, *Bruce Lee: Mfalme wa Kung Fu* (Dar es Salaam: Grand Arts Promotion, 1982). For an exploration of the meaning of kung fu to Ujamaa-era Dar es Salaam youth, see May Joseph, "Kung Fu Cinema and Frugality," in *The Visual Culture Reader*, ed. Nicholas Mirzoeff (London: Routledge, 2002), 433–50.

57. L. A. Mbuguni and Gabriel Ruhumbika, "TANU and National Culture," in *Towards Ujamaa: Twenty Years of TANU Leadership*, ed. Gabriel Ruhumbika (Dar es Salaam: East African Literature Bureau, 1974), 275–87.

58. For interpretations of popular film in Africa, see Charles Ambler, "Popular Films and Colonial Audiences: The Movies in Northern Rhodesia," *American Historical Review* 106 (2001): 81–105; Ch. Didier Gondola, *Tropical Cowboys: Westerns, Violence, and Masculinity in Kinshasa* (Bloomington: Indiana University Press, 2016); Brian Larkin, "Indian Films and Nigerian Lovers: Media and the Creation of Parallel Modernities," *Africa* 67, no. 3 (1997): 406–40; Laura Fair, "Making Love in the Indian Ocean: Hindi Films, Zanzibari Audiences and the Construction of Romance in the 1950s and 1960s," in *Love in Africa*, ed. Jennifer Cole and Lynn Thomas (Chicago: University of Chicago Press, 2009), 58–82.

59. Martin Rubin, "Thrillers," in *Schirmer Encyclopedia of Film*, ed. Barry Keith Grant (New York: Schirmer Reference, 2007), 4:255–61.

60. Writers Faraji H. H. Katalambula and Muhammed Said Abdulla were famous for their Swahili detective novels, including Katalambula's famous *Simu ya Kifo* (Dar es Salaam: East African Literature Bureau, 1965), which was reprinted eight times between 1965 and 1975, and Abdulla's *Mizimu ya Watu wa Kale* (Nairobi: East African Literature Bureau, 1960) and *Kisima cha Giningi* (London: Evans Bros., 1968).

61. Rajab, *Ufunguo wa Bandia* (Dar es Salaam: East African Publications, 1979).

62. John Simbamwene, *Mwisho wa Mapenzi* (Dar es Salaam: Longman, 1971). Similarly, in Edi Ganzel's *Ndoto ya Mwendawazimu* (Dar es Salaam: East African Literature Bureau, 1972) the character Mishack, an urban migrant from Rufiji and a reformed ex-criminal, is convinced by his fiancée, Hilda, the beautiful nightclub singer who is also an urban migrant, that in order for them to have the finances needed to get married, he must help her steal diamonds from mines in Mwanza.

63. Jennifer Cole and Lynn Thomas, "Introduction: Thinking Through Love in Africa," in *Love in Africa*, ed. Jennifer Cole and Lynn Thomas (Chicago: University of Chicago Press, 2009), 5.

64. Ganzel, *Ndoto ya Mwendawazimu*; Rajab, *Ufunguo wa Bandia*; Kajubi Mukajanga, *Tuanze Lini?* (Dar es Salaam: Grand Arts Promotion, 1983).

65. Agoro Anduru, *The Fugitive* (Dar es Salaam: Intercontinental, 1982).

66. Ndyanao Balisidya, *Shida* (Nairobi: Foundation, 1975).

67. This theme of suffering for the sake of love appears in many of Simbamwene's novels. For examples of a young male lover being tortured and physically abused for the sake of love, see Ndibalema, *Nimeponzeka*; Kajubi Mukajanga, *Tuanze Lini?*

68. Richard Stren, "Urban Inequality and Housing Policy in Tanzania: The Problem of Squatting," in *Research Series* (Berkeley: Institute of International Studies, University of California at Berkeley, 1975), 87.

69. Jumaa Mkabarah, *Kizimbani* (Dar es Salaam: Black Star Agencies, 1974). The 1974 novella was not the first time Mkabarah explored the tensions between young men and older men with "traditional" ways of thinking, in a way that was sympathetic to the former. In his first book, which was a biography of the Tanzanian pop musician Salum Abdallah, Mkabarah emphasized Abdallah's refined cosmopolitanism, his religiosity, and his rejection of all forms of delinquency, dramatizing his struggles to gain autonomy from a strict Arab father who tried to plan his marriage and prevent him from following his chosen career path: a sign of backwardness, Mkabarah seems to suggest. In these texts, Mkabarah models a kind of manhood rooted in the struggle to claim autonomy from older generations; Jumaa Mkabarah, *Mwanamuziki wa Tanzania: Salum Abdallah* (Dar es Salaam: Taasisi ya Uchunguzi wa Kiswahili Chuo Kikuu cha Dar es Salaam, 1972).

70. See, for example, Ivaska's description of Nyerere's denouncement of protesting university students as arrogant; Andrew Ivaska, "Of Students, 'Nizers,' and a Struggle over Youth: Tanzania's 1966 National Service Crisis," *Africa Today* 51, no. 3 (2005): 93–99.

71. For example, Baka, *Salome*; Ganzel, *Ndoto ya Mwendawazimu*; Simbamwene, *Kwa Sababu ya Pesa* (Dar es Salaam: Longman, 1972); Martha Mandao, *Ani Opens Her Purse* (Achimota, Ghana: African Christian Press, 1971).

72. A number of news articles reporting on the problem of teenage pregnancy attributed the problem to the desires of young schoolgirls for money and material comforts; for example, S. Rweyemamu, "Hatu ya Kufukuza Wasichana Shuleni Yafaa Irekebishwe," *Uhuru*, January 30, 1974.

73. This is true even in many of what I call "crime thrillers," without the narrative elements of romances; for example, Mishack in Ganzel's *Ndoto ya Mwendawazimu* is convinced to stage the robbery out of a desire to marry Hilda; Sami in Rajab's *Ufunguo wa Bandia* tells Atende that the robbery of the mosque will allow him to marry her properly; and Willy Gamba, in Musiba's *Kufa na Kupona*, after finding the culprits who are traitors to FRELIMO, is rewarded with the love of a beautiful woman.

74. These debates raged in the newspapers of the late 1960s and throughout the 1970s. For a discussion of debates over marriage laws, see Ivaska, *Cultured States: Youth, Gender and Modern Style in 1960s Dar es Salaam* (Durham, NC: Duke University Press, 2011), 166–205.

75. For example, Mkabarah, *Kizimbani*; Simbamwene, *Mwisho wa Mapenzi*; Ndyanao Balisidya, *Shida* (Nairobi: Foundation, 1975); I. C. Mbenna, *Sitaki* (Dar es Salaam: East African Publishing House, 1976); Rajab, *Ufunguo wa Bandia*; Anduru, *Fugitive*; and Mkufya, *The Dilemma* (Dar es Salaam: Press and Publicity Center, 1982).

76. This bodily contrast is emphasized in the novels of Mkufya, including *The Wicked Walk* (Dar es Salaam: Tanzania Publishing House, 1977), and *The Dilemma* (Dar es Salaam: Press and Publicity Center, 1982).

77. Edi Ganzel, *Faili Maalum* (Dar es Salaam: Tamasha, 1981).

78. In the novel he is portrayed as someone who wants to own *ghorofa*, or multiple-story buildings. This is significant, as ghorofa were, in the popular imagination, associated with Indian landlords. In 1971, the Tanzanian state had nationalized most urban property worth over 100,000 shillings: in other words, many of the city's most conspicuous ghorofa; James R. Brennan, *Taifa: Making Nation and Race in Urban Tanzania* (Athens: Ohio University Press, 2011), 3–6.

79. May Joseph, "Kung Fu Cinema and Frugality."

80. Kassam, *Joto la Fedha*.

81. Msuya, *Mazungumzo za Mchana* (Dar es Salaam: Tanzania Publishing House, 1973).

82. Mukajanga, *Tuanze Lini?* This was written and copyrighted in 1975.

83. Mukajanga, *Kitanda cha Mauti* (Dar es Salaam: Grand Arts Promotion, 1982). For the ultimate sugar daddy story, see Kassam's *Shuga Dedi* (Dar es Salaam: International Publishers Agency, 1984).

84. Mukajanga, "Logic," in *Summons: Poems from Tanzania*, ed. Richard Mabala (Dar es Salaam: Tanzania Publishing House Limited, 1980), 46.

Chapter 5: From Socialist to Street-Smart

1. Craig Jeffrey and Stephen Young, "Jugaad: Youth and Enterprise in India," *Annals of the Association of American Geographers* 104, no. 1 (2013), 182–94.

2. Kenneth King, *Jua Kali Kenya: Change and Development in an Informal Economy, 1970–1995* (Athens: Ohio University Press, 1996).

3. Marc Le Pape, "Les Status d'une Génération: Les Déscolarisés d'Abidjan entre 1976 et 1986," *Politique Africaine* 24 (1986), 104–12.

4. Jeremy L. Jones, "'Nothing Is Straight in Zimbabwe': The Rise of the *Kukiya-Kiya* Economy 2000–2008," *Journal of Southern African Studies* 36, no. 2 (2010), 285–99.

5. Marissa Moorman, "Anatomy of Kuduro: Articulating the Angolan Body Politic after the War," *African Studies Review* 57, no. 2 (2014), 21–40.

6. Though Ujamaa was the official philosophy of the state, it was not a single, top-down vision of the world, but rather a "loose typology of development repertories," in the words of Priya Lal. Lal has shown how everyday Tanzanians took on the categories and ideas of ujamaa in various and unintended ways; Lal, "Self-Reliance and the State: The Multiple Meanings of Development in Early Post-Colonial Tanzania," *Africa* 82, no. 2 (2012): 212–34.

7. Frederick Cooper, *Decolonization and African Society: The Labor Question in French and British Africa* (Cambridge: Cambridge University Press, 1996), and Lisa Lindsay, "Working with Gender: The Emergence of the 'Male Breadwinner' in Colonial Southwestern Nigeria," in *Africa after Gender*, ed. Catherine Cole, Takyiwaa Manuh, and Stephan Miescher (Bloomington: Indiana University Press, 2007).

8. Ryan Thomas Skinner, *Bamako Sounds: The Afropolitan Ethics of Malian Music* (Minneapolis: University of Minnesota Press, 2015), and Bob White, *Rumba Rules: The Politics of Dance Music in Mobutu's Zaire* (Durham, NC: Duke University Press, 2008).

9. Skinner, *Bamako Sounds*.

10. James R. Brennan, "Democratizing Cinema and Censorship in Tanzania, 1920–1980," *International Journal of African Historical Studies* 38, no. 3 (2005): 481–511; and Kelly Askew and John Francis Kitime, "Popular Music Censorship in Tanzania," in *Popular Music Censorship in Africa*, ed. Michael Drewett and Martin Cloonan (Hampshire, UK: Ashgate, 2006), 137–56.

11. L. A. Mbuguni and Gabriel Ruhumbika, "TANU and National Culture," in *Towards Ujamaa: Twenty Years of TANU Leadership*, ed. Gabriel Ruhumbika (Dar es Salaam: East African Literature Bureau, 1974), 275–87.

12. Werner Graebner, "Tanzania: Popular Music; The Land of Use-Your-Brain," in *The Rough Guide to World Music: Africa and the Middle East*, vol. 1 (London: Rough Guides, 2006), 681–89.

13. Ann Komaromi, "The Material Existence of Soviet Samizdat," *Slavic Studies* 63, no. 3 (2004): 597–618.

14. Garth Myers, *Verandahs of Power: Colonialism and Space in Urban Africa* (Syracuse, NY: Syracuse University Press, 2003).

15. James Ferguson, "De-moralizing Economies: African Socialism, Scientific Capitalism, and the Moral Politics of Structural Adjustment," in *Global Shadows: African in the Neoliberal World Order* (Durham, NC: Duke University Press, 2006), 69–88.

16. Michael Schatzberg, *Political Legitimacy in Middle Africa: Father, Family, Food* (Bloomington: Indiana University Press, 2001).

17. J. L. Krapf, *A Dictionary of the Suahili Language* (London: Trubner, 1882), 19.

18. Brennan, *Taifa: Making Nation and Race in Urban Tanzania* (Athens: Ohio University Press, 2011), 71.

19. This proverb was taken up in a popular song by Mbakara Mwinshehe.

20. Brennan, *Taifa*.

21. For example, Luise White, *The Comforts of Home: Prostitution in Colonial Nairobi* (Chicago: University of Chicago Press, 1990).

22. Jonathon Glassman, *Feasts and Riot: Revelry, Rebellion, and Popular Consciousness on the Swahili Coast, 1856–1888* (Portsmouth, NH: Heinemann, 1995); and Jeremy Prestholdt, *Domesticating the World: African Consumerism and the Geneaologies of Globalization* (Berkeley: University of California Press, 2008).

23. For a discussion of this from a case study in Central Kenya, see Derek R. Peterson, *Creative Writing: Translation, Bookkeeping, and the Work of Imagination in Colonial Kenya*, Social History of Africa (Portsmouth, NH: Heinemann, 2004), 167.

24. W. E. Taylor, *African Aphorisms or Saws from Swahililand* (London: Sheldon, 1924).

25. Marcia Wright, *Strategies of Slaves and Women: Life-Stories from Central Africa* (New York: Lilian Barber, 1993), and Margaret Strobel, *Muslim Women in Mombasa, 1890–1975* (New Haven, CT: Yale University Press, 1979). For a more recent analysis, see Kenda Mutongi, *Worries of the Heart: Widows, Family and Community in Kenya* (Chicago: University of Chicago Press, 2007).

26. For a similar dynamic of gifts in relationships, in a very different context, see Mark Hunter, *Love in the Time of AIDS: Inequality, Gender, and Rights in South Africa* (Bloomington: Indiana University Press, 2010).

27. Nancy Rose Hunt, *A Colonial Lexicon: Of Birth, Medicalization and Mobility in the Congo* (Durham, NC: Duke University Press, 1999), 12.

28. See, for example, parables that suggest that urban Africans who desire real estate have a slave mentality, attained through attempting to imitate Arab

slave-traders who build stone houses on the Swahili coast; TANU, *Vitabu Vya Darubini: Unyonge wa Mwafrika* (Dar es Salaam: East African Publishing House, 1970).

29. Mwakyembe, "Azimio La Arusha," *Uhuru*, May 14, 1970.

30. Martha Mandao, *Ani Opens Her Purse* (Achimota, Ghana: African Christian Press, 1971).

31. B. R. Nchimbi, *Penzi La Dawa* (Dar es Salaam: Tanzania Publishing House, 1974).

32. See Ato Quayson's discussion of the inapplicability of the *flaneur* in Accra in his book *Oxford Street, Accra: City Life and the Itineraries of Transnationalism* (Durham, NC: Duke University Press, 2014).

33. Mandao, *Ani Afungua Mkoba Wake* (Dodoma: Central Tanganyika Press, 1974), 1.

34. Teresia Mshuza, "Mtindo Wa Wanawake Kufanya Kazi Usiku Unahitaji Marekebisho," *Uhuru*, February 12, 1972.

35. The sugar daddy appears in Senegalese writer Mariama Ba's *So Long a Letter*, (Portsmouth, NH: Heinemann, 1989); in the form of the protagonist's own husband, who leaves his wife and becomes the sugar daddy of a friend and age-mate of his own daughter. The Kenyan writer Rosemarie Owino's 1975 novel *Sugar Daddy's Lover* (Nairobi: Spear, 1975) is only one among surely dozens of examples of the appearance of the sugar daddy in popular fiction in Africa.

36. Schatzberg, *Political Legitimacy in Middle Africa*; Tejumola Olaniyan, "Corpulence, Cartoonists and Politics," *Africa Past and Present*, Episode 101, May 24, 2016, interview by Peter Alegi and Peter Limb.

37. Lynn Thomas, *Politics of the Womb: Women, Reproduction and the State in Kenya* (Berkeley: University of California Press, 2003).

38. The women's union of St. Alban's Anglican Church in Dar es Salaam, for example, listed preventing their daughters from accepting gifts from boys and men as one of their central aims as mothers; Chama cha Mama Wakristo, "Msaada kwa Viongozi" (Women's Mother's Union, "Guidelines for Leaders"), St. Mark's Center Archive, Dar es Salaam. Theresia Mshuza devoted a full-page spread in the newspaper *Uhuru* to the topic: "Urafiki Wavulana Na Wasichana Uwe Na Namna Gani?," *Uhuru*, April 4, 1970.

39. W. E. Mkufya, *The Wicked Walk* (Dar es Salaam: Tanzania Publishing House, 1977); Kassim M. Kassam, *Shuga Dedi* (Dar es Salaam: International Publishers Agency, 1984); and Kajubi D. Mukajanga, *Kitanda cha Mauti* (Dar es Salaam: Grand Arts Promotion, 1982).

40. See chapter 1 of this volume.

41. Amy Stambach, "*Kutoa Mimba*: Debates About Schoolgirl Abortion in Machame, Tanzania," in *The Sociocultural Aspects of Abortion*, ed. Alaka Malwade Basu (Westport, CT: Praeger, 2003), 79–102.

42. Joe Lugalla, *Crisis, Urbanization, and Urban Poverty in Tanzania: A Study of Urban Poverty and Survival Politics* (Lanham, MD: University Press of America, 1995), 166–79.

43. T. L. Maliyamkono and Mboya S. D. Bagachwa, *The Second Economy in Tanzania*, Eastern African Studies (London: J. Currey, 1990).

44. Aili Tripp, *Changing the Rules: The Politics of Liberalization and the Informal Urban Economy in Tanzania* (Berkeley: University of California Press, 1997).

45. Ben Mtobwa, *Pesa Zako Zinanuka* (Dar es Salaam: Heko, 1984).

46. Mtobwa, *Pesa Zako Zinanuka*.

47. Interview with Jackson Kalindimya, June 11, 2013, Dar es Salaam, Tanzania.

48. See Kandili Maulana in Mtobwa's *Pesa Zako Zinanuka*, and Sami Kiama in Hammie Rajab's *Ufunguo wa Bandia*.

49. "Usafiri Dar es Salaam."

50. Amina H. Ng'ombo, *Heka Heka za Ulanguzi* (Peramiho: Benedictine Publications Ndanda-Peramiho, 1982).

51. Kassam, *Joto la Fedha* (Dar es Salaam: Kobe, 1982).

52. Tripp, *Changing the Rules*.

53. Tripp, *Changing the Rules*.

54. This is similar to what Yurchak observed for the end of the Soviet Union; Alexei Yurchak, *Everything Was Forever, Until It Was No More: The Last Soviet Generation* (Princeton, NJ: Princeton University Press, 2005).

55. Kajubi Mukajanga became editor of Hamasa and Wakati ni Huu; Ben Mtobwa of Heko; Nico ye Mbajo of Mcheshi; Nico ya Mbajo and Saidi Bawji of Sani; Hammie Rajab of Busara; and Kassim Musa Kassam of Cheka.

56. Graham Mytton, *Mass Communication in Africa* (London: Edward Arnold, 1983); and Nkwabi Ng'wanakilala, *Mass Communication and Development of Socialism in Tanzania* (Dar es Salaam: Tanzania Publishing House, 1981).

57. Alex Perullo, *Live from Dar es Salaam: Popular Music and Tanzania's Music Economy* (Bloomington: Indiana University Press, 2011).

58. Koen Stroeken, "Immunizing Strategies: Hip-Hop and Critique in Tanzania," *Africa: Journal of the International Africa Institute* 75, no. 4 (2005), 488–509.

59. As James Brennan shows, colonizers were accused of "sucking with straws" the sweat of Africans; Brennan, "Blood Enemies: Exploitation and Urban Citizenship in the Nationalist Political Thought of Tanzania, 1958–75," *Journal of African History* 47, no. 3 (2006): 389–413.

60. Jumaa Mkabarah, *Siibi Tena* (Dar es Salaam: Maarifa, 1972).

61. Fundi Mussa, "*Ujanja Warudisha Nyuma Vijana*," *Mwafrika*, July 2, 1963.

62. For example, see the *Mitaani na Kashkash* series from *Mwafrika*, discussed in chapter 2.

63. Kassim Chande, *Kazikwa Yu Hai* (Dar es Salaam: Southern Publications, 1984).

64. Anne Lewinson, "Going with the Times: Transforming Visions of Urbanism and Modernity among Professionals in Dar Es Salaam, Tanzania" (PhD diss., University of Wisconsin-Madison, 1999).

65. Interview with Fatuma Mdoe, March 27, 2009.

66. Emily Callaci, "Dancehall Politics: Mobility, Sexuality, and Spectacles of Racial Respectability in Late Colonial Tanganyika, 1930s–1961," *Journal of African History*, no. 3 (2011): 365–84.

Conclusion

Epigraph: "The Full Texture of a City: Ratik Asokan Interviews Sarnath Banerjee," *Guernica*, April 1, 2016.

1. Lawrence Mtawa, "Maktaba Kuu ya Taifa Itatufaidia," *Nchi Yetu*, November 1969.
2. Anthony Almeida, in the film *Many Words for Modern*, director Jord den Hollander, Jord den Hollander Films, 2007.
3. For example, Mityaev, Anatoli, and Khuse, *Masimulizi Ya Lenin: Kwa Watoto*, in Swahili, trans. from Russian, ed. Abdul-Razak (Moscow: Idara ya Maendeleo, 1972); *Hadithi Juu Ya Lenin* (Moscow: Idara ya Maendeleo, 1967); Mao Zedong, *Mazungumzo Muhimu Ya Mwenye Kiti Mao Tse-Tung Pamoja Na Wageni Kutoka Asia, Afrika, Na Latin Amerika* (in Swahili text) (Peking: Ofisi ya Uchapaji wa Lugha za Kigeni, 1966); Mao Zedong, *Maneno Yaliyoteuliwa Ya Mwenye* (Peking: Ofisi Ya Uchapaji Wa Lugha za Kigeni, 1967); Bertolt Brecht, Abedi Shepardson, and Hassan Ahmed Marshad, *Mtu Mzuri Wa Setzuan* (in Swahili) (Nairobi: Kenya Literature Bureau, 1980); G. B. Johnson and Booker T. Washington, *Maisha Ya Booker T. Washington: Mtu Mweusi Maarufu* (London: Sheldon, 1937); Franz [sic] Fanon, *Viumbe Waliolaaniwa*, trans. Gabriel Ruhumbika and Clement Maganga (Dar es Salaam: Tanzania Publishing House, 1978); *Mafukara ya Ulimwengu*, trans. Ahmed Yusuf Abeid, 1977; and M. W. Kanyama Chiume, *Kwame Nkrumah* (London: Transafrica, 1977).
4. Presses include Daystar Press in Nigeria; CLAIM in Blantyre; Centre de Publications Evangéliques in Blantyre; and African Christian Press based in Achimota, Ghana, and Kitwe, Zambia.
5. Louise Young, *Beyond the Metropolis: Second Cities and Modern Life in Interwar Japan* (Berkeley: University of California Press, 2013).
6. Ananya Roy, *City Requiem, Calcutta: Gender and the Politics of Poverty*, Globalization and Community (Minneapolis: University of Minnesota Press, 2003).
7. Young, *Beyond the Metropolis*, 10.
8. Brian Larkin, *Signal and Noise: Media, Infrastructure and Urban Culture in Nigeria* (Durham, NC: Duke University Press, 2008), 6.
9. AbdouMaliq Simone, *For the City Yet to Come: Changing African Life in Four Cities* (Durham, NC: Duke University Press, 2004), chapter 4.
10. Emily Callaci, "Dancehall Politics: Mobility, Sexuality, and Spectacles of Racial Respectability in Late Colonial Tanganyika, 1930s–1961," *Journal of African History*, no. 3 (2011): 365–84.
11. Rudolf Mrázek, *Engineers of Happy Land: Technology and Nationalism in a Colony* (Princeton, NJ: Princeton University Press, 2002), 1.

12. Simone, *For the City Yet to Come*; Gyan Prakash, *Mumbai Fables* (Princeton, NJ: Princeton University Press, 2010); Emily Callaci, "Street Textuality: Socialism, Masculinity and Urban Belonging in Tanzania's Pulp Fiction Publishing Industry, 1975–1985," in *Comparative Studies in Society and History* 59, no. 1 (2017), 183–210. See also chapters 1 and 4 of Rudolf Mrázek's innovative book on the history of Indonesia, *Engineers of Happy Land*.

13. Aili Tripp, *Changing the Rules: The Politics of Liberalization and the Informal Urban Economy in Tanzania* (Berkeley: University of California Press, 1997).

14. Saskia Sassen, *The Global City: New York, London, Tokyo* (Princeton, NJ: Princeton University Press, 1991).

15. Andrew Burton, "Townsmen in the Making: Social Engineering and Citizenship in Dar es Salaam, c. 1945–1960"; James Ferguson, *Expectations of Modernity: Myths and Meanings of Urban Life on the Zambian Copperbelt* (Berkeley: University of California Press, 1999); Lisa Lindsay, "Working with Gender: The Emergence of the 'Male Breadwinner' in Colonial Southwestern Nigeria," in *Africa after Gender*, ed. Catherine Cole, Takyiwaa Manuh, and Stephan Miescher (Bloomington: Indiana University Press, 2007); Gwendolyn Wright, "Tradition in the Service of Modernity: Architecture and Urbanism in French Colonial Policy," in *Tensions of Empire: Colonial Cultures in a Bourgeois World*, ed. Frederick Cooper and Ann Laura Stoler (Berkeley: University of California Press, 1997); Keith Hart, "Informal Income Opportunities and Urban Employment in Ghana," *Journal of Modern African Studies* 11, no. 1 (1973): 61–89; and Paul Ehrlich, *The Population Bomb* (New York: Ballantine, 1968).

Bibliography

Archives, Libraries, and Special Collections

East Africana Collection, Library of the University of Dar es Salaam, Dar es Salaam, Tanzania

Maktaba Kuu ya Taifa (Tanzania National Library), Dar es Salaam, Tanzania

Melville J. Herskovits Library of African Studies, Northwestern University, Evanston, IL

Redio Sauti ya Injili Archives, Moshi, Tanzania

St. Mark's Center Archive, Dar es Salaam, Tanzania

Tanzania National Archives (TNA), Dar es Salaam, Tanzania

UMATI Archives, Dar es Salaam, Tanzania

Interviews and Correspondence

Ali Abbas, May 14, 2009, Dar es Salaam

Kiroboto Akida, April 8, 2009, Tanga

Modest Belege, July 28, 2015, Dar es Salaam

Walter Bgoya, June 3, 2013, Dar es Salaam

Andrew Damas, December 2, 2008, Dar es Salaam

Shabaani Debe, January 5, 2009, Tanga

Stanley Ganzel, June 5, 2013, Dar es Salaam

Muhiddin Maalim Gurumo, November 11, 2008, Dar es Salaam

Lawrence Gwakisa, September 4, 2009, correspondence with author

Bi. Halima, April 8, 2009, Tanga

Shakila Saidi Hamisi, November 20, 2008, Dar es Salaam

Steven Hiza, January 25, 2009, Tanga

Sagaya Hussein, October 19, 2008, Dar es Salaam

Leonard Isidori, February 13, 2009, Tanga

Belesa Kakere, January 19, 2009, Tanga

Hamza Kalala, August 10, 2009, Dar es Salaam

Jackson Kalindimya, June 13, 2013, Dar es Salaam

Patrick Kamaley, January 19, 2009, Tanga

Abraham Kapinga, June 15, 2009, Dar es Salaam

Elias Kasore, September 7, 2009, Dar es Salaam
Francis Kaswahili, November 11, 2008, Dar es Salaam
Kiberiti, October 17, 2008, Dar es Salaam
King Kiki, January 5, 2009, Dar es Salaam
Ramesh Kothari, September 2, 2009, Dar es Salaam
Ravi Kothari, September 2, 2009, Dar es Salaam
Bakari Kubo, November 26, 2008, Dar es Salaam
Maele Kushuma, December 21, 2010, Dar es Salaam
Makoye Kwilukilwa, January 5, 2009, Dar es Salaam
Bi. Loco, April 1, 2009, Tanga
Angelo Luhala, November 19, 2008, Dar es Salaam
Richard Mabala, June 20, 2013, Dar es Salaam
Freddy Macha, correspondence with author, January 3, 2009;
    interviews on March 11, 2009, London; March 29, 2009, Dar es Salaam
Bakari Majengo, February 11, 2009, Dar es Salaam
Mohamed Majura, April 5, 2009, Tanga
Dr. Sifuel Mamuya, January 3, 2011, Marangu
Hamed Manyema, January 27, 2009, Tanga
Mzee Mapili, December 2, 2008, Dar es Salaam
Lucia E. Matewele, April 21, 2009, Tanga
Fatuma Mdoe, March 27, 2009, Tanga
Clemence Merinyo, June 11, 2013, Dar es Salaam
Amy Mfinanga, January 3, 2011, Moshi
Ismaili Issa Michuzi, September 9, 2009, Dar es Salaam
Muhidin Michuzi, September 3, 2009, Dar es Salaam
Said Kassim Rajab Mihiko, June 10, 2013, Dar es Salaam
Jumaa Mkabarah, June 17, 2013, Muheza
Majaliwa Mnyijanga, April 7, 2009, Tanga
Grace Mtawali, December 26, 2010, Dar es Salaam
Ibrahim Hamisi Mtumwa, June 1, 2009, Dar es Salaam
Telson Peter Mughogho, January 1, 2009 and May 4, 2009, Tanga
Kajubi Mukajanga, June 8, 2013, Dar es Salaam
M. M. Mulokozi, June 6, 2013, Dar es Salaam
Evans Musiba, June 7, 2013, Dar es Salaam
Maria Rogers Mwangoye, April 1, 2009, Tanga
Amne Mbaraka Mwinshehe, November 26, 2008 and December 3, 2008,
    Dar es Salaam
Taji Mbaraka Mwinshehe, November 25, 2008.
Hassan Ngoma, April 9, 2009, Tanga
Mzee Charles Mpembwe Njali, February 13, 2009, Tanga
Christina Nsekela, December 6, 2010, Mbeya
Yusuf Omari, June 15, 2009, Dar es Salaam
Ali Said Pazi, August 22, 2009, Dar es Salaam
Farid Hammie Rajab, June 10, 2013, Dar es Salaam

Taabu Ramadhani, June 21, 2009, Dar es Salaam
Emmanuel Martin Saidi, January 28, 2009, Tanga
Wilfred Martin Saidi, January 29, 2009, Tanga
Zigi Saidi, January 25, 2009, Tanga
Abdul Salvator, September 7, 2009, Dar es Salaam
Filipo Samuel Semdani, April 8, 2009, Tanga
Ally Sykes, February 12, 2009, Dar es Salaam
Omari Urembo, June 17, 2009, Dar es Salaam

Fictional Works and Popular Literature

Abdulla, Muhammed Said. *Kisima cha Giningi.* London: Evans Bros., 1968.
———. *Mizimu ya Watu wa Kale.* Nairboi: East African Literature Bureau, 1960.
———. *Mke Mmoja, Waume Watatu.* Dar es Salaam: East African Publishing House, 1975.
Abdul-Wahab, Z. B. *Ulimbo.* Dar es Salaam: East African Literature Bureau, 1976.
Abubakar, Bi. S. *Haki Ya Mtu Haipokei.* Peramiho: Benedictine Publications Ndanda-Peramiho, 1981.
Akwilombwe, Rashidi Alli. *Jambazi.* Dar es Salaam: Msasani Stationaries, 1988.
Anduru, Agoro. *The Fugitive.* Dar es Salaam: Intercontinental, 1982.
———. *Kukosa Radhi.* Dar es Salaam: Press and Publicity Center, 1983.
Ba, Mariama. *So Long a Letter.* Portsmouth, NH: Heinemann, 1989.
Baka, Abdul. *Salome.* Dar es Salaam: Tanzania Publishing House, 1972.
Balisidya, Ndyanao. *Shida.* Nairobi: Foundation, 1975.
Banzi, Alex. *Pumbazo La Moyo.* Dar es Salaam: East African Literature Bureau, 1977.
———. *Titi La Mkwe.* Dar es Salaam: Tanzania Publishing House, 1972.
———. *Usiku Wa Balaa.* Dar es Salaam: Wamasa Publications, 1981.
———. *Zika Mwenyewe.* Dar es Salaam: Tanzania Publishing House, 1977.
Chachage, C. L. S. *Kivuli.* Dar es Salaam: B.C.I., 1982.
Chande, Kassim. *Kazikwa Yu Hai.* Dar es Salaam: Southern Publications, 1984.
———. *Lazima Afe.* Dar es Salaam: Hamassa Publications, 1983.
———. *Mnuko Wa Damu.* Dar es Salaam: Southern Publications and Agency, 1982.
Charo, Kateta Mwana. *Umelogwa Au Umetumwa?* Dar es Salaam: East African Literature Bureau, 1976.
Chiduo, Nobert. *Mikononi Mwa Mauti.* Dar es Salaam: East African Literature Bureau, 1975.
Chiwonda, Edgar. *Tabia.* Dar es Salaam: Tanzania Publishing House, 1983.
Chogo, Angelina. *Kortini Mtu Huu!* Nairobi: Foundation, 1975.
Dibwe, S. S. *Mauaji Ya Kishenzi.* Dar es Salaam: Dibwe Publications, 1986.
Felix, Florence. *Kuchanganyikikwa.* Peramiho: Benedictine Publications Ndanda-Peramiho, 1983.
Ganzel, Edi. *Faili Maalum.* Dar es Salaam: Tamasha, 1981.
———. *Jogoo La Shamba.* Dar es Salaam: East African Publications, 1978.

———. *Kijasho Chembamba*. Dar es Salaam: Tamasha Publications, 1980.

———. *Kitanzi*. Dar es Salaam: Utamaduni Publishers, 1984.

———. *Ndoto ya Mwendawazimu*. Dar es Salaam: East African Literature Bureau, 1972.

Kalindimya, Jackson. *Mtafutano*. Dar es Salaam: Tajack, 1989.

———. *Tafrija Ya Damu*. Dar es Salaam: Tajack, 1984.

———. *Wimbi La Huzuni*. Dar es Salaam: Tajack, 1988.

Kassam, Kassim M. *Huku Ataka Na Huku Ataka*. Dar es Salaam: Kassam Publishing Center, 1985.

———. *Joto la Fedha*. Dar es Salaam: Kobe, 1982.

———. *Shemeji Kula, Dada Hayuko*. Dar es Salaam: Cheka Magazine, 1987.

———. *Shuga Dedi*. Dar es Salaam: International Publishers Agency, 1984.

Katalambulla, Faraji H. H. *Buriani*. Dar es Salaam: East African Literature Bureau, 1975.

———. *Lawalawa Na Hadithi Nyingine*. Dar es Salaam: East African Literature Bureau, 1976.

———. *Mirathi*. Dar es Salaam: East African Literature Bureau, 1976.

———. *Mizani Ya Imani*. Nairobi: Nelson Africa, 1978.

———. *Pendo Pevu*. Dar Es Salaam: East African Publications, 1976.

———. *Pili Pilipili*. Arusha: East African Publications, 1977.

———. *Simu Ya Kifo*. Dar es Salaam: East African Literature Bureau, 1965.

———. *Unono*. Nairobi: Nelson Africa, 1978.

Keto, Ali. *Chumo La Husuda*. Dar es Salaam: East African Publications, 1976.

———. *Nitamshtaki Kuzimu*. Dar es Salaam: East African Publishing House, 1976.

———. *Pole Dada*. Dar es Salaam: East African Publications, 1976.

Kezilahabi, Euphrase. *Dunia Uwanja wa Fujo*. Kampala: East African Literature Bureau, 1975.

———. *Kichwamaji*. Dar es Salaam: East African Publishing House, 1974.

———. *Rosa Mistika*. Dar es Salaam: Dar es Salaam University Press, 1971.

Kiango, Saifu D. *Jeraha Ya Moyo*. Nairobi: Foundation, 1974.

Kitsao, Jay. *Uasi*. Nairobi: Oxford University Press, 1980.

Kiwanga, Hemed A. *Je, Kisasi?* Dar es Salaam: E. S., 1983.

Komanya, A. *Tabu*. Dar es Salaam: Tanzania Publishing House, 1977.

Komba, Serapius. *Pete*. Dar es Salaam: IKR, 1978.

Kuhenga, Casmiri. *Kovu La Pendo*. Dar es Salaam: Longman, 1971.

———. *Sofia Kipepeo*. Peramiho: Benedictine Publications Ndanda-Peramiho, 1980.

Lemki, Mark. *Yarabi Maskini*. Dar es Salaam: East African Literature Bureau.

Macha, Freddy. *Twen'zetu Ulaya*. Dar es Salaam: Grand Arts Promotion, 1984.

Malyi, Victor Joseph. *Kisa Cha Upelelezi Wa Inspekta Dumbi*. Dar es Salaam: Jacaranda Publications, 1985.

Manghulo, A. *Raha Zetu*. Dar es Salaam: Longman, 1979.

Mapalala, Bernard. *Cheo Dhamana*. Dar es Salaam: East African Publishing House, 1976.

Mashambulio, Damiano. *Msichana Anapolaghai.* . . . Dar es Salaam: Heko Publications, 1986.

Massawe, Hilda. *Mapenzi Ya Fedha Nauli Ya Ahera.* Peramiho: Benedictine Publications Ndanda-Peramiho, 1983.

Mbajo, Nicco. *Dhamana Ya Mapenzi.* Dar es Salaam: Press and Publicity Center, 1982.

———. *Sifi Mara Mbili.* Dar es Salaam: Mcheshi, 1984.

Mbega, Omar. *Ndoto Kivulini.* Dar es Salaam: International Publishers Agencies, 1982.

Mbelwa, H. C. M. *Donda Ndugu.* Dar es Salaam: Tanzania Publishing House, 1973.

———. *Mwana Wa Shetani.* Dar es Salaam: Longman, 1977.

Mbenna, I. C. *Sitaki.* Dar es Salaam: East African Publishing House, 1976.

———. *Siuwezi Ujamaa.* Dar es Salaam: East African Publishing House, 1976.

Mbogo, Emmanuel. *Giza Limeingia.* Dar es Salaam: Tanzania Publishing House, 1980.

Mchome, G'ray. *Awe Hai Au Amekufa.* . . . *Namtaka!* Moshi: May 25th Publications, 1982.

———. *Kaburi La Fedha.* Moshi: May 25th Publications, 1982.

Mdoe, Chase A. P. *Kifo Cha Paulina.* Dar es Salaam: Heko Publications, 1987.

———. *Kilemba Cha Ukoka.* Dar es Salaam: Grand Arts Promotion, 1984.

Mhoza, Ally R. *Pendo La Kifo.* Dar es Salaam: Tanzania Publishing House, 1972.

Mkabarah, Jumaa. *Kafara.* Dar es Salaam: Black Star Agencies, 1976.

———. *Kizimbani.* Dar es Salaam: Black Star Agencies, 1974.

———. *Marehemu Susana.* Dar es Salaam: Utamaduni Publishers, 1974.

———. *Mbio Za Kipofu.* Dar es Salaam: Utamaduni Publishers, 1981.

———. *Mwanamuziki wa Tanzania: Salum Abdallah.* Dar es Salaam: Taasisi ya Uchunguzi wa Kiswahili Chuo Kikuu cha Dar es Salaam, 1972.

———. *Ramani Ya Maiti.* Dar es Salaam: Utamaduni Publishers, 1985.

———. *Siibi Tena.* Dar es Salaam: Maarifa, 1972.

Mkasiwa, A. S. *Adui Wa Haki.* Peramiho: Benedictine Publications Ndanda-Peramiho, 1981.

Mkufya, W. E. *The Dilemma.* Dar es Salaam: Press and Publicity Center, 1982.

———. *The Wicked Walk.* Dar es Salaam: Tanzania Publishing House, 1977.

Mloka, Charles. *Mjini Taabu.* Peramiho: Benedictine Publications Ndanda-Peramiho, 1985.

———. *Operationi Pata Potea.* Morogoro: Kasoro Bahari, 1988.

Mlolwa, Didace. *Hatari! Pesa Au Kifo.* Dar es Salaam: Attractive Artists Co., 1988.

———. *Nitaua Tu . . . Akokme Ubishi.* Dar es Salaam: Masumin, 1986.

Mnzava, Kapombe. *Usiku Wa Mbalamwezi.* Dar es Salaam: Tanzania Publishing House, 1979.

Mohamed, Mohamed S. *Kiu.* Dar es Salaam: East African Publishing House, 1972.

Msokile, Mbunda. *Thamani Ya Ukubwa.* Dar es Salaam: Meza Publications, 1979.

Mtendamema, G. W. *Sipendi Kuishi*. Dar es Salaam: Longman, 1978.

Mtobwa, Ben. *Dar es Salaam Usiku*. Nairobi: Mkuki, 1998.

———. *Dimbwi La Damu*. Dar es Salaam: East African Publications, 1984.

———. *Lazima Ufe Joram*. Dar es Salaam: Heko Publications, 1983.

———. *Malaika wa Shetani*. Dar es Salaam: Heko Publications, 1988.

———. *Mikononi Mwa Nunda*. Dar es Salaam: Heko Publications, 1986.

———. *Najisikia Kuua Tena*. Dar es Salaam: Tanzania Africa Publications, 1984.

———. *Pesa Zako Zinanuka*. Dar es Salaam: Heko Publications, 1984.

———. *Salamu Toka Kuzimu*. Dar es Salaam: Heko Publications, 1987.

———. *Tutarudi Na Roho Zetu?* Dar es Salaam: Heko Publications, 1987.

Mukajanga, Kajubi D. *Bruce Lee: Mfalme wa Kung Fu*. Dar es Salaam: Grand Arts Promotion, 1982.

———. *Kitanda cha Mauti*. Dar es Salaam: Grand Arts Promotion, 1982.

———. *Mpenzi*. Dar es Salaam: Grand Arts Promotion, 1984.

———. *Tuanze Lini?* Dar es Salaam: Grand Arts Promotion, 1983.

Munisi, Salliel. *Kama Ndoto*. Nairobi: East African Literature Bureau, 1976.

———. "Logic," in *Summons: Poems from Tanzania,* ed. Richard Mabala. Dar es Salaam: Tanzania Publishing House Limited, 1980.

Musiba, Erastablus Elvis. *Kikomo*. Dar es Salaam: Continental, 1980.

———. *Kikosi Cha Kisasi*. Kilimanjaro, 1979.

———. *Kufa Na Kupona*. Dar es Salaam: East African Literature Bureau, 1974.

———. *Njama*. Dar es Salaam: Continental, 1981.

Muwanga, P. C., and A. S. Geranija. *Doa La Mauti*. Nairobi: Heinemann, 1976.

Mvungi, Martha. *Hana Hatia*. Dar es Salaam: Tanzania Publishing House, 1975.

Mwanga, Zainab. *Hiba Ya Wivu*. Dar es Salaam: Ruvu, 1984.

———. *Kiu Ya Haki*. Morogoro: Spark, 1983.

Mwaware. *Maputo*. Dar es Salaam: Longman, 1980.

———. *Operesheni Vipusa*. Dar es Salaam: Black Star Agencies, 1977.

Mwenegoha, Hamza. *Kifo Cha Furaha*. Nairobi: Transafrica, 1975.

Nchimbi, B. R. *Penzi la Dawa*. Dar es Salaam: Tanzania Publishing House, 1974.

Ndibalema, Charles. *Fimbo La Ulimwengu*. Nairobi: Heinemann, 1974.

———. *Nimeponzeka*. Dar es Salaam: Longman, 1970.

Ngahyoma, Ngalimecha. *Huka*. Dar es Salaam: Tanzania Publishing House, 1973.

Ng'ombo, Amina H. *Chuki Ya Ndoa*. Peramiho: Benedictine Publications Ndanda-Peramiho, 1981.

———. *Heka Heka za Ulanguzi*. Peramiho: Benedictine Publications Ndanda-Peramiho, 1982.

Omari, Cuthbert K. *Barabara Ya Tano*. Dar es Salaam: Tanzania Publishing House, 1973.

———. *Kuanguliwa Kwa Kifaranga*. Nairobi: Heinemann, 1976.

———. *Mwenda Kwao*. Dar es Salaam: Chuo cha Uchunguzi wa Lugha ya Kiswahili, 1971.

Owino, Rosemarie. *Sugar Daddy's Lover*. Nairobi: Spear, 1975.

Rajab, Hammie. *Ama Zao, Ama Zangu*. Dar es Salaam: Busara, 1982.

———. *Balaa*. Dar es Salaam: Busara, 1983.

———. *Dunia Hadaa*. Dar es Salaam: Busara, 1982.

———. *Gubu La Wifi*. Dar es Salaam: Busara, 1985.

———. *Ninajuta Kuolewa*. Dar es Salaam: Busara, 1983.

———. *Roho Mkononi*. Dar es Salaam: Busara, 1984.

———. *Sanda La Jambazi*. Dar es Salaam: Busara, 1985.

———. *Somo Kaniponza*. Dar es Salaam: Busara, 1984.

———. *Ufunguo wa Bandia*. Dar es Salaam: East African Publications, 1979.

Rajab, Hammie, and Edi Ganzel. *Kipigo cha Fashisti Iddi Amin Dudu*. Dar es Salaam: Tamasha, 1979.

Rujakingira, A. D. *Asiyekuwepo*. Dar es Salaam: Longman, 1980.

Rutayisinga, John. *Ngumi Ukutani*. Dar es Salaam: Longman, 1979.

———. *Papa La Mji*. Dar es Salaam: Grand Arts Promotion, 1985.

———. *Tumgidie Bwege*. Dar es Salaam: Grand Arts Promotion, 1985.

Saffari, A. J. *Harusi*. Dar es Salaam: University of Dar es Salaam Press, 1984.

———. *Kabwela*. Dar es Salaam: Longman, 1978.

———. *Kaka Msomi*. Dar es Salaam: Longman Tanzania, 1976.

Salwenga, Lonely S. S. *Hadaa Za Maisha*. Peramiho: Benedictine Publications Ndanda-Peramiho, 1982.

Sangija, D. *Bado Mmoja*. . . . Peramiho: Benedictine Publications Ndanda-Peramiho, 1971.

Sembera, Fidelis. *Maisha Nuksi*. Dar es Salaam: Longman, 1976.

———. *Po!* Morogoro: Jomssi, 1984.

———. *Salima, Mtoto Wa Watu*. Dar es Salaam: Longman, 1977.

———. *Tamaa*. Dar es Salaam: Swala, 1982.

———. *Umbea*. London: Transafrica, 1978.

Seme, William B. *Njozi Za Usiku*. Dar es Salaam: Longman, 1973.

Simbamwene, John. *Akuanze Mmalize*. Peramiho: Benedictine Publications Ndanda-Peramiho, 1984.

———. *Anatafutwa Kusaidia Polisi*. Morogoro: Jomssi, 1984.

———. *Dogodogo Wanitesa*. Morogoro: Jomssi, 1982.

———. *Kivumbi Uwanjani*. Nairobi: Transafrica, 1978.

———. *Kwa Sababu ya Pesa*. Dar es Salaam: Longman, 1972.

———. *Kweli Unanipenda?* London: Transafrica, 1978.

———. *Madhambi Ya Elita*. Morogoro: Jomssi, 1982.

———. *Madhambi Ya Mwenye Nyumba*. Morogoro: Jomssi, 1984.

———. *Mapenzi Ya Pesa*. Peramiho: Benedictine Publications Ndanda-Peramiho, 1976.

———. *Mwisho wa Mapenzi*. Dar es Salaam: Longman, 1971.

———. *Operesheni Sukuma Namba Nane*. Morogoro: Jomssi, 1985.

Sizya, D. P. *Tumekosa, Mtusamehe*. Dar es Salaam: Black Star Agencies, 1976.

Tegambwage, Ndimara. *Duka La Kaya*. Dar es Salaam: Tausi, 1985.

Twarindwa, G. *Kesi*. Arusha-Dar es Salaam: East African Publications, 1979.

Zorro, Zahir Ally. *Kabwe Makanika Jitu Kumbuka Vita Dhidi Ya Unyama Wa Mafia Mob Part 1*. Dar es Salaam: Dibwe, 1986.

Textbooks, Primers, and Educational Pamphlets

"A Guide to the Operation of Literacy/Adult Education Programme in Tanzania." n.d.

Elizabeti. *Barua kwa Dada*. Dodoma: Central Tanganyika Press, 1970.

Frémon, Isabelle Victorine, and Sister Mwuguzi. *Mdoe na Mama Yake: Mashauri katika Kuwalea Watoto Wadogo*. London: Sheldon, 1951.

Hamilton, St. Clair, and Archer Wallington. *Maarifa Yawapasayo Mama Katika Kutunza Watoto Wao*. London: Sheldon, 1943.

Kouene, Esther, and H. M. Twining. *Mama wa Afrika na Nyumba Yake*. Dar es Salaam: East African Literature Bureau, 1955.

Mamuya, Dr. S. J. *Jando Na Unyago*. Nairobi: East African Publishing House, 1973.

———. *Tatizo La Kutoa Mimba*. Dar es Salaam: Elimu ya Malezi ya Ujana, 1980.

———. *Usafi Wa Maisha Ya Ujana*. Dar es Salaam: Elimu ya Malezi ya Ujana, 1980.

Mandao, Martha. *All Alone in the City*. Achimota, Ghana: African Christian Press, 1969.

———. *Ani Afungua Mkoba Wake*. Dodoma: Central Tanganyika Press, 1974.

———. *Ani I stap wanpis long biktaun*. Madang, Papua New Guinea: Kristen Press, 1976.

———. *Ani Opens Her Purse*. Achimota, Ghana: African Christian Press, 1971.

———. *Ani y la Ciudad*. Salta, Argentina: Editorial Mundo, 1975.

———. *Peke Yangu Mjini*. Dodoma: Central Tanganyika Press, 1969.

———. *Seule dans la Ville*. Abidjan: Centre de Publications Evangéliques, 1974.

———. *Umoyo wa m'tauni*. Blantyre, Malawi: CLAIM, 1973.

———. *Zowawa za m'tauni*. Blantyre, Malawi: CLAIM, 1973.

Msuya, S. K. *Mazungumzo Za Mchana*. Dar es Salaam: Tanzania Publishing House, 1973.

———. *Mazungumzo Ya Usiku*. Dar es Salaam: Tanzania Publishing House, 1978.

———. *Mazungumzo Za Jioni*. Dar es Salaam: Tanzania Publishing House, 1976.

Pelham-Johnson, Margery. *Binti Leo Kwake*. Nairobi: Eagle, 1950.

Rutashobya, J. M. "Tanzania Adult Literacy Adult Education Programme." Dar es Salaam: Ministry of Community Development and National Culture, n.d.

TANU. *Vitabu Vya Darubini: Unyonge wa Mwafrika*. Dar es Salaam: East African Publishing House, 1970.

UMATI, *Umati Story: From Family Planning to Sexual and Reproductive Health*, 2005.

Discography

Atomic Jazz Band. *Dunia Ina Tabu/Dada Tabia Zako Mbaya*. Saba 7–39, 1971.

Jamhuri Jazz Band. *Jamhuri Jazz Band 1970/71*. Philips PKLP 101, 1971.

Marijani Rajabu and Dar International. Vol. 2 *Masudi*. MSK CAS 515, n.d.
Morogoro Jazz Band. *Choyo Uache*. Polydor, POL 7–051B, 1970.
Salum Abdallah and Cuban Marimba. *Ngoma Iko Huko: Vintage Tanzanian Dance Music, 1955–1965*. Dizim Records 4701, 2000.
Zanzibara. *Ujamaa, the Sound of 1960s Tanzania*. Vol. 3. Buda Music 860142, 2007.

Newspapers and Periodicals

Binti Leo
Civil Servants Magazine of the United Republic of Tanzania
Daily News [Dar es Salaam]
Dar es Salaam Medical Journal
Drum [Nairobi]
Habari za Mwadui
Habari za Posta
Jenga
Kiongozi
Kwetu [Dar es Salaam]
Mhola Ziswe
Mlezi
Mulika
Mwafrika [Dar es Salaam]
Mzalendo [Dar es Salaam]
Nationalist [Dar es Salaam]
Nchi Yetu [Dar es Salaam]
Ngurumo [Dar es Salaam]
Sunday News [Dar es Salaam]
Tanesco News
Tanganyika Standard [Dar es Salaam]
Tanzania Engineers
Tanzania Police Journal
Tatejo
Uhuru [Dar se Salaam]
Umoja

Unpublished Sources

Ivaska, Andrew. "Negotiating 'Culture' in a Cosmopolitan Capital: Urban Style and the State in Colonial and Postcolonial Dar es Salaam." PhD diss., University of Michigan, 2003.
Lewinson, Anne. "Going with the Times: Transforming Visions of Urbanism and Modernity among Professionals in Dar es Salaam, Tanzania." PhD diss., University of Wisconsin-Madison, 1999.
Martin, Stephen Harvey. "Music in Urban East Africa: A Study of the Development of Urban Jazz in Dar Es Salaam." PhD diss., University of Washington, 1980.

Research Notes and Data for 1973/1974 Social Survey of Dar es Salaam. Marja-Liisa Swantz, Deborah Bryceson, Hilda Ausi, Severa Mlay and Fatuma Macha.

Published Sources

Abdulaziz, M., ed. and trans. *Muyaka: 19th-Century Swahili Popular Poetry.* Nairobi: Kenya Literature Bureau, 1979.

Abu-Lughod, Lila. *Dramas of Nationhood: The Politics of Television in Egypt.* Chicago: University of Chicago Press, 2005.

African Development Bank Group. "Tracking Africa's Progress in Figures." Tunis: African Development Bank, 2014.

Ahlman, Jeffrey. *Living with Nkrumahism: Nation, State, and Pan-Africanism in Ghana.* Athens: Ohio University Press, 2017.

Allman, Jean. "Phantoms of the Archive: Kwame Nkrumah, a Nazi Pilot Named Hanna, and the Contingencies of Postcolonial History Writing." *American Historical Review* 118, no. 1 (2013): 104–29.

Amadiume, Ifi. *Male Daughters, Female Husbands: Gender and Sex in African Society.* London: Zed, 1987.

Ambler, Charles. "Popular Films and Colonial Audiences: The Movies in Northern Rhodesia." *American Historical Review* 106 (2001): 81–105.

Aminzade, Ronald. *Race, Nation, and Citizenship in Post-Colonial Africa: The Case of Tanzania.* New York: Cambridge University Press, 2013.

Anderson, William B. *The Church in East Africa, 1840–1974.* Nairobi: Uzima, 1981.

Andreasen, Manja Hoppe, and Jytte Agergaard. "Residential Mobility and Homeownership in Dar es Salaam." *Population and Development Review* 42, no. 1 (March 2016): 101.

Andrews, Loretta Kreider, and Herbert D. Andrews. "The Church and the Birth of a Nation: The Mindolo Ecumenical Foundation and Zambia." *Journal of Church and State* 17, no. 2 (1975): 191–216.

Apter, Andrew. *The Pan-African Nation: Oil and the Spectacle of Culture in Nigeria.* Chicago: University of Chicago Press, 2005.

Arnoldi, Mary Jo. "Youth Festivals and Museums: The Cultural Politics of Public Memory in Postcolonial Mali." *Africa Today* 52, no. 4 (2006): 55–76.

Askew, Kelly. *Performing the Nation: Swahili Music and Cultural Politics in Tanzania.* Chicago: University of Chicago Press, 2002.

Askew, Kelly, and John Kitime. "Popular Music Censorship in Tanzania." In *Popular Music Censorship in Africa,* ed. Michael Drewett and Martin Cloonan, 137–56. Hampshire, UK: Ashgate, 2006.

Banerjea, Koushik. "'Fight Club': Aesthetics, Hybridisation and the Construction of Rogue Masculinities in *Sholay* and *Deewar.*" In *Bollyworld: Popular Indian Cinema through a Transnational Lens,* ed. Raminder Kaur and Ajay J. Sinha. Thousand Oaks, CA: Sage, 2005.

Barber, Karin. *The Anthropology of Texts, Persons and Publics.* Cambridge: Cambridge University Press, 2007.

———. "Popular Arts in Africa." *African Studies Review* 30, no. 3 (1987): 1–78.

Barz, Gregory, and Frank Gunderson, eds. *Mashindano! Competitive Music Performance in East Africa*. Dar es Salaam: Mkuki na Nyota, 2000.

Becker, Felicitas. "Female Seclusion in the Aftermath of Slavery on the Southern Swahili Coast: Transformations of Slavery in Unexpected Places." *International Journal of African Historical Studies* 48, no. 2 (2015): 229.

Bgoya, Walter. *Books and Reading in Tanzania*. Paris: UNESCO, 1986.

———. "From Tanzania to Kansas and Back Again." In *No Easy Victories: African Liberation and American Activists over a Half-Century, 1950–2000*, 103-6. Trenton, NJ: Africa World Press, 2008.

Bhola, H. S. *Campaigning for Literacy: Eight National Experiences of the Twentieth Century*. Paris: UNESCO, 1984.

Bienefeld, M. A. "The Self Employed of Urban Tanzania." In *IDS Discussion Paper*. Brighton, UK: University of Sussex, 1974.

Bier, Laura. "Feminism, Solidarity and Identity in the Age of Bandung: Third World Women in the Egyptian Press." In *Making a World after Empire: The Bandung Moment and Its Political Afterlives*, ed. Christopher Lee. Athens: Ohio University Press, 2010.

Brennan, James R. "Between Segregation and Gentrification: Africans, Indians and the Struggle for Housing in Dar es Salaam, 1920–1950." Chapter 4 in *Dar es Salaam: Histories from an Emerging African Metropolis*, ed. James R. Brennan, Andrew Burton, and Yusuf Lawi. Dar es Salaam: Mkuki na Nyota, 2007.

———. "Blood Enemies: Exploitation and Urban Citizenship in the Nationalist Political Thought of Tanzania, 1958–75." *Journal of African History* 47, no. 3 (2006): 389–413.

———. "Democratizing Cinema and Censorship in Tanzania, 1920–1980." *International Journal of African Historical Studies* 38, no. 3 (2005): 481–511.

———. "Realizing Civilization through Patrilineal Descent: The Intellectual Making of an African Racial Nationalism in Tanzania, 1920–1950." *Social Identities* 12, no. 4 (2006): 405–23.

———. *Taifa: Making Nation and Race in Urban Tanzania*. Athens: Ohio University Press, 2011.

——. "Youth, the TANU Youth League and Managed Vigilantism in Dar es Salaam, Tanzania." *Africa* 76, no. 2 (2006): 221–46.

Brennan, James R., Andrew Burton, and Yusuf Lawi, eds. *Dar es Salaam: Histories from an Emerging African Metropolis*. Dar es Salaam: Mkuki na Nyota, 2007.

Burgess, G. Thomas. "Mao in Zanzibar: Nationalism, Discipline and the (De) Construction of Afro-Asian Solidarities." In *Making a World after Empire: The Bandung Moment and Its Political Afterlives,* ed. Christopher Lee, 196–234. Athens: Ohio University Press, 2010.

Burton, Andrew. *African Underclass: Urbanisation, Crime and Colonial Order in Dar es Salaam*. Oxford: James Currey, 2005.

———. "The Haven of Peace Purged: Tackling the Undesirable and Unproductive Poor in Dar Es Salaam, ca. 1950s–1980s." *International Journal of African Historical Studies* 40, no. 1 (2007): 119–51.

———. "Raw Youth, School-Leavers and the Emergence of Structural Unemployment in Late-Colonial Urban Tanganyika." *Journal of African History* 47 (2006): 363–87.

———. "Townsmen in the Making: Social Engineering and Citizenship in Dar Es Salaam, c. 1945–1960." *International Journal of African Historical Studies* 36, no. 2 (2003): 331–65.

Burton, Andrew, and Gary Burgess. "Introduction." In *Generations Past: Youth in East African History*, ed. Andrew Burton and Hélène Charton-Bigot. Athens: Ohio University Press, 2010.

Burton, Andrew, and Hélène Charton-Bigot, eds. *Generations Past: Youth in East African History*. Athens: Ohio University Press, 2010.

Burton, Antionette. *Dwelling in the Archive: Women Writing House, Home and History in Late Colonial India*. Oxford: Oxford University Press, 2003.

Caldeira, Teresa Pires do Rio. *City of Walls: Crime, Segregation, and Citizenship in São Paulo*. Berkeley: University of California Press, 2000.

Callaci, Emily. "Dancehall Politics: Mobility, Sexuality, and Spectacles of Racial Respectability in Late Colonial Tanganyika, 1930s–1961." *Journal of African History*, no. 3 (2011): 365–84.

———. "'Chief Village in a Nation of Villages': History, Race and Authority in Tanzania's Dodoma Plan." *Urban History* 43, no. 1 (2015): 96–116.

———. "Injectable Development: Depo-Provera and the Mapping of the Global South." Forthcoming.

———. "Street Textuality Socialism, Masculinity and Urban Belonging in Tanzania's Pulp Fiction Publishing Industry, 1975–1985." *Comparative Studies in Society and History* 59, no. 1 (2017): 183–210.

Casson, W. T. "Architectural Notes on Dar es Salaam." *Tanzania Notes and Records* 71 (1970): 181–84.

Chachage, C. S. L. "The Tanzanian Publishing Industry." Occasional Paper. Kingston, UK: University of Hull, 1994.

Chattopadhyay, Swati. *Representing Calcutta: Modernity, Nationalism and the Colonial Uncanny*. London: Routledge, 2005.

Chiume, W. K. *Dunia Ngumu*. Dar es Salaam: Tanzania Publishing House, 1969.

Cole, Jennifer. "Fresh Contact in Tamatave, Madagascar: Sex, Money and Intergenerational Transformation." In *Generations and Globalization: Youth, Age and Family in the New World Economy*, ed. Jennifer Cole and Deborah Durham, 74–101. Bloomington: Indiana University Press, 2007.

Cole, Jennifer, and Lynn Thomas. "Introduction: Thinking Through Love in Africa." In *Love in Africa*, ed. Jennifer Cole and Lynn Thomas. Chicago: University of Chicago Press, 2009.

Colla, Elliott. "Anxious Advocacy: The Novel, the Law, and Extrajudicial Appeals in Egypt." *Public Culture* 17, no. 3 (winter 2005): 417–43.

Comaroff, Jean, and John L. Comaroff. *Of Revelation and Revolution*. Vol. 2, *The Dialectics of Modernity on a South African Frontier*. Chicago: University of Chicago Press, 1997.

Connelly, Matthew. "To Inherit the Earth: Imagining World Population, from the Yellow Peril to the Population Bomb." *Journal of Global History* 1, no. 3 (2006): 299–319.

Cooper, Frederick. *Decolonization and African Society: The Labor Question in French and British Africa*. Cambridge: Cambridge University Press, 1996.

———. "Industrial Man Goes to Africa." In *Men and Masculinities in Modern Africa*, ed. Lisa Lindsay and Stephan Miescher, 128–37. Portsmouth, NH: Heinemann, 2003.

———. *On the African Waterfront: Urban Disorder and the Transformation of Work in Colonial Mombasa*. New Haven, CT: Yale University Press, 1987.

Coulson, Andrew. *Tanzania: A Political Economy*. Oxford: Clarendon, 1982.

Decker, Alicia. *In Idi Amin's Shadow: Women, Gender, and Militarism in Uganda*. Athens: Ohio University Press, 2014.

Decker, Corrie. "Biology, Islam and the Science of Sex Education in Colonial Zanzibar." *Past and Present* 222 (February 2014): 215–47.

———. "Reading, Writing, and Respectability: How Schoolgirls Developed Modern Literacies in Colonial Zanzibar." *International Journal of African Historical Studies* 43, no. 1 (2010): 89–114.

Doyle, Shane. "Premarital Sexuality in Great Lakes Africa, 1900–1980." In *Generations Past: Youth in East African History*, ed. Andrew Burton and Hélène Charton-Bigot, 237–61. Athens: Ohio University Press, 2010.

Edmondson, Laura. "National Erotica: The Politics of 'Traditional' Dance in Tanzania." *Drama Review* 45, no. 1 (spring 2001): 153–70.

———. *Performance and Politics in Tanzania*. Bloomington: Indiana University Press, 2007.

Ehrlich, Paul. *The Population Bomb*. New York: Ballantine, 1968.

Fair, Laura. "Drive-in Socialism: Debating Modernities and Development in Dar es Salaam, Tanzania." *American Historical Review* 118, no. 4 (2013): 1077–104.

———. "Making Love in the Indian Ocean: Hindi Films, Zanzibari Audiences and the Construction of Romance in the 1950s and 1960s." In *Love in Africa*, ed. Jennifer Cole and Lynn Thomas, 58–82. Chicago: University of Chicago Press, 2009.

———. *Pastimes and Politics: Culture, Community, and Identity in Post-Abolition Urban Zanzibar, 1890–1945*. Athens: Ohio University Press, 2001.

Fanon, Frantz. *The Wretched of the Earth*. Translated by Constance Farrington. New York: Grove, 1963.

———. *Viumbe Waliolaaniwa*, trans. Gabriel Ruhumbika and Clement Maganga. Dar es Salaam: Tanzania Publishing House, 1978.

———. *Mafukara ya Ulimwengu*, trans. Ahmed Yusuf Abeid. London: Transafrica, 1977.

Feierman, Steven. *Peasant Intellectuals: Anthropology and History in Tanzania.* Madison: University of Wisconsin Press, 1990.

Ferguson, James. "Country and City on the Copperbelt." In *Culture, Power, Place: Explorations in Critical Anthropology,* ed. James Ferguson and Akhil Gupta, 137–56. Durham, NC: Duke University Press, 1997.

———. *Expectations of Modernity: Myths and Meanings of Urban Life on the Zambian Copperbelt.* Berkeley: University of California Press, 1999.

———. *Global Shadows: Africa in the Neoliberal World Order.* Durham, NC: Duke University Press, 2006.

Gaitskell, Deborah. "'Christian Compounds for Girls': Church Hostels for African Women in Johannesburg, 1907–1970." *Journal of Southern African Studies* 6, no. 1 (1979): 44–69.

Geiger, Susan. *TANU Women: Gender and Culture in the Making of Tanganyikan Nationalism, 1955–1965.* Portsmouth, NH: Heinemann, 1995.

George, Abosede. *Making Modern Girls: A History of Girlhood, Labor, and Social Development in Colonial Lagos.* Athens: Ohio University Press, 2014.

Glassman, Jonathon. "Creole Nationalists and the Search for Nativist Authenticity in Twentieth-Century Zanzibar: The Limits of Cosmopolitanism." *Journal of African History* 15, no. 2 (2014): 229–47.

———. *Feasts and Riot: Revelry, Rebellion, and Popular Consciousness on the Swahili Coast, 1856–1888.* Portsmouth, NH: Heinemann, 1995.

———. *War of Words, War of Stones: Racial Thought and Violence in Colonial Zanzibar.* Bloomington: Indiana University Press, 2011.

Gondola, Ch. Didier. *Tropical Cowboys: Westerns, Violence, and Masculinity in Kinshasa.* Bloomington: Indiana University Press, 2016.

Gopal, Sangita, and Sujata Moorti. "Introduction." In *Global Bollywood: Travels of Hindi Song and Dance,* 1–62. Minneapolis: University of Minnesota Press, 2008.

Goux, Marie-Ange. "Public Housing Policies: Decentralization, Government Policies, and the People's Solutions." In *From Dar es Salaam to Bongoland: Urban Mutations in Tanzania,* ed. Bernard Calas, 99–124. Dar es Salaam: Mkuki na Nyota, 2006.

Grace, Joshua. "Heroes of the Road: Race, Gender and the Politics of Mobility in Twentieth Century Tanzania," *Africa* 83, no3 (2013): 403–25.

Graebner, Werner. "Tanzania: Popular Music; The Land of Use-Your-Brain." In *The Rough Guide to World Music: Africa and the Middle East.* Vol. 1. London: Rough Guides, 2006.

Guyer, Jane I. "Introduction." In *Money Struggles and City Life: Devaluation in Ibadan and Other Urban Centers in Southern Nigeria, 1986–1996,* ed. Jane Guyer, LaRay Denzer, and Adigun A. B. Agbaje. Portsmouth, NH: Heinemann, 2002.

Hansen, Karen Tranberg. "Dressing Dangerously: Miniskirts, Gender Relations and Sexuality in Zambia." In *Fashioning Africa: Power and the Politics of Dress,* ed. Jean Allman, 166–85. Bloomington: Indiana University Press, 2004.

Hansen, Karen Tranberg, and Mariken Vaa. "Introduction." In *Reconsidering Informality: Perspectives from Urban Africa*, 7–20. Uppsala: Nordic Africa Institute, 2004.

Hanson, Holly. "Queen Mothers and Good Government in Buganda: The Loss of Women's Political Power in Nineteenth-Century East Africa." In *Women in African Colonial Histories*, ed. Susan Geiger, Nakanyike Musisi, and Jean Marie Allman, 219–36. Bloomington: Indiana University Press, 2002.

Haram, Liv. "'Prostitutes' or Modern Women? Negotiating Respectability in Northern Tanzania." In *Rethinking Sexualities in Africa*, ed. Signe Arnfred, 7–34. Uppsala: Nordiska Afrikainstitutet, 2004.

Hart, Keith. "Informal Income Opportunities and Urban Employment in Ghana." *Journal of Modern African Studies* 11, no. 1 (1973): 61–89.

Hirji, Karim F., ed. *Cheche: Reminiscences of a Radical Magazine*. Dar es Salaam: Mkuki na Nyota, 2010.

Horton, Mark, and John Middleton. *The Swahili: The Social Landscape of a Mercantile Society*. Oxford: Blackwell, 2000.

Hungwe, Chipo. "Putting Them in Their Place: 'Respectable' and 'Unrespectable' Women in Zimbabwean Gender Struggles." *Feminist Africa*, no. 6 (2006): 33–47.

Hunt, Nancy Rose. "Colonial Fairy Tales and the Knife and Fork Doctrine in the Heart of Africa." In *African Encounters with Domesticity*, ed. Karen Tranberg Hansen, 143–71. New Brunswick, NJ: Rutgers University Press, 1992.

———. *A Colonial Lexicon: Of Birth, Medicalization and Mobility in the Congo*. Durham, NC: Duke University Press, 1999.

Hunter, Mark. *Love in the Time of AIDS: Inequality, Gender, and Rights in South Africa*. Bloomington: Indiana University Press, 2010.

Hyslop, Jonathan. "Gandhi, Mandela and the African Modern." In *Johannesburg: The Elusive Metropolis*, ed. Achille Mbembe and Sarah Nuttall, 119–36. Durham, NC: Duke University Press, 2008.

Iliffe, John. *East African Doctors: A History of the Modern Profession*. Cambridge: Cambridge University Press, 1998.

———. *A Modern History of Tanganyika*. Cambridge: Cambridge University Press, 1979.

Ivaska, Andrew. "Anti-Mini Militants Meet Modern Misses: Urban Style, Gender and the Politics of 'National Culture' in 1960s Dar es Salaam, Tanzania." *Gender and History* 14, no. 3 (2002): 584–607.

———. *Cultured States: Youth, Gender and Modern Style in 1960s Dar es Salaam*. Durham, NC: Duke University Press, 2011.

———. "Of Students, 'Nizers,' and a Struggle over Youth: Tanzania's 1966 National Service Crisis." *Africa Today* 51, no. 3 (2005): 93–99.

James, Deborah, and Elizabeth Hull. "Introduction: Popular Economies in South Africa." *Africa* 82, no. 1 (2012): 1–19.

Jeffrey, Craig, and Stephen Young. "Jugad: Youth and Enterprise in India." *Annals of the Association of American Geographers* 104, no. 1 (2013): 182–94.

Johansson, Carl J. "The Bible School and the Church." *International Review of Mission* 45 (1956): 396–400.

Jones, Jeremy L. "'Nothing Is Straight in Zimbabwe': The Rise of the *Kukiya-Kiya* Economy 2000–2008." *Journal of Southern African Studies* 36, no. 2 (2010): 285–99.

Joseph, May. "Kung Fu Cinema and Frugality." In *The Visual Culture Reader*, ed. Nicholas Mirzoeff, 433–50. London: Routledge, 2002.

Kambili, Cyprian. "Ethics of African Tradition: Prescription of Dress Code in Malawi 1965–1973." *Society of Malawi Journal* 55, no. 2 (2002): 80–99.

Kezilahabi, Euphrase. "The Swahili Novel and the Common Man in East Africa." In *The East African Experience: Essays on English and Swahili Literature, 2nd Janheinz Journal of African Historyn-Symposium*, ed. Ulla Schild, 75–83. Mainz: Verlag, 1980.

King, Kenneth. *Jua Kali Kenya: Change and Development in an Informal Economy, 1970–1995.* Athens: Ohio University Press, 1996.

Kline, Wendy. *Bodies of Knowledge: Sexuality, Reproduction and Women's Health in the Second Wave.* Chicago: University of Chicago Press, 2010.

Komaromi, Ann. "The Material Existence of Soviet Samizdat." *Slavic Studies* 63, no. 3 (2004): 597–618.

Konde, Hadji. *Press Freedom in Tanzania.* Arusha, Tanzania: Eastern African Publications, 1984.

Krapf, J. L. *A Dictionary of the Suahili Language.* London: Trubner, 1882.

Krause, Monika. "The Ruralization of the World." *Public Culture* 25, no. 2 (2013): 233–48.

Kusno, Abidin. *Behind the Postcolonial: Architecture, Urban Space and Political Cultures in Indonesia.* London: Routledge, 2000.

Lacey, Stephen. *British Realist Theatre: The New Wave in Its Context 1956–1965.* London: Routledge, 1995.

Lal, Priya. *African Socialism in Postcolonial Tanzania: Between the Village and the World.* Cambridge: Cambridge University Press, 2015.

———. "Militants, Mothers and the National Family: Ujamaa, Gender and Rural Development in Postcolonial Tanzania." *Journal of African History* 51, no. 1 (2010): 1–20.

———. "Self-Reliance and the State: The Multiple Meanings of Development in Early Post-Colonial Tanzania." *Africa* 82, no. 2 (2012): 212–34.

Larkin, Brian. "Indian Films and Nigerian Lovers: Media and the Creation of Parallel Modernities." *Africa* 67, no. 3 (1997): 406–40.

———. *Signal and Noise: Media, Infrastructure and Urban Culture in Nigeria.* Durham, NC: Duke University Press, 2008.

Lecocq, Baz, and Erik Bähre. "The Drama of Development: The Skirmishes behind High Modernist Schemes in Africa." *African Studies* 66, no. 1 (2007): 1–8.

Le Pape, Marc. "Les Status d'une Génération: Les Déscolarisés d'Abidjan entre 1976 et 1986." *Politique Africaine* 24 (1986): 104–12.

Leslie, J. A. K. *A Survey of Dar es Salaam.* London: Oxford University Press, 1963.

Lienhardt, Peter. *The Medicine Man (Swifa Ya Nguvumali).* Oxford: Clarendon, 1968.

Lindsay, Lisa. "Domesticity and Difference: Male Breadwinners, Working Women, and Colonial Citizenship in the 1945 Nigerian General Strike." *American Historical Review* 104, no. 3 (1999): 783–812.

———. "Working with Gender: The Emergence of the 'Male Breadwinner' in Colonial Southwestern Nigeria." In *Africa after Gender*, ed. Catherine Cole, Takyiwaa Manuh, and Stephan Miescher, 241–52. Bloomington: Indiana University Press, 2007.

Lucas, Reverend Father. "Msimbazi Community Centre, Dar es Salaam," paper presented at the conference "The Church Meets Life in the Town," Dar es Salaam, Tanzania, May 14–21, 1964. Dar es Salaam: Tanganyika Rapid Social Change Study, Commission "C," 1964.

Lugalla, Joe. *Crisis, Urbanization, and Urban Poverty in Tanzania: A Study of Urban Poverty and Survival Politics.* Lanham, MD: University Press of America, 1995.

Magaziner, Daniel. "Two Stories about Art, Education and Beauty in Twentieth-Century South Africa." *American Historical Review* 118, no. 5 (2013): 1403–29.

Maliyamkono, T. L., and Mboya S. D. Bagachwa. *The Second Economy in Tanzania.* Eastern African Studies. London: J. Currey, 1990.

Markle, Seth. "'Book Publishers for a Pan-African World': Drum and Spear Press and Tanzania's Ujamaa Ideology." *Black Scholar* 37, no. 4 (2008): 16–26.

Marks, Shula. "Patriotism, Patriarchy and Purity: Natal and the Politics of Zulu Ethnic Consciousness." In *The Creation of Tribalism in Southern Africa*, ed. Leroy Vail, 215–40. Berkeley: University of California Press, 1989.

Mbembe, Achille, and Sarah Nuttall. "Introduction." In *Johannesburg: The Elusive Metropolis*, ed. Achille Mbembe and Sarah Nuttall. Durham, NC: Duke University Press, 2008.

Mbuguni, L. A., and Gabriel Ruhumbika. "TANU and National Culture." In *Towards Ujamaa: Twenty Years of TANU Leadership*, ed. Gabriel Ruhumbika, 275–87. Dar es Salaam: East African Literature Bureau, 1974.

McKittrick, Meredith. "Forsaking Their Fathers? Colonialism, Christianity and Coming of Age in Ovamboland, Northern Namibia." In *Men and Masculinities in Modern Africa*, ed. Stephan Miescher and Lisa Lindsay, 33–51. Portsmouth, NH: Heinemann, 2003.

Meghji, Zakia Hamdani. "Sisterly Activism." In *Cheche: Reminiscences of a Radical Magazine*, ed. Karim Hirji, 77–82. Dar es Salaam: Mkuki na Nyota, 2010.

Miescher, Stephan. "'Nkrumah's Baby': The Akosombo Dam and the Dream of Development in Ghana, 1952–66." *Water History* 6, no. 4 (2014): 341–66.

Mkabarah, Jumaa R. R. *Salum Abdallah: Mwanamuziki Wa Tanzania.* Dar es Salaam: Taasisi ya Uchunguzi wa Kiswahili, Chuo Kikuu cha Dar es Salaam, 1975.

Mlama, Penina Muhando. *Culture and Development: The Popular Theatre Approach in Africa.* Uppsala: Nordiska Afrikainstitutet, 1991.

Modern Girl around the World Research Group. "The Modern Girl as Heuristic Device: Collaboration, Connective Comparison, Multidirectional Citation." In *The Modern Girl around the World: Consumption, Modernity and Globalization*, 1–24. Durham, NC: Duke University Press, 2008.

Monson, Jamie. *Africa's Freedom Railway: How a Chinese Development Project Changed Lives and Livelihoods in Tanzania*. Athens: Ohio University Press, 2011.

Moorman, Marissa. "Anatomy of Kuduro: Articulating the Angolan Body Politic after the War." *African Studies Review* 57, no. 2 (2014): 21–40.

M'Passou, Denis. *Mindolo: A Story of the Ecumenical Movement in Africa*. Lusaka, Zambia: Multimedia, 1983.

Mpogolo, Z. J. *Functional Literacy in Tanzania*. Dar es Salaam: Swala, 1980.

Mrázek, Rudolf. *Engineers of Happy Land: Technology and Nationalism in a Colony*. Princeton, NJ: Princeton University Press, 2002.

Murray, Martin J. *City of Extremes: The Spatial Politics of Johannesburg*. Durham, NC: Duke University Press, 2011.

Mutongi, Kenda. "'Dear Dolly's Advice: Representations of Youth, Courtship, and Sexualities in Africa, 1960–1980." *The International Journal of African Historical Studies* 33, no. 1 (2000), 1–23.

———. *Worries of the Heart: Widows, Family and Community in Kenya*. Chicago: University of Chicago Press, 2007.

Myers, Garth. *Verandahs of Power: Colonialism and Space in Urban Africa*. Syracuse, NY: Syracuse University Press, 2003.

Myers, Garth, and Martin J. Murray. "Introduction: Situating Contemporary Cities in Africa." In *Cities in Contemporary Africa*, ed. Garth Myers and Martin J. Murray. New York: Palgrave Macmillan, 2006.

Mytton, Graham. *Mass Communication in Africa*. London: Edward Arnold, 1983.

National Museums of Tanzania. *Maelezo ya Kijiji cha Makumbusho*. Dar es Salaam: Printpak Tanzania, 1966.

Newell, Sasha. *The Modernity Bluff: Crime, Consumption, and Citizenship in Côte d'Ivoire*. Chicago: University of Chicago Press, 2012.

Ng'wanakilala, Nkwabi. *Mass Communication and Development of Socialism in Tanzania*. Dar es Salaam: Tanzania Publishing House, 1981.

Nkrumah, Kwame, and M. W. Kanyama Chiume. *Harakati Ya Kitabaka Katika Afrika*. Dar es Salaam: Tanzania Publishing House, 1974.

Nurse, Derek, and Thomas T. Spear. *The Swahili: Reconstructing the History and Language of an African Society, 800–1500*. Philadelphia: University of Pennsylvania Press, 1985.

Nyerere, Julius. *The Arusha Declaration: Ten Years After*. Dar es Salaam: Government Printer, 1977.

———. "The Importance and Pleasure of Reading." Speech at the opening of the Printing Works and Book Warehouse, Arusha, 1965, in *Nyerere on Education*, vol. 2, ed. E. Lema, M. Mbilinyi, and R. Rajani. Dar es Salaam: E. and D., 2006.

———. "President's Inaugural Address." In *Freedom and Unity: A Selection from Writings and Speeches, 1952–65*. Dar es Salaam: Oxford University Press, 1967.

———. "Ujamaa: The Basis for African Socialism," in *Ujamaa: Essays on Social-ism*, 1–12. Dar es Salaam: Oxford University Press, 1968.

Obiechina, Emmanuel N. *An African Popular Literature: A Study of Onitsha Market Pamphlets*. Cambridge: Cambridge University Press, 1973.

Olden, Anthony. "For a Poor Nation a Library Service Is Vital: Establishing a National Public Library Service in Tanzania in the 1960s." *Library Quarterly* 75, no. 4 (2005): 421–45.

Parpart, Jane. "Wicked Women and Respectable Ladies: Reconfiguring Gender on the Zambian Copperbelt, 1936–64." In *"Wicked" Women and the Reconfiguration of Gender in Africa*, ed. Dorothy Hodgson and Sheryl McCurdy, 274–92. Portsmouth, NH: Heinemann, 2001.

Perullo, Alex. *Live from Dar es Salaam: Popular Music and Tanzania's Music Economy*. Bloomington: Indiana University Press, 2011.

———. "Rumba in the City of Peace: Migration and the Cultural Commodity of Congolese Music in Dar es Salaam, Tanzania, 1968–1985." *Ethnomusicology* 52, no. 2 (2008): 196–223.

Peterson, Derek. *Creative Writing: Translation, Bookkeeping, and the Work of Imagination in Colonial Kenya*. Portsmouth, NH: Heinemann, 2004.

———. *Ethnic Patriotism and the East African Revival: A History of Dissent, c. 1935–1972*. New York: Cambridge University Press, 2012.

———. "The Intellectual Lives of Mau Mau Detainees." *Journal of African History* 49 (2008): 73–91.

Plageman, Nate. *Highlife Saturday Night: Popular Music and Social Change in Urban Ghana*. African Expressive Cultures. Bloomington: Indiana University Press, 2013.

Prakash, Gyan. "Imagining the City, Darkly." In *Noir Urbanisms: Dystopic Images of the Modern City*, ed. Gyan Prakash, 1–16. Princeton, NJ: Princeton University Press, 2010.

———. *Mumbai Fables*. Princeton, NJ: Princeton University Press, 2010.

Prashad, Vijay. *The Darker Nations: A People's History of the Third World*. New York: New Press, 2008.

Prestholdt, Jeremy. *Domesticating the World: African Consumerisms and the Genealogies of Globalization*. Berkeley: University of California Press, 2008.

Prichard, Andreana. *Sisters in Spirit: Christianity, Affect and Community Building in East Africa, 1860–1970*. East Lansing: Michigan State University Press, 2017.

Quayson, Ato. *Oxford Street, Accra: City Life and the Itineraries of Transnationalism*. Durham, NC: Duke University Press, 2014.

Ranger, Terrence. *Dance and Society in Eastern Africa, 1890–1970: The Beni Ngoma*. Berkeley: University of California Press, 1975.

Rappaport, Joanne, and Thomas B. F. Cummins. *Beyond the Lettered City: Indigenous Literacies in the Andes*. Durham, NC: Duke University Press, 2012.

Reid, Richard. "Arms and Adolescence: Male Youth, Warfare and Statehood in Nineteenth-Century Eastern Africa." In *Generations Past: Youth in East African History*, 25–46. Athens: Ohio University Press, 2010.

———. *War in Pre-Colonial Eastern Africa: The Patterns and Meanings of State-Level Conflict in the Nineteenth Century.* Athens: Ohio University Press, 2007.

Rex, Frederick. "Africa Literacy and Writing Centre." *International Review of Missions* 49, no. 193 (1960): 91–94.

Robinson, Jennifer. "Living in Dystopia: Past, Present and Future in Contemporary African Cities." In *Noir Urbanisms: Dystopic Images of the Modern City*, ed. Gyan Prakash, 218–40. Princeton, NJ: Princeton University Press, 2010.

Rockel, Stephen J. *Carriers of Culture: Labor on the Road in Nineteenth-Century East Africa.* Portsmouth, NH: Heinemann, 2006.

Rodney, Walter. *How Europe Underdeveloped Africa.* London: Bogle L'Ouverture Publications, 1972.

———. *Walter Rodney Speaks: The Making of an African Intellectual.* Trenton, NJ: Africa World Press, 1990.

Roy, Ananya. *City Requiem, Calcutta: Gender and the Politics of Poverty.* Globalization and Community. Minneapolis: University of Minnesota Press, 2003.

Roy, Ananya, and Nezar AlSayyad. *Urban Informality: Transnational Perspectives from the Middle East, Latin America, and South Asia.* Lanham, MD: Lexington Books, 2004.

Rubin, Martin. "Thrillers." In *Schirmer Encyclopedia of Film*, ed. Barry Keith Grant, 4:255–61. New York: Schirmer Reference, 2007.

Sabot, R. H. *Economic Development and Urban Migration.* Oxford: Clarendon, 1979.

Sassen, Saskia. *The Global City: New York, London, Tokyo.* Princeton, NJ: Princeton University Press, 1991.

Saul, John S. "Radicalism and the Hill." In *Socialism in Tanzania: An Interdisciplinary Reader*, ed. John S. Saul and Lionel Cliffe, 289–92. Nairobi: East African Publishing House, 1973.

Schatzberg, Michael. *Political Legitimacy in Middle Africa: Father, Family, Food.* Bloomington: Indiana University Press, 2001.

Schneider, Leander. *Government of Development: Peasants and Politicians in Postcolonial Tanzania.* Bloomington: Indiana University Press, 2014.

———. "The Maasai's New Clothes: A Developmentalist Modernity and Its Exclusions." *Africa Today* 53, no. 1 (2006): 101–31.

Scott, James C. *Seeing Like a State: How Certain Schemes to Improve the Human Condition Have Failed.* New Haven, CT: Yale University Press, 1998.

Shipley, Jesse Weaver. *Living the Hiplife: Celebrity and Entrepreneurship in Ghanaian Popular Music.* Durham, NC: Duke University Press, 2013.

Shivji, Issa. "Tanzania—the Silent Class Struggle." In *Socialism in Tanzania: An Interdisciplinary Reader*, ed. John S. Saul and Lionel Cliffe, 304–40. Nairobi: East African Publishing House, 1973.

Silberschmidt, Margrethe. "Masculinities, Sexuality and Socio-Economic Change in Rural and Urban East Africa." In *Re-Thinking Sexualities in Africa*, ed. Signe Arnfred, 233–50. Uppsala: Nordiska Afrikainstitutet, 2004.

Simone, AbdouMaliq. *For the City Yet to Come: Changing African Life in Four Cities*. Durham, NC: Duke University Press, 2004.

———. "People as Infrastructure: Intersecting Fragments in Johannesburg." *Public Culture* 16, no. 3 (2004), 407–29.

Skinner, Ryan Thomas. *Bamako Sounds: The Afropolitan Ethics of Malian Music*. Minneapolis: University of Minnesota Press, 2015.

———. "Cultural Politics in the Post-Colony: Music, Nationalism and Statism in Mali, 1964–75." *Africa* 82, no. 4 (2012): 511–34.

Spear, Thomas. "Neo-Traditionalism and the Limits of Invention in British Colonial Africa." *Journal of African History* 44 (2003): 3–27.

Stambach, Amy. "*Kutoa Mimba*: Debates about Schoolgirl Abortion in Machame, Tanzania." In *The Sociocultural Aspects of Abortion*, ed. Alaka Malwade Basu, 79–102. Westport, CT: Praeger, 2003.

Stavans, Ilan. *Antiheroes: Mexico and Its Detective Novel*. Translated from Spanish by Jesse H. Lytle and Jennifer A. Mattson. Cranbury, NJ: Associated University Presses, 1997.

Straker, Jay. *Youth, Nationalism and the Guinean Revolution*. Bloomington: Indiana University Press, 2009.

Stren, Richard. "Urban Inequality and Housing Policy in Tanzania: The Problem of Squatting." Berkeley: Institute of International Studies, University of California at Berkeley, 1975.

Stren, Richard, Mohamed Halfani, and Joyce Malombe. "Coping with Urbanization and Urban Policy." In *Beyond Capitalism vs. Socialism in Kenya and Tanzania*, ed. Joel Barkan, 175–200. Boulder, CO: Lynn Rienner, 1994.

Strobel, Margaret. *Muslim Women in Mombasa, 1890–1975*. New Haven, CT: Yale University Press, 1979.

Stroeken, Koen. "Immunizing Strategies: Hip-Hop and Critique in Tanzania." *Africa: Journal of the International Africa Institute* 75, no. 4 (2005): 488–509.

Sturmer, Martin. *A Media History of Tanzania*. Peramiho: Ndanda Mission Press, 1998.

Swantz, Lloyd. *The Medicine Man among the Zaramo of Dar es Salaam*. Uppsala: Scandinavian Institute of African Studies, 1990.

Swantz, Marja-Liisa. *In Search of Living Knowledge*. Dar es Salaam: Mkuki na Nyota, 2016.

———. "Women Workers in Dar es Salaam: 1973/74 Survey of Female Minimum Wage Earners and Self-Employed." *University of Dar es Salaam Research Paper No. 23*. Dar es Salaam: University of Dar es Salaam, 1974.

Tanganyika Rapid Social Change Study. Commission "C.," Christian Council of Tanganyika, East Africa Committee for the Urban Africa Programme and All Africa Conference of Churches. *The Church Meets Life in the Town*. Dar-es-Salaam: s.n., 1964.

Tarlo, Emma. *Unsettling Memories: Narratives of the Emergency in Delhi*. Berkeley: University of California Press, 2003.

Taylor, W. E. *African Aphorisms or Saws from Swahililand*. London: Sheldon, 1924.

Thomas, Lynn. "The Modern Girl and Racial Respectability in 1930s South Africa." *Journal of African History* 47 (2006): 461–90.

———. *Politics of the Womb: Women, Reproduction and the State in Kenya*. Berkeley: University of California Press, 2003.

Tripp, Aili. *Changing the Rules: The Politics of Liberalization and the Informal Urban Economy in Tanzania*. Berkeley: University of California Press, 1997.

Tsuruta, Tadasu. "Popular Music, Sports and Politics: A Development of Urban Cultural Movements in Dar es Salaam, 1930s–1960s." *African Study Monographs* 24, no. 3 (2003): 203–5.

Turino, Thomas. *Nationalists, Cosmopolitans, and Popular Music in Zimbabwe*. Chicago: University of Chicago Press, 2000.

UMATI. *Umati Story: From Family Planning to Reproductive Health*. Dar es Salaam: UMATI, 2005.

Vestbro, Dick Urban. *Social Life and Dwelling Space: An Analysis of Three House Types in Dar es Salaam*. Stockholm: Ordfront, 1975.

Walkowitz, Judith R. *City of Dreadful Delight: Narratives of Sexual Danger in Late-Victorian London*. Women in Culture and Society. Chicago: University of Chicago Press, 1992.

———. "The Indian Woman, the Flower Girl and the Jew." *Victorian Studies* 42, no. 1 (1998): 3–46.

———. *Nights Out: Life in Cosmopolitan London*. New Haven, CT: Yale University Press, 2012.

Weiss, Brad. "Thug Realism: Inhabiting Fantasy in Urban Tanzania." *Cultural Anthropology* 17, no. 1 (2002): 93–124.

Werner, Alice, and William Hichens. *The Advice of Mwana Kupona upon the Wifely Duty from the Swahili Texts*. Medstead, UK: The Azanian Press, 1934.

West, Richard. *The White Tribes of Africa*. London: Jonathan Cape, 1965.

Westad, Odd Arne. *The Global Cold War: Third World Interventions and the Making of Our Times*. Cambridge: Cambridge University Press, 2005.

Westcott, N. J. "An East African Radical: The Life of Erica Fiah." *Journal of African History* 22, no. 1 (1981): 85–101.

White, Bob. *Rumba Rules: The Politics of Dance Music in Mobutu's Zaire*. Durham, NC: Duke University Press, 2008.

White, Luise. *The Comforts of Home: Prostitution in Colonial Nairobi*. Chicago: University of Chicago Press, 1990.

———. "Separating the Men from the Boys: Constructions of Gender, Sexuality, and Terrorism in Central Kenya, 1939–1959." *International Journal of African Historical Studies* 23, no. 1 (1990): 1–25.

Williams, Raymond. *The Country and the City*. New York: Oxford University Press, 1973.

Willis, Justin. *Potent Brews: A Social History of Alcohol in East Africa 1850–1999*. Eastern African Studies. Oxford: James Currey, 2002.

World Bank. *World Development Report 1994*. New York: Oxford University Press, 1994.

Wright, Gwendolyn. "Tradition in the Service of Modernity: Architecture and Urbanism in French Colonial Policy." In *Tensions of Empire: Colonial Cultures in a Bourgeois World*, ed. Frederick Cooper and Ann Laura Stoler, 322–45. Berkeley: University of California Press, 1997.

Wright, Marcia. *Strategies of Slaves and Women: Life-Stories from Central Africa*. New York: Lilian Barber, 1993.

Yeh, Wen-Hsin. "Progressive Journalism and Shanghai's Petty Urbanites: Zou Taofen and the Shenghuo Enterprise, 1926–1945." In *Shanghai Sojourners*, ed. Frederick Wakeman Jr. and Wen-Hsin Yeh, 190–216. Berkeley: Institute of East Asian Studies, University of California, 1992.

Young, Louise. *Beyond the Metropolis: Second Cities and Modern Life in Interwar Japan*. Berkeley: University of California Press, 2013.

Yu, George T. *Africa's China Policy: A Study of Tanzania*. New York: Praeger, 1975.

Yurchak, Alexei. *Everything Was Forever, Until It Was No More: The Last Soviet Generation*. Princeton, NJ: Princeton University Press, 2005.

Index

Abbas, Ali, 117
Abdallah, Chiku, 51–52
Abdallah, Salum, 109–10, 114, 244n69
Abdulla, Muhammed Said, 244n60
abortion, 34, 50–51, 89, 173, 195. *See also* family; relationships; reproduction
Abu-Lughod, Lila, 48
Activities of the Black Market (Ng'ombo). See *Heka Heka za Ulanguzi* (Ng'ombo)
Adult Education Revolution, 148, 178. *See also* education; literacy
adultery, 34, 51, 171
adulthood, 26, 30, 47–49, 128, 133, 145, 163–89. *See also* youth
advice literature, 60–71, 79, 82, 153, 193, 209. *See also* Christianity; working girls
"Advice of Mwana Kupona upon the Wifely Duty," 69
Africa: authenticity and, 32, 53, 105, 113, 121, 131, 172, 190; domesticity in, 81–91; economy in, 2, 8, 26–27, 37; liberation of, 148–51, 163–65; modernization in, 14, 209, 213; morality in, 3, 188–89, 203; nationalism in, 15, 25, 178; relationships in, 132–34, 165; socialism in, 3–7, 17, 21–23, 36–42, 129, 174–87, 196–201, 205; tradition in, 35, 107, 112, 114, 188; uplift in, 18–19, 28; urban, 1, 12–13, 25, 29, 44, 54–57, 81, 194–95, 212. *See also* Dar es Salaam; East Africa; economy; socialism; Tanzania; uplift; urbanization; *and individual countries*
African Christian Press, 59, 73–74
Africanization, 74, 87, 124
Aggrey, James, 221n19
All Africa Literature Center, 71–72
All Alone in the City (Mandao). See *Peke Yangu Mjini* (Mandao)
Allman, Jean, 13

Almeida, Anthony, 206
Amadiume, Ifi, 230n49
Ama Zao, Ama Zangu (Rajab), 160
Amin, Idi, 145, 161, 176
Amin, Samir, 77
Anduru, Agoro, 153–54, 165
Anglican Central Tanganyika Press, 73–74
Ani Afungua Mkoba Wake (Mandao), 73, 80–81, 191, 193
antiurbanism, 4–6, 13–20, 26–27, 39, 44, 56–57, 64, 100, 130, 200
apartheid, 93, 219n49
Arusha, 146, 215n2
Arusha Declaration, 4, 36–37, 40, 73, 154, 170, 191
Asians, 22–24, 170, 203
Askew, Kelly, 114
"Aunty, Lend Me Your Tight Skirt" (Jamhuri Jazz Band). *See* "Shangazi Naomba Taiti" (Jamhuri Jazz Band)
Ausi, Hilda, 77
authenticity, 7, 15, 19–23, 29, 49–57, 105, 112–13, 130–32, 190, 237n74
autonomy, 30–31, 62, 66, 78, 106, 128–34, 169, 194, 244n69. *See also* independence; self-reliance; self-sufficiency

Ba, Mariama, 248n35
Bagachwa, Mboya S. D., 197
Bagdelleh, Kheri Rashidi, 32
Baka, Abdul, 238n92
Barber, Karin, 7, 11
"Barua kwa Dada," 70
Bashome, Rwehikira, 95–96
Bawazir, Omar, 33
Becker, Felicitas, 215n2
Bed of Death (Mukajanga). See *Kitanda cha Mauti* (Mukajanga)

Belege, Modest, 73
belonging, 76, 136–37, 168, 195–96, 212.
    See also adulthood; culture; social networks
Bgoya, Walter, 46, 147, 149–50
Bier, Laura, 228n7
bila jasho, 204–5
Binti Leo, 85
black market, 17, 120, 186, 197–200. See also
    economy, the; informal sector
Black Panther Party, 23, 114–15
Bollywood, 166, 185. See also films
bongo, 17, 180, 182, 200–206
Brecht, Bertolt, 209
Brennan, James, 24, 223n37
brewers, 31, 68, 126, 155. See also women
bridewealth, 67, 82–83, 98, 117, 167, 171,
    231n53. See also marriage
briefcase publishers, 16, 144–79, 198, 201–2
Britain, 22, 81, 145
Brown, James, 113, 115, 185
Bryceson, Deborah, 68, 77–78, 83, 100, 126
Buguruni, 89, 119
bump dance, 115–17, 194
Burton, Antoinette, 81
Busara. See Rajab, Hammie

capitalism, 20, 57, 80, 116, 130, 166, 184,
    200, 210
censorship, 144, 176, 185, 210
Central Tanganyika Press, 59, 73, 75
Chachage, C. S. L., 152
Chande, Kassim, 203
Chase, James Hadley, 165
Cheyney, Peter, 165
Chiume, Murray, 149
Christian Council of Tanzania, 67,
    73, 98
Christianity: advice literature and, 15, 59,
    62–82, 98–99, 153, 183, 191, 193, 209; in
    Dar es Salaam, 13, 15, 27, 67, 116; domestic-
    ity and, 82, 90, 147; family planning and,
    92–97; housing and, 83–89; women and,
    60–61, 75. See also advice literature
citizenship: gender and, 174, 193, 195; literacy
    and, 149–51, 178; postcolonial, 57–58;
    socialist, 40, 48–49, 53; urban, 13, 21,
    35–36, 139
City of Dreadful Delight (Walkowitz), 9
City of Tomorrow, The, 89. See also Jijini
    Kesho (Mandao)
city stories, 9–12, 213. See also advice litera-
    ture; literature; media; pulp-fiction
Civil Servants Magazine, 35

class: Christianity and, 15, 60–63, 70–71;
    contraception and, 92–94; literacy and,
    44–45; nightlife and, 103–7; socialism and,
    38, 129–30, 193; women and, 74, 82, 88–89,
    99, 126
cleverness, 203–5. See also bongo
clubs. See dancehalls; nightlife
cohabitation, 82, 85, 91, 231n53. See also
    family; households
Cold War, the, 3, 37
Cole, Jennifer, 169, 239n100
Colla, Elliot, 145
colonialism: authenticity and, 130–33;
    domesticity during, 81, 87; economy and,
    26, 32, 37, 44, 131, 134; inequalities of, 7,
    20, 23; lexicon of, 190; modernization and,
    37, 147, 212; neo-, 8, 57, 77, 79; policies of, 3,
    22, 24–25; race and, 28, 30, 39, 188; villages
    and, 27–29. See also Britain; capitalism;
    Christianity; decolonization; Europe;
    imperialism; socialism
commoditization, 25, 106, 116–17, 139–40,
    183. See also consumerism; gifts; sugar
    daddies
community: centers, 35, 45, 88, 118,
    130, 148, 186; Christian, 67, 73–74, 90;
    imagined, 29, 81, 209; moral, 11, 49, 106,
    108–9, 187; political, 32, 222n24; socialist,
    25, 43, 150; social networks and, 17–18,
    191–92; urbanization and, 2, 8, 13–14, 27,
    68, 121, 182, 211. See also social networks
consumerism, 102–7, 122–40, 174, 188,
    237n70. See also commoditization
contraception, 92–97, 100. See also abortion;
    family; reproduction; sex
Cooper, Frederick, 13
cordon sanitaire, 24, 117
corruption, 10, 14, 140, 171, 193–94
cosmopolitanism, 21–25, 30, 38, 105–6,
    123–28, 176, 185, 244n69
Côte d'Ivoire, 74, 181, 209, 237n70
Counterfeit Key, The (Rajab). See Ufunguo wa
    Bandia (Rajab)
Country and the City, The (Williams), 20
crime thrillers, 10, 16. See also fiction;
    pulp-fiction
criminality, 10, 15, 46, 145, 198–200
culture: African, 41, 149; authentic, 114–15,
    132; dancehalls and, 105–7, 116–22, 128,
    136; Dar es Salaam and, 21, 205; importa-
    tion of, 177, 185; inequality and, 211–13;
    Islamic, 23, 31, 117; music and, 108–15, 122,
    127; nationalism and, 36–37; politics of,

105, 217n25; protectionism and, 130, 185, 202; socialism and, 35, 38, 144, 146, 184. *See also* dance; dancehalls; films; literature; music; Operation Vijana; urban texts
Cummins, Thomas B. F., 10

Daily News, 49, 239n1
dance, 31, 64, 102, 107–32, 194, 204–5, 209, 212, 223n23. *See also* bila jasho
dancehalls, 103–7, 115–28, 136–39, 143, 183, 186, 204, 212
Dar es Salaam: antiurbanism and, 4–6, 13–15, 19–20, 26–27, 39, 44, 56–57, 64, 200; briefcase publishers in, 143–79; Christianity in, 60–61, 72; class in, 6, 39, 41; cosmopolitanism in, 21–25; culture in, 35, 102–28; domesticity in, 90–98, 135; gender in, 126, 134, 136–39; health care in, 41–42; housing in, 19, 82–88, 123; infrastructure in, 13, 210–12; literacy in, 10, 42–46, 186; literature in, 16, 58–59; map of, 22; media in, 11, 20, 31–34, 49–53; migration to, 1–5, 9, 25–30, 215n1; race in, 22, 28, 30; self-reliance and, 129–32; sexuality in, 16; socialism in, 15, 19, 21, 31, 36, 55; women in, 56, 62–90, 99–100. *See also* culture; dance; dancehalls; infrastructure; literacy; literature; music; nightlife; socialism; social networks; TANU (Tanzania African National Union); women
Dar es Salaam Usiku (Mtobwa), 159
Davis, Angela, 113
decentralization, 41, 55, 121
Decker, Corrie, 63, 229n19
decolonization, 2, 9, 19–21, 30–31, 54, 64, 72, 158, 206
Democratic Republic of Congo, 22, 121
Depo-Provera, 93, 95. *See also* contraception
detribalization, 3, 28. *See also* migration; villagization
development, 12, 48–50, 129, 135, 147, 153, 159, 178, 184, 227n102. *See also* infrastructure
Dibwe, Subira Salum, 241n28
Dilemma, The (Mkufya), 245n76
disinvestment, 2, 167. *See also* antiurbanism; TANU (Tanzania African National Union)
divorce, 82, 85, 91–92. *See also* family; households
Dodoma, 39, 42, 57, 73
domesticity: Christian, 70–85, 90, 98–99; flexible, 16, 62, 92, 135; gender and, 69, 99, 238n90. *See also* family; households

Doyle, Arthur Conan, 167
dress: consumerism and, 59, 137; cosmopolitan, 16, 64, 75, 113, 115, 122–27, 136, 138, 194, 211; men and, 164, 237n74; national, 130–31, 137; policing of, 26, 41, 53, 55, 120; westernization of, 51–52, 186; women and, 51, 53, 55, 66, 137, 236n48. *See also* miniskirts; Operation Vijana
Drum, 64, 125, 165

East Africa: *bongo* and, 181–82; Christianity in, 70, 72; consumerism in, 132–34; dance of, 102, 107; literature of, 69, 147, 157, 159; morality in, 188–89, 195, 203; politics in, 3, 25, 203; urbanization in, 26–27, 159, 190, 201. *See also* Africa
East African Literature Bureau (EALB), 148, 151, 154, 157, 173, 241n23
East African Publishers, 33, 241n23
economic crisis, 19, 57, 64, 140–44, 174
economy, the: black-market, 17, 120, 186, 197–200; colonial, 36–37, 134; global, 19, 22, 26; informal sector, 57, 120, 126, 143, 146–47, 153, 188, 212; leisure, 119, 122, 127; liberalization of, 178, 200–202, 206; recession and, 9, 167, 180; self-reliant, 78, 132, 140, 189; socialism and, 20, 40, 49, 181; strength of, 2, 64, 99, 196, 212; urbanization and, 8–9. *See also* wealth
education, 9, 21, 27, 43–45, 48, 146. *See also* literacy
employment, 4, 12, 65, 70, 100, 125, 169, 184, 193. *See also* economy; informal sector; working girls
End of Love, The (Simbamwene). See *Mwisho wa Mapenzi* (Simbamwene)
English, 23, 33, 46, 49, 55, 73, 119, 143–51, 211, 240n11
entrepreneurialism, 4, 14, 31, 65, 100, 153, 181–82, 188, 209
equality, 56, 188, 198, 202. *See also* inequality
"Essays on African Socialism" (Nyerere), 129
ethnicity, 22–23, 26–29, 34, 40
Etienne's, 115, 120
Europe, 22–23, 149, 203. *See also specific countries*
exploitation, 38–39, 48, 115, 120, 126, 175, 195, 203

Faili Maalum (Ganzel), 173
family: flexible concept of, 16–17, 91, 209; ideals, 15, 62, 68, 72, 74, 92, 134–35, 182, 198; intergenerational struggle over,

family: flexible concept of (continued)
170–71; planning, 90–100, 131, 209; rural,
26–29. *See also* cohabitation; divorce;
marriage
family planning, 90–98, 100, 131, 209
Family Planning Association of Tanzania
(UMATI), 92–93, 131
Fanon, Frantz, 3, 36–38, 46, 77, 149, 209
fashion, 130, 137, 186. *See also* dress
Feierman, Steven, 8
female uplift, 76, 81, 91, 195, 226n89. *See also*
women
feminism, 43, 64, 78, 80, 153
Ferguson, James, 20, 71, 187, 230n50
Fiah, Erica, 24, 27, 29, 31
fiction, 58–59, 143–79, 186, 191, 209, 245n73.
See also literature; pulp-fiction; romance
films, 165–66, 185, 202
Fleming, Ian, 165
forcible repatriation, 1, 4, 19, 29, 39–41,
47–48, 56, 110. *See also* repatriation;
villagization
foreignness, 15, 48, 56
Freire, Paolo, 44, 62, 79
frugality, 68–70, 123, 128–32, 148–50, 173,
176, 188, 238n92
furniture, 83, 165, 170–71, 191–92, 195.
See also family; frugality; greed; women

Gado. *See* Mwampembwa, Godfrey
Gandhi, Indira, 5
Gandhi, Mohandas, 3, 20, 24
Ganzel, Edi, 148, 151–53, 159, 161, 167, 172–73,
177, 209, 245n73
Garvey, Marcus, 24–25
Geiger, Susan, 68
gender: belonging and, 16, 104, 136; housing
and, 84, 191, 230n50; inequality, 44, 78,
125; mobility and, 162, 193; norms, 63–64,
171, 189, 213; order, 54, 86, 131, 135, 170,
195; politics, 21, 25–26, 28, 30, 40; relations, 64, 67, 106, 133; roles, 68, 71, 81,
98–99, 134, 138, 140. *See also* masculinity;
men; women
generations, 21, 47, 57, 90, 169–70, 172, 176,
205, 244n69. *See also* youth
generosity, 104, 106, 125, 133–34, 140, 189.
See also masculinity
George, Abosede, 61
Germany, 22–23
Ghana, 3, 5, 13, 36, 59, 73–74, 209, 218n29
gifts, 102, 133–37, 165, 169, 189, 194, 248n38.
See also masculinity; relationships; sex

Glassman, Jonathon, 220n13
global south, the, 1–2, 5–6, 74
Grand Arts Promotion, 152
greed, 28, 104, 129–35, 140, 169–71, 176, 188,
194, 238n92, 247n28. *See also* commoditization; consumerism; frugality; self-
reliance; self-sufficiency; women
Gurumo, Muhiddin Maalim, 107–8, 119
Guyer, Jane, 12

Hana Hatia (Mvungi), 43
"Hanifa" (Rajabu), 102–3, 105, 107–8, 119,
140, 238n92
Hansen, Karen, 116
Hart, Keith, 4, 218n29
Harvey, Stephen, 114
Haya, 28–29
health care, 41–42, 90–100. *See also* contra-
ception; family planning
Heinemann African Writers Series, 71
Heka Heka za Ulanguzi (Ng'ombo), 200
Heko, 177, 198
He/She Is Not to Blame (Mvungi). See *Hana
Hatia* (Mvungi)
Hinduism, 22, 25
households: Christian, 72, 74, 84, 147, 183;
flexible, 31, 62–63, 82–83, 91–92, 100, 123,
134–35, 187, 212; frugal, 68, 70, 129, 174,
238n92; marriage, 132, 137. *See also* Christianity; family; frugality
house marriages, 83–84, 91, 135, 231n53.
See also *ndoa ya kinyumba*
housing: modern, 18–19, 40, 49, 157–58,
219n2, 245n78; women and, 63, 84–89,
188–94. *See also* households
huna, 103–4, 106. *See also* masculinity; relationships; wealth
Hunt, Nancy Rose, 190
Hyslop, Jonathan, 20

ideologies: of masculine generosity, 106, 125,
133–35; Ujamaa, 6–7, 20, 37, 131, 169, 182,
190. *See also* socialism; Ujamaa
Ilala, 50, 52, 118
imperialism, 7, 115, 163–64, 176, 230n50.
See also colonialism
"I'm Thinking of Going Back" (Jamhuri Jazz
Band). *See* "Nafikiri Kurudi" (Jamhuri
Jazz Band)
independence, 18–19, 30–38, 61, 70, 110,
154, 180–83, 218n30, 240n11. *See also*
decolonization
India, 5, 20, 22, 81, 145, 181, 188, 221n19

inequality, 2, 6–7, 10–11, 66, 78, 144, 169, 188, 213

informal sector, the, 5, 65, 120, 126, 147, 178, 181, 212, 218n29. *See also* economy, the; publishing industry

infrastructure: mobility and, 192–94; publishing, 147, 151; social, 13, 99, 170, 183–84, 211; soft, 123–24, 136, 186; urban, 2–4, 8, 12, 18, 30, 37, 180, 210–11

intellectuals. *See specific intellectuals*

International Monetary Fund, 201, 212

International Planned Parenthood Federation (IPPF), 92, 95

Islam, 22, 27, 31, 67–68, 74, 81, 92, 215n2, 240n11

Ivaska, Andrew, 86, 114

Jackson, Mahalia, 115

Jamhuri Jazz Band, 110, 137

Jando na Unyago (Mamuya), 97–98

jasho, 203, 205

Jenga, 34

Jijini Kesho (Mandao), 89

Jomssi Publications, 152

Joseph, Pauline, 86, 99

Joto la Fedha (Kassam), 174

journalism, 33–34, 50–52, 153. *See also* media; reporting

Kajubi. *See* Mukajanga, Kajubi

Kalala, Hamza, 127

Kalindimya, Jackson, 153, 177, 198–99

Kambona, Oscar, 227n102

kanga, 53–54. *See also* dress

Kariakoo, 50, 52, 103, 109, 115, 117, 121

Kashkash, 33, 151. *See also* Sichalwe, Maurice

Kasikwa Yu Hai (Chande), 203

Kassam, Kassim Musa, 142, 174, 176

Katalambula, Faraji H. H., 244n60

Kaunda, Betty, 71

Kaunda, Kenneth, 71

Kawawa, Rashid, 50, 92

Kenya, 22, 33, 152, 181, 189

Kezilahabi, Euphrase, 144, 163

Kidude, Bi, 108

Kikomo (A. E. Musiba), 142

Kilema, James, 114

Kiongozi, 75, 229n33

Kipigo Cha Fashisti Iddi Amin Dudu (Amin), 161

kisura, 136–37, 203, 239n100. *See also* dress; women

Kisutu, 57, 66, 120, 235n35

Kiswahili, 46, 149–50, 240n11

Kitanda cha Mauti (Mukajanga), 175

Kitanzi (Ganzel), 159

Kivukoni College, 43, 45, 150

Kizimbani (Mkabarah), 170, 244n69

Klerruu, Wilbert, 123

Kouene, Esther, 70

Kufa na Kupona (Musiba), 166, 245n73

kujitegemea. *See* self-reliance

Kushuma, Maele, 88

kutafuta maisha, 1, 30, 47, 215n2. *See also* migration

Kwetu, 25, 27

labor, 3–4, 25–27, 37, 66, 76, 130, 134, 146–47, 203, 219n2

Lal, Priya, 3, 38

landlords, 22, 50, 52, 65, 68, 85–86, 191. *See also* housing; women

language, 13, 29, 53–57, 76, 113, 129–31, 155, 201–6, 211, 213. *See also* English; Swahili

La Onda, 145

Larkin, Brian, 211

leisure sector, 33, 107, 119–27, 140. *See also* economy, the

Lenin, Vladimir, 209

Leslie, J. A. K., 22, 30, 84

"Let Us Adhere to Our Culture" (Sunburst), 114

"Let Us Cultivate Our Farms" (Cuban Marimba). *See* "Tulime Mashamba" (Cuban Marimba)

liberation, 18–19, 36, 40, 49, 54, 150, 165

Lin Biao, 37

Lindsay, Lisa, 230n50

literacy, 9–10, 42–48, 79–80, 129–30, 146–53, 178, 186, 208–11, 218n30, 225n73, 240n11

literature: advice, 60–82, 89–90, 99, 183, 191, 193, 209; Africanist, 25; fiction, 58–59, 143–71, 174, 186, 200; sex education, 97–98; TANU, 49, 129–30. *See also* fiction; poetry; pulp-fiction; romance; *and individual authors*

"Logic" (Mukajanga), 175

logics, 13, 48, 55, 57, 182, 187, 193

Loleza Girls' School, 74, 92

love, 46, 105, 145, 150, 164–75, 244n67

"Lover, I'm Warning You!" (NUTA Jazz Band). *See* "Mpenzi Ninakukanya" (NUTA Jazz Band)

Lumumba, Patrice, 121

Macha, Freddy, 104, 124
Machangu, Samuel, 118
Macmillan, 148–49, 152
Magaziner, Daniel, 219n49
magazines, 18, 34–35, 64, 125, 154, 162, 177, 198, 241n29. *See also individual magazines*
Magome, Guido, 50
Makange, Robert, 31
Maktaba Kuu ya Taifa, 207–10, 212
Malawi, 22, 41, 74, 121, 149, 209
Mali, 36, 184
Maliyamkono, T. L., 197
"Mama wa Afrika na Nyumba Yake" (Kouene), 70
Mamuya, Sifuel, 97–98
Mandao, Martha, 59–60, 62, 72–74, 80–81, 89–90, 98–99, 191, 193
Mandela, Nelson, 20
manhood, 174–83, 244n69. *See also* gender; masculinity; men
Mao Zedong, 3, 37–38, 131, 163–64, 209
Marehemu Susanna (Mkabarah), 163
Margot's, 55, 120
marriage, 15, 26, 65, 69–101, 132–37, 148, 191, 209, 231n53, 245n74. *See also* divorce; house marriages
Marx, Karl, 209
Marxism, 8, 23, 62, 164
masculinity, 104–6, 125–26, 133–34, 140, 163, 176, 189. *See also* gender; generosity; manhood; men; wealth; women
"Masudi" (Rajabu), 108
Masuka, Dorothy, 137
materialism, 2, 45, 129–39, 170, 203, 213. *See also* commoditization
maternity leave, 92, 94, 100
Mazungumzo (Msuya), 46–47
Mbuguni, L. A., 185
Mdoe, Fatuma, 204
media, 9–14, 21, 24, 33–34, 43, 49–55, 75, 105, 177, 210. *See also* films; literature; magazines; newspapers; propaganda
Meghji, Zakia Hamdani, 230n40
men, 31, 52–54, 134, 144–45, 152–59, 162–65, 172–79, 183–89, 192. *See also* gender; masculinity; wealth
methodology, 14–18, 207–9
Mhije, Allen, 55–56
migration, 1, 13, 19–21, 26–31, 45–46, 65, 67, 121, 167. *See also* repatriation; urbanization; villagization
Mindolo Ecumenical Center, 71, 73

miniskirts, 53–54, 116, 136, 194, 227n106. *See also* dress
Ministry of Culture, 35, 127
Ministry of Information, 1, 34, 49
Mitaani na Kashkash, 33, 151
Mkabarah, Jumaa, 148, 151–54, 157–59, 163, 165, 169–70, 172–73, 177–78, 244n69
Mkufya, W. E., 245n76
Mlama, Penina Muhando, 62, 209, 228n4, 230n40
Mlay, Severa, 77, 79
Mnazi Moja Park, 24, 117–19
mobility, 6–7, 26–34, 84, 94, 99, 106, 161–64, 192–93, 211. *See also* masculinity; youth
Mobutu, Sese Seko, 121
modernization: colonial-era, 81, 212–13; dance and, 112–16; housing and, 157–58, 191; literacy and, 147–49; socialist, 5, 14, 18–21, 30–46, 178, 184, 225n75; women and, 64, 70, 75, 93, 136. *See also* dress; housing; literacy
Mohamed, Bibi Titi, 31, 68, 190
monogamy, 15, 101, 164. *See also* marriage; relationships
Monson, Jamie, 215n2
Moorman, Marissa, 181
morality: community and, 11–14, 49, 187, 191; economies of, 196; legitimacy and, 181, 190; logics of, 8–9, 14, 55; music and, 108–9; public, 25, 52, 57, 107; socialism and, 120, 204; urbanization and, 72, 123; vocabulary of, 3, 29, 213
Mozambique, 5, 27, 163
Mpenzi (Mukajanga), 157, 163, 175
"Mpenzi Ninakukanya" (NUTA Jazz Band), 107–8
Mrázek, Rudolf, 211
Mshuza, Theresia, 75, 91, 99, 193
Msimbazi Center, 73–74, 88
Msuya, S. K., 47
Mtwali, Grace, 94
Mtobwa, Ben, 153, 159, 163, 177, 197–99
Mughogho, Telson, 124
Muhando, Penina, 153
Mukajanga, Kajubi, 142, 152–61, 169, 174–77
Mulokozi, M. M., 157
Mumbai Fables (Prakash), 10
Musiba, A. Elvis, 142, 148, 151–54, 163–67, 173, 177, 209
music, 16, 23, 102–27, 137, 139, 183, 202, 204, 234n27. *See also* dance; dancehalls
Mussa, Fundi, 203
Muthusi, Bob, 33

Mutongi, Kenda, 29
Muyaka, 109, 133
Mvungi, Martha, 43–44, 153, 162
Mwafrika, 31–33, 49, 53, 120, 124, 151, 203
Mwampembwa, Godfrey, 177
Mwanga, Zainab, 153
Mwaruka, Mbaraka Mwinshehe, 113, 122, 138–39
Mwinshehe, Ramadhani, 118
Mwinyi, Ali Hassan, 177, 200–201
Mwisho wa Mapenzi (Simbamwene), 153, 168, 244n62
Mzalendo, 49, 53, 64, 75

"Nafikiri Kurudi" (Jamhuri Jazz Band), 110
Nairobi, 33, 124, 151–54, 165, 241n23
National Development Corporation, 34, 149
National Housing Commission (NHC), 40, 85–86
nationalism, 24–38, 49, 110–12, 128, 147, 178, 185–86, 203. *See also* protectionism
Nationalist, 49, 93
National Library, 58, 207
nativism, 21, 23, 220n13
Nchi Yetu, 34, 49, 51, 53, 55, 64, 227n103, 237n74
Ndibalema, Charles, 153, 166
ndoa ya kinyumba, 83, 92, 135. *See also* house marriages
Ndoto ya Mwendawazimu (Ganzel), 153, 245n73
Nehru, Jawaharlal, 4
neocolonialism, 8, 57, 77
Neto, Agostinho, 163
Newell, Sasha, 237n70
newspapers, 25–35, 49–64, 67, 75, 100, 110–15, 151–53, 201, 239nn1–2. *See also* media; *and individual newspapers*
Ng'ombo, Amina, 200
Ngurumo, 18, 31–34, 49–53, 120
Nigeria, 12, 74, 152, 209, 238n90
nightlife, 16, 55, 110–40, 183, 235n42. *See also* dance; dancehalls; dress; music
Nimeponzeka (Ndibalema), 153
Nkrumah, Kwame, 3, 46, 149, 209
Novatus, Padre R. P., 90
Nsekela, Christina, 92–93, 95–96
nuclear family, 97, 101, 129, 134–35, 147. *See also* family
NUTA, 107–8, 119
Nyerere, Julius, 1–9, 18–19, 23–24, 36–42, 48–49, 56–57, 112, 129, 146–48, 186–89, 217n23. *See also* Arusha Declaration;

socialism; TANU (Tanzania African National Union); Ujamaa

Oman, 22, 38
Omari, Yusuf, 115
"On Housing and the Single Girl," 86
On the Witness Stand (Mkabarah). See *Kizimbani* (Mkabarah)
Operation Bloodsucker. *See* Operation Kupe
Operation Economic Sabotage, 196–97
Operation Every Person Must Work. *See* Operation Kila Mtu Afanye Kazi
Operation Hard Work. *See* Operation Nguvu Kazi
Operation Kila Mtu Afanye Kazi, 41. *See also* repatriation; villagization
Operation Kupe, 41, 48. *See also* repatriation; villagization
Operation Nguvu Kazi, 196–97. *See also* employment; repatriation; villagization
Operation Vijana, 41, 55, 86, 127. *See also* dress
Operation Vijiji, 39, 48, 56. *See also* repatriation; villagization
Operation Villages. *See* Operation Vijiji
Operation Youth. *See* Operation Vijana
Owino, Rosemarie, 248n35

patriarchy, 25, 30, 63, 78–80, 180, 222n25. *See also* feminism; gender
patronage, 184–85, 241n28. *See also* literature
Pedagogy of the Oppressed (Freire), 44
Peke Yangu Mjini (Mandao), 59–60, 73, 191
Penzi la Dawa (Nchimbi), 150, 192
Perullo, Alex, 202
Pesa Zako Zinanuka (Mtowba), 197–98
Peterson, Derek, 29, 189, 219n39, 222n24
Pilgrim's Progress, 72
poetry, 109, 133, 155, 161
Pole Dada (Mwinshehe), 138
policing, 26, 41, 50–56, 66, 120, 127–28, 182–83, 222n24, 223n37. *See also* dress; TANU (Tanzania African National Union)
"Popular Arts in Africa" (Barber), 8
popular urbanists, 7–8. *See also* urbanization
poverty, 19, 29, 41, 44–45, 53, 129, 169–70, 188–89, 200, 215n2. *See also* huna; self-reliance
Prakash, Gyan, 10, 56, 145
pregnancy. *See* reproduction

press, 42, 144, 156, 209. *See also* media; newspapers; publishing industry
Princess Hotel, 102–3, 119
propaganda, 1, 15, 43–46, 68, 96, 130–31, 191,
196. *See also* socialism; TANU (Tanzania
African National Union)
prostitution, 26, 51, 119–20, 171, 235n42.
See also working girls
protectionism, 57, 178, 185, 197, 201–2,
237n76. *See also* economy, the; nationalism;
socialism
publishing industry, 31, 35, 42, 144–79, 203
pulp-fiction, 143–79, 186, 191, 209, 245n73

race: authenticity, 15, 22–27, 49, 53, 55, 130;
betrayal, 38, 47–48, 136; colonization
and, 28, 36, 81; gender and, 29, 34, 49, 52,
64, 70, 223n37; injustice and, 41, 56, 149;
respectability and, 32, 54, 224n50; stereotypes and, 188, 203; TANU and, 30–31
racism, 30, 93, 116, 149
radio, 197, 202
Radio Tanzania, 58
Rajab, Hammie, 152, 154–55, 159–61, 167, 172,
176–77, 199, 202, 209
Rajabu, Marijani, 102–3, 108, 119, 153
Rappaport, Joanne, 10
real estate, 30, 190–91
reformists, 62–63, 69, 75, 78, 82, 90, 97,
99–101, 183. *See also* advice literature;
Christianity; working girls
relationships: between author and audience,
62–66, 146; romantic, 87, 91, 122, 132–35,
138–40, 195, 223n37, 243n53, 248n38;
social, 116, 152–79, 187, 189, 192. *See also*
generosity; gifts; social networks
religion, 15, 22, 27, 59, 67–68, 74, 81, 92, 154.
See also Christianity; Islam
repatriation, 1, 4, 41–42, 47–48, 52, 110, 196.
See also forcible repatriation; villagization
reporting, 33–34, 50–52, 153. *See also* newspapers; *and individual newspapers*
reproduction, 25, 66, 170–76, 193, 245n72. *See
also* contraception; family; sex
respectability, 17, 66, 98, 126, 189, 193, 204,
215n2, 224n50
rhetoric, 5, 38, 40, 56–57, 65, 126–31, 135, 180,
188–90. *See also* antiurbanism; nationalism; self-reliance; self-sufficiency; Ujamaa
Robinson, Jennifer, 145
Rodney, Walter, 4, 46, 77, 149, 230n39
romance, 16, 73, 138, 143, 169–75. *See also*
fiction; love; relationships

Roy, Ananya, 13, 20, 210
Rubin, Martin, 166
Ruhumbika, Gabriel, 185
rural relocation. *See* repatriation;
villagization
rural return. *See* repatriation; villagization
rural romanticism, 3, 6–7, 15, 20, 29, 54, 189.
See also antiurbanism
Rweyemamu, Robert, 66

Saad, Siti binti, 108
Salimu, Dora, 50–52
Salome (Baka), 238n92
Sassen, Saskia, 212
Sauti ya Injili, 67, 73
scarcity, 2, 10, 143–44, 179, 185–87, 199.
See also economy
Schatzberg, Michael, 222n25
Scott, James, 39
segregation, 10, 23–24, 117
self-reliance, 4, 38, 66, 126–34, 138, 140, 189,
201, 205–6
self-sufficiency, 40, 70, 128, 140, 174, 176,
221n19
sex, 25, 66, 87, 97–98, 133, 165, 175, 187, 209,
229n19. *See also* commoditization; family;
relationships; reproduction; sexuality
sexual danger, 9–10, 162, 165
sexuality: commodification and, 104, 106,
132, 139–40; dance and, 115–18; discourse,
53, 57, 95, 170–71, 186; gender and, 172–73,
176, 194, 223n37; policing of, 8–10, 16–17,
25, 29, 54–56, 120, 127–28, 132
"Shangazi Naomba Taiti" (Jamhuri Jazz
Band), 137
Shipley, Jesse Weaver, 107
Shivji, Issa, 20, 46, 77, 149
Shuga Dedi (Kassam), 142
Sichalwe, Maurice, 33, 151. *See also* Kashkash
Simbamwene, John, 152–54, 167–68, 244n62,
244n67
Simone, AbdouMaliq, 4, 12, 128, 211
Simu ya Kifo (Katalambula), 244n60
Skinner, Ryan, 184
slavery, 38–39, 215n2, 225n73, 247n28
Smith, Ian, 93
socialism: African, 15, 77, 144, 154, 163, 178;
bongo and, 180–82, 204–5; collapse of, 17,
186, 196–201, 205; community and, 150;
culture and, 16, 117, 119, 121–22, 127, 146,
184–85; economy and, 49, 141, 143, 155,
185; education under, 148; family and,
90–94, 96–98, 182; frugality and, 173,

176; infrastructure and, 34, 186, 191–92;
literacy and, 9, 42–48, 129, 210, 240n11;
media and, 48–50, 144, 174, 177; music
and, 105–6, 108–10, 202; self-reliance
and, 4, 38, 128–32; urbanization and, 7,
20, 36, 200, 212; villagization and, 1, 5–6,
37–39, 52–54, 56, 187, 216n9; women and,
64, 125, 175, 183. *See also* capitalism; Dar
es Salaam; frugality; self-reliance; self-
sufficiency; Ujamaa
social networks, 13, 62, 105–6, 122, 134,
145–79, 211, 213. *See also* men; pulp-fiction
Sollima, Sergio, 166
Songambele, Mustapha, 127
South Africa, 93, 121, 165, 219n49
Soviet Union, the, 186, 219n49
Special Files, The (Ganzel). See *Faili Maalum*
(Ganzel)
squatter settlements, 6, 13, 39, 52, 55, 66, 143.
See also Operation Vijana
stereotypes, 136, 163, 174, 188
Stoler, Ann Laura, 210
Stren, Richard, 40, 67
Stroeken, Koen, 202
Structural Adjustment Policy, 201
sugar daddies, 172–76, 193–94, 248n35
Sugar Daddy's Lover (Owino), 248n35
Sukari, Kaka, 33
Sunburst, 113–14, 120
Super Volcano, 113–14
surveillance, 13, 55, 210
surveys, 63, 78–79, 209. *See also* University of
Dar es Salaam; working girls
Swahili, 33, 46, 53–56, 82–85, 107–9, 114, 151,
155, 208
Swantz, Marja-Liisa, 62, 68, 77–78, 83, 100,
126
Sykes, Ally, 117

TANITA cashew-processing factory, 65,
77, 90
TANU (Tanzania African National Union):
culture and, 104–5, 112–13, 117–22, 127,
144, 185; education and, 42–48, 98; image
of, 123; infrastructure and, 18–19, 40,
49; literature, 21, 146; media and, 31–32,
49–50, 64, 75, 85, 93, 149; modernity and,
34, 36; policies of, 54, 92, 130; propaganda, 130, 170, 174, 196; urbanization
and, 15, 20, 30, 55, 57; villagization and,
1, 6, 38–39; women's branch, 68, 88, 131;
Youth League, 1, 17, 31–32, 41, 55, 66, 104,
120, 127–28, 148, 182–85. *See also* culture;

dancehalls; Nyerere, Julius; Operation
Vijana; self-reliance; self-sufficiency;
socialism; Ujamaa
Tanzania: colonization of, 27, 32, 37; culture
in, 27, 102–28; domesticity in, 16, 82–83,
91–98, 132–33; economy of, 8, 17; gender
roles in, 71, 126, 134; housing in, 83–86,
245n78; literacy in, 42–46, 150; media in,
50–56; modernization of, 18, 30; protectionism, 57, 178, 201; publishing in, 21,
144–79; race in, 22–26, 31; socialism in, 3–4,
9, 13, 34–38, 55, 180, 186–88, 199, 246n6;
urbanization in, 1–2, 5–6, 17–20, 26, 57; villagization policies in, 6, 39; women in, 15,
56, 61–90, 99–100. *See also* Dar es Salaam
Tanzania African National Union (TANU).
See TANU (Tanzania African National Union)
Tanzania Publishing House (TPH), 46,
147–51, 157, 192
taraab, 117–18
TAZARA railroad, 154, 215n2
television, 177, 202
Thakers, Randhir, 32
Third World, the, 3, 8, 37, 225n66
Third World solidarity, 37, 40, 57
Thomas, Lynn, 133, 169, 193, 239n100
Tripp, Aili, 100, 197, 201, 212
Tuanze Lini? (Mukajanga), 142, 153
"Tulime Masamba" (Cuban Marimba),
109–10, 114

Ufunguo wa Bandia (Rajab), 167–68, 199,
245n73
Uganda, 33, 41, 176
Uhuru, 49, 53, 75, 90, 115–16, 208, 227n103
Ujamaa: economy and, 17, 65, 139–40, 155;
policies, 41, 43, 178, 246n6; propaganda,
46, 49; rhetoric, 70, 77, 126, 128–30, 135,
173–74, 180, 182, 188, 190, 198, 201, 203,
205; street archives of, 144–46, 150, 198;
urbanization and, 3–8, 36, 58, 187; villagization, 54, 57, 110, 196, 225n75. *See also*
Dar es Salaam; repatriation; socialism;
TANU (Tanzania African National Union);
urbanization; villagization
UMATI (Family Planning Association of
Tanzania), 92–98
Umoja wa Wanawake wa Tanzania (UWT),
68–69, 88, 131
underdevelopment, 4, 8, 62, 77
United States, the, 93, 95, 115
University of Dar es Salaam, 23, 43–46, 62,
77–80, 91, 149–57, 183–85, 209, 228n4,

University of Dar es Salaam (continued)
230nn39–40. *See also* surveys; working
girls
Unyonge wa Mwafrika, 174
uplift, 4, 19, 21, 28, 32, 43, 68, 76, 81, 91,
226n89. *See also* female uplift
urbanization, 1–9, 19–21, 27, 66, 72, 105–6,
140, 186, 190, 205. *See also* antiurbanism;
Dar es Salaam; repatriation; villagization
urban masculinity. *See* masculinity
urban revolution, 1–3, 25, 81. *See also*
urbanization
urban texts, 11–12, 14. *See also* literature;
magazines; newspapers; publishing
industry

villagization, 4–6, 19, 36–43, 52–57, 110, 154,
190, 216n9, 225n75. *See also* Operation
Nguvu Kazi; repatriation
violence, 24–26, 29, 38–41, 44, 56, 76, 126–27,
153, 183, 194
visura. See *kisura*

Wakati ni Huu, 176–77, 239n1
Walkowitz, Judith, 9
Washington, Booker T., 25, 209, 221n19
wealth, 7, 25–26, 105, 135, 171–76, 188–90,
194, 200, 203, 213. *See also* adulthood;
masculinity
Weiss, Brad, 11, 215n2
westernization, 26–27, 51, 127, 162, 186
"What Kind of Life in Dar es Salaam"
(Abdallah), 51
Wicked Walk, The (Mkufya), 245n76

Williams, Raymond, 6, 20, 47
Willy Gamba, 163, 165–66
women: commodification and, 102–6, 165;
consumerism and, 108, 131, 136–39, 170,
176, 193; control of, 26–29, 34, 53, 223n23;
dependence of, 125–26, 134–35, 140, 189;
dress and, 125, 131, 236n48; greed and, 133,
170–71, 238n92, 245n72; mobility of, 40,
162; policing of, 50–56, 222n24, 223n37;
sexuality of, 90–98, 173, 194; violence
against, 39, 41, 127–28, 175, 183; working,
15, 31, 59–90, 188, 238n90; writers, 43, 153,
226n89. *See also* advice literature; Christianity; contraception; family planning;
female uplift; gender; surveys
working girl hostels, 87–90, 99, 212
working girls, 60–90, 126, 209. *See also* contraception; family planning
Wretched of the Earth, The (Fanon), 36–37

Yemen, 22, 24
Young, Louise, 10, 210
youth: adulthood and, 176, 182–83, 189;
commoditization and, 116, 138–40; control
of, 25–30; culture, 103–4, 185; male, 134,
169–70, 173–74; mobility, 123, 205; relationships, 116–17, 171, 243n53
Yurchak, Alexei, 219n49
YWCA, 73, 88–90, 99

Zairean music, 235n40
Zambia, 20, 22, 36, 41, 71, 74, 121, 230n50
Zanzibar, 22, 37–38, 108, 115
Zimbabwe, 121, 181, 231n53